Using
FOCUS
GROUPS

Sara Miller McCune founded SAGE Publishing in 1965 to support the dissemination of usable knowledge and educate a global community. SAGE publishes more than 1000 journals and over 800 new books each year, spanning a wide range of subject areas. Our growing selection of library products includes archives, data, case studies and video. SAGE remains majority owned by our founder and after her lifetime will become owned by a charitable trust that secures the company's continued independence.

Los Angeles | London | New Delhi | Singapore | Washington DC | Melbourne

Ivana Acocella & Silvia Cataldi

Using FOCUS GROUPS

Theory, Methodology, Practice

Los Angeles | London | New Delhi
Singapore | Washington DC | Melbourne

Los Angeles | London | New Delhi
Singapore | Washington DC | Melbourne

SAGE Publications Ltd
1 Oliver's Yard
55 City Road
London EC1Y 1SP

SAGE Publications Inc.
2455 Teller Road
Thousand Oaks, California 91320

SAGE Publications India Pvt Ltd
B 1/I 1 Mohan Cooperative Industrial Area
Mathura Road
New Delhi 110 044

SAGE Publications Asia-Pacific Pte Ltd
3 Church Street
#10-04 Samsung Hub
Singapore 049483

© Ivana Acocella and Silvia Cataldi 2021

First published 2021

Editor: Natalie Aguilera
Assistant editor: Eve Williams
Production editor: Katherine Haw
Copyeditor: Solveig Gardner Servian
Proofreader: Rebecca Storr
Indexer: Silvia Benvenuto
Marketing manager: Susheel Gokarakonda
Cover design: Francis Kenney
Typeset by: C&M Digitals (P) Ltd, Chennai, India
Printed in the UK

Library of Congress Control Number: 2020932301

British Library Cataloguing in Publication data

A catalogue record for this book is available from the British Library

ISBN 978-1-5264-4560-5
ISBN 978-1-5264-4561-2 (pbk)

At SAGE we take sustainability seriously. Most of our products are printed in the UK using responsibly sourced papers and boards. When we print overseas we ensure sustainable papers are used as measured by the PREPS grading system. We undertake an annual audit to monitor our sustainability.

Contents

Although the book is the result of joint reflection by the authors, sections 1.2, 1.3, 3.1, 3.2, 3.3, 3.4, 4.5, 12.1, 12.2 and Chapters 5, 6, 7, 8 can be attributed to Ivana Acocella, section 1.1, 1.4, 1.5, 3.5, 3.6, 4.1, 4.2, 4.3, 4.4, 12.3 and Chapters 2, 9, 10, 11 can be attributed to Silvia Cataldi.

About the authors

Ivana Acocella is a Lecturer of Sociology at the University of Florence (Italy). Since 2002, she has taught Methodology and Research Methods for the Social Sciences. She currently teaches Sociology of Migration and Qualitative Research. Her research focuses on epistemological and methodological assessment of qualitative research approaches.

Silvia Cataldi is a Lecturer of Sociology at the Sapienza University of Rome (Italy). Since her PhD, she has taught Social Sciences Research Methodology and Sociology. Her research focuses on methodological aspects of social research, public sociology and social action regimes. She is partner of many European projects and she is a board member of RN20 Qualitative Methodology of the European Sociological Association.

Part I

WHAT IS A FOCUS GROUP?

1

Outlining the Focus Group

The focus group is an essential tool in the researcher's toolbox. Designed to study social representations, the focus group is a technique that takes advantage of group interactions to gather information.

However, in a toolbox, not all tools are useful for every occasion nor can any of them meet every need: each has its own specificities, its own strengths and weaknesses. This is why it is important to understand what the focus group technique is, when to use it and when not.

In this chapter, which outlines the main features of the focus group and its epistemological roots, we will focus on the two constitutive elements of the technique:

- the group as a source of information;
- the dialogical interaction among the participants.

The pros and the cons of using this technique depend on these elements. We will then try to give some indications as to when it is advantageous for a researcher to choose the focus group and when it is better to choose other techniques. Finally, specific attention will be dedicated to a contemporary variation of the tool: the online focus group.

--------- **Chapter goals** ---------

- *Knowledge*: main characteristics and epistemological roots of the face-to-face and online focus group.

(Continued)

- *Applying knowledge and understanding*: when to choose and when not to choose the focus group for research purposes.
- *Making judgements*: developing awareness of the advantages and disadvantages of group interaction, which is the engine of the focus group technique.

1.1 The main features of the technique

Definition

The focus group is an essential technique in the researcher's toolbox. A good investigator needs to know when to use one research tool rather than another. This choice is made based on the cognitive objectives of the research and the fundamental characteristics of the instrument. Indeed, there is no one tool that is better than another, nor one that can be used for each and every research opportunity. For this reason, before using a focus group, the researcher must know what the fundamental characteristics of this tool are and what it is used for. Based on this, the researcher will be able to decide whether or not the focus group is the right tool for his/her research.

So, what is a focus group? The specific definition we can give is that it is a 'non-standard' technique for information gathering based on an apparently informal discussion among a group of people selected on the basis of specific characteristics, outlined according to the cognitive purposes of the research. The debate occurs in the presence of a moderator, who leads a focused discussion on the research issues, and (possibly) an observer, who observes the interactions and integrates the verbal information arising from the conversation. Let us analyse this definition point by point.

Research technique

First of all, we define the focus group as a 'technique'. The term technique in the scientific field indicates a tool that the investigator uses for research purposes. The term technique can be distinguished from 'method' because a method is a set of procedures, rules and principles that allow the researcher to know/explain reality. A technique therefore derives from reflections on the method as it represents its applicative result.

The second important thing is that it is a 'research technique'. When we use this expression, we intend to anchor it in the field of scientific investigation. This means that, while not excluding more applicative fields, in this text we will mainly deal with the focus group as an application of 'scientific research', understood as a systematic investigation undertaken to discover facts or relationships and reach conclusions using scientific method.

This does not mean that the technique is only of use to intellectuals or academics. It rather means that we place the focus group within the 'research cycle'. Scientific research has some characteristic phases: identification and definition of the investigation problem, formulation of research questions or hypotheses, collection and analysis of information, and communication of results. The focus group is therefore a useful tool for the 'information gathering' phase of a research project. Learning to use a focus group consciously and appropriately can therefore constitute a resource for scholars of all ages: it can be useful both for junior researchers and for qualified and senior researchers. Furthermore, the focus group is a useful tool for many disciplines. It therefore has an interdisciplinary value. Indeed, over the last decades the focus group has been gaining more and more attention in a variety of disciplines: marketing, political science, evaluation research, business and administration, medicine, health, education and social research.

A 'non-standard' technique and qualitative approach

Another specific feature of the focus group is that it is a research technique that uses 'non-standard' gathering procedures. This means that: from the moderator's point of view, in the information collection tools and discussion outline, the questions do not follow either a predetermined order or an *a priori* precisely established text; from the point of view of those taking part in the discussion, no classification scheme is provided for possible alternative answers. In other words, the technique develops within the qualitative approach of social research.

Concepts and Theories

Within the debate between qualitative and quantitative research, Alberto Marradi (1997) suggested using 'standard' and 'non-standard' to qualify the families of approaches used in the social sciences: 'standard' is the classical one referring to the families of the experimental method, characterized by variable manipulation, and the data matrix method, relating to associations among variables; 'non-standard' stands for specific research activities and related conceptual and operational tools based on non-standardized information collection procedures.

We will look into the kind of distinct information that the researcher can obtain when using the focus group later on (see section 1.2). Here, suffice it to say that, developing in the context of a qualitative approach, the focus group is a technique based on non-standardized data collection procedures. Furthermore, it is based on a mainly bottom-up research path. This means that the researcher collects the empirical material and then examines it to establish which interpretation is suggested by the set of most relevant information.

Connected to this, some scholars also emphasize the 'emic' aspect of the focus group (among others, Stewart and Shamdasani, 1990: 13; Cyr, 2019: 10) deriving from the close connection that links the data produced to the social context of origin. Indeed, the use of non-standardized information collection procedures allows the researcher to enhance the 'insiders' point of view', in order to understand and explain a phenomenon starting from its conceptual, analytical and linguistic categories. In this way, it is possible to highlight the gap between the researcher's and the insiders' 'frames of reference' and reach a 'thick description' (Geertz, 1975: 27) of the phenomenon, starting from the perspectives and the categorization processes of the people who are directly involved in that phenomenon, because it is part of their daily life. Taking up the famous distinction of Klaus Krippendorff (2004), these scholars highlight some aspects that characterize the technique, including the proximity of the social situation described by the group debate to the participants' life-world, as well as the low degree of structuring given to the discussion outline and the moderate role played by the researcher in directing the collective debate.

Moreover, in order to maximize the advantages of the technique, the non-standard and qualitative connotation of this tool should pertain to both the collection of information, as well as to the entire logic that guides its use. However, it should be emphasized that the focus group can be combined with other qualitative or quantitative tools in the context of a mixed-method research design, as well as quantitative tools based on standard logics which can be used during the information analysis.

Incidentally, we prefer to talk about 'information' rather than 'data', since the term data etymologically refers to something that is given, that already exists in nature and simply needs to be collected by the researcher. In contrast, scientific research data are always influenced by the specific information collection procedure of each technique. In the case of the focus group, the data are the texts produced by the verbal and non-verbal interactions between the moderator and the participants.

An informal discussion in appearance only

One other point is that the interaction among the group members brings the focus group discussion closer to everyday communication: people can express themselves in a similar way to any communication with peers or other analogous exchange of opinions relating to everyday life.

For this reason, some authors point out that the focus group has a phenomenological basis (Calder, 1977; Beck et al., 1986; Frey and Fontana, 1993; Vaughn et al., 1996; Palmer et al., 2010). In detail, they stress the naturalness and informality of the information collection context, which is characterized by little conditioning by the researcher and takes place in an atmosphere of dialogical interaction.

However, we must not be deceived by this closeness to the world of everyday life. The debate in a focus group only apparently looks like a natural discussion, since the interaction among the participants:

- takes place in a place identified by the research group;
- is based on pre-established cognitive purposes;
- takes place among people chosen with specific criteria.

Indeed, the meeting is the first element of artificiality: the people participating in a focus group are not observed in their natural environment but are called to interact in a place and at a time proposed by the research group. Second, their co-presence is not spontaneous, they are carefully selected, recruited. Third, the discussion itself will not be free, but will be conducted by a researcher, and above all it will be focused on some specific theme or aspects of it, established *ex ante* by the research group. This focus aspect is so important that the term 'focus' becomes part of the name of this technique, stressing that the discussion is con-centrated on a few specific topics.

In other words, the technique requires planning as part of a research design and a series of procedures aimed at maximizing the usefulness of the results in relation to the pre-established objectives. For this reason, the focus group cannot be naively considered a natural context of interaction.

The focus group actors

Finally, the focus group actors are fundamental. First of all, there is the mod-erator. He/she is the person who supports and relaunches the discussion, fol-lowing an outline planned on the basis of cognitive purposes and adapted to the people with whom he/she is interacting in that moment. The moderator may or may not be the researcher or a member of the research group. However, he/she should be specialized in group dynamics management, and fully aware of the choices made by the research group. In other words, it is fundamental that the moderator has internalized the cognitive issues of the research and has participated in project meetings from the beginning.

Another important figure is the observer. Indeed, to maximize the effective-ness of the focus group, we recommend that, alongside the moderator, an observer also attends the discussion session. The observer is the person who detects non-verbal behaviours and information on the type of interaction that is established among the participants in order to integrate and strengthen the analysis of the verbal information. Since interactions are an integral part of the information production process in a focus group, it is important to have the presence of this second person, who not only acts as an assistant to the moderator but also focuses on observing the interactions among the participants. Indeed, this activity requires continuous attention, which the moderator – engaged in other tasks – cannot guarantee.

Finally, the key players in the focus group are the participants. They are chosen based on criteria established by the researcher because they are deemed useful for the research purposes. They are also required to interact in the group, and are asked not only to respond to the stimuli proposed by the moderator, but above all to problematize and discuss the topic of investigation through comparison and an exchange of ideas with the others present. This is why a small group of people is considered most suitable to meet the cognitive objectives set.

Summing up

In conclusion, we can state that the focus group is a research technique having the following distinctive properties:

- the presence of a moderator;
- the (recommended) presence of an observer;
- the presence of a small group of people deemed suitable to provide information on the research topic;
- the focus of the discussion on a specific topic or on particular aspects of a theme decided on the basis of the interests of the research group;
- non-standardized information collection procedures;
- a discussion that is not spontaneous.

These six distinctive properties ensure that the focus group can be considered a useful research tool for studying collective representations and opinions. However, we should bear in mind that the engine of the technique is group interaction, as it is the source of information. The next section is dedicated to this important aspect.

1.2 The group and interaction as sources of information

The information produced by the focus group has some specificities deriving from two features of this technique:

- the particular group formed for the focus group;
- the dialogic interaction that is established among the participants.

The process of cognitive identification with a 'social group'

The discussion group constitutes the main source of information for the focus group. The discussion is formed by emphasizing some of the social categories with which the members identify. In such a way, a common group of belonging or reference emerges, bringing to light those shared elements distinguishing the participants.

Indeed, the choice of the same social category of belonging/identification makes it possible to spread the perception among the participants that they have not been invited as 'individual persons', but as 'representative members of a social group' evaluated by the researcher as the most suitable to discuss the research issue. According to the composition of the group, therefore, each focus group can solicit the collection of an individual's opinions as a representative member of a social category, for example as a 'child', 'mother', 'student', 'worker' and so on. This favours the presence of experience common to the research topic, as well as the emergence of points of view and ways of categorizing the phenomena that are similar or at least comparable.

Concepts and Theories

Adapting the theory of Henri Tajfel (1974) to a focus group discussion, it is cognitive identification with a common social category that spreads a sense of belonging to the same social/reference group. Therefore, the sense of identification is not based on real physical and interactive belonging to a group in everyday life, but on 'self-categorization' and a form of 'external recognition' with reference to a given social category (Tajfel, 1974; Turner, 1982).

The research group chooses which social category of belonging/identification to bring out during the group discussion. This choice is made on the basis of the research objectives, thus evaluating which is the most suitable perspective to exploit in order to problematize and discuss the research issue.

Indeed, in our opinion, during a focus group we are interested in bringing out those cognitive processes influenced by feelings of belonging to 'social groups of reference/identification' which – even if they are sometimes taken for granted – contribute to the formation of the individual's social identity and condition his/her way of categorizing reality and of acting (therefore, they provide models of interpretation and action orientation). In other words, those cognitive processes are at the basis of the reproduction, which may be unconscious, of the symbolic forms of the socially shared knowledge disseminated in particular social groups.

Concepts and Theories

Referring to the theory of social identity developed by Henri Tajfel and John C. Turner in the 1970s, social attitudes can be considered the product of the response to cognitive processes of social categorization. In other words, they are the result of shared cognitive organizations based on the common perception of social collocations. According to this theory, through the process of identification with particular social categories, an individual adopts attitudes and behaviours associated with them. Thus, these social categories become an integral part of the definition of an individual's social identity and influence his/her way of thinking and acting.

Therefore, the focus group can be an effective technique to draw out socially influenced cognitive systems if it values this cognitive categorization/identification process for the formation of the discussion group. These cognitive systems sometimes crystallize and sometimes remain fluid, but in any event influence the social representations of individuals on the reality that surrounds them. Thus it is possible during the group discussion to thematize and discuss the particular object of study, starting from the chosen social category of identification/belonging, in order to render these cognitive processes evident. By proceeding in this way, the technique can favour the emergence of inter-subjective or – better still – inter-group representations, which reproduce the images spread and the beliefs shared among the social group that the participants of the meeting have been called to represent (Cunningham-Burley et al., 2001: 196; Marková et al., 2007: 19–24; Cyr, 2019: 10–20).

This potential of the technique increases if 'experts' on the topic are invited to the group discussion. They should not be 'specialists', but people having familiarity with the phenomenon studied, since it is part of their everyday lives (Stewart and Shamdasani, 1990: 53; Carey and Asbury, 2012: 41). In this way, the focus group will allow the researcher to explore inter-subjective representations and the socially shared knowledge relating to aspects of people's daily lives.

Comparison between groups formed from different cognitive processes of categorization/identification can make use of the technique even more interesting. Indeed, inter-subjective representations and shared beliefs are not the same for all groups – even though they may reach a certain degree of agreement in each of these (Terry and Hogg, 1996; Cooper et al., 2001) – because they derive from the experience that a group makes of a specific social phenomenon. In this way, comparison between different groups will allow the emergence of a plurality of representations and perspectives on the phenomenon starting from the social category of identification/belonging chosen each time.

Expert advice

As an example, we can consider the different representations that social workers, third-sector operators or volunteers may develop on the topic of immigration. They may come into contact with immigrants daily, but for different reasons and with specific methods of intervention/relationships. This can influence the production of different social representations on specific topics. For example, they can even provide different meanings for the term 'foreign' or the expression 'social integration'.

Ultimately, the choice of how to form the various focus group sessions will allow the discussion group to be used for a dual purpose:

- the group as a 'means' to bring out a social category with which the individual participants can identify and to engender a feeling they have not been invited to participate in the discussion meeting as single persons but as members of a specific social group;
- the group as a 'unit of analysis', because it is representative of the social group that the researcher wants to investigate in a discussion (i.e. starting from the particular social category requested) in order to bring out the collective representations connected to it.

Interaction as an integral part of information

The interaction between the various actors involved (among the participants, between the moderator and the participants) plays a fundamental role in the information production and detection process of a focus group (Puchta and Potter, 2004: 9–20).

Only rarely has the methodological literature explored the peculiar role that dialogue among the social actors plays in the collective formation of the statements and negotiation of meanings during a focus group. However, focus groups explicitly use group interaction as part of the technique (Kitzinger, 1994a).

As detailed above, since focus groups involve people who share the same social category of identification/belonging, it allows the researcher to examine different forms of socially shared knowledge. Hence, a focus group is not only a local activity at that particular time, but an interactive situated activity whose aim is to bring out social representations and discursive sense-making processes, thus involving socio-cultural aspects of dialogue (Albrecht et al., 1993: 58–9; Liamputtong, 2011: 16–18; Halkier, 2017: 394–8). However, the notion of social representation itself cannot be conceived of as a set of homogeneous, static and decontextualized 'ideas' that a person (or a group of subjects) has on a given topic. Indeed, social representations arise from social interaction between individuals and groups, circulate through communication, and, therefore, are embedded in dialogical activities (Cunningham-Burley et al., 2001: 198).

Concepts and Theories

Serge Moscovici (1961, 2000) defines social representations as a series of concepts, statements and explanations which arise in everyday life, through interpersonal communications. They are forms of socially elaborated and participated knowledge that contribute to the construction of social reality. Therefore, they designate a form of social thought. The term 'social' also refers to the interactive and dialogic nature of the formation of social representations.

Therefore, if socially shared knowledge has a dialogical nature, it implies that its contents have a dynamic structure and show progression and change. At the same time, if socially shared knowledge has a dialogical nature, it is – due to its same nature – characterized by regularities and recurrences, as well as by tensions, contradictions, vagueness and ambiguities; indeed, since social representations are 'thoughts in movement' elaborated through public debate, different points of view may emerge during the transformation of abstract information into concrete meanings. For this reason, human dialogue can under no circumstances be reduced to sheer transmission of information.

Based on these premises, since the focus group may be regarded as socially situated interaction, this technique appears to be a particularly suitable means of exploring the dynamics of the contents and forms of social representations through the study of communicative processes (Frisina, 2018: 190). In this way, interactions among the participants may be considered both a means of generating data and a focus of analysis (Kitzinger, 1995: 299).

By considering a focus group as a situated communication activity that relies on historically and culturally shared social knowledge, this technique can allow the researcher to identify the hegemonic representations related to the social beliefs, knowledge and ideologies circulating in societies. In this way, it provides information on the relatively stabilized forms of socially shared knowledge. Usually, this refers to knowledge about the social reality that the individual has assimilated into the environment and that makes daily life relatively orderly, habitual and systematic. In the 'natural attitude', this knowledge is taken for granted, while providing a supply of 'information-at-hand' that serves to direct action in everyday life.

Concepts and Theories

According to Alfred Schütz (1962, 1975), a 'natural attitude' (natürliche Aufstellung) prevails in any form of social relationship. Based on this attitude, it is taken for granted that both the promoter and the interlocutor attribute the same meaning to an action, and that, therefore, there is perfect interchangeability between the subjective points of view. This happens because, in the social world, experiences of consciousness of the 'other' are grasped through the mediation of already codified models of meaning or 'typification' of experiences, compressing their uniqueness. The typifications are sets of interpretative schemes that the individual has assimilated from the environment, thus providing 'the stock of knowledge-at-hand' which serves to orient in daily actions. In this way, the action develops because there exist pre-established interpretations and expectations of the behaviour of the other. Starting from this pre-established cultural code, the individual is able to move easily in different social situations. Hence, typification is a socially influenced cognitive process at the basis of 'naive' action (therefore of the 'natural attitude'), which – even implicitly – limits experiences, pre-constituting them as 'typical'.

At the same time, through the study of communicative processes, during focus groups the researcher may also learn the dialogic and interactive process that underlies the formation of shared social knowledge. Indeed, in a focus group, even if participants share a great deal of social knowledge, the dialogue is always characterized by an open and heterogeneous interplay of multiple meanings and voices in continuous tension (Smithson, 2000: 109; Liamputtong,

2011: 16–18; Hennink, 2014: 26–7; Halkier, 2017: 406–7). By paying attention not only to 'what' a participant says, but also to 'how' he/she says it when discussing with others, study of the interaction allows the researcher to explore the dynamic structures of the group debate and which themes under discussion show progression and change.

In this way, the focus group may also favour the emergence of diverse voices, as well as of the multiple meanings that people attribute to social representations since, as detailed above, social representations are not crystallized knowledge but 'thoughts in movement'. Therefore, by foregrounding diversities and heterogeneities in the shared social knowledge, the dialogical perspective allows us to investigate the change in social representations, as well as the direct or subtle challenges to the social order and to the different forms of conditioning (Kitzinger, 2004). For this reason, during a focus group, in the same way as it is possible to observe the manner in which the social representations are taken for granted or reproduced, it is also possible to investigate the acts of resistance (pushing towards change) in relation to certain social norms (Frisina, 2018: 204).

There is no doubt that, through dialogical thinking and communication, the focus group allows the researcher to examine language, thinking and knowledge in action. In this way, it is possible to discover the dynamic and heterogeneous characteristics of socially shared knowledge and the way in which this knowledge is in continuity or discontinuity with the past, as well as the different forms of interactive communication. For this reason, we are convinced that this technique offers significant opportunities to explore the power of dialogue dynamics.

Summing up

In conclusion, if the researcher develops a process of cognitive identification with a 'social group' among the participants and he/she enhances a dialogic interaction during the debate, a focus group enables the exploration of:

- stabilized forms of socially shared knowledge;
- tensions and different meanings inside the same shared knowledge;
- reinterpretations of the symbolic forms of social knowledge.

1.3 The advantages and disadvantages of interaction

To promote dialogical interaction during the focus group, the moderator should conduct the debate in such a way as to solicit a 'group discussion' rather than a 'group interview' (Kitzinger, 1995: 299; Parker and Tritter, 2006: 25–6; Barbour, 2007: 20; Flick, 2019: 318). Indeed, the term 'interview' evokes not only the detection of individual opinions, but also a procedure based on an interviewer asking a question and an interviewee producing an answer (Corrao, 2000: 16). In contrast, in focus groups, the moderator launches a discussion topic and he/she should wait for an answer, which is generated by the dynamics established among the participants. Only in this way will it be possible to enhance the interactive nature of the discussion that is the focus group's hallmark.

However, the interaction is twofold: sometimes it can enhance the information assets of the focus group; at other times it can reduce the effectiveness of the technique. Below, we will analyse when interaction is an added value and when some cognitive or communication problems may arise due to the group dynamics (see Table 1.1).

Interaction as an added value

If the interaction among the participants proceeds in a serene atmosphere and the discussion is conducted in a way that is not too direct or structured by the moderator, an information amplification effect can be produced. Indeed, the synergy of the group can favour the expression of varied information and a plurality of positions, activating the memory of forgotten details and aspects not previously considered (Hennink, 2014: 30–1). With its memory solicitation and idea-confrontation processes, the 'reticular' interaction plays a fundamental role during this phase.

Moreover, group discussions often develop through the association of ideas, since each participant can link to the others' interventions to add information, provide his/her point of view, ask for clarifications, report any strengths or weaknesses and so on. This triggers a process of chain responses in which one 'intervention draws on the other' soliciting the formulation of many opinions, with a consequent enrichment of the knowledge of the phenomenon under investigation. For these reasons, when referring to the advantages of group interaction, several scholars use terms such as 'synergism', 'snowballing', 'stimulation' (Stewart and Shamdasani, 1990). For the same reasons, other authors consider the focus group a technique particularly suited to obtaining new ideas, additional knowledge and unexpected opinions, thus stimulating the researchers' interpretative imagination (Morgan, 1997: 27; Puchta and Potter, 2004: 118–20; Marková et al., 2007: 87).

In a focus group discussion, interaction also allows participants to form their own point of view by comparing themselves with others, enabling them to better define their position and gain greater awareness of their ideas (Hennink, 2014: 30–1). This happens because the group synergy encourages the participants to publicly discuss the motivations that led them to reflect in a certain way or to adopt a certain behaviour in everyday life (Barbour, 2007: 150). Thus, comparison with others allows a participant to discover the vital 'background' that underlies his/her own actions and to focus attention on aspects that are often taken for granted and on which, therefore, he/she had not reflected before. At the same time, the focus group can help participants clarify, reinforce or modify an opinion that had remained uncertain until then. For this reason, when referring to the focus group, David E. Morrison defines it as 'a consciousness-raising exercise' (1998: xiv). For the same reason, other scholars suggest that the focus group is a particularly suitable technique for studying the ordinary processes of idea and socially shared knowledge formulation (Marková et al., 2007).

In addition to facilitating the collection of a large amount of information, the interaction can clarify the content of the discussion. Indeed, interaction with other participants allows the individual members of the group to explicate their conceptual, linguistic and argumentative schemes, according to a sharing and comparing procedure that leads to the definition of subjective meanings and the creation of new common areas of mutual understanding (Frey and Fontana, 1993; Vaughn et al., 1996; Smithson, 2000: 111). In the same way, the 'reticular' interaction allows the identification of similarities and differences among the various opinions, as well as the strengths and weaknesses of the various positions (Cardano, 2003: 155). In this way, the comparison between the participants and the group synergy can favour the development of arguments and inter-subjective representations deriving from the continuous feedback, collective reasoning and negotiation of all the persons involved in the debate (Marková et al., 2007: 46–7; Carey and Asbury, 2012: 28).

Cognitive and communicative problems

However, it should be remembered that interaction is not always an advantage. During the process of attributing meaning to a question or to a response provided to/by a participant, a cognitive problem that may occur concerns polysemy or 'semantic dispersion'. Indeed, since the link between concepts and terms is not rigid, the linguistic code is not fully shared, making communication imperfect (Marradi, 2007: 30–40). In focus group discussions, this problem can multiply according to the number and variety of participants (Marková et al., 2007: 18–19, 25). These considerations support the hypothesis that during the focus group it is appropriate to invite people who share a common or analogous experience with regard to the research topic. This can favour the emergence of similar ways of categorizing the phenomenon.

A second problem relates to the dynamics that are produced among the members of a group when they are asked to share a series of pieces of individually owned information to perform a common task. Indeed, some psychologists have found that as the number of group components increases, the quality of individual performance decreases (Latané et al., 1979; Williams et al., 1981; Kerr and Park, 2001: 112–16). This is attributed primarily to problems of coordination, which end up slowing the free production of ideas (Kravitz and Martin, 1986; Forsyth, 2014: 208–9). This mechanism can also occur in a focus group discussion, since, even if it solicits the formulation of ideas, the reticular interaction does not always give everyone the opportunity to express themselves. While listening to others, memories and reasoning are prompted very quickly. However, since it is not necessarily possible to intervene at any given time, not everyone can always express what they are thinking and, maybe, when a participant takes the floor, he/she does not remember all the thoughts that the discussion had solicited in him/her. In the same way, it can also happen that, in the discussion, a person is continually interrupted by other participants who want to make their own contributions to what was stated, making him/her lose the thread of his/her reasoning.

In addition, the speed of interaction during the discussion can reduce adequate information retrieval. Indeed, as already pointed out, in the discussions of a focus group, interaction often proceeds through association of ideas. Despite this favouring the emergence of a multitude of ideas and opinions, however, continuous changes of topic can occur. Furthermore, some relevant themes that may have emerged can be abandoned quickly, while others can be expanded on even if they are only marginal with respect to the research issues (Acocella, 2012: 1131–3). Therefore, there is no guarantee that the focus group discussion always permits a complete and adequate analysis of the research issues, especially if many topics are considered. These considerations support the hypothesis that the focus group discussion should focus on a few aspects considered relevant to the research, to allow all participants to reflect and express their opinions on each topic in an appropriate way in the short time available (an hour and a half on average).

Finally, in group discussions, even if the dialogic interaction is the main source for the collective construction of the statements and the negotiation of meanings, some group dynamics can occur which risk reducing the effectiveness of the technique. Indeed, interacting and discussing in a collective debate is not easy and the way of relating with others changes from person to person, depending on the characteristics of the single participants and the interactive context. Indeed, dynamics of conformism and attitudes of acquiescence can arise, as well as subjugation or extreme conflict. The fear of being judged or of exposing himself/herself too much can, therefore, lead an individual to conform (at least publicly) to the most widespread opinions in the group, since they are considered more standard and shared by society. At the same time, stereotyped ideas can emerge, due to the pressure and conditioning exercised by social conventions. Furthermore, dynamics of power can arise relating to the presence of people who exercise particular influence, due to their status or social position or just because they are 'perceived' as more expert, competent and capable of dealing with the research topic (Liamputtong, 2011: 80–2; Carey and Asbury, 2012: 28; Hennink, 2014: 30–3). At other times in group discussions, individual participants may interact less, out of shyness, while others tend to intervene too much because they are less inhibited by public speaking or because they know more about the discussed topic (Cyr, 2019: 79–80).

For this reason, the choice to invite people who share common or at least comparable experiences can partly defuse these dynamics or reduce their negative effects. Indeed, this reduces the degree of uncertainty that can derive from living a new 'experience' like that of participating in a focus group. Furthermore, it may favour the formation of a comfortable environment and the perception of being among 'equals', as well as increasing the possibility of discussing the research topic from similar perspectives.

These dynamics are part of everyday life. Therefore, they cannot be considered 'right' or 'wrong' *a priori*. This is because adoption of the technique is useful not only to gather opinions on the research topic, but also to explore the dynamic and interactive processes that underlie the formation of inter-subjective and social representations and different forms of socially shared knowledge. Sometimes, these dynamics are the product of ineffective focus group planning or unproductive discussion management. Other times, in contrast, they arise spontaneously during the debate, because, even if the research group has adequately planned the focus group session, it is not possible to predict in advance what the participants will be like and how they will react in the common discussion. Over the course of the book, we will return to these dynamics and how to moderate them when they compromise the success of the focus group. Here, suffice it to anticipate that both the moderator and the observer play a fundamental role in recognizing these dynamics and evaluating when, during the group discussion, they can be considered inappropriate because they compromise the free circulation of ideas and the establishment of a comfortable environment for all participants. In this case, it will be up to the moderator to intervene to mitigate them and reduce the cognitive and communicative risks connected to them.

Table 1.1 Pros and cons of interaction

The pros of interaction	The cons of interaction
☐ Formation of varied information and a plurality of positions	☐ Polysemy or 'semantic dispersion'
☐ Recollection of forgotten details and aspects not previously considered	☐ Coordination problems that can reduce the free production of ideas
	☐ Impossibility of always expressing what you are thinking

The pros of interaction	The cons of interaction
☐ Association of ideas and the chain response process in which one 'intervention draws the other'	☐ Risk of being interrupted and losing the thread of one's reasoning
☐ Acquisition of a greater awareness of one's own ideas and the explication of knowledge taken for granted	☐ Continuous changes in the discussion topics
	☐ Expanding on topics marginal to the research interests
☐ Explication of conceptual, linguistic and analytical schemes	☐ Risk of conformism dynamics and the occurrence of attitudes of acquiescence
☐ Ability to strengthen or change an uncertain opinion	☐ Risk of subjection or extreme conflict
☐ Identification of the similarities-differences or the strengths-weaknesses of various opinions	☐ Shyness in public speaking
	☐ Presence of 'dominant talkers' who are or consider themselves more expert on the discussed topic
☐ Formation of arguments and inter-subjective representations	

1.4 When to choose the focus group: comparison with related techniques

The focus group and other group techniques

As a fashionable research technique, the focus group 'is often adopted without any prior consideration of whether it really is the most suitable technique for achieving the cognitive goals of the research' (Acocella, 2012: 1126). In reality, the researcher may have other similar tools in his/her toolbox. He/she should therefore be familiar with the characteristics of each of them, in order to understand which is more functional for the purposes of that particular research project.

First of all, there are other techniques that use a group as a source of information. The most important are:

- the nominal group technique (NGT);
- the Delphi method;
- brainstorming.

The specificities of a focus group and the kind of information it is able to collect allow the researcher to distinguish this technique from others using a group as a source of information.

The focus group and NGT

The main difference between the focus group and NGT relates to the form interaction between participants takes (see Table 1.2). While interaction is very much encouraged in the focus group and can be considered the real engine of the technique, in NGT free interaction is avoided and, in any event, very much structured (Stewart and Shamdasani, 1990: 22; Dean, 2004: 389). Indeed, in NGT, even when the participants are in the same place, in the first phase they are asked not to interact and instead to answer open questions or a questionnaire privately; in the second phase, they are asked to discuss the ideas collected. However, in this second phase, the facilitator tries to maintain the anonymity of the idea collected individually in the first phase and participants cannot freely intervene in response to the solicitations of others, because only rounds of circular intervention are planned (therefore not reticular interactions like the focus group). A feature of the technique is the 'nominality' of the group, so much so that there are also versions of NGT in which the participants are not co-present, and the interaction is completely mediated by the facilitator.

Given these specificities of the technique, the choice of NGT over focus group is to be preferred in some specific cases: first, when the research is closer to the world of work, business or political decisions, rather than purely cognitive purposes, and the researcher wants to get problem-solving ideas and rank them by importance, emphasizing the participants' individual contributions more than the interaction among them (Barbour, 2007: 171); and second, the NGT technique is to be preferred when conflicts might arise among group members that prevent the normal development of the discussion, since it allows greater control over interaction (Corrao, 2000: 20; Acocella, 2008: 13).

The focus group and the Delphi method

The kind of interaction established among participants also distinguishes the focus group from another group technique: the Delphi method (see Table 1.2). Like NGT, in this case the group is again 'nominal', since its members are generally located in different spaces (Stewart and Shamdasani, 1990: 23). Indeed, normally, the technique does not require the co-presence of the participants but is carried out remotely (usually via email). It proceeds in different rounds in which, first, the moderator obtains a series of answers to one or more questions from each person separately, and second, he/she summarizes the individual contributions and sends them back to all the group members, asking for subsequent answers/reflections in the light of the expressed positions (Barbour, 2007: 46–7). Each round provides an opportunity for the participants to respond and to ask for an answer to their questions. Over multiple rounds, the process can lead to consensus or near-consensus (Linstone and Turoff, 2002: 4–7; Shariff, 2015: 246). A feature of the technique is the maintenance of anonymity, so a participant does not know who the other members of the group are and only interacts with the facilitator.

As in the case of NGT, this technique serves research needs closer to the world of work, business or political decisions, rather than purely cognitive issues. Indeed, the Delphi method is used to build consensus around some solutions, so that they become shared. Indeed, over multiple rounds, the process should gradually lead to a convergence of opinions and, in the last step, the collected answers are converted into closed questions in order to narrow down the topic and reach a majority agreement.

Furthermore, the choice of the Delphi method is to be preferred to the focus group when dealing with real experts, such as scientists or technicians (Acocella, 2008: 13). Such experts may either be too busy to participate in a face-to-face session that requires a meeting in a specific place and time, or they may live far apart from each other, and, above all, they may be in competition with one another. For this reason, interaction mediated by a facilitator and at a distance can be the best solution.

The focus group and brainstorming

The focus group also differs from a third technique that uses the group as a source of information: brainstorming (Sullivan, 2009: 53). Like the focus group, brainstorming was designed to promote creativity and serendipity. However, unlike the focus group, this technique involves a group of individuals who are asked to produce, sometimes even without the presence of a moderator, new ideas on a topic, without worrying about their quality. In this case, therefore, the interaction, although reticular, is aimed more at the rapid association of ideas rather than exploring opinions. Indeed, this technique is based on the principle that the greater the quantity of ideas produced, the higher the probability that some are good (Stewart and Shamdasani, 1990: 24–7; Corrao, 2000: 23).

These differences are due to the fact that, while use of the focus group is aimed at gaining knowledge of a given phenomenon, brainstorming is usually limited to the elaboration of new ideas or the suggestion of possible solutions to a given problem (Bezzi and Baldini, 2006; Acocella, 2008: 13). This is why brainstorming should be preferred when looking for creative solutions in an informal atmosphere (see Table 1.2).

Table 1.2 Other group techniques

	Nominal group technique (NGT)	Delphi method	Brainstorming
What	A structured group meeting conducted by a facilitator, for problem identification, solution generation and decision making	An iterative method for obtaining consensus among a group of experts	A technique for producing creative ideas in group idea-generation sessions
Goal	To obtain ideas to solve a problem and rank them by importance	To build consensus, often used as a means of problem solving, decision making and/or forecasting	To produce alternative proposals and new creative ideas, and prompt divergent thinking
When it is to be chosen instead of a focus group	☐ When research needs are not only cognitive but also practical (search for solutions) ☐ When conflicts among the group members may arise that could prevent the normal development of the discussion	☐ When research needs are not only cognitive but oriented to consensus building ☐ When the research has to involve experts who are busy, and/or live far away and/or may be competitive with each other	☐ When the purpose of the research is to collect a large amount of ideas on a topic, without worrying about their quality ☐ When looking for creative solutions in an informal atmosphere

The focus group and in-depth interview

Finally, the researcher should evaluate when the focus group is appropriate by comparing it with another similar qualitative technique: the individual interview with a low degree of structuring, or in-depth interview.

Both techniques have something in common: they belong to the family of interrogation techniques (which can be individual or group); they develop in coherence with an emic and qualitative approach to research (epistemological roots); they use non-standardized information collection procedures; they have a high degree of freedom as to the respondents' answers (open answers, wide and aimed at problematization).

Precisely due to these similarities, the information collected in a focus group is often considered identical to the data collected in an individual interview (Johnston et al., 1995: 57; Smithson, 2000: 105). In reality, the techniques are different. Therefore, there is no absolute superiority of one over the other, or one which gives better information than the other (Kaplowitz and Hoehn, 2001). There are divergences both in the objective of the two techniques and in the type of interaction context that is created through the two instruments.

Regarding the objectives, the first thing is that, while interviews excel at eliciting 'private' accounts, focus groups give researchers access to the interactive and dialogic narratives that participants produce in group situations (Frisina, 2018: 190). So, the in-depth interview should be preferred when a researcher aims to detect individual attitudes and motivations, personal experiences or life stories (Hennink, 2014: 28–9). Moreover, the individual interview is functional to the study of extraordinary and unique circumstances, especially those involving sensitive or personal topics (Robson and Foster, 1989; Stokes and Bergin, 2006). In all these cases, the focus group should not be chosen.

Regarding interaction, in a very elementary way it can be stated that, while in the focus group the interaction is in a group, in the individual interview the interaction takes place between two actors alone: the interviewer and the interviewee. Even if the literature tends to underestimate the relational dimension of the individual interview, today many scholars agree on the centrality of the relational dimension and, therefore, they are aware that information resulting from the interrogation techniques can neither be reified nor objectified (Gobo and Mauceri, 2014; Cataldi, 2018). Indeed, the human relations established during the interrogation process contribute to the production of information. Precisely for this reason, we cannot say that interaction does not count. Rather, we can state that the dynamics of interaction represent the condition and the product for both the in-depth interview and a focus group. In both techniques, the relational dimension is unavoidable and constitutive of the information development processes (Cataldi, 2018: 309).

However, there are some differences. First of all, dialogic interaction among participants is the hallmark of focus groups, in order to examine the development, maintenance and changes in socially shared knowledge (Marková et al., 2007: 46–7; Carey and Asbury, 2012: 28). Indeed, as detailed above, the collective interaction among people who share the same social category of identification/belonging is both a form of information generation as well as a focus of analysis (Kitzinger, 1995: 299). This is why 'the added value of focus groups is that they are able to observe the interactional context in which they are produced' (Frisina, 2018: 190).

In contrast, in an in-depth interview, the interaction between the interviewer and the interviewee is the main source of information. This interaction is based on a 'pact of trust' (Bichi, 2002), in which the interviewer places himself/

herself in a position of 'active listening' and an 'empathic role' aimed to problematize biographical attitudes and experiences, while the interviewee provides his/her definitions of situations, tells his/her own daily practices and explains the reasons for his/her choices and actions. Ultimately, the purpose of the interaction is to explore personal opinions, biographical events and the subjection-subjectivities processes that occur during a person's life, in order to bring out an individual perspective on a particular phenomenon or biographical identity profile (Acocella, 2013; Hennink, 2014: 28–9; Caillaud and Flick, 2017: 164–8).

For a summary of the main differences between the focus group and in-depth interview, see Tables 1.3 and 1.4.

Table 1.3 Comparison between the focus group and in-depth interview

Common points	☐ Shared belonging to the great family of interrogation techniques
	☐ Emic and qualitative approaches to research
	☐ Non-standardized information collection procedures
	☐ High degree of freedom in the answers of the respondents
	☐ The relational dimension is constitutive of the information development processes
Differences in the goals	☐ Focus group suitable for: social representations and shared opinions and in general narratives and arguments that participants present in group situations
	☐ In-depth interview suitable for: 'private' accounts, such as attitudes and individual motivations, personal experiences, life stories or circumstances of unique applicability, especially those involving sensitive or personal topics
Differences in the interaction	☐ Focus group: reticular and symmetrical group interaction among people who share the same social category of identification/belonging; interaction is both a means of generating empirical information and a focus of analysis; possibility of exploring the dynamic and interactive development of socially shared knowledge
	☐ In-depth interview: the interaction is based on the interviewer's 'active listening' and 'empathic role', aimed at problematizing the interviewee's personal and biographical attitudes/experiences; possibility of bringing out individual perspectives on a particular phenomenon or biographical identity profile

Table 1.4 Focus group and in-depth interview strengths

Focus group	In-depth interview
☐ Synergy – the group process generates a wider range of information than would accrue from a comparable number of in-depth interviews	☐ There are circumstances in which only this technique can be applied, especially those involving sensitive or personal topics
☐ Snowballing – respondent interaction creates a chain of thought and ideas	☐ High-quality outcome, in terms of the depth and comprehensiveness of the information that it can yield. In particular, it affords the opportunity to build a close rapport and a high degree of trust, thus improving the quality of the collected information and making it easier to express non-conformity. This is for two main reasons:
☐ Serendipity – a great idea can come out of the blue	
☐ Stimulation – respondents' views are brought out by the group process	
☐ Security – respondents are more likely to be candid as there will probably be other similar people during the group discussion, and there is less individual pressure than in an in-depth interview	
☐ Spontaneity – because nobody is required to respond to a question, this encourages a spontaneous response when people have a definite point of view	a. the possibility for the respondent – frequently for the first time – to really analyse his/her motivations for a particular action
☐ Specialization – a trained moderator can solicit several respondents in a given session	b. the unusual opportunity to be listened to, which, together with the anonymity afforded, offers the respondent a feeling of empowerment
☐ Salience – the comparison among participants may elicit why a particular issue is relevant in that group	

Source: Elaboration from Stokes and Bergin, 2006: 27–8

1.5 Online focus groups

General features

The increasing use of information and communication technologies (ICTs) has a significant impact on research practices. One of the innovations created by technology is the online focus group.

Online focus groups have found application in a wide range of settings, including advertising, marketing, healthcare, higher education and basic social science research, among others. Many research projects have revealed that online focus groups have the same effectiveness as face-to-face focus groups with respect to drawing out information from group participants (Campbell et al., 2001; Reid and Reid, 2005; Abrams and Gaiser, 2017). However, at the same time, these research projects have also highlighted that there are circumstances where one type of focus group may offer more advantages over the other (Murgado-Armenteros et al., 2012; Lobe, 2017).

The online focus group can be performed via teleconferencing or via web using remote groups (Allen, 2014). There are a variety of bandwidths and specialized platforms developed for online groups. However, these platforms could be an issue, because it reduces the flow of the discussion and the availability of visual information (Stewart and Shamdasani, 2017: 51).

Synchronous voice and chat technologies enable the transmission of relatively nuanced expressions and emotions in video mode (Lobe, 2017: 239). Tools like Skype, or other software such as Adobe Connect, GoToMeeting and WebEx, are able to virtually replicate real-time, face-to-face interaction (Liamputtong, 2011: 151–2).

Online variations

Whatever practical mode is chosen to implement the focus group, one important aspect to bear in mind is the interactional nature of the focus group. Indeed, we know that the focus group's engine is precisely the discussion among the participants. As the literature claims, focus groups rely on interaction within a group, rather than a question-and-answer format. By debating issues and interacting to understand how other group members interpret key terms, participants are more likely to contribute to group discussions to generate information across a range of experiences and opinions (Morgan, 1997: 26; Puchta and Potter, 2004: 118–20; Hennink, 2014: 16–19).

Therefore, the key question is: how can we ensure that the interactional nature of the focus group is fully preserved, even online?

The first thing that must be maintained is the synchronicity of the interaction. In our opinion, indeed, variants that provide for asynchrony cannot properly be described as using the focus group technique, as they change the nature of the interaction. In asynchronous interaction, a person does not interact immediately with the other participants or moderator, but has time to reflect and post his/her opinion on others' contributions later (Liamputtong, 2011: 152–3). Therefore, the mechanism of sharing and comparing opinions is more akin to a 'group interview' rather than a focus group.

On the contrary, synchronous online groups are the closest approximation of traditional face-to-face focus groups and involve real-time discussions led by one or more moderators, usually with up to eight participants (Sintjago and Link, 2012: 5; Stewart and Shamdasani, 2017: 51).

In some cases, the online focus group can be realized in a virtual environment. We call this application 'Focus Groups in Virtual Worlds': 'a virtual world, sometimes referred to as a massively multiplayer online world (MMOW), is a computer-simulated environment in which individuals interact through personal avatars. […] Virtual worlds provide meeting rooms and other locations for interaction among avatars. The interactions may occur through typed text or through voice chat' (Stewart and Shamdasani, 2017: 54). This is a possible variation of online focus groups, in which the virtual world allows avatars to better link the topic of discussion in a simulated context (Bartle, 2003: 154–6; Liamputtong, 2011: 153–5).

Advantages

The choice to carry out an online focus group offers some advantages and some disadvantages.

We will first indicate the advantages.

- *Logistical issues*. First, the online tool can help to solve logistical problems affecting the recruitment of participants. A key limitation of focus group research concerns the difficulty of getting all participants together at the same time and place. Technology reduces this limitation (Johnson, 2005: 177; Matthews et al., 2018: 1621). At the same time, this allows the categories of participants to be broadened to individuals who would otherwise not easily participate in focus groups, such as people who are always on a tight schedule, who have severe disabilities, who cannot travel away from home or who live a long way from each other. The online focus group also reduces the time and cost involved in convening a meeting of participants in a single place for a pre-established appointment. Obviously, there will be other costs to consider in respect of the technology and Internet connection. Additionally, in choosing a time for the appointment, researchers must bear in mind that people who live on different continents will be in different time zones.
- *Recording and transcription*. Recording and transcribing the discussion of a focus group is usually a challenging and labour-intensive process, particularly because the moderator is dealing with several participants. 'Rapid exchanges of ideas among the participants and overlapping conversation presents a great challenge to the researcher, even with the help of technologies like audio or video recording' (Cher Ping and Seng Chee, 2001: 56).

In an online discussion, the electronic board automatically records the discussion as well as the textual chat. Moreover, automatic recording usually offers the possibility of pre-classifying the collected information, thus eliminating the labour-intensive tasks of recording and transcribing. Recording is usually facilitated by built-in tools in online interfaces, which can be downloaded almost immediately (Lobe, 2017: 231–2; Stewart and Shamdasani, 2017: 48).

- *Sensitive issues.* In the literature, the advantage of being able to better preserve anonymity is considered a plus, especially when dealing with delicate and sensitive issues (Pearson, 1999). The potential anonymity of virtual groups can create a high sense of psychological safety for sensitive topics or potentially embarrassing issues (Liamputtong, 2011: 150–3).
- *Limitation of interaction biases.* In some cases, online interaction can control some biases and prevent conflicts or competitiveness among the participants. This is especially true in the case of highly qualified professional groups. Keeping anonymity can prevent fights and racing for the best idea. This also applies in the case of groups with different hierarchical levels. While a face-to-face focus group would trigger bias due to social structuring, some studies show a lack of social dominance and the possibility of 'group thinking' in online applications (Cher Ping and Seng Chee, 2001: 54–5).
- *Adaptability for specific targets.* 'Online focus groups can be appropriate for specific types of participants, especially teens, low-incidence groups, professionals, policy makers and handicapped individuals' (Stewart and Shamdasani, 2017: 49). In general, online focus groups have been particularly applicable to research involving disadvantaged people. Moreover, opinion leaders and experts located in different places, as well as busy executives, professionals or policy makers, can more readily be recruited for participation. Lastly, online focus groups provide an especially appropriate venue for reaching young people, who are generally quite comfortable and at ease in the online world but are difficult to reach by other means (Fox et al., 2007; Kelly et al., 2010).

Disadvantages

However, the application of the online focus group also has some limitations. We will highlight some more evident weaknesses cited in the literature.

- *Digital gap.* The first point of weakness concerns the selection of the participants. The success of an online focus group assumes that the participants have the skills and familiarity with the electronic format of discussion, including keyboarding skills. Moreover, most of the electronic platforms enabling online focus groups require a stable high-speed internet connection (Lobe, 2017: 235–6). This requires technical equipment, and it cannot be taken for granted that all the participants will have it. Therefore, availability of the technical equipment and the ICT skills and competencies are in themselves elements that automatically select possible participants. This limitation is not only of concern at the individual level, but, most importantly, at the social level. We know that more than half of the world's population has access to the Internet, but there are entire sections of the population and geographical areas that are excluded from it. It is therefore necessary to take into account the digital divide and differences in opportunities for social access to the Internet and the technological and ICT skills required when using this technique (Abrams and Gaiser, 2017: 437).

- *Artificiality of the interaction situation.* Group participants may not be who they claim to be, due to concerns about sharing personal information with strangers in an electronic context (Lobe, 2017: 245–6). However, this limit is becoming less relevant, thanks to the profusion of technologies in everyday life. This is leading to increased confidence and familiarity with such interaction situations, especially for younger and middle-aged groups.

- *Lack of non-verbal communication.* 'A lack of face-to-face interaction can reduce the spontaneity of the group and may reduce or eliminate the non-verbal communication that plays a key role in eliciting responses' (Stewart and Shamdasani, 2017: 50). That said, online focus groups often offer the possibility of using accessory tools to cope with this shortcoming, such as text chat, images and so on. Such tools can work alongside video recording.

Summing up

Regarding virtual interaction and its effects, the literature discusses the role of self-representation. On the one hand, some scholars emphasize the fact that online interaction gives people the opportunity to express themselves more freely (Ellison et al., 2006; Turkle, 2011). For example, some scholars state that online interaction can limit the potential for 'Hawthorne-type effects', in which the researcher induces a desirability bias that could inhibit normatively inappropriate behaviours (e.g. expressions of racial and ethnic prejudice). In other words, participants choose to self-censor in face-to-face interaction situations (Golder and Macy, 2014).

On the other hand, other research shows that online interaction is characterized by the same processes as face-to-face interaction (Hoffman and Novak, 2012: 199). For example, these studies underline that online interpersonal interactions are affected by gender, race, age, and even height and attractiveness stereotypes (Fiske et al., 2002; Fox and Bailenson, 2009; Stewart and Shamdasani, 2017). According to these studies, we need to be careful about reading virtual communications as 'authentic'. People's types of online participation are not transparent windows; rather, they are often carefully curated and systematically managed. The degree of this public self-construction varies. Nevertheless, just as we do in all other areas of our everyday life, we exercise some control all the time when we are online – what we say, what we upload, what we show as our interests and so on (Manovich, 2012). This also applies to online focus groups.

Further reading

Barbour, R.S. and Morgan, D.L. (eds) (2017) *A New Era in Focus Group Research*. London: Palgrave Macmillan.

This volume provides a critical approach to using focus groups, inspecting how this technique has been used to explore a diverse set of research questions covering a broad spectrum of fields.

Fielding, N.G., Lee, R.M. and Blank, G. (eds) (2016) *The SAGE Handbook of Online Research Methods* (2nd edn). London: Sage.

This book takes into account the significant impact of the use of information and communication technologies (ICTs) and the diffusion of the Internet on research practices. A specific chapter is dedicated to the online focus group.

Exercises

1. Explain in your own words why the focus group offers a seemingly informal research context.

2. You are conducting research on use of the TikTok application among teenagers. Indicate why you decide to use the online version of the focus group and what the pros and the cons of this choice are.

2

Dealing with Ethical Challenges

Focus groups, like other 'emic' research techniques, can seem quite informal. Indeed, some of the best groups can resemble a group of friends chatting more than a formal information collection effort. However, researchers always need to remember that in focus groups the same ethical requirements apply as in other research methods.

In this chapter, we will focus on ethical issues. In particular, we will try to answer the following three questions:

- How do general ethical principles apply to the focus group?
- What specific ethical challenges are encountered at different stages of research with focus groups?
- What ethical issues does an online focus group have to deal with?

Therefore, ethical questions will be addressed with a practical approach, trying to predict the most common dilemmas that arise in focus group research applications.

Chapter goals

- *Knowledge*: ethical general principles applied to focus group practice.
- *Applying knowledge and understanding*: how to apply ethical issues in the various stages of research with focus groups.
- *Making judgements*: developing awareness of the effects of research choices, particularly with regard to participants.

2.1 General ethical principles

The context

During the twentieth century, professional communities in the humanistic fields have developed ethical codes relating to the morality of the members of the profession (Smith, 1995: 480; Beauchamp and Childress, 2002). These regulatory codes are based on social obligations and are supported by formal and informal sanctions, and aim to clarify whether professional actions are appropriate (Miles and Huberman, 2014).

In the social field, the academic and professional communities have, albeit with some delay, adopted the practice of drafting ethical documents, with the aim of self-regulating. Their documents mostly concern the ethical and moral implications that arise from their relationship with people who are involved in the jobs or the scientific activity of professionals (e.g. the community under study, the topics analysed, patients, people followed by social workers). Indeed, the object of the work of the social professions is human people as social actors, along with their behaviours and their opinions (Israel, 2015). Hence the main concern of those who have to deal with the social field must be to safeguard people in all ways, and this means ensuring that the work that they do – as a scholar of the social or a professional – is not too intrusive and does not negatively affect any person's life in any way. At any rate, in general, it can be stated that research participants' rights are anchored in fundamental human rights and the fundamental ethical principles that govern all scientific research (European Commission, DG RTD, 2018).

Principles

In general, these documents follow the four principles that are considered ethical pillars of any research method:

- *Autonomy*. This requires that the people concerned have autonomy of thought, intention and action when making decisions regarding research procedures. Therefore, the decision-making process must be free of coercion or coaxing.
- *Justice*. The idea that the burdens and benefits of research must be distributed equally among all groups in society.
- *Beneficence*. This requires that the procedure be provided with the intent of doing good for the subjects involved.
- *Non-maleficence*. This requires that research does not harm the persons involved or others in society.

In the context of social research and the social professions, these four general principles are articulated into multiple statements, which can be summarized as follows (Nosek et al., 2002; Cataldi, 2014; Eynon et al., 2017: 22):

- Recognition of the purely relational character of professional activity and research in the social sphere.
- Attention to value-freedom, emphasizing the requirement that both researchers and professionals, while being value-oriented, should not express value judgements or be linked to conflicts of interest.
- Duty of confidentiality. In particular, compliance with the procedures for collecting informed consent is emphasized, as is the obligation to bring the research and professional objectives to the attention of the people involved. Social researchers and the social professions have a responsibility to ensure that the confidentiality of the information collected is guaranteed to all participants throughout the whole process, both during the interaction and when the information collected is transmitted, analysed and stored.
- Avoiding the risk of participants being harmed. Social researchers and the social professions have the responsibility to ensure, as far as they can, that persons will not come to harm by taking part in any study/intervention. In the social fields, both psychological and physical harm is considered (Carey and Asbury, 2012: 35; Hennink, 2014: 45). This requires attention to the symbolic dimension.
- Awareness of the consequences that can ensue from the research process and from results, together with a willingness to focus on the repercussions for the public and civil society.

Ethical principles in focus group

What specifically happens in the focus group? The focus group is a research technique. Therefore, all the general principles mentioned above apply to it. Moreover, like many other research tools, focus groups are based on human interactions.

However, there are some particular features. The first derives from the fact that the focus group belongs to the qualitative research family of approaches. Ethical principles relating to the relationship with the people involved are even more challenging in the context of this approach to research. Indeed, qualitative research supports commitments to (Buchanan, 2000; Aluwihare-Samaranayake, 2012: 65):

- capturing the voices of participants and expressing their experiences;
- studying persons by directly interacting with them;
- understanding the participants' social world through their voices and points of view;
- using the participants' words to tell their stories and points of view.

Moreover, the focus group has another particular feature: participation in a collective discussion 'is interactive in the sense that an individual's input exists within a social context' (Smith, 1995: 482).

Obviously, this characteristic has some consequences. The most important ones concern the interaction. In particular, according to Mickey W. Smith (1995), in focus groups ethical issues may arise from 'overdisclosure' by group participants. There are two main challenges:

- participants reveal themselves to each other;
- there may be stresses due to the intensity of the interaction of the group.

In what follows, we will analyse the main ethical issues that researchers face in the different phases of application of the focus group, trying to take a practical step-by-step perspective and giving some advice.

2.2 Choosing and recruiting participants

Choosing and recruiting participants are two delicate steps of focus group research. They may involve issues related to the socio-cultural and political context, trust, knowing and being known (Aluwihare-Samaranayake, 2012: 68).

Choice of cases

As in qualitative information collection techniques, in the focus group the choice of participants follows the logic of interest and relevance to the cognitive objectives of the research. This is why we do not talk about real sampling but instead about seeking out the best match between empirical cases and theoretical ones. Indeed, the researcher is in charge of defining the reference target of the research work, which means defining who the theoretical cases are. Therefore, an ideal profile for the participants is defined. The choice of empirical cases is then made on this basis, following the criteria of usefulness and fruitfulness from the theoretical point of view in order to investigate the unit of analysis (Ragin and Becker, 1992: 220).

This is even more true in qualitative research designs, where the characteristics of the population are usually not known beforehand and the cases to be explored are chosen not for their distribution in the population, but for the interest that they seem to hold for the researcher.

In subsequent chapters (see section 5.2) we will explain how the choice of cases can be made and what criteria must be followed. Here it is sufficient to suggest that the selection of some empirical cases and the exclusion of others may have repercussions on the investigated topic, raising ethical problems (see Table 2.1).

When the investigative context is close to the researcher's daily life, there may be significant negative effects arising from the choice of some cases and the exclusion of others. Indeed, the selection of the participants can undermine relationships among the persons involved or between these people and the researcher. It is therefore up to the researcher to carefully assess the advantages and disadvantages of carrying out a study in a 'familiar context'.

Regarding the choice of the participants, another precaution to be taken concerns the choice of having the group include acquaintances (people who are personally known by the researcher and/or who know each other). The general principle is to protect participants' privacy in the community. Typically, focus groups are composed of participants who do not know each other. Nevertheless, depending on the topic, a researcher may end up with a group of friends, acquaintances, or even relatives. The researcher should be careful when asking people to reveal things that could affect them later (Gimbel, 2017).

The recruitment process

Other ethical problems may arise from the recruitment process (Aluwihare-Samaranayake, 2012: 68). For example, when approaching participants, traditional procedures emphasize the importance of involving some key figures such as the cultural mediator, the key informant and the qualified witness. These key figures have the characteristic of assuming a role very close to that of the researcher, becoming almost consultant and auxiliary in both the phase of access to the field and the phase of identification and recruitment of the focus group participants. These are in fact special persons who, due to their characteristics, can be considered reliable and competent, and who can provide important information because of their strategic position in the group, enabling the researcher to identify interesting people for the research.

From an ethical point of view, the use of these key figures is very positive. Indeed, this strategy favours a participatory perspective on the investigation by involving the people studied in the different phases of the research. However, whatever key figure is used to get in touch with the people studied, it is always necessary to evaluate the reliability of the person selected for the key role and keep in mind that their perspective when making observations of reality will be partial. It is therefore necessary to be aware, from a dispassionate standpoint, of the key figure interests, in order to assess the strengths and weaknesses of their involvement and to prevent any conflicts of interest (see Table 2.1).

In the field

In research on the identity of second-generation Muslim women in Italy (Acocella et al., 2016), for example, the researchers relied for the choice of participants in the focus groups on two women cultural mediators: one belonging to the Pakistani community, and the other to the Moroccan community. However, while in the Moroccan community the recruitment took place through informal and friendly channels, explaining the research goals, the Pakistani community mediator followed a more formal approach, using a hierarchical channel or through a religious leader. This may indicate that the Pakistani women were not completely free to accept participation in research.

The contact

Finally, there are some practical considerations to bear in mind when contacting possible focus group participants (see Table 2.1).

- *Email or telephone?* Usually, the first contact is made by email or by telephone. In both cases the researcher has personal data available and he/she has the duty of ensuring confidentiality. Email addresses are often identifiable because they may contain names, geographical location and organizational affiliation. At the same time, having a person's private telephone number means holding sensitive information about him/her (Gimbel, 2017). For this reason, it is recommended to reduce email and telephone channels to a minimum and use other tools for first contacts (Eynon et al., 2017). However, if the researcher uses the phone or email, it is important to explain how he/she acquired the personal contact details of the people and reassure them of their right to privacy of information.
- *Convince or sell?* Usually, researchers make a great deal of effort to recruit a group that consists of the ideal empirical cases for research purposes. However, the purpose of the focus group is to hear what its members have to say, not to market to them or sell them one's ideas. For this reason, it is important to avoid both the typical attitude of the seller and the paternalistic approach of the researcher, assuming that everyone will benefit from the participation. The researcher may feel tempted to use minor subterfuges so that people cannot refuse to participate in the focus group. An example could be telling them that all the other individuals have accepted, in order to convince them to participate because of a sense of social responsibility. These strategies should be avoided as they are forms of exercise of power by the researcher, who is seeking to coerce the individual.

On the contrary, it is always necessary to respect the subject, bearing his/her priorities in life in mind and the possibility that he/she does not have the same idea about the importance of research (Gimbel, 2017).

- *Right to refuse or duty to participate?* Focus groups are conducted in a place chosen by the researcher (Orentlicher, 2005). This may result in a refusal to participate by some of those invited, for multiple reasons, including the fact that the choice of place and/or time does not fit the participant's schedule or habits (Aluwihare-Samaranayake, 2012: 68). The context selected for the discussion can influence the decision to participate. For example, if the researcher chooses to conduct the focus group in the participants' own professional environment, the choice of whether or not to participate is not completely free and is conditioned by work relationships (Gilli, 1971), especially if the participants are from different hierarchical levels. In this case, more or less deliberately, the researcher can benefit from the fact that the participant may perceive that there may be indirect sanctions if he/she decides not to participate in the research. For these reasons, the research group should evaluate the effects of direct or indirect pressure on people when choosing the research environment. In addition, the customer also has an important role. Sometimes knowing who the customer is can lead to refusing participation. For example, if it is a large company with an explicit interest, the subjects may refuse to participate in order to express their dissatisfaction with the company's brand and business policy. On the other hand, the client's reputation can be appealing to participants and encourage their participation. For example, if the customer is a prestigious moral body, university, research centre or government institution, the selected persons may feel encouraged to be involved in the research.

Table 2.1 Ethical challenges in choosing and recruiting participants

Research activity	Risk	Advice
Choice of cases close to the researcher's daily life	☐ Persons chosen for the focus group may feel elected; by contrast, non-participants may feel excluded ☐ People may feel compelled to participate by acquiescence or politeness	☐ Evaluate the direct and indirect effects of selecting acquaintances ☐ Diversify the recruitment environments

(Continued)

Table 2.1 (Continued)

Research activity	Risk	Advice
Use of key figures for choice and recruitment	☐ The key figure identifies the participants according to his/her particular interests ☐ The key figure uses inappropriate recruitment strategies/criteria (i.e. hierarchical channels)	☐ Evaluate the reliability of the key figure and consider his/her particular interests ☐ Follow the key figure's activities and evaluate their recruitment criteria/strategies in detail ☐ Use more key figures
First contact with the people	☐ Contacted people may feel that their privacy has been violated because the researcher is in possession of personal contact details (i.e. email address or telephone number)	☐ Explain how you acquired the personal contact details of the person ☐ Set up the contacts through the research website and activate an anonymized forum for participants to ask questions about the research
Convincing people to participate in the research	☐ Act like a salesman ☐ Use minor subterfuges so that the people cannot refuse participation	☐ Respect the person, keeping in mind his/her priorities in life ☐ Inform participants, even at first contact, that they may refuse to participate in the research

Voluntary informed consent

The most fundamental ethical behaviour and the core of any research project is informed consent. Participants should know that they are part of a research process, and the researcher should be honest about what is being studied. Anyone doing research should be aware of and knowledgeable about informed consent and should ensure that any research project meets these standards (Carey and Asbury, 2012: 57; Gimbel, 2017).

Principles

For focus group researchers, it is of the utmost importance to specify in advance what information will be collected and how it is to be used (see Appendix 1). The principle of informed consent stresses the researcher's responsibility to fully inform participants of different aspects of the research in comprehensible language (Hennink, 2014: 46; Sanjari et al., 2014: 10). Clarifications need to include the following issues:

- the nature of the research;
- the identity of the researcher;
- the financing body;
- the objective of the research;
- the participants' potential role;
- how the results will be published and used.

Furthermore, informed consent must reassure participants about:

- privacy and the prohibition of disclosing information relating to research;
- safety;
- anonymity and confidentiality.

Sometimes, that is, in research on sensitive topics where written consent puts the informants at risk, oral consent can be audio recorded (Sanjari et al., 2014: 10) and can take the place of a written document.

When highly sensitive issues are concerned, children and other vulnerable individuals should have access to a tutor who is present during initial phases of the study, and ideally, during information-gathering sessions (Carey and Asbury, 2012: 76–7).

2.3 Interaction

In focus groups, trying to ensure that harm is not caused by the study is particularly challenging because there may well be unintended consequences of the research due to the social interaction (Eynon et al., 2017: 22). Indeed, many research collection techniques provide for researcher/participants interaction. However, in the case of the focus group the relationships are multiple, since the engine is collective discussion and group interaction (see section 1.3). For precisely this reason, the greatest risks of harm and suffering for the participants can derive from this very interaction (Carey and Asbury, 2012: 35).

In the field of social research, it is always necessary to bear in mind that the relationship established between researcher and social actor has an eminently social character. Therefore it is not possible to exclude also the hierarchical structuring dimension of the interaction. Some scholars, in particular, speak of the power exercised by the researcher over the social actor (Galtung, 1967; Gilli, 1971; Scraton, 2004). This type of power can be of various types, but above all it is 'technical', that is, it depends on the disparity of knowledge that exists between the actors of social research (Gilli, 1971).

The power exercised on the participants is both symbolic, because the researcher has a greater knowledge and command of the research objectives, and technical, since the leader of the discussion (who may or may not coincide with the researcher; see Chapter 7) has greater knowledge about the technique's operation.

In any event, from an ethical point of view hierarchical and power structuring cannot be eliminated. It is indeed part of the diversity of roles between social actors. However, it is important to be aware of this in order to prevent the researcher and especially the moderator (who interfaces directly with the participants and who may not coincide with the researcher) from causing suffering or damage derived from the exercise of the technical power.

In the following chapters, we will analyse the power dynamics within the groups and the asymmetric position between the moderator and the participants during the discussions (see sections 7.1 and 9.4). However, we can anticipate some precautions that the moderator can take in the course of his/her task to reduce the risk that the group discussion may have unintended effects of harming the participants. Many of these risks can be predicted and prevented by the researcher. Others can be predicted and prevented by the moderator. The main criteria to be considered are discussed below (see Table 2.2).

Tips for moderator and researcher

- *Ensure confidentiality in the group.* The researcher cannot guarantee complete confidentiality of the information collected because the participants do not reveal themselves only to the moderator, but also to each other (Carey and Asbury, 2012: 57 and 67; Hennink, 2014: 49). For this reason, focus group researchers cannot promise or ensure strict and absolute confidentiality. Indeed, the researcher does not have control over what participants may disclose after they leave the focus group. To minimize this potential problem, the researcher should inform participants that this may occur (Smith, 1995: 483). The researcher should also include this issue in the introductory statements, in order to make the participants aware and ask them not to reveal outside the focus group what is said during the group meetings. Although this does not entirely solve the problem, this approach procedure can alleviate concerns and reduce participants' apprehensions.
- *Prevent harm from the group discussion.* It sometimes happens that the discussion is very heated and can become conflictual. Some expressions,

epithets or harsher comparisons can cause suffering or discomfort in some participants. In order to assess and prevent this risk, the moderator should encourage a comfortable atmosphere and establish a 'netiquette' in group discussion (Mann and Stewart, 2000). Another way to prevent conflicts in the group is to chose the assortment of participants carefully. The design of the group and the recruitment of participants are both important. Groups with people of different hierarchical levels, such as groups with the boss and his/her employees, should be avoided (see section 5.2). In addition, attention should be paid to the atmosphere of group discussion. The best advice is to do everything to create a good climate during the focus group session. This will be the best way to prevent ethical issues arising from interaction. At the beginning of the discussion, the icebreaker and warm-up exercises can help create a comfortable climate for the participants. This can help to prevent the degeneration of relationships within the group (see section 7.2). At any rate, it is important to remember to provide participants with an easy way to leave the group discussion. Hence, it will be up to the moderator to reiterate, before the start of the discussion, that a participant can leave the group if they feel uncomfortable (see section 7.2). Finally, at the end of the discussion, it is also advisable to make an assessment of the interaction climate in the group, asking the participants how much they felt at ease during the discussion. This is particularly useful for estimating the possible negative effects, not only during the discussion, but also some time after the session.

Expert advice

After completing the focus group, participants can assess the general interpersonal climate of the session by answering the following questions: Did you feel the group was warm? Did you feel that the comments of the group made it easier for you to share your feelings on the topic?

- *Prevent harm from the moderator's involuntary behaviour.* Despite the best intentions, it can happen that the moderator's behaviour involuntarily hurts the participants in the focus group. In the following chapters, we will analyse how the moderator can play his/her role, assessing the level of directivity of group coordination (see section 7.1). However, there are situations in which the moderator can unwillingly affect participants' susceptibility. For example, the moderator may make comments about what the participants say, and such comments can be read as disrespectful or not sufficiently sensitive (Gimbel, 2017: 1). At other times, even just simple behaviour by the moderator can be interpreted differently. For example, the moderator's gaze can induce a participant to 'shut up' if he/she interprets the look as disappointment, or alternatively the same gaze can be interpreted as an input to continue the discussion deepening the sentence just said (even more than the participant would do spontaneously), if the person interprets the look as approval. In addition, people participating in a focus group may feel uncomfortable in this new social situation. For many of them, it may be the first time that they have taken part in such a group. Obviously, the presence of the moderator and the technical equipment for the audio-video recording can make them uncomfortable. This happens in (almost) all focus groups. Usually, however, this concern disappears after the first few minutes of a focus group, thanks to the moderator, who can make the discussion feel comfortable. However, in some cases performance stress can be more persistent. This happens especially when the discussion is highly structured and with many questions. In this case participants can feel quizzed or tested (Gimbel, 2017: 1). The moderator should therefore avoid asking too many pressing questions and allow the participants to express themselves, because the goal of a focus group is to learn from them. Finally, often unintentionally, the moderator can abuse the patience and commitment of the participants. For example, a practical suggestion to prevent participants from becoming impatient is to end the focus group on time.

Table 2.2 Ethical challenges in focus group discussion

Risk	Advice
The discussion can become overheated and conflictual	☐ Design groups that are not too heterogeneous, or at least limit the differences that may lead to excessive clashes (i.e. opposite political positions, different hierarchical levels)
	☐ Prevent conflictual events by ensuring a good relational climate in moderation (i.e. providing icebreaker and warm-up exercises)
	☐ Exclude questions that may provoke excessive conflict, change topic or in extreme cases interrupt the focus group
A participant may feel offended or hurt by the words of another participant	☐ Define a 'netiquette' in group discussion
	☐ Before the start of the discussion, reiterate that a participant can leave the group if she/he feels uncomfortable. It's important to make an assessment of the interaction climate in the group, asking the participants how much they felt at ease during the discussion

Risk	Advice
The moderator can make the participants feel devalued	☐ Be respectful of participants (i.e. avoid passing judgement or commenting on or making jokes about participants)
	☐ Make participants feel expert on the topic
	☐ Show interest in everything that participants say
Participants may disclose information after leaving the focus group	☐ Inform participants that researchers cannot promise or ensure strict and absolute confidentiality
	☐ Include this issue in the introductory statements
	☐ After the discussion, organize a debriefing to explain to participants how to respect confidentiality

2.4 Choosing sensitive or delicate topics

Sometimes the topics covered by a focus group can be sensitive. In this case, the researcher must carefully evaluate the advantages and disadvantages of conducting a focus group on sensitive topics (see Table 2.3).

Risks of sensitive topics

Indeed, on the one hand, the focus group can be a way to allow participants to open up to sensitive issues (Carey and Asbury, 2012: 22). The group can be a tool to reassure them that they are not alone in facing a specific problem or a delicate situation and therefore be free to express themselves (Goldman, 1962: 62–3).

On the other hand, the researcher must also carefully evaluate the unwanted effects of a group and then decide whether to conduct an in-depth interview. In fact, in a focus group delicate topics are not only known by the researcher, but they also become the domain of the group. There are two risks related to this:

- the possibility that the other members of the focus group report what emerged during the discussion to others (Morgan and Krueger, 1993: 12);
- the possibility that the group itself becomes a vehicle for labelling. As the labelling theory maintains the label of deviance is attributed within a group and leads to a change in the perception of oneself and others.

Expert advice

When conducting a focus group with alcoholic persons, it is important to ensure that participants do not report to their family members, acquaintances and friends who was present in the focus group and what topics, attitudes or behaviours emerged during the discussion. In addition, care should be taken to make an appointment in a neutral place that does not necessarily require participants to explain to third parties what the focus group topic is and what problems are discussed in the session.

There is also the risk that the interaction within the group is perceived by the participants as a sort of group therapy, as happens in self-help groups. In this case, the role and task of the focus group is misunderstood and can become clinical. If this happens, it is the researcher's task to clarify that it is a matter of research and to interrupt, where necessary, discussions when there is the risk of creating false expectations. For this reason, it is necessary to evaluate whether it is appropriate to investigate sensitive issues in discussion groups. Indeed, some scholars suggest preferring the in-depth individual interview for these topics (Goldman, 1962: 62–3).

Furthermore, for other scholars the focus group does not work for sensitive topics because each member recounts his/her own experience in an individual way and therefore does not create the conditions for a group discussion (Acocella, 2008: 176–80).

Tips for sensitive topics

At any rate, if the researcher wants to collect sensitive information, he/she should consider asking these questions in homework or by using in-group questionnaires, so that participants do not have to speak aloud to the group. If the focus group is discussing a sensitive issue, it may also be possible to include individual work within the session, where individual participants are asked to perform an exercise, answer some closed questions or describe a deviant or at-risk situation, individually, without showing what was written to the other participants. After this individual moment, the discussion can take place more generally on the topic of investigation without describing in detail what the individual participants wrote/answered during the exercise phase or the individual questions. The moderator can then collect individual responses and help the discussion without going into the details of sensitive behaviours. After the discussion, the researcher will be able to read calmly what the participants have written individually, and this will help to better understand what has been discussed and the perspectives/experiences of participants (which can be considered as their starting points).

The choice of a delicate theme can also influence the design of the focus group. For example, if the researcher chooses a sensitive topic, it may be more appropriate to conduct a focus group with a small number of participants, in order to keep the relationships under control and to go deeper.

Another stratagem is to organize a debriefing with the participants after the focus group. In some cases, the debriefing can be collective in order to cool down and distill what has been said in the group, reminding participants of the secrecy of the information. The debriefing can be organized by the moderator and in some cases – depending on the topic – it may require the support of specialized professionals, such as psychologists, who can support the moderator in dealing with any possible negative effects that the research may have on participants.

In other cases, however, the debriefing can be individual and can also give rise to legal, behavioural, clinical or medical advice to the participant who has confessed to deviant or at-risk behaviour during the focus group.

In the field

An example is provided by Mickey W. Smith (1995: 484–5). While discussing risk behaviour issues (i.e. sexual activity, drug use) with an HIV population, a participant may disclose that he/she is engaging in risky behaviours (e.g. knowingly having unsafe sex). How does the moderator handle this situation? The researcher may wish to take note of the comment and discreetly discuss the issue with the individual after the focus group meeting. Another option may be to acknowledge the point immediately and provide information to the participant.

Finally, the moderator can offer participants contact information or resources to use if they have questions after the group. This is especially important if the focus group concerns a sensitive topic or involves an at-risk population. This is the way to provide support.

Table 2.3   Ethical challenges when choosing a sensitive topic

Risk	Advice
A person may not feel comfortable talking about the topic within a group	☐ Evaluate whether the focus group is the best technique for such a topic or whether an in-depth interview is better

(Continued)

45

Table 2.3 (Continued)

Risk	Advice
Other members of the focus group report to the outside or to others what emerged during the discussion	☐ Organize a collective debriefing with the participants after the focus group, reminding them of the secrecy of the information
The group itself becomes a vehicle for the labelling of third persons	☐ Organize the focus group in a neutral place
The participants perceive the interaction within the group as a sort of group therapy, (i.e. as in self-help groups)	☐ Clarify that the group does not have clinical purposes ☐ Where necessary, interrupt the discussion when there is a risk of misunderstanding, so as not to create false expectations
Interaction with different people can be difficult to sustain and psychologically demanding	☐ Design the focus group with a small number of participants, in order to keep the relationships under control and to go deeper ☐ Organize a collective debriefing after the focus group with specialized professionals
During the focus group there is the disclosure of risky behaviours or behaviours with medical/clinical or legal consequences	

2.5 Incentives

In the context of social research, there are two forms of incentives for those taking part in the field research: symbolic incentives and material incentives (Galtung, 1967: 147).

In both cases, the very fact of talking about incentives presupposes that the relationship between researcher and research participant is:

- a social relationship and therefore is carried out according to the formal and informal rules and expectations typical of a society, albeit according to the canons of a professional or research relationship;
- a relationship that can result from an exchange of goods, which are largely immaterial, but in some cases also material;

- a relationship in which the researcher can exercise a form of power by, for example, granting incentives or rewards, symbolic materials, to the participants.

Non-material incentives

The first form of power is cultural in nature and is based on the sharing of values and norms: it gives rise to symbolic incentives. The reward that the researcher can therefore foresee for those who participate in the focus group can assume forms that are not purely material in nature, such as satisfaction, achievement, performing an activity different from routine ones, feeling useful, giving opinion on the investigation topic and so on. Those who participate in the research can feel satisfied by making their own contribution to knowledge about a topic. Even just being listened to by someone and being able to communicate one's idea can be gratifying. The researcher can therefore appeal to these incentives – without exploiting them – to motivate the participants and demonstrate gratitude for their participation in the focus group (Krueger and Casey, 2000).

Expert advice

The researcher can seek the collaboration of the participants by appealing to social values, such as the common good, the advancement of scientific knowledge or improvement of the status quo. At the same time, participants can feel gratified by group discussion and their contribution to the research.

Material incentives

As well as the symbolic forms of incentive to research, there are also material ones. Where this is the case, the power exercised by the researcher will be remunerative. It facilitates an exchange system in which the researcher provides compensation for those who participate in the research in exchange for their time, effort and experience.

The practice of giving material incentives to research participants is becoming increasingly common. Whereas this practice previously pertained only to market research, it is now much more widespread than is believed. Indeed, it is used also in many academic fields and in some disciplines in particular, such as economics, marketing and medicine. This practice is becoming more common as the complexity of the task required of the participant increases and in areas with more resources available for research.

The most common practice is to give cash or gift vouchers to research participants (Carey and Asbury, 2012: 22). Other forms can be the reimbursement of expenses, compensation for time, inconvenience and possible discomfort, to show a token appreciation for the participants' help (www. ethicsguidebook.ac.uk). In reality, this practice is ethically questionable (Head, 2009: 335). In particular, it is important to bear the following key points in mind:

- *Material incentives – yes or no?* The literature concurs that material incentives can be considered a form of coercion that influence the voluntary nature of research participation (Alderson and Morrow 2004; Grant, 2006). Indeed, payments exert undue influence on potential participants' decisions about whether to take part in research. The situation is particularly difficult 'when participants are people from impoverished groups or where participation might mean participants were "out of pocket" in some way' (Wiles et al., 2005: 16). This particular concern arises because financially disadvantaged groups may be more vulnerable to this kind of coercion. Because they need the money, their consent is not truly freely given if payment is involved (Liamputtong, 2011: 55). Where this is the case, it is good to evaluate the advantages and disadvantages of using material incentives (Hennink, 2014: 47).
- *Money or voucher?* A further issue is how the payment is made. Cash payments may have implications in terms of, for example, participants' benefit payments or taxation (if they are seen as 'income'). Moreover, to avoid cash money, it should be noted that bank credit procedures often do not allow anonymity and give access to very sensitive information (www.ethics guidebook.ac.uk). For this reason, the majority of scholars stress that it is not appropriate to give payments and instead to emphasize the possibility of replacing money with discount coupons or purchase vouchers (Liamputtong, 2011: 56). Often such vouchers may also be for products related to research or be useful to participants. Finally, 'some research projects may provide other incentives, rewards or compensations for time and effort, such as food' (Wiles et al., 2005: 17). Hence, one might argue that focus group research uses forms of inducement when providing refreshments on attendance. In any event, organizing some moderate amount of refreshment is a polite way of welcoming participants and can be useful to warm up or to end the group discussion.
- *Declare or not declare incentives?* Some researchers manage the coercion problem by not informing persons that they will be paid and give payment as a 'thank you' after they have participated in the research. 'Of course, the difficulty with this is that it is not possible to keep this a surprise for

long as word soon gets round, especially in specific communities' (Wiles et al., 2005: 17). Above all, there are very important ethical issues that militate against following this strategy (Truman, 2003). Payment should not override the principles of freely given and fully informed consent. Before they start the research, participants should know that they can withdraw from the study at any time without losing their payment. As a result, it is recommended that the use of an incentive should appear on the informed consent form (see Appendix 1). Furthermore, it is essential to report incentives in the interim and final project report.

In the field

From a report of research on a group of women as part of an advertising campaign for an underwear company: 'Participants were compensated with a $20 gift card to either Dunkin' Donuts or iTunes. The university's institutional review board approved the study' (Kruger et al., 2018).

Therefore, if it is proposed to make any kind of payment to participants, the researcher should think carefully about why it is necessary, and how it is done. Furthermore, because of these dilemmas, research ethics committees carefully scrutinize any plans to pay research participants (www.ethicsguidebook.ac.uk).

2.6 Data transmission, data storing and data analysis

The elaboration, transmission and storing of the information collected is a particularly delicate process. These research phases are particularly sensitive because they often involve several members of the research staff. Indeed, many different people usually handle focus group recordings and transcripts. Furthermore, the research group can be composed of several people who will participate in the final analysis collectively or individually, deepening specific parts of the investigation. The principle of confidentiality requires particular attention to all these steps.

Data transmission

The first step concerns the transmission of audio or audio-video recordings of group discussions. They are often transmitted to research support personnel who produce full transcription of the focus groups. After the transcription, the texts are again transmitted to the researcher or to other specialized personnel who will attend to the analysis. Finally, the analysis will be transmitted and used by the research staff to write intermediate and final reports and so on. This gives an idea of the number of people to whom the information collected is transmitted.

As regards securely transmitting the information collected, potential solutions include use of labels that are meaningless to anyone but the researcher, and the separate transmission of personal data on participants (Eynon et al., 2017: 23).

Therefore, it is advisable to state in the informed consent form how the transmission of the information collected will be made and who will be responsible for it.

Data storage

Data storage operations should also not be underestimated from the ethical point of view. The information collected needs to be protected against other people accessing them or tampering with them (Carey and Asbury, 2012: 86; Hennink, 2014: 135). This can be an issue in the networked systems commonly used in universities and research centres (Eynon et al., 2017: 23). The name and the specific information on the person responsible for secure data storage should be included in the informed consent form.

Data analysis

With regard to analysis of the information collected, it should be noted that the final material available to researchers for processing consists of transcription texts (see Chapters 10 and 11). There are several effective strategies to protect personal information: for instance, removal of identifier components and biographical details, as well as the use of pseudonyms (applicable to names of individuals, places and organizations).

Furthermore, often the analysis operations will consist of the classification and construction of grids. This requires a reading and in-depth knowledge of the texts by analysts and also of the contexts and subjects from which they originate. For this reason, the analysis phase is particularly sensitive when it comes to protecting confidentiality, because the code and retrieval work often cannot be separated from personal information. However, this information cannot be explicitly included in the analysis, nor can it be published.

Reporting

Finally, particular attention must be paid to the phase of writing the interim report, the final research report, articles and scientific books (see Chapter 12). The considerations to keep in mind are the following:

- *Protect participants' privacy in reporting.* In scientific reports, personally identifiable information should be removed from quotes. However, research reports often also require support from various materials, such as video materials or online ones. As Kinsey Gimbel (2017: 1) maintains, participants should have 'completed a release form prior to the focus group, but that does not mean that they consented to having video clips or quotes put on YouTube or on a billboard. Video recordings should be kept within the research team or the intended audience of a final report, unless identities are disguised'. This applies unless the researcher asks in advance for the participant's authorization to shoot the video and show it in public. Obviously, the question becomes more sensitive in the case of minors (where parental authorization might not be enough) or protected categories.

- *Give feedback to participants.* After the field research, the researcher often forgets the participants. In reality, an ethical approach to research requires the return of knowledge to social actors. This mode activates the 'double hermeneutic' (Montesperelli, 1998), a typical circle where 'concepts, theories and findings generated by sociology spiral in and out of social life' (Giddens, 1987: 32). Therefore, it will not be enough to send the persons involved the publications related to the research to which they have contributed; instead it would be advisable to invite them to an *ad hoc* meeting in order to discuss with them the results that emerged from the focus groups and the research in general. This engagement can become a new occasion for mutual learning between researcher and social actors.

- *Take the effects of research on the participants into account.* The dissemination and publication of results is never neutral for those who have participated in the study. Sometimes the publications will be read only by experts, professionals or academics. At other times – especially in relation to the sources of publications and to the clients – more far-reaching dissemination will be required. In the university field, this is part of the so-called 'third mission', that is, the vocation of academic research to engage with the human and social context in which it is embedded and to contribute to its development. Furthermore, it must be borne in mind that the dissemination of the results can contribute to highlighting a little-known social problem or, on the contrary, to social labelling with the risk of making some categories of persons more vulnerable (Barbour, 2007: 115). As Anthony Giddens (1984) explains, social science is not only affected by society, but it is an effective agent in shaping it. Indeed, social science is internal to its 'subject matter' in a way that natural science is not, as well as the findings of social science 'cannot be kept wholly separate from the universe of meaning and action which they are about' (Giddens, 1984: xxxii–iii). This is why there is an ethical risk that social research may – without wishing to – contribute to categorizing and labelling social types and thus increase their isolation and marginalization. For this reason, it is important to pay attention to the unforeseen outcomes of social research and categorization. In this regard, an interesting point of view has been propounded by the pedagogist Paulo Freire (1968), who highlights the basic purpose of social disciplines: inducing humans 'to be more human', that is, to fully develop their own potentialities so that they are no longer passive, but rather think to produce changes. In this sense, social categories should not contribute to oppression, but they could increase awareness and emancipation.

In the field

An example of a topic that can be highlighted by social research is violence against men. Usually this violence is not reported by the victims as a result of shame. Yet doing research on this issue, against the current, can help to give voice to some oppressed people and can contribute to creating civic awareness on the issue. Empirical evidence on this topic can also contribute to plan adequate preventative interventions.

Only in this way will a report have the capacity to enable the participants to change from their position of vulnerability or oppression and amplify their own voice, bringing their cultural and socio-political construction of self and experience to the foreground (Barbour, 2007: 115–16).

2.7 Ethics in online focus groups

As mentioned in Chapter 1, 'the rise of Web 2.0, the advent of greater bandwidth and new technology platforms have made it possible to extend the range of focus group research to the online environment'. An investigation conducted in 2010 by the Council of American Survey Research Organizations found that 'commercial research firms were experiencing either no growth or a decline in location-based focus groups and in-depth interviews, but also reported that revenues from online focus groups had nearly doubled' (Steward and Shamdasani, 2017: 49).

Online risks and tips

For this reason, the topic of ethics in online focus groups needs to be addressed separately. Generally, the same principles apply as for face-to-face focus groups.

Nevertheless, some points must be taken into consideration. We list them below with references to the main literature on the topic.

- *Privacy.* Online focus groups require that users register and either create or are given a password so that confidentiality of the information collected can be easily ensured (Im and Chee, 2006). Online filters can make people feel more secure, so that they can perceive themselves as being more protected in their privacy by meeting remotely through the Web. As Rebecca Eynon, Jenny Fry and Ralph Schroeder (2017) explain, this perception may encourage people to discuss topics or disclose more details than they would be willing to in face-to-face situations. In any event, researchers need to ensure that the perception of anonymity is fulfilled.
- *Security issues.* As shown by Eun-Ok Im and Wonshik Chee (2006: 270), 'compared with other types of Internet data collection methods that are accessible to the public without passwords, online focus groups are safer' because they require the access to a closed platform dedicated only to participants (Lobe, 2017: 245). However, maintaining security and confidentiality could be a challenge to researchers during the information collection process. Hacking attempts can take place. For this reason, it is necessary to update the software regularly, including the firewall, in order to prevent any potential virus infection or hacking attempt.
- *Harm issues.* Since the online focus group format is usually favoured to protect the privacy of the participants, it is often chosen to deal with sensitive topics. For example, online focus groups can be used for people who have attempted suicide, people who are considering/have committed a crime or people who are bullying other people (Carmack and Degroot, 2014). At any rate, as in the face-to-face focus group, the researcher's most important concern should be avoiding the risk of participants incurring psychological harm during and after the group discussion (Carey and Asbury, 2012: 35). Indeed, the researchers' duties are not different compared to a face-to-face focus group. Therefore, the precautions mentioned above must be put into practice carefully.
- *Informed consent.* A potential problem online is the difficulty of explaining and understanding informed consent. Usually the informed consent form is filled in online before the group discussion. Having an individual filling in the form remotely, without in-depth information or without a face-to-face explanation with simple words, can generate misunderstandings (Lobe, 2017: 244). For this reason, the researcher must thoroughly explain the consent that the participants are signing, perhaps with a tutorial or some examples also online. In addition, it is possible to create a forum on the research site for anonymous answers to questions. This helps to reduce the number of people who abandon the group discussion or refuse their

consent to the use of the information collected. In the same way, a good informed consent document for an online focus group 'should include information about the technology, how it may and may not impact such things as anonymity (including IP addresses) and expectation. It might be helpful to indicate in the informed consent form that participants should not record the focus group for any purpose, avoiding the possibility that other people for any other reason use the discussion' (Abrams and Gaiser, 2017: 447).

- *Special targets.* Another important issue concerns certain vulnerable groups (Barbour, 2007: 107–15). Online research is particularly suitable for young people and minors. However, for them it is always necessary to have the informed consent of the parents. For example, some researchers suggest sending specific invitations to adults and care givers in order to give them private access through a password to a controlled website containing all the information about the research and the participants. There are also other vulnerable targets who need special consent procedures: for example, people with mental disabilities or special handicaps, and prisoners.

- *Online communities.* Usually the recruitment of participants for online focus groups takes place within virtual communities. This ensures that those who are recruited are comfortable with ICT. Moreover, virtual communities are often based on specific topics, so that it is possible to recruit people interested in certain issues or who share the same group membership. However, online communities must be respected and it is important to avoid the investigator's intrusiveness for instrumental purposes. For example, the researcher must not be persistent in his/her recruitment announcement posts, since this is 'not unlike the telemarketing recruitment call during dinner hours' (Abrams and Gaiser, 2017: 447). Being respectful of online groups and virtual communities is fundamental in online research.

In conclusion, the development of online focus groups is raising new challenges. The ethical principles to be pursued are the same, but the modes of interaction can pose new risks. It is up to the researcher to evaluate properly whether the focus group has to be done online, taking into account all the consequences of this choice.

Further reading

The Research Ethics Guidebook: A Resource for Social Scientists, available at www.ethicsguidebook.ac.uk (accessed 30 March 2020).

Designed as an online resource for social science researchers, this site provides guidance and information relating to different stages of the research process.

Boddy, J. (2015) 'The ethics of social research', in N. Gilbert and P. Stoneman (eds), *Researching Social Life* (4th edn). London: Sage. pp. 59–89.

The chapter of this book on social research has the virtue of having a comprehensive view of ethics as moral integrity, which affects all the steps in the conduct of research.

Exercises

1. After reading the chapter, in your opinion, why is paying attention to ethical issues important and not just a bureaucratic requirement to pass an ethics committee? List at least five reasons.

2. At the end of a focus group on drug abuse, the moderator notes that as the participants leave, they exchange information about the purchase of cocaine. What would you do?

Part II

PLANNING AND DESIGNING

3

Designing a Focus Group Research

When starting research, it is crucial to know how many focus groups to perform, what criteria to use to select the groups, how to draw-up the discussion outline and so on. In order to know what choices are the best, however, the researcher needs to have a strategy, which first of all means drawing up a good research design. The research design is like an action plan. There is no perfect action plan that is suitable for every occasion.

Before starting research with focus groups, it is necessary to set up a plan. First of all, the researcher must ask himself/herself some basic questions:

- What are the goals of my research?
- What use of the focus group is more appropriate to respond to this goal?

On the basis of the following two questions, the researcher can individuate the functions of the focus group in his/her research and develop a good plan of action. In particular, in the current use of this technique, four main functions can be considered:

- exploratory-descriptive function;
- analytical-in-depth function;
- experimental function;
- evaluative function.

Considering these four different functions is fundamental for drawing up a good focus group design. Indeed, each function corresponds to a different cognitive goal and, thus, to different choices in collection planning.

In this chapter, after briefly analysing the elements of qualitative research design, we examine how these elements can be appropriately applied in the four different functions of the focus group. In detail, the chapter describes the main characteristics of research in which the focus group is used in an autonomous information-gathering role.

──────────────── **Chapter goals** ────────────────

- *Knowledge*: focus group research design when it is decided to use the technique in an autonomous information-gathering role.
- *Applying knowledge and understanding*: how to design a focus group on the basis of its different functions with reference to the composition of the groups and the structuring level of the information collection tools.
- *Making judgements*: developing a critical analysis on the possibility to conduct neutral observation and obtain immediate empirical knowledge.

3.1 The characteristics of a focus group research design

As presented in the first chapters, the focus group is an effective technique when a researcher is interested in bringing out the socially shared knowledge or collective representations disseminated in particular social groups. Indeed, the focus group is a group discussion held for research purposes that involves people who belong to a social category identifying their membership of a particular community (citizens, politicians, women, young people, social workers, etc.). The collective discussion can favour the emergence of intersubjective representations, reproducing widespread images and shared beliefs within the social group that focus group participants are required to represent (representations of citizens, politicians, women, young people, social workers, etc.).

Specific features

In order to choose how to conduct a research with focus group, it is important to outline the general characteristics of a research design using this technique. The expression 'research design' refers to a general strategy that integrates the various components of the study in a coherent and logical way, thus ensuring an appropriate study of the research topic.

A focus group research design has some specificities, which mainly concern two points:

- the type of research object (unit of analysis);
- the relationship between theory and research (conceptualization of the unit of analysis).

The unit of analysis

Generally, through qualitative approaches, the research issue (unit of analysis) is investigated intensively (identifying the main characteristics and development processes that underlie it), rather than extensively (i.e. the extent of its referents). At the same time, qualitative research is usually conducted when the intention is to reconstruct and understand a phenomenon 'from the inside', enhancing the conceptual, linguistic and analytical categories of the 'insider' (who is directly involved or interested in that phenomenon). Therefore, the aim of such a research is to draw out aspects relevant to developing conceptual categories appropriate to describe and understand the phenomenon under study, enhancing the point of view of the insider (Harris, 1979: 39; Lett, 1990: 132; Cardano, 2011: 20–4; Cyr, 2019: 10–16).

The relationship between theory and research

For these reasons, in these approaches, the relationship between empirical observations and theorization is predominantly inductive. At the beginning of the search, the analysis unit is identified generically, and its features will be defined in detail only after the fieldwork (Bowen, 2006: 14). Indeed, the formulation of an initial theory could inhibit the ability to 'understand' the insider's point of view on the phenomenon studied (Atkinson, 2014). Rather, the theory is discovered during the investigation (Hennink, 2014: 42). We can say that the researcher tries to gain insight and to 'listen' to how social actors tell their real-life world. Later he/she tries to analyse the narrations and the different perspectives in order to understand what theory is suggested by the set of all the detected empirical materials (Glaser and Strauss, 1967). As the researcher analyses the empirical materials, major themes are expected to emerge and to be categorized in such a way that they yield a theory (Bowen, 2006: 13–14; Barbour, 2007: 127–8). Ultimately, taking inspiration from observations of facts and from information collected, the researcher will sort and categorize such empirical materials to formulate a theory.

This inductive approach influences the way in which, in qualitative research, the empirical referents are selected (the research cases) and how the features of the object of study are collected (i.e. the structuring level of the information collection tool).

The choice of cases

Regarding the empirical referents, in the design phase it is not usually possible to know in advance the population referable to the unit of analysis, since it is generally specified more in detail only during the research (Ragin and

Becker, 1992: 220; Hennink, 2014: 41–2). However, this is not a cause for concern (see Table 3.1). Indeed, if the aim is to identify the main characteristics of a phenomenon and not estimate its extent, there is no interest in identifying a clear set of referents – a defined population – to which the results are extended (Stewart and Shamdasani, 1990: 16–18; Krueger and Casey, 2000: 76–7; Barbour, 2007: 69).

Expert advice

For example, in an investigation on social exclusion, the objective of a qualitative study usually is not focused on the extent of the phenomenon, rather it is focused on its main characteristics. Furthermore, for the inductive approach typical of qualitative research, at the beginning of the investigation the unit of analysis (object of study) can only be identified generically. This means that the phenomenon of social exclusion can be basically outlined as social marginalization. Moreover, usually the researcher is not interested in specifically identifying the population referable to the unit of analysis, for example the users of social services; in contrast the qualitative researcher may be more interested in people living in conditions of social marginalization.

Also for this reason, in these approaches the term 'choice of cases' is preferable to 'sampling procedure' because a theoretical representation is sought rather than statistical representation (through probabilistic sampling procedures of cases extracted from a defined population). The choice of empirical cases is based on the criteria of usefulness and fruitfulness on the theoretical point of view for investigating the unit of analysis (Ragin and Becker, 1992: 220). The cases to be explored are therefore chosen for the interest that they seem to express to the researcher (Macnaghten and Myers, 2004: 67; Barbour, 2007: 69). The empirical cases will not be equivalent from the point of view of theoretical fecundity, since they do not necessarily have to refer to the same 'trait' of the analysis unit. Indeed, it is possible that some empirical cases will be more useful to examine one aspect and others to investigate other aspects of the unit of analysis (Mason, 2002: 128–34). Furthermore, the various 'empirical cases' – in light of the conceptual elaborations and interpretations – will be able, in various ways, to constitute different types of 'theoretical cases' or 'specific theoretical constructs' that will contribute to identifying, delineating and understanding the unit of analysis of the research or a part of it (Walton, 1992).

Expert advice

Following the above example on a search on social exclusion, for the choice of cases, a qualitative researcher is not interested in the statistical representation of the cases, but in their theoretical fecundity. For this reason, the choice of cases aims to draw attention to some features of the phenomenon under investigation. For example, the researchers may choose two different cases because they allow examination of two aspects of the phenomenon, such as the 'condition of social vulnerability' and the 'condition of chronic social exclusion'. At the end of the search, the researcher can evaluate the theoretical fruitfulness of the chosen cases and therefore reinterpret these 'empirical cases' as 'theoretical cases', giving them the meaning of 'the vulnerable' and 'the chronic excluded'.

Table 3.1   The choice of cases in qualitative research

Since the qualitative research has an inductive approach, at the beginning of the search, the analysis unit is identified generically	→	For this generic definition, usually it is not possible to know in advance the population referable to the unit of analysis
Non-statistical representativeness of empirical cases	→	Empirical cases are not randomly extracted from a predefined population, because the researcher is not interested in their statistical representativeness with reference to the unit of analysis
Theoretical representation of empirical cases	→	Empirical cases are chosen because they are considered interesting to examine the characteristics of the unit of analysis
Empirical cases not necessarily 'equivalent'	→	Different cases can be identified with the aim of examining different aspects of the phenomenon
'Empirical cases' can be reinterpreted as 'theoretical cases'	→	The empirical cases identified can be reinterpreted based on their theoretical fecundity

The information collection tool

Like the unit of analysis, also its characteristics will emerge and will be defined during the research. Indeed, due to the inductive nature of qualitative approaches, the aspects to be explored and the analytical perspectives on the phenomenon studied emerge in the course of the research, starting from the observation of the empirical referents considered significant to investigate the unit of analysis (Frisina, 2010: 40). For this reason, the structuring level of the information collection tools (in other words, the detail level of the topics and the aspects to be investigated with reference to the unit of analysis) cannot be definitively identified during the initial design phase (Bichi, 2007). It may even vary from one to another collection step, enabling the researcher to draw out different aspects or topics.

However, it is important to specify that, despite the inductive nature of such approaches, the information collection tools (such as the discussion outline used by the moderator) will never be totally devoid of structuring, since at the basis of a research activity there are always cognitive objectives to be achieved (Morgan, 1997: 53–4; Barbour, 2007: 87–8). Generally, therefore, from the early stages of research design, it is possible to identify some 'orientative concepts' that can predispose to perception, providing a guide for approaching empirical reality and suggesting directions to 'look at', but leaving the possibility of enriching the previous knowledge with the information collected.

Sensitizing concepts

Herbert Blumer (1969: 149–50) uses the expression 'sensitizing concepts' to state that such concepts do not prescribe what to see, do not capture reality in the concepts' definitions themselves. Rather, they have to be used as analytical tools – often taken from the researcher's professional encyclopaedia – and they help to provide theoretical depth in the course of the collection phase through their continuous comparison with actual empirical observations (Charmaz, 2000, 2006).

This 'tension' between theory and research can persist throughout the entire investigation process (see Table 3.2):

- in the initial phase, to provide a 'disciplinary' or 'professional' perspective and help the researcher to approach the object of study;
- in the ongoing phases to argue why, in the course of the research, it was decided to develop one analytical perspective on the phenomenon rather than another among those that emerged during the research;
- in the final analysis, to arrive at the final re-elaborations, in order to give an interpretation of the information gathered, formulating models and theories within which the information collected appears intelligible.

Concepts and Theories

Empiricist philosophical and epistemological currents of the late nineteenth and twentieth centuries (such as pragmatism, neopositivism, operationism, analytic philosophy) professed a complete translation of observational language into theoretical language and, therefore, an isomorphism between the scientific discourse and the observed reality. However, later reflections on scientific observation highlighted its importance for the construction of theoretical knowledge and the influence of the researcher's personal/professional background on the observation itself (Duhem, 1906; Hanson, 1958; Kuhn, 1962; Lakatos, 1976). This position is simplified with the notion of 'theory-laden observation' coined by Norwood Russell Hanson (1958: 7), which asserts the absence of 'theoretically neutral' observational data. Indeed, as Hanson writes, observation is an activity of recognition, rather than knowledge, since it is influenced by the observer's cognitive and conceptual framework. Even when a researcher observes a phenomenon for scientific purposes, this process of categorization influences observation, leading to notice certain aspects rather than others, as well as to choose to deepen some of these aspects and ignoring others. These conceptual schemes can belong to the culture and biographical experiences of the observer or to his/her scientific community. The latter specifically pertains to scientific research observation, and, compared to the former, allows a more intersubjective observation according to a disciplinary perspective.

The possibility to recognize the level of theoretical fruitfulness of an empirical case *in itinere* and to have different structuring levels of the information collection tools during the research is also connected to the flexibility of the qualitative design. The researcher can combine multiple strategies within a single qualitative research path. The qualitative design is open, interactive, modelled during the study, and involves constant adjustments among its elements (Baxter and Jack, 2008: 553–4).

During the field research, the researcher can choose which empirical cases are best suited to the specific phase of the research. At the same time, he/she can identify new conceptual dimensions or analytical perspectives to follow and to include in future steps (Cardano, 2020: 28–30). The analysis and interpretation do not start after the end of the fieldwork but accompany the entire research process. Likewise, there is a circularity between theory and research in order to identify which empirical cases can be considered relevant as 'theoretical cases' referable to the unit of analysis and which dimensions/analytical perspectives can be developed in light of emerging theoretical interpretations (Templeton, 1994: 168; Morgan, 1997: 67–8).

The three phases of the research (pre-fieldwork, fieldwork and post-fieldwork) are therefore neither separated nor sequential. Rather, they mostly consist of a spiral in which it is possible to return to choices, modifying and specifying them. This is the prerequisite for implementing future steps and enhancing knowledge. The use of 'sensitizing concepts' will help in this continuous review.

Initially, those concepts will be used as analytical tools to approach the fieldwork. Then, after the first information collection phases, the sensitizing concepts can be reworked, enriched and progressively articulated in the course of the research. Furthermore, since the categorizations drawn from the 'professional researcher encyclopaedia' (Barbour, 2007: 140–1) have the advantage of being more intersubjective, the use of such 'sensitized concepts' can help the researcher to proceed in a 'controlled' and 'transparent' way throughout the search process, while respecting a more flexible and inductive approach between observation and theorization (Bowen, 2006: 14; Hennink, 2014: 180).

Expert advice

In the initial phase of a research on social exclusion, the researcher can consider the concept of 'working poor' useful to investigate the topic, because it can lead to paths of marginalization. This is a way of using sensitizing concepts in order to provide a 'disciplinary' perspective on a research issue. During the information gathering, the researcher can decide to develop an analytical perspective among those that emerge. For example, he/she can choose to consider the 'long period of unemployment' more interesting than the simple 'episode of unemployment'. Finally, in the analysis, the researcher can use sensitizing concepts for the elaboration of an interpretative and theoretical framework. For example, the researcher can trace back the 'long period of unemployment' to a strongly debilitating condition. The longer a person is unemployed, the lower his/her ability to react to the condition of marginalization becomes.

In this way, the researcher does not proceed 'randomly' according to his/her own specific sensitivity, but rather by choosing some research paths and discarding others on the basis of choices considered more appropriate and useful from his/her point of view as a 'scholar' and, therefore, according to his/her theoretical reference paradigms.

To conclude, it can be stated that 'the framework should continue to develop and be completed as the study progresses and the relationships between the proposed constructs will emerge as data are analyzed. A final conceptual framework will include all the themes that emerged from data analysis. [...] Returning to the propositions that initially formed the conceptual framework ensures that the analysis is reasonable in scope and that it also provides structure for the final report. One of the drawbacks of a conceptual framework is that it may limit the inductive approach when exploring a phenomenon. To safeguard against becoming deductive, researchers are encouraged to journal their thoughts and decisions and discuss them with other researchers to determine if their thinking has become too driven by the framework' (Baxter and Jack, 2008: 553).

Table 3.2 The sensitizing concepts in qualitative research

In the initial phase	In the ongoing phases	In the final analysis
Providing a 'disciplinary' or 'professional' perspective on the object of study	Arguing why it was decided to develop one analytical perspective rather than another among those emerged	Arriving at the final interpretation, formulating theories within which the empirical materials appear intelligible

3.2 The four functions of focus groups

We have investigated the inductive nature of qualitative research designs and its influence on the choice of empirical cases and on the characteristics to be detected with reference to the unit of analysis. In the following, we will examine how these elements are declined in focus group research designs, according to the four different functions attributed to the focus group:

- *exploratory-descriptive function*: to collect a wide range of aspects and perspectives of analysis on a phenomenon;
- *analytical-in-depth function*: to identify more relevant features or to deepen some analytical perspectives;
- *experimental function*: to test, within an experimental observation, a structured explanation of a phenomenon, after a deliberate manipulative intervention;
- *evaluative function*: to provide arguments for a judgement (of effectiveness, efficiency, etc.) on policies, programmes, products, services or public and non-public projects and so on.

On the basis of the function attributed to the focus group, the researcher can choose the best strategies for his/her purposes: he/she can decide the empirical cases to be considered relevant in terms of theoretical cases, as well as define the structuring level of the information collection tools.

Although these choices are always the result of the researcher's decision, they represent different ways to 'control' and make the overall research process 'transparent'.

Obviously, the distinction among the four types of research design is suggested in ideal-typical terms, useful above all for expository and illustrative purposes. Indeed, we are aware that in reality the distinction among the various research designs cannot always reflect the complexity of real research situations. However, this distinction can be useful for identifying the main problems to be addressed and the most adequate answers to provide during the design of a research project.

3.3 The exploratory-descriptive function

Specific features

The exploratory-descriptive function of the focus group (see Figure 3.1) is especially helpful in gathering a wide range of aspects and perspectives of analysis.

According to Herbert Hyman (1955), a researcher undertakes an investigation with exploratory and descriptive purposes in order to study a phenomenon which is still little known or in regard to which there are scant references in the existing scientific literature. The strategies of these types of research, however, are also considered when, regardless of the already achieved knowledge, the researcher's interest is focused on bringing out new features, discovering aspects not previously considered, and offering new analytical perspectives on the phenomenon (Langford and McDonagh, 2003).

Therefore, when a focus group is adopted with these purposes, the technique is enhanced to promote creativity, innovation and serendipity. The group discussion will promote synergy among the group's members and favour their free expression. The moderator will assume a low profile, so that opinions and ideas can be expressed without constraint (Stewart and Shamdasani, 1990: 24–7; Hennink, 2014: 16–17).

Moreover, in this function, the aim of the research is always knowledge about a given phenomenon, in order to bring out various aspects and analytical perspectives during the discussion, rather than deepening such aspects and perspectives. Ultimately, the exploratory and descriptive function adopts an investigation strategy that gives priority to the breadth and heterogeneity of information in order to elicit a large amount of varied information on a given phenomenon, without claiming to treat all of it in a detailed or in-depth manner (Vaughn et al., 1996: 62; Barbour, 2007: 69).

The purposes are descriptive rather than analytical, exploratory rather than investigative, in order to evidence the complexity of the phenomenon under study. These purposes will therefore influence the planning strategies of the research relative to both the choice of empirical cases and the aspects/perspectives to be investigated (Frisina, 2018: 193).

The choice of cases

With reference to empirical cases, indeed, the heterogeneity and breadth of empirical referents will be valorized. The researcher can improve the degree of heterogeneity of the discussion groups both internally and externally. The heterogeneity within a group can ensure a certain dynamism in the discussion and facilitate the emergence of different perspectives and positions on the topic discussed (Bloor et al., 2001: 36; Zammuner, 2003: 116–17; Barbour, 2007: 69–70). The heterogeneity among different groups will enable comparison between different cases.

Although referable to the same unit of analysis, the heterogeneity of the cases can help to identify different types of 'theoretical cases' because they will be positioned differently in relation to the object of study. In this way, it is possible to bring out variegated aspects of the same phenomenon or widen the analytical perspectives.

It is also advisable to plan a large number of discussion groups or involve a large number of participants in the groups, in order to ensure a wider exploration of the phenomenon. It is thus possible to foster the collection and the analysis of a large amount of information on the research issue (Caplan, 1990: 529; Barbour, 2007: 69).

In the field

An example is the research conducted to determine women's opinions on risk behaviours and HIV contamination in heterosexual relationships (Maxwell and Boyle, 1995). A large series of group discussions were carried out, involving medium to large groups (from 6 to 12 participants) of white and black women aged between 30 and 51 years old. The meetings focused on the asymmetry of gender power in heterosexual relationships and changes over time in sexual habits.

The information collection tool

Turning to the aspects of the unit of analysis to be investigated, the exploratory and descriptive function does not generally follow a predefined theoretical or analytical setting. Indeed, usually, theory and analysis perspectives will emerge over time; therefore, they will be a late product of research and empirically anchored. At the initial stage, the research can define some general objectives. However, they should be considered in a flexible way and they can range in several directions during fieldwork (Stewart and Shamdasani, 1990: 62–3; Frisina, 2010: 55–8).

This aspect influences the structuring level of the information collection tools used in each focus group, which will be low-structuring, allowing participants in the focus group to choose spontaneously how to deal with the topics of the discussion (Morgan, 1998b: 46–54). Indeed, especially when the topic to be investigated is not adequately known by the research group, it is inappropriate and even impossible to structure the issues to be dealt with or the analytical perspectives to be followed from the beginning of the research (Cyr, 2019: 57–61). In any event, our advice is to prefer research tools with low structuring levels. This is especially important when the aim is to give more space to the insider's perspective and not understand how people place themselves in relation to a conceptual, analytical and linguistic frame set organized by the researcher (Frisina, 2010: 91). The lower the structuring level of the research tools prepared by the researchers, the higher the contribution by participants to discussions and their role in the production of the results. The researcher therefore places himself/herself in a position of 'listening', valuing above all the point of view of the participants invited to be part of the focus group (Puchta and Potter, 2004: 67–87; Hennink, 2014: 74).

In the field

During research on the perception of the sense of history in common people (Leone and Curigliano, 2005), the moderator formulated only a generic question in the group discussion: 'Have there been moments when you have had the impression of being part of the history?'.

In this type of research function, each discussion can be considered independently. Sometimes, different aspects of the analysis unit may emerge from one discussion session to another. On other occasions, alongside aspects already dealt with, new perspectives not investigated in previous discussions may be introduced. Ultimately, the researcher can choose to approach each discussion session in a different way. Obviously, in exploratory designs this is not a problem, since the aim is to gather as wide a range of opinions on the research issue as possible (Puchta and Potter, 2004: 126–30; Cyr, 2019: 105).

The use of the focus group with exploratory and descriptive functions there-fore well expresses the inductive vocation of qualitative research approaches. However, as said, this inductive vocation should not be confused with the illu-sion of 'letting the data speak for themselves'. Even in the exploratory and descriptive design adopting an 'emic' perspective on the phenomenon, the conceptualizations produced by the researcher will never be the result of a sim-ple speculative reproduction of the reality of the facts detected (Jevons, 1874). Conceptualizations will not have a merely empirical foundation, since, as stated, it is not possible to observe and investigate a phenomenon in a 'neutral' or 'pure' manner, discarding all pre-notions and recording 'facts' independently of inter-pretative processes.

Hence, although the researcher cannot compare the results arising from different sessions, since often not all the groups necessarily articulate the discussion around the same aspects of the phenomenon and the groups themselves are very heterogeneous (Stewart and Shamdasani, 1990: 62–3; Carey and Asbury, 2012: 83–5), the investigator will still make choices, assessing situation by situation. Only from these choices can conceptualiza-tions emerge (Blaikie, 2000).

It will be up to the researcher to decide which features of discussion group can be underlined in his/her interpretation, in order to consider one empirical case as a relevant theoretical case of the unit of analysis. In this way, a profile will emerge highlighting the specific theoretical fruitfulness of the case. At the same time, it will be up to the researcher to assess which characteristics and perspectives on the phenomenon that have emerged in the various discussions deserve to be emphasized, as well as which aspects should be omitted in the conceptualizations, specifying the analytical model best able to yield a theoretical generality. In other words, the innovative potential dedicated to 'discovery' attributed to the exploratory and descrip-tive function does not lie in the information itself, but in its interpretation and in the researcher's ability to underline its theoretical fruitfulness (Marková et al., 2007: 198–9).

Obviously, even in exploratory strategies, the researcher will orient himself/herself through categories and analytical perspectives deriving from his/her professional background (Barbour, 2007: 140–1). His/her reasoning will be based on an inferential process of unification, that is, incorporation of a fact into a category which can be 'already known', 'redefined' or created *ex novo*, but always finding useful notions and concepts within the professional ency-clopaedia. In this way, the researcher will be able to enhance the observation of known and unknown facts, improving the technique's potential to promote creativity, innovation and serendipity.

Therefore, the empirical results will be inductively ordered and categorized through attempts at theorization and conceptual abstraction. Conceptual abstractions and theories, however, will be strongly 'anchored' in what the researcher has detected empirically (Carey and Asbury, 2012: 85–6). Thus, the exploratory-descriptive function enhances an 'emic' perspective connecting conceptualization to the insiders' 'frames of reference' (linguistic and meaningful categories). Conceptual abstractions and theories will derive from how the researcher chooses to organize, order and categorize the empirical material, evaluating the most useful and appropriate way to reproduce the experience of respondents or the context of study (Bowen, 2006).

To sum up

In conclusion, considering the exploratory-descriptive purposes of this function, the research design should be planned by taking the following recommendations into consideration:

- high internal and external heterogeneity of groups (with reference to theoretical cases);
- a large number of participants in the groups and/or a large number of discussion groups;
- low structuring of the collection tools.

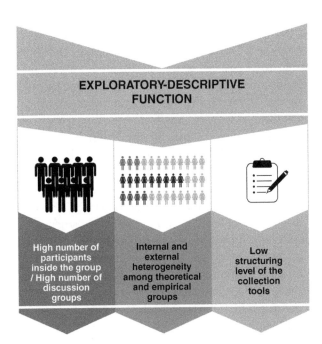

Figure 3.1 Planning focus group research design with exploratory-descriptive functions

3.4 The analytical-in-depth function

Specific features

The analytical-in-depth function of the focus group (see Figure 3.2) is especially helpful in identifying the more important features of the investigated phenomenon or examining the adequacy of some analytical perspectives that the researcher evaluates appreciable (Hennink, 2014: 16–17).

It is possible to pursue research with analytical purposes when a researcher is interested not only in bringing out and describing the complexity of a social phenomenon, but also in explaining it, identifying its development process.

Explanation in social sciences

Explanation in the social sciences does not presuppose the universality imputable to a law. Indeed, the impasse of the positivist explanation, based on scientist assumptions concerning the deterministic nature of social reality, has been superseded. The epistemological presupposition of every law – therefore of its truth in every time and in every place – is the existence of regularities which can be identified because they exist 'in nature'. If such regularities do not exist, they cannot be detected. This is the case of the social sciences: it is not possible to find laws because there are no laws that underlie the origin and development of social phenomena (Campelli, 1991).

Furthermore, in social sciences, it is impossible to record the presence of a causal influence of one variable on another, in an objective manner such as postulated in the experimental sciences, without any intervention of the researcher's knowledge. Indeed, unlike physical sciences, it is not possible to isolate a pair of properties of humans by manipulating one to detect its effects on the other, maintaining constant all other properties that can influence (Hedström and Ylikoski, 2010).

Concepts and Theories

Ultimately, in social sciences the type of relationship between two properties – and therefore two variables – is not directly observable; this excludes the only conclusive way to control a cause–effect relationship and to decide about its truth/falsity. Indeed, the researcher can record information on properties transformed into variables in a data matrix (cases for variables) and, through statistical techniques, detect the presence of correlations among variables (i.e. the students' school performance is associated with their parents' education

(Continued)

level). However, a covariation cannot be translated into a causal relationship (Marradi, 2007: 89). Therefore, only the researcher can give, if he/she considers it plausible, a causal interpretation of this association (on the influencing variable and the influenced variable). This interpretation is assumed on the basis of the researcher's personal and professional knowledge (i.e. starting from a sociological paradigm or from his/her professional encyclopaedia).

According to Max Weber (1904), the number and nature of the causes of every single event are always infinite. Moreover, because many features characterize the phenomena – 'always infinitely multiple' – their processing into concepts is necessarily selective and *Wertbeziehung* (value relations) leads a researcher in this cognitive action. For this reason, a cause–effect relationship 'is a question of imputation' of a certain event to one or more causes operated by a researcher. This explanation cannot be considered true or false, but only more or less adequate (Weber, 1904: 47–58).

In qualitative approaches – such as those using focus groups – the aim of imputation of causes is rarely pursued, especially in terms of control of a relationship between two or more variables. Indeed, these approaches favour penetration into 'meaning-provinces' (Schütz, 1975) for the overall comprehension of specific situations, rather than the production of variable frequency distributions. Hence, in these approaches the causation – when considered – is usually imputed through narrative reconstruction tools and, only rarely, through statistical tools by association or covariance detection.

However, it is possible to adopt a research strategy using the focus group with analytical-in-depth purposes, in order to reach more detailed knowledge of a phenomenon or to evaluate the adequacy of some analytical perspectives appreciated by the researcher (Morgan, 1997: 54; Hennink, 2014: 19–22). In this case, differently from the exploratory designs, rather than highlighting the heterogeneity and multiplicity of information, the researcher can favour the collection of homogeneous and more detailed information in order to trace aspects relevant to delineating or understanding the phenomenon under study. Therefore, this investigative strategy will have a different influence on the choice of empirical cases and the structuring level of the collection tool guiding the researcher in the fieldwork.

The choice of cases

With regard to research cases, it is preferable to choose 'similar' empirical cases. The similarity should be referable to the same 'trait' of the analysis unit.

Thus, homogeneity can be enhanced both internally and externally to discussion groups. The homogeneity within the group will allow the participants to discuss the topic of discussion starting from more similar or comparable perspectives (Bloor et al., 2001: 36; Barbour, 2007: 70; Carey and Asbury, 2012: 41–3). The external homogeneity among groups will be useful for comparing empirical cases referring to the same type of 'theoretical case', in order to identify which aspects of the phenomenon studied are in common or combined in a similar way. In this way, these aspects can be considered more relevant or useful for understanding the phenomenon studied, according to the perspective of that specific 'theoretical group'.

When the aim is analytical, the researcher can also resort to segmentation, subdividing the various empirical cases based on the identification of several 'theoretical cases' in order to bring out, in a comparative perspective, their similarities and differences (Hennink, 2014: 112–13). In this way, the comparison will be composite, allowing the researcher to analyse the phenomenon from different perspectives. In this regard, David L. Morgan states: 'If you suspect that different types of participants will have different perspectives on the topic, then sorting them into separate groups will maximize both their compatibility within groups and your ability to make comparisons between groups' (1998b: 59–60).

Expert advice

For example, if the aim is to investigate social representations of social exclusion by social workers, this social group can be subdivided into various subgroups (e.g. based on different areas of professional intervention). In this way, the researcher can elicit similarities and differences among inter-subjective representations and action-lines of the various subsets.

If the researcher chooses the aspects to enhance for the internal homogeneity and external heterogeneity of empirical groups in the initial research design, his/her 'frames of reference' will be privileged. Indeed, he/she can choose the characteristics of the participants starting from preliminary knowledge already possessed. Moreover, given the flexible nature of the qualitative research design, the researcher can also resort to a spiral strategy (Frisina, 2010: 55–8). He/she can identify the distinctive aspects in progress and decide how to proceed during the fieldwork. In this case, the analytical perspective will be more empirically anchored, at least in the early phases of the study.

In any event, in both strategies, the relationship between empirical cases and 'theoretical cases' can only be presumed. Indeed, generally, the researcher forms the various groups starting from already known structural characteristics (gender, qualification, profession, etc.), rather than from possible attitudes. Moreover, it should be stressed that homogeneity on some property does not guarantee homogeneity in conceptual, analytical or linguistic schemes. In this case, therefore, the formation of 'theoretical cases' may follow different criteria from those identified in the choice of groups, especially enhancing the content of group discussions.

Another recommendation when conducting research with analytical-in-depth purposes is to lead smaller discussion groups. Indeed, a small number will allow the participants to intervene several times, having more time available to explain their points of view and discuss the topic in detail. In this way, smaller discussion groups allow the researcher to collect more in-depth and detailed information in each focus group (Morgan, 1998b: 72–3). In addition, it is likely that a small number of focus groups will suffice, since the analytical perspective on investigated topic will be more focused in each discussion. Indeed, this research design is interested in exploring in depth some specific aspects of a phenomenon rather than bringing out its complexity.

The information collection tool

The same considerations apply to the structuring level of the information collection tool. The researcher gives priority to the use of the focus group for analytical purposes, when he/she aims to acquire a detailed knowledge of a phenomenon, as well as to deepen the adequacy of some analytical perspectives, in order to identify the main aspects to outline the conceptual category referred to the research analysis unit.

Therefore, compared to exploratory and descriptive investigations, our advice is to devise collection tools with a higher structuring level, since the analytical aspects and perspectives on the phenomenon investigated that the research group wants to bring to the attention of the participants increase in collective discussions (Corrao, 2000: 53–4; Morrison-Beedy et al., 2001: 48). Moreover, it is important to compare the detected information. For this reason, the aspects and analytical perspectives will be the same in the different focuses in order to be comparable.

In the field

An example is a research on the representations of poverty among marginalized people (Cardano et al., 2003). The topic was investigated by means of a highly structured discussion outline focusing on many dimensions: impoverishment processes, the local welfare system and the policies implemented at local level to counteract these phenomena. For some of these dimensions, the research group not only formulated generic questions, but introduced a series of stories on hypothetical situations.

Obviously, as the structuring level of collection tools increases, the focus of the discussion progressively shifts from the frames of reference of the participants to those of the researcher (Cyr, 2019: 54–5). Hence, the researcher's contribution will grow in determining the agenda for discussion, as well as his/her role in the production of results.

Sometimes it is possible to decide to structure the discussion grid already in the early design stages to deepen previous knowledge drawn from the existing literature or from previous research studies. In this case, therefore, the research approach will be more 'etic', since the researcher's conceptual and analytical frame will be further enhanced (Morgan, 1997: 46–54).

However, given the flexibility of qualitative research designs, it is possible to follow a spiral strategy. In the first steps, the researcher can prepare a low structuring-level discussion outline, choosing some aspects and perspectives that he/she wants to deepen about the topic. Then, the researcher can decide to specify the topic in the course of fieldwork, progressively structuring the collection tools in a targeted and timely manner. Hence, in this case, even if the researcher will choose the overall analytical perspective, the conceptual and analytical frame will emerge in a more 'emic' way according to the insiders' perspective (Stewart and Shamdasani, 1990: 62–3).

Nevertheless, unlike exploratory design, when the focus group is used for analytical purposes, a more rigid approach to research is necessary, even from the initial phases. Indeed, since the aim is to enhance the homogeneity of the information, any single group discussion cannot be considered independent from the others. The research goal is to identify similar elements in different discussion groups or, in any event, compare similar cases to detect possible shared perspectives. However, excessively planning the overall design of the research from the beginning may preclude the possibility of bringing out information not strictly connected to the analytical perspective adopted by the researcher. This information could anyway be very valuable in the final analysis (Merton et al., 1956). It is therefore necessary to be careful not to over-alter the nature of the focus group, which anyway aims to valorize an 'emic' approach to phenomena study.

To sum up

In conclusion, considering the analytical-in-depth purposes of this function, the research design should be planned in light of the following suggestions:

- an internal homogeneity within groups and external heterogeneity among groups (with reference to theoretical cases);
- a low number of participants in the groups and/or a reduced number of discussion groups;
- a gradual high structuring level of the collection tools.

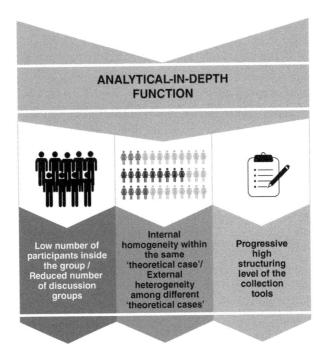

Figure 3.2 Planning of focus group research design with analytical-in-depth functions

3.5 The experimental function

Specific features

A type of research design rarely considered in relation to the applications of the focus group technique is the experimental one (see Figure 3.3). In the classic handbooks, indeed, there are only few references to this function.

This type of research design is not widespread in studies with focus groups, because the experimental approach has developed in the epistemological context of natural sciences. This context is profoundly different from human disciplines and is difficult to adapt to qualitative research.

While maintaining a certain critical reserve towards such an application, in this chapter we will address the experimental function in the interests of providing fuller information. Indeed, such a research design is very widespread in some disciplines, such as social psychology, group sociology, marketing and mass communication sciences, which are disciplines historically inspired by the experimental and behavioural empirical tradition.

Born within the epistemological context of natural sciences, the experimental approach as a method to develop scientific knowledge consists in a procedure realized through a deliberate intervention modifying the observation situation, according to the logic of the 'difference method' enunciated by John Stuart Mill (1843). Hence the experimental design is inspired by a form of experience on natural facts yielded by deliberate manipulative strategies performed by humans (Cohen and Nagel, 1934).

Concepts and Theories

The experimental design is based on the following elements: identification of experimental properties and operational properties (equivalent to dependent and independent variables in the data matrix approach); random assignment of the people to an experimental group and a control group (randomization); planning of the manipulation intervention of the independent variable on the experimental group; and detection of the change effects through the comparison of the two groups. We use the expression 'experiment' if both the manipulation of the independent variable and the randomization are present; we use the expression 'quasi-experiment' if only the first of the two elements is present (Campbell and Stanley, 1966: 151–3; Cook and Campbell, 1979).

Many criticisms can be levelled at this type of research design. The main ones concern the possibility of controlling all the properties, especially the ones external to the experiment (other properties influencing the relationship between the experimental properties and the operational properties that, for this reason, it is necessary to maintain constant). Indeed, in the context of the human being, it is difficult to argue that the two groups, the experimental and the control ones, are exactly the same for all conditions/ aspects. For this reason, the effect of the independent property can hardly be attributed unequivocally to the reactions registered in the experimental group. Indeed, as discussed previously, unlike in social sciences, it is not possible to isolate a pair of properties of humans by manipulating one to evaluate its effects on the other, maintaining effectively constant all other properties that can influence the relationship between the first two (Marradi, 2007: 89).

Concerning research with focus groups, the criticisms become even more radical and the applications even more difficult. Indeed, this technique was born in the qualitative field, where research is characterized by a flexible relationship between theory and research, giving priority to induction and sensitizing concepts. Conversely, the experimental or quasi-experimental design

79

follows a hierarchical–deductive relationship between theory and research, a high degree of structuring of hypotheses, the operationalization of properties in variables and strict control of all procedures.

However, despite these great differences, a large amount of experimental research makes use of the focus group as the main information collection technique. The reason is that the experimental design leverages the group as the principal analysis tool, and this aspect is common to the focus group technique. This means that the technique of group discussion is considered suitable for experimental or quasi-experimental research beyond its great differences with respect to the assumptions of qualitative inquiry.

In particular, the experimental or quasi-experimental design is used for the investigation of opinion changes. The most common applications are employed in studies on mass communication. In these contexts, the focus group emphasizes the social nature of action and does not reduce social scientific research to the study of the individual. This is an important consideration especially in the context of media research, where mechanical conceptions of media effects are giving way to more social, semiotic and diffusion-based conceptions of media processes. The study of the media audience is less concerned with registering effects at the psychological level in aggregates of individuals, and increasingly concerned with the study of social processes of communication. Accordingly, the focus group is a method in tune with current sensibilities in media research, which are redefining media processes and the conception of the audience (Lunt and Livingstone, 1996: 90).

In the field

A classic example is communication research on audience response to public discussion programmes (Livingstone and Lunt, 1994). The focus group was used to simulate some of the processes of public opinion formation. In particular, group members were asked to work collaboratively towards a consensual product, as in the 'news game'. Hence, a collectively generated news report was devised and then discussed in order to explore the processes whereby people arrive at their beliefs.

The experimental or quasi-experimental design is used for the investigation of the group dynamics, especially in the field of social psychology. In these cases, the research team can use the focus groups in order to analyse the variations produced by intentional manipulation of the research conditions, comparing the results obtained in the experimental groups with those achieved in the control groups, through the study of the discussions aroused in the various sessions.

The experimental or quasi-experimental design with a focus group will have a different influence on the choice of empirical cases and the structuring level of the collection tools guiding the researcher in the fieldwork.

The choice of cases

The experimental or quasi-experimental design requires a rigid structuring of all research processes. Research hypotheses should be considered as statements on relationships between properties which can be empirically tested. Within this design, therefore, it is necessary to draw a distinction among the independent property (the one that the researcher manipulates, assuming it to have a direct effect on the dependent one), the dependent property (the one of which the variation is to be observed following the manipulation of the independent property) and extraneous properties (all those which are not independent but could affect the results). Furthermore, operationalization is very important, in order to clarify definitions, gather data and define variables.

The manipulation procedure should be defined. For this reason, not only should the groups be planned in detail, but they should also be defined through a segmentation design that takes account of the maximum homogeneity among groups, with reference to the assumption of substantial similarity/ affinity between control groups and experimental groups. Without necessarily resorting to randomization, the preservation of this assumption makes it possible to exclude the influence of any other factor which can significantly affect the research outcome. Therefore, our advice is to plan more than one control group, as well as more than one experimental group, in order to have a greater number of comparison elements.

The most suitable experimental focus groups are both the 'only after' one characterized by a single information collection after the manipulative stimulus, and the 'before–after' one characterized by a double information collection, which can be performed before (pre-test) and after (post-test) stimulation. Our advice is to consider the 'only after' research design for cases where a previous information collection can affect the result of the experiment in some way. Instead, we recommend using the 'before–after' research design when the purpose of the research is to determine the effectiveness of changes in the people involved, as in pilot programmes.

Moreover, the manipulative stimulus may vary according to the objectives of the research. As a manipulative stimulus, the researcher can solicit the experimental group through images or videos, as well as the recounting of a short story.

The information collection tool

Finally, regarding the collection tool, our advice is to focus the discussion on the topics of the manipulative stimulus, soliciting the participants with a highly structured discussion grid, in order to collect as much detailed information as possible.

To sum up

In conclusion, considering the experimental and quasi-experimental purposes of this function, the research design should be planned in consideration of the following suggestions:

- design of two groups or super groups (the control and the experimental groups);
- strict homogeneity among groups;
- a high structuring level of the collection tools;
- evaluation whether it is more opportune to conduct the discussion only after having introduced the manipulative stimulus, or before and after having introduced it.

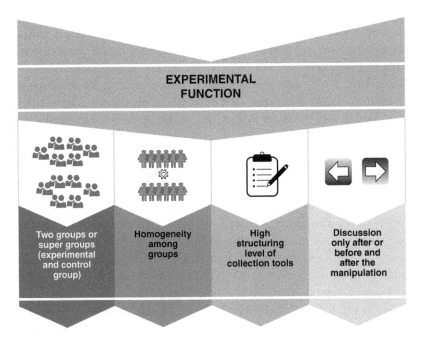

Figure 3.3 Planning focus group research design with experimental functions

3.6 The evaluative function

Specific features

Many focus group applications concern evaluative research designs, that is, complex research plans aimed at developing a value judgement on the achievement of a certain goal linked to an action (see Figure 3.4).

Evaluation is a social research activity serving the public interest with a view to a conscious decision-making process. The evaluation is useful for ascertaining the coherence of an action with the design idea, as well as the quality of the same design idea (Hennink, 2014: 22–4). This is a procedure starting from an evaluation request by a public/private client. It is divided into an evaluation design (proposed by the evaluator to the client and agreed between them) and empirical research (carried out by the evaluator, with the possible participation of client and user representatives). Finally, it results in a discussion on the results and a proposal presented to stakeholders.

Therefore, the evaluation is linked to decision and action. Indeed, often, its reference is collective action targeted on desirable and possible change (Patton, 2002; Macnaghten, 2017).

Evaluating is a valuable tool for decision making. It is a systematic way of information accumulation leading to a judgement on policies, services, programmes, products, public or private projects and so on. It also can be an instrument for legitimating public choices (since it highlights the efficiency requirements of procedures and choices effectiveness) and for rationalizing actions (Hennink, 2014: 22–4; Cyr, 2019: 74).

It is possible to consider two functions of evaluation: support for decision making and self-analysis by a body/institution/collective. Indeed, it helps to draw out the needs of a context and to address the action according to explicit objectives and with respect to subjects belonging to the economic and social context analysed.

Hence, the characteristics of the design of evaluation research are the following: it is part of a broader strategy halfway between a purely cognitive design and an intervention one; it is characterized by a cognitive interest in the object of study, but its results (technical reports) constitute an important basis of action for political purposes.

In order to structure such a design, it is first necessary to define the evaluation mandate and define the decisional and stakeholder context in order to understand the real reasons why the assessment is requested. In this way, it is possible to define the evaluation question, that is, the problem related to the evaluation and its exact definition in terms of questions.

Concepts and Theories

Richard A. Krueger and Mary A. Casey (2000: 378–80) note that evaluators use focus groups to:

- assess needs;
- design an intervention;
- evaluate project options;
- pilot test information collection tools;
- understand findings;
- monitor and evaluate operations.

The evaluation is structured into three main phases:

- the *ex-ante* evaluation;
- *in-itinere* evaluation;
- the *ex-post* evaluation.

The *ex-ante* evaluation

The first phase analyses the conditions under which a programme/intervention can occur. It therefore has purposes that are not exclusively exploratory, but also descriptive and analytical. Hence, starting from a consistent cognitive basis, it aims at evaluating the initial context of an action. To this end, the focus group technique can be useful for investigating the perceptions, opinions and behaviours of the groups of actors that will be involved in the intervention, paying particular attention to the expectations of change of the various groups.

In structuring this phase, therefore, the collection tool mainly concerns the elements of the project under evaluation. For example, we recommend dividing the discussion outline into various sections based on different subtopics or aspects of the project analysed and specifying key questions.

In the field

An example is the research on evaluation of the US Department of Energy's pilot low-income energy programme (Magill, 1993). The purpose of the focus groups was to detect how clients felt about the programme, what changes they would recommend, and whether they practised energy saving techniques. The results were used in planning the following year's State Energy Program.

Another recommendation concerns the group's segmentation: this should take target groups and stakeholder groups into account. For this reason, it is better to plan different groups according to the different stakeholder categories: service users, workers, donors, funders, citizens and so on.

The *in-itinere* evaluation

The *in-itinere* evaluation takes place during the programme application process. Its aim is to monitor progress of the implementation of the intervention itself. Here again, the purpose is not only theoretical-cognitive but also practical, because from a correct interpretation of information, decisions can be taken regarding possible adjustments, suspensions or implementations of the programme itself. The use of focus groups is particularly indicated in order to gather opinions, difficulties and first results of the intervention programme by listening to the voice of the insiders (as target groups or stakeholder groups).

In this phase, the collection tools mainly concern the implementation of the project under evaluation. Our advice is to include in the discussion outline the opinions of the participants on the strengths and weaknesses of programme implementation, in order to bring out elements not previously considered. To evaluate these aspects, it is therefore preferable to involve people directly affected by the intervention in the discussion groups.

The *ex-post* evaluation

The third type of evaluation is the best known. Generally, *ex-post* evaluation is required at the end of a programme, either public or private, in order to evaluate the impact of the results obtained. In this case, the use of focused groups can be useful for collecting considerations, suggestions, feelings and expectations of the people involved in the programme/service/policy (Macnaghten, 2017: 358–9). The group discussions can therefore involve the actors of change in order to bring out limits, obstacles, results and effects.

The choice of cases in all the phases

Generally, a good evaluation design should take the importance of all three phases into account. We therefore suggest adopting a progressive approach in the selection of cases. Indeed, at the beginning of the process, the evaluator can decide to plan the groups according to some unspecified criteria which will gradually become more and more defined and clear.

Expert advice

For example, usually during the *ex-ante* phase, the evaluator frequently uses multiple criteria of participants selection and group formation, such as belonging to specific stakeholder categories (service users, workers, citizens, investors etc.) or specific social categories (according to age, gender, qualification etc.). Furthermore, he/she can decide to organize a large number of discussion groups. Afterwards, during the *in-itinere* phase and the *ex-post* phase, the macro criteria can continue to exist, but the groups can be progressively more segmented and restricted.

The collection tools in all the phases

A certain gradualness is also recommended in the planning of the collection tools, such as drawing up the discussion outline and defining the moderator's agenda. Those tools can be updated and structured progressively, according to the knowledge accumulated during the evaluation process. Our advice is to adopt the so-called 'funnel approach', to be applied to the entire research path. The evaluation process begins with open sessions that become more focused progressively, increasingly restricting the themes of the discussion to the specific interests of the evaluator.

In reality, not always is the focus group used for evaluative functions in its autonomous information-gathering role. Some scholars (Bezzi, 2001: 346–7) recommend the use of evaluative focus groups within a triangulation, or rather a mixed-method strategy, to improve the effectiveness of its evaluative function (see Chapter 4).

However, it should be emphasized that the focus group has a significant role in evaluation (Patton, 2002). This is especially due to group synergy during the discussion, which can enhance the participative role of stakeholders in the programme/action being assessed. Moreover, the use of focus groups can simulate/anticipate the decision making, allowing a significant reduction of uncertainty margins (Palumbo, 2001). In other words, with respect to other techniques, the peculiarity of focus groups with evaluative functions is precisely the 'coproduction' of the observed with observers (Hennink, 2014: 22–4).

In conclusion, considering the evaluative purposes of this function, the research design should be planned in consideration of the following suggestions:

- define groups on intervention targets;
- gradually increase the structuring level of collection tools;
- consider the possibility of conducting the discussion in all the evaluation phases: *ex-ante, in itinere* and *ex-post*.

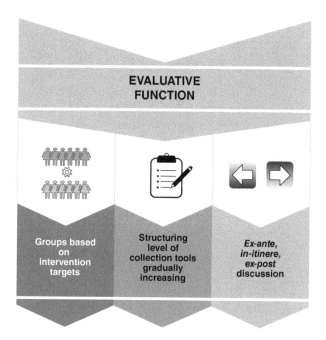

Figure 3.4   Planning of focus group research design with evaluative functions

For this reason, usually the evaluative function provides the combination of two moments: in the first phase it is quite similar to a research design with an exploratory-descriptive function; in the second phase it becomes quite similar to an analytical-in-depth function.

Further reading

Blumer, H. (1969) *Symbolic Interactionism: Perspective and Methods.* Englewood Cliffs, NJ: Prentice Hall.

In this seminal work, in contrast with the 'objectivist' depersonalization of cognitive research, Herbert Blumer recommend the use of 'sensitizing' concepts to study the complex empirical universe in its everyday social dimension, humanly 'participated'.

Ragin, C.C. and Becker, H.S. (eds) (1992) *What is a Case? Exploring the Foundation of Social Inquiry*. Cambridge: Cambridge University Press.

This book offers useful insights on the 'nature' of the case in social research and how the ways in which it is defined influences the researchers, as both specific empirical phenomena and general theoretical categories.

Exercises

1. In research on representations of social exclusion processes, you decide to conduct focus groups involving social workers. What kind of information collection tool can be planned if the focus group is used with an exploratory-descriptive function? Then consider how to remodulate the same tool, this time assuming use of the focus group with an analytical-in-depth function.

2. Suppose you conduct a research in the educational field to support the use of cooperative educational methodologies (i.e. cooperative learning) in elementary school classes. Which criteria should be privileged in the groups' segmentation?

4

Mixing the Focus Group with Other Techniques

Sometimes, the research goals require the focus group to be combined with other collection techniques. In this case, the general research design can have the same characteristics described in the last chapter. In other words, it can be exploratory-descriptive, analytical-in-depth, explanatory-experimental, evaluative.

What changes is the role of the focus group design. In a mixed-methods research design, there are other recommendations to be followed.

Before starting mixed-methods research, the researcher must ask himself/herself two basic questions:

- In my mixed-methods research, what is the combination of techniques for?
- How can I enhance the focus group's distinctive features in my mixed-methods research?

On the basis of these two questions it is possible to identify the roles of the focus group in the research and develop a good plan of action.

This chapter describes the main characteristics of research where the focus group is used in a supportive information-gathering role alongside both quantitative and qualitative techniques.

―――――――――――――――――― **Chapter goals** ――――――――――――

- *Knowledge*: focus group research design when it is decided to use the technique in a mixed-methods approach.
- *Applying knowledge and understanding*: how to use the focus group in support of quantitative or qualitative collection techniques, identifying the right role.
- *Making judgements*: developing a critical analysis of the purposes of mixing methods.

4.1 Combination with other techniques

So far, we have examined what kind of research design can be followed if the focus group is used as an autonomous information-gathering technique.

However, as well as using the technique independently, focus groups can also be used alongside other techniques. In such cases, the research will have a complex design with integrated techniques.

This role can be characterized by two fundamental variations:

- *ex-ante*, where the proposed focused discussions precede the main phase of information gathering;
- *ex-post*, where the group discussions follow the information-gathering phase.

The origins

The combined use of focus groups is contemporaneous with the time when the technique was designed. Already with Emory S. Bogardus (1926), precursor of the technique, the focus group had a subsidiary role supporting the development of collection tools for large-scale investigations (Morgan, 1998a).

However, the real paternity of the focus group can be attributed to Robert K. Merton (Merton and Kendall, 1946; Merton et al., 1956; Merton, 1987), who even then suggested its use in a supporting role. Following Paul Felix Lazarsfeld's invitation to attend an unplanned work session on the study of public reactions to radio propaganda programmes (Lazarsfeld et al., 1948), in 1941 Merton suggested a new tool based on a non-directive (individual or group) interview focused on a few key topics.

As a technique with a supplementary function, the focus group was developed for generating new research questions and guiding hypotheses (Merton and Kendall, 1946). The importance of the focus group's function in supporting other information-gathering techniques, mainly the survey, has also been recognized in the field of market research, where the tool spread widely after the 1950s, starting with Paul Felix Lazarsfeld's studies on decision-making processes, above all on consumption (Lazarsfeld et al., 1948). From that period onwards, there was an increasing need in the marketing sector to go deeply into the psychological, cultural and social motivations inducing consumers to make small everyday choices. So-called qualitative techniques appeared to be the most appropriate for this type of 'understanding'; researchers increased the awareness that, in order to develop marketing strategies and company policies, knowledge of decision-making behaviour is just as necessary as knowledge of all the quantitative aspects of consumption. Marketing therefore assigned the focus group technique a functional role that was well suited for the exploratory phase of the investigation and the focusing of the problem (Chisnall, 2005).

Subsidiary potentials

The subsidiary potentials of focused group discussion were also considered later, in the 1980s, when the technique once again spread to the social sciences. In most cases, however, researchers focused on the auxiliary role of focus groups in the exploratory phase of the investigation, especially in relation to two main tasks: suggesting new hypotheses to be controlled in the subsequent phases of the research (Goldman, 1962; Stewart and Shamdasani, 1990; Dowson et al., 1993); and soliciting proposals and gathering ideas for construction of the questionnaire (Bellenger et al., 1976; Morgan, 1997; Krueger and Casey, 2000).

In the field

Among the first research using the focus group in this role was Evelyn Folch-Lyon and John F. Trost's (1981) study on sexual habits. This research focused on sensitive topics, and it used the information obtained from the focus groups in support of a survey design to explore Mexican contraceptive practices.

In contrast, the other role of the focus group remained in the background for a long time: its combined use in an auxiliary role to the analytical-interpretative phase of the research (ex-post role). Although unanimously recognized by classic handbooks as a possible alternative application (Bellenger et al., 1976;

Morgan, 1997; Corrao, 2000), for a long time this did not receive adequate dedicated space in methodological reflection.

However, before going into the distinction between the use of *ex-ante* and *ex-post* support roles, there is a key question to answer: what is a mixed-methods strategy good for? To answer this, we shall now conduct a brief critical discussion.

It is often considered that the focus group is useful in controlling the validity, reliability and fidelity of data collected with other techniques (such as the survey). However, this underpins the traditional concept of triangulation and combination of different techniques, which, on closer inspection, is wide open to criticism. Indeed, assigning focus groups the task of evaluating the quality of information obtained through other collection tools presupposes not only the full comparability and uniformity of data derived from such different information collection techniques, but, in essence, a very positivist attitude to using multiple techniques.

The assumption that triangulation is in itself an instrument to improve the data of a single instrument, having certain, more accurate and reliable information, is one that cannot be taken for granted at all. Indeed, these objectives cannot be considered in themselves the methodological assumptions of triangulation; rather, they must be clarified, specifying how the processes of data comparison and harmonization can be implemented (Hesse-Biber, 2010). In what follows we will clarify what triangulation is and what its functions are.

4.2 Triangulation

Definition

The term 'triangulation' derives from topographical studies and refers to a trigonometric method through which the exact distance between a fixed point and an observation point can be identified. We are familiar with its applications in various spheres, from nautical, to military, to geometry. In each context, it is understood as referring to the need to draw on several points of reference to obtain a more accurate result (Smith, 1975).

In social sciences, 'triangulation' refers to a strategy of integrating different techniques in studying the same phenomenon, with a view to increasing the reliability of the research results. Dealing specifically with methodological triangulation, Norman K. Denzin (1989) distinguished two main uses of this strategy: the within-method approach and the between-methods approach.

The first was defined by Herman W. Smith (1975) as the most primitive form of triangulation. This is because it envisages both a comparison between different indicators relating to the same property, and a comparison between the results obtained by those same indicators in different field researches, the aim being to check both internal validity and data reliability. Therefore, this technique simply requires the use of the same instrument on different occasions.

The second type of methodological triangulation can be defined as the most popular, albeit one of the most complex. It enables researchers to compare the results obtained by different techniques and has an illustrious precedent in the multi-trait/multi-method procedure of Donald T. Campbell and Donald W. Fiske (1959). On this last form of triangulation, a debate began that has continued until the present day.

The debate

The scholar who first fully grasped and espoused this proposal, adapting it to the needs of anthropological research, was Jack D. Douglas (1976), who enunciated 'the principle of "mixed strategies". In his view, each study must start from a low degree of methodological structuring and then slowly and gradually arrive at an increasingly precise definition of the strategy to be adopted, going from natural forms of observations to increasingly structured and standardized information collection procedures' (Cataldi, 2016: 6).

In most cases, however, the debate focused on the techniques on which integration strategies should be used, in an attempt to neutralize the weaknesses of each instrument while at the same time enhancing its strengths.

'This strategy attracted a great deal of criticism, especially in relation to the integration imperative, which in a few years became for many authors a "must" that was often not backed by sufficient study. As Todd D. Jick (1979) underscored, combining techniques can be effective and useful only if applied within a research design that has been studied in its finest details and supported by a sufficiently sound conceptual and theoretical apparatus. This is the case with research projects whose design itself envisages certain important elements such as the breakdown of the field researches, the different data-collection stages and the specific data analysis and comparison methods. Again, according to Jick, if the project design lacks this precision, the risk is that triangulation will create more confusion and the researcher will be inundated with information that he/she will be able to process only superficially' (Cataldi, 2016: 7).

Indeed, the adoption of a multiple technique strategy should consider the nature of the information available (Fielding and Fielding, 1986). Empirical data deriving from different techniques cannot always be simply compared and related, especially without considering adequately the research setting and the design method from which data have been obtained. In other words, there is the risk of having an extremely approximate and moderately superficial result. Indeed, each combination strategy inevitably does have a choice and a simplification. David Silverman asserts that a naive use of triangulation only leads to 'an illusory search for the full picture' (2000: 100). Taking up the concept of Martyn Hammersley and Paul Atkinson (1983), Silverman argues that triangulation ignores the fact that different sets of information will always be generated in different settings. For this reason, supporting the use of multiple methods, for instance combining interviews, participant observation and document reading in an ethnographic study, does not ensure having the most valid and reliable data. In short, different points of view do not necessarily give us a whole vision, but only a part of the picture. Hence, the combination of different methods is not the system to find the reality, or the 'true' state of affairs. On the contrary, Silverman points out that 'it is usually far better to celebrate the partiality of your data and delight in the particular phenomena that it allows you to inspect (hopefully in detail)' (2000: 112).

These criticisms call into question the basic assumption of triangulation designs, according to which the weaknesses in each single method will be compensated by the counter-balancing strengths of another (Jick, 1979; Hennink, 2014: 25). Therefore, this assumption has to be deconstructed, in order to avoid an ingenuous vision that attributes to the mediation of different sets of data the illusion of obtaining certain, more accurate or reliable results (Creswell et al., 2003; Giddings, 2006). At same time, these criticisms of combined technique strategies indicate that triangulation has in many cases become a 'methodological fashion' rather than a real requirement (Barbour, 2007: 56–8; Caillaud and Flick, 2017: 155–7).

In the field

In a mixed-method research on the meaning role and salience of rape myths within the subculture of college student athletes (McMahon, 2007), the researcher found that the survey's finding a 'low acceptance of rape myths [...] was contradicted by the findings of the focus groups and individual interviews, which indicated the presence of subtle rape myths' (2007: 362).

In the box there is a good example of how mixed methods can be used to give different perspectives on the respondents' opinions based on the type of research technique used (Hesse-Biber, 2010: 462). This does not depend on data reliability, but on the specificity of how each technique gathers/produces information. In other words, triangulation can help the researcher to enrich the perspective on the research issues, through a multiplicity of information. For this reason, triangulation in the social sciences should not be used solely to evaluate and check the validity and reliability of the data, but it should be extended to other purposes (Seawright, 2016).

Triangulation's purposes

But for what purposes, therefore, should the triangulation strategy (i.e. a strategy combining different techniques) be used? We can identify four specific use areas for a focus group's combination role:

- *Use for techniques.* The triangulation strategy allows the researcher to design a data collection tool (i.e. questionnaire), through better knowledge of the subjects' language, ways of thinking, possibilities of action.
- *Use for contexts.* The triangulation strategy allows the researcher to approach a little-known context or the frames of references of social actors. Enhancing the 'emic' aspect of the technique, the focus group can become acquainted with the environment and the object of study.
- *Use for contents.* The triangulation strategy allows the researcher to combine different techniques in order to increase the amount of empirical materials available or to find new stimuli and new opportunities to expand knowledge of the people under study by envisaging a flexible and open research design. In this respect, Robert Dingwall (1997) and David Silverman (2000) considered triangulation to be an opportunity arising not so much during the 'how' stage (i.e. in the early stages of the research) as in the 'why' stage (i.e. at those times when some empirical results do not 'add up' and require additional data to obtain a more satisfactory interpretation of the phenomenon being analysed).
- *Use to investigate unexpected results.* The triangulation strategy is also applied in cases where the researcher wants to examine specific aspects of the results of an initial investigation that cannot be satisfactorily explained, or which do not provide satisfactory empirical support for the hypotheses formulated.

4.3 The *ex-ante* role in the orientation phase

General features

For a long time, the focus group was exclusively used in the exploratory and preliminary phases of research. Even today, it is considered useful when a researcher is at the beginning of a new project and he/she needs to get closer to the phenomenon studied and the context of study (Corrao, 2000).

This supporting role attributed to the focus group usually precedes a wide-ranging data collection phase with standardized techniques and especially a survey with the questionnaire. This choice of combining quantitative techniques with qualitative ones can indicate a hidden need in the research, even if it is not declared: pre-gathering can help to integrate 'informational adequacy' (the accuracy and completeness of the information) with 'efficiency' (the cost sustained for each additional information) (Zelditch, 1962; Johnson and Turner, 2003).

For this reason, the integrated use of a focus group with a survey with a questionnaire remains the most common design, as well as the one most recommended in classic handbooks (Morgan, 1998a). In this triangulation strategy, the characteristics of the focus group make it possible to enrich the information obtained from the survey and vice versa (Hesse-Biber, 2010). For example, group discussions allow detailed study, but the results cannot be generalized statistically; conversely, data resulting from a survey may refer to a large population, but they cannot reflect the holistic complexity of a research issue (Corrao, 2000: 45).

The *ex-ante* functions

Generally, there are three main ways in which focus groups function to support the orientation of the survey (see Figure 4.1):

- becoming familiar with the object of investigation;
- building the empirical basis of the research in an emic way; that is, identifying the conceptual schemes and the language of the groups of persons involved;
- evaluating the adequacy and the complexity of the collection tools (scales, questions, instructions, etc.) to be used for the extensive survey according to the respondents' characteristics.

Regarding the first function, it has been identified by Theodore D. Fuller et al. (1994), who consider the acquisition of familiarity to be the first tangible result achieved by integrating techniques (Carey and Asbury, 2012: 20–1; Caillaud and Flick, 2017: 157–9). Making use of a pilot study with focus group discussions supports the researcher in the formulation phase of the research, aligning him/her to a progressive approach to the research issue (Johnson and Turner, 2003: 299; Barbour, 2007: 46).

Tamas Vicsek (2005) describes the advantages of using the focus group as an *ex-ante* support tool for a wide-ranging investigation as follows: 'One of the major objectives of the pilot phase was to get closer to the research topic, to familiarize myself with the topic and find useful aspects to concentrate on and aid the hypothesis development process' (2005: 108).

Indeed, focus groups are very open and flexible, therefore allowing a gradual approach to the topic of investigation.

Another function of the *ex-ante* role of the focus group is building the empirical basis of the research in an emic way. In particular, collective discussions can support the researcher in identifying the frames of reference of the people he/she wants to study (Currall and Towler, 2003; Carey and Asbury, 2012: 20–1). Indeed, reducing the complexity of the investigation problem can be achieved by very different routes. Hence, the analysis of the dimensions of the problem made by the researchers may not correspond at all to the issues perceived as crucial by the actors. In these cases, the researcher can conduct some group discussions with experts in the field, or actors involved in it, in order to frame the phenomenon studied according to their point of view.

In the field

In the medical area, mixed methods research using focus group in this role was conducted on Children's Safety Initiative – Emergency Medical Services (Hansen et al., 2016). There was little previous knowledge regarding this topic, especially with regard to specific contributors to paediatric safety events. For this reason, it was important to involve people with particular expertise in order to approach such a complex problem. Therefore, five preliminary focus group discussions were conducted with specific experts belonging to different professional providers' categories engaged in paediatric patient safety. The results obtained through group discussions were used as a basis for conducting a Delphi survey.

In such cases, the use of an instrument close to the group's everyday situation can facilitate, through the exchange of opinions, the knowledge of the actors' conceptual schemes and extrapolate their definitions or thinking structures (Barbour, 2007: 46). In this role, focus groups are useful for specifying the various dimensions and characteristics of concepts. Moreover, they also support the creation of classifications or typologies, not only about the issues raised, but also about references, levels and dimensions that are linked to each aspect emerging from the discussions.

Building an empirical basis in an 'emic' way also means focusing on actors' language in order to plan the following information-gathering steps using a way of speaking close to the one used by subjects involved (Kitzinger, 1994b). Therefore, it will be necessary to evaluate which groups to involve, according to whether the researcher's interest is to investigate the professional or technical language of a given social category or to detect the linguistic register to be used in the questionnaire. This strategy allows the researcher to improve the quality of the information collected and reduce the perceived gap between his/her language and the language of the actors.

In the field

During research conducted on school choices in the island of Sardinia, focus groups with students were used before a large-scale sampling survey (Calidoni and Cataldi, 2016). They were particularly useful for understanding not only the frames of references of students in choosing secondary school and university, but also for learning juvenile slang. For example, in their everyday lives Sardinian young people say 'on the continent' to mean 'in another Italian region', even if Sardinia is itself an Italian region. For this reason, this label was used in the questionnaire.

Another specific function concerns the support for framing the questionnaire and the scaling techniques. In such cases, the focus group makes it possible to evaluate the adequacy and complexity of the collection tools to be used for the extensive survey according to the characteristics of the respondents, especially when wording and phrasing items (see section 11.2).

4.4 The *ex-post* role in the analytical-interpretative phase

General features

A strategy of combining techniques to collect different data is the use of focus groups to support other tools in the analytical-interpretive phase. Although unanimously recognized by classic handbooks as a possible alternative of application (Morgan, 1997; Corrao, 2000), for a long time this option did not have adequate specific space in methodological reflection.

In particular, there is a certain vagueness in the literature regarding such a use and above all regarding applications, aims and advantages. In this section, we provide some guidelines and examples.

The *ex-post* functions

First of all, there are four general purposes related to this application (see Figure 4.1). They are:

- deepening specific topics of investigation;
- suggesting new interpretative keys;
- exploring new research questions not previously considered by the investigation;
- evaluating the progress of the survey and obtaining feedback on the research.

With regard to the first purpose, it derives from a lack of information perceived by the researcher at the end of a study (Barbour, 2007: 46–7). Planning focus group discussions at the end of a wide-ranging data collection process can mean focusing on specific topics of investigation in relation to which the information obtained through the previous phases is unsatisfactory and/or superficial. In such cases, therefore, the use of discussion makes it possible to broaden the information platform and to deepen the results that have emerged from the data analysis (Stewart et al., 2008).

This objective can therefore be achieved both through a horizontal operation of extending the database with respect to a delimited area of new interest, and through a vertical operation of deepening some attitudes and representations of the insiders or some features of contexts underlying certain empirical results obtained from the wide-ranging investigation (Hesse-Biber, 2010).

In the field

An interesting application of this combined use of focus groups is some research conducted in the second half of the 1980s in Thailand on the fertility decline of Thai families and its connection with modernization processes (Knodel et al., 1987). The aim of the study was to generate qualitative information (on perceptions, opinions and attitudes) to complement the quantitative data on changes in fertility patterns. In particular, focus groups made it possible to clarify the influence of the social and economic changes on the reproductive patterns of Thai families.

Regarding the second purpose, it can support the researcher in data interpretation, opening the study to the emergence of new interpretative keys. In such cases, the researcher has no lack of information, but he/she has difficulty in interpreting the results arising from the investigation based on the theoretical framework.

In support of this claim, the collective debates, exploiting the synergy effect (Stewart and Shamdasani, 1990), can encourage the emergence of innovative ideas different from those expressed in individual interviews.

In addition, collective discussions can help to understand unexpected results, which seem to contradict common sense or previous knowledge on the topic (Barbour, 2007: 46–7; Carey and Asbury, 2012: 20–1). Focus groups in fact can be a valuable resource to bring out composite representations and different opinions previously unknown or to deepen the results already obtained, stimulating the fluidity of the processes of hypotheses and concepts formation.

Another purpose of using the focus group in this role is to broaden the research field to include new topics connected to the research issue. Sometimes, the need to start new in-depth analysis arises from previous collection phases using focus groups. While in the first case the researcher has a lack of information and in the second case the researcher has an interpretative difficulty, in this third case the researcher has new research questions not previously previewed, and the focus group is considered the most useful tool with which to investigate these new scientific interests (Torres, 2006).

This case is connected with the typical ability of the focus group to trigger a series of chain responses that stimulate the emergence of a multiplicity of topics related to the main interest of the research (Onwuegbuzie et al., 2009). Those topics are often under-researched and require specific new attention from the researcher. In other cases, the need to start new in-depth analysis arises after research using a survey, so that new focus groups can be devoted to new topics not previously included in the questionnaire but considered important by the researcher in order to understand the research problem better (Vicsek, 2005).

In the field

Jane T. Bertrand and colleagues (1992), after conducting a survey with a questionnaire on the sexual practices of the Quiché-speaking Mayan population, conducted focus groups in order to investigate new aspects of the phenomena not covered in the previous survey. In particular, the focus group study dealt with some little-known topics, that is, highly intimate aspects of Guatemalan men's sexual behaviour. Discussions focused in particular on extra-marital relations, use of prostitutes and violence against women.

Finally, there is the possibility in mixed-methods strategies to use the focus group in the *ex-post* role in order to obtain feedback from the participants in the survey and an all-round evaluation on the results, limits and strengths of the research.

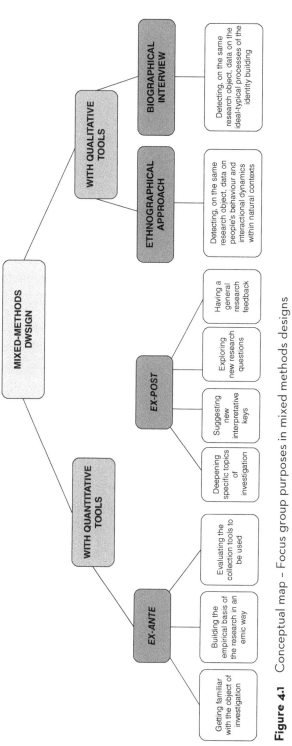

Figure 4.1 Conceptual map – Focus group purposes in mixed methods designs

4.5 Mixing qualitative methods

General features

The combined use of the focus group with other non-standard techniques is less widespread, or at any rate less explored in the literature. Indeed, studies on triangulation are focused on the limits of quantitative approaches (above all related to the standardization level of information gathering), that, although they allow a statistical generalization of the results, sometimes risk overestimating the systems of reference (analytical or conceptual) of the investigators on the observed phenomenon, because of the 'etic' nature of the research setting.

For these reasons, many scholars have tried to overcome these limitations by designing information collection techniques that are closer to the conceptual and linguistic categories and the context of the persons involved in their research, integrating quantitative and qualitative approaches. In the same way, these integrations have been useful in enriching interpretations and theoretical models, when standardized techniques have not been sufficient to draw out the complexity of a studied phenomenon. The ancillary rather than complementary use attributed to qualitative research approaches has probably also discouraged the exploration of the opportunities or challenges involved in using a qualitative mixed method for a long time in the social sciences (Bryman, 2006; Giddings, 2006).

As detailed in Chapter 3, qualitative research approaches are judged more suitable to provide in-depth information. The non-standardization of the information collecting procedures – typical of techniques used in these approaches – makes it possible to identify new forms of knowledge that exploit the point of view of those directly involved as well as the specificity of the context analysed (Vidich and Lyman, 2000). At the same time, these approaches make it possible to focus on aspects that are often taken for granted or extend beyond the sphere of common knowledge (Silverman, 2000).

Each qualitative approach satisfies specific cognitive aims, allowing the same phenomenon to be analysed from different perspectives. For these reasons, it may be interesting to examine the possibility of integrating several non-standardized techniques in order to increase their potential to penetrate the surface of very complex phenomena (Hesse-Biber, 2010; Cyr, 2019).

In what follows, we present how different qualitative approaches can be combined in order to take advantage of their potentiality and their particular perspective of observation.

In detail, our proposal will concern the possibility of integrating focus groups with: ethnography and the biographic approach (see Figure 4.1).

Focus groups and ethnography

The ethnographic approach is more useful to detect people's behaviour as well as the dynamics of interactions within natural contexts. Indeed, the distinctive feature of this approach is the chance it offers to observe phenomena in their natural environment in order to achieve more contextualized, but also deeper, knowledge (Hammersley and Atkinson, 1983). Only complete 'immersion' in the environment that constitutes the object of study allows the researcher to record the evolution of a social fact (Park, 1950).

Observation is the main technique of information collection used by the ethnographic approach. It is considered a non-reactive technique, since during an observation the researcher does not intend to cause a behaviour but he/she merely observes it when it occurs (Adler and Adler, 1994). The obtrusiveness of data collection tools is always an issue for social scientists. The use of techniques to investigate a phenomenon can modify the context observed by influencing attitudes and definitions of the situation by which the people under investigation reproduce those phenomena. Non-reactive observation is a less intrusive technique than the others because no questions are asked (Miller and Brewer, 2003). It reduces the risk of activating the defence strategies of the observed subject, though not obviating the risk of altering the observed 'object' with the mere presence of the researcher (Acocella, 2013: 9).

The observation's findings can be integrated by the use of other reactive techniques in order to reveal aspects that could not be detected by observation alone, such as the personal feelings and perceptions of studied groups (Barbour, 2007: 55–6). For this reason, within the same study, the observations can be combined with focus groups and biographical interviews. Indeed, the focus group allows the researcher to detect a social group's collective representations, while the biographical interview can match interest in subjective meanings with temporal depth and the multi-dimensional structure of an individual's life story (Liamputtong, 2011: 93–7).

As detailed in section 1.2, the added value of focus groups consists in the collective debate involving people who have a direct experience of the topic, 'experts' or actors involved in the phenomenon whose point of view emerges from their familiarity with the phenomenon studied (Cote-Arsenault and Morrison, 1999). Communication can become more spontaneous if the people involved feel that they have encountered similar situations as a result of having had, for example, similar professional or social experiences (Munday, 2006). This will also favour the creation of a compact group and the perception of belonging to the same social group (Acocella, 2008). For this reason, during focus group discussions, interaction among people who share similar experiences or a common background in relation to the topic discussed can generate inter-subjective representations reflecting the images and beliefs of the social group involved in the focus group (see section 5.2).

In the field

An example of the application of mixing qualitative methods is pro-vided by research that took place on the forms of 'submerged' violence that can arise in care institutions for minors (Acocella, 2013). In the research, non-reactive observation was considered a useful technique for exploring relationships between residents and workers of those structures for minors. For example, the major focus of observations was the level of concentration of decision making and the degree of standardization of activities pursued in these institutions. The purpose was to identify if and in what ways a strictly managed environment with prescriptive rules and without sharing of life decisions between caregiver and user can bring about exclusion processes or lead to vulnerability. Instead, in the research, the focus group was the best way to investigate the social representations of 'care' work. The aim was to identify a set of inter-subjective representations related to the structuring and organization of work within institutions. Mutual repre-sentations, as well as decision making and sharing processes, were also explored.

Focus groups and biographical interview

Through the biographical interview, it is possible to investigate the subjec-tive 'universe of meaning' that is the basis of behaviour and according to which life events are interpreted (Denzin, 2001; Caillaud and Flick, 2017: 164–72). At the same time, this technique allows the researcher to retrace the way in which – in a biography – the different life spheres have evolved over time while simultaneously intersecting with each other (school, work, relationships with people and institutions etc.). In this way, it is possible to identify the main events of every life sphere and in what ways the events of several spheres are integrated with each other into processes of multiple concatenation and mutual influence (Ritchie, 2003). For this reason, the biographical interview can be useful in elaborating different types of identity building processes such as analytical syntheses, by identifying their particular features and the main concatenation among biographic events, life facts, milestones, trajectories, turning points and so on, thus safeguarding the tem-poral depth and multi-dimensional structure of an individual's life story (Chamberlayne et al., 2000). The aim is to identify the main ideal-typical features of such processes, thus allowing the researcher to switch from an individual story to a sociological type into which this biographic story can be inserted (Liamputtong, 2011: 93–7).

In the field

In the research study on submerged violence, the biographic narrative approach was used to explore the changes in the residents' lives following their admission to the residential structure. The purpose was to detect the consequences in terms of structuring or de-structuring of the residents' identity and the potential risk of configuring identity as 'prisoner', 'excluded' or 'borderline'. At the same time, the aim was to bring out the possible strategies of resistance, as well as the processes of adaptation or surrender to the new condition by young residents.

Summing up

In conclusion, the use of a qualitative mixed-method approach can help to penetrate the surface of very complex phenomena, if the researcher is able to exploit the knowledge of specific cognitive aims which different qualitative methods allow him/her to fulfil in relation to the same research issue. In this way, a combination of different qualitative approaches can reveal the multi-dimensional nature of a social phenomenon, emphasizing at the same time the 'emic' nature of these methods and their potential to provide in-depth information and new forms of knowledge.

Further reading

Jick, T.D. (1979) 'Mixing qualitative and quantitative methods: triangulation in action', *Administrative Science Quarterly*, 24 (4): 602–11.

In this pioneering article on triangulation in administrative sciences, Todd D. Jick provides a literature review on the strategy of mixing methods, highlighting its pitfalls and opportunities.

Denzin, N.K. (2012) 'Triangulation 2.0', *Journal of Mixed Methods Research*, 6 (2): 80–8.

This article is suggested because it shows the recent developments of the debate on triangulation.

Exercises

1. A research team wants to study what young people expect to happen when they drink alcohol (alcohol expectancies) and how confident they are in believing they can manage pressures to drink alcohol (self-efficacy). Explain how you would use focus groups in designing a national survey to collect information about alcohol expectancies and self-efficacy.

2. In a research report on nursing practices, you read the following sentence: 'There are many benefits to using mixed methods. Quantitative data can support qualitative research components by identifying representative patients or outlying cases, while qualitative information can shed light on quantitative components by helping with the development of the conceptual model or instrument'. Discuss the sentence.

5

Choosing and Recruiting the Focus Group Participants

The group of participants is the main source of information for the focus group. How to choose and how to recruit participants are therefore crucial decisions.

These decisions are intended to bring out the particular social category around which the participants will have to be able to identify themselves in order to feel that they have not been invited in the meeting as individuals, but as members of a particular social group. At the same time, some criteria must be followed in setting up the discussion group in order to facilitate interaction among the participants and maximize the collection of high-quality information in the little time available.

In this chapter, we will explain the criteria for choosing and recruiting the participants. The first part of the chapter will examine the characteristics that allow the discussion group to qualify as a 'group' rather than as a simple assembly of individuals. At the same time, the criteria to be followed in the composition of the group to meet these conditions will be identified. The second part of the chapter will examine some methodological questions concerning the breadth of each discussion group and the number of focus groups to be conducted, according to the planning strategy of the research. In addition, some recruitment and logistical strategies will be indicated with the aim of facilitating the participation of people in group discussions.

───────── **Chapter goals** ─────────

- *Knowledge*: composition and recruitment of group discussion participants.
- *Applying knowledge and understanding*: identifying the conditions to qualify participants as a 'social group'.
- *Making judgements*: being aware of the criteria to use in choosing and finding participants to maximize the collection of quality information.

5.1 A 'collectivity' built *ad hoc*

When a focus group works well, during a discussion session, the participants do not act as individuals but as if they were part of the same social group. In this subsection, we will examine the particular 'social group' that is formed during the focus group and the conditions that allow the change in the participants' perceptions of being invited not as single persons, but because they are considered representative of a particular collectivity.

The group as a source of information

The group discussion is the main source of information for deepening knowledge on a particular topic of interest. For this reason, the researcher chooses the participants based on the research objectives. In everyday life, people belong to multiple groups and several social categories. However, during an investigation with a focus group, the researcher chooses the specific social category that identifies the members by emphasizing those elements of belonging/identification most suitable for the research objectives. In this way, a common group of belonging or reference emerges, bringing to light those joint elements that distinguish the participants. Therefore the researcher assesses which criteria are most useful for obtaining relevant information. In other words, the group formed in a focus group is always selected and somehow artificial. For this reason, we can say that a focus group is always a group that is built *ad hoc* by the researcher.

The 'extraneousness' of the participants

Some scholars argue that it is more effective to involve pre-existing groups in a focus group discussion, as this choice guarantees a more relaxed and cordial atmosphere (Zammuner, 2003: 114) and a more natural context for discussion (Kitzinger, 1994b: 105).

However, in our view, there are only a few specific situations that warrant the use of pre-existing groups: for example, if the purpose is to investigate groups that are naturally constituted, as in organizations, training courses and so on. In these cases, nevertheless, the researcher will probably have to select participants (because natural groups are usually too numerous for a focus group). It is also important to bear in mind that the task of gathering information will be something new for the group and will therefore establish relations oriented to the purpose of the research (that in the end are not natural).

In any event, if the researcher uses pre-existing groups it is necessary to pay attention to certain considerations.

First, when people who know each other participate in a discussion, it is more difficult to guarantee anonymity and to allow a discussion of the arguments without inhibitions due to previous daily reports (Morgan, 1998b: 67; Krueger and Casey, 2000: 11; Bloor et al., 2001: 43; Hennink, 2014: 41).

Second, in a group discussion where there are some people who know each other, privileged communication lines can be established among them that prevent a broader debate with all those present. It may also happen that some participants decide to refrain from expressing their disagreement for fear of breaking the relationship with others (Corrao, 2000: 47; Albanesi, 2004: 56; Carey and Asbury, 2012: 33). In a similar manner, if pre-existing groups are involved, the possible presence of entrenched antipathies or hostilities may induce some participants to adopt negative attitudes towards others, regardless of what they have declared during the debate (Cardano, 2003: 162).

In the field

This type of situation can be found in research on forms of marginalization in the third age in which focus groups were carried out with elderly people (Brunelli, 2003). Indeed, one participant declared himself disgusted by the ignorance of the other members. His considerations triggered a chain of controversy that ended in a brawl. Conflicts already existed among the participants, but their gravity had not been grasped before the discussion. This compromised the degree of fidelity of the answers provided by the participants to such an extent that the research group excluded the information gathered in that meeting from the analysis.

Finally, people who know each other well, when they interact, can take for granted a lot of information that might otherwise be interesting to the researcher (Zammuner, 2003: 114; Hennink, 2014: 40–1).

These dynamics may hinder the establishment of a confidential climate during the meeting and the freedom of expression of opinions. They may also make it difficult to distinguish genuine opinions from those influenced by previous relationships. This is also because the researcher is not aware of factors unrelated to the discussion that may have affected the interventions. In this regard, conducting discussion with pre-established groups implies that the results of the research are difficult to decontextualize, since what emerges during the discussion is characterized by the everyday routines and ordinary interactions of group members (Bloor et al., 2001: 18). Thus, in this regard we can agree with David W. Stewart and Prem N. Shamdasani when they state that a pre-existing group can 'produce less variance in opinion than a group of strangers who might otherwise be equally homogeneous' (1990: 56).

To conclude, the choice of conducting a focus group with people who belong to a pre-existing group should be limited to special occasions (as in an organization, a training course, a school class etc.). However, in these cases, to avoid the distortions mentioned above, it is advisable to mix the focus group with other detection techniques. For example, combined focus group use with observation can be an effective method to identify the dynamics of group members and the most common behaviours, and/or with in-depth interviews, to investigate the underlying motivations and attitudes.

The 'social dimension' of the group

Having highlighted that the group discussion is always formed *ad hoc*, it is important to identify what is meant by 'social group' when we refer to a focus group and how it is constituted during the discussion. Some elements contribute to this process.

The 'interaction' is the first element of the group's constitution that can be considered. As Robert F. Bales (1950) and George C. Homans (1950) argue, the basis of a group is a structure of social relations characterized by direct interaction among a limited number of individuals. In the focus group, therefore, the unifying element consists precisely of direct interaction, which is normally face to face, and even in an online version is still synchronic. Indeed, although the structure does not last over time, among the participants in a focus group a kind of social relationship is established on the basis of the exchange of opinions and the sharing of the same social situation. However, since it is limited to the duration of the meeting, the interaction alone is not sufficient to spread among the participants the perception of being members of the same social group.

A second element that can facilitate the transition from a simple agglomeration of individuals to a group is the performance of a 'common task'. For Morton Deutsch and Harold B. Gerard (1955), the formation of a group occurs when some people are together to achieve a common purpose. According to Kurt Lewin (1948) and Donald T. Campbell (1958), a characterizing feature of the group is the existence of a common destiny, which spreads a sense of belonging among those who share it. In the discussions of a focus group, the moderator provides a common purpose: dealing with a specific topic in relation to which participants are invited to compare their opinions by interacting with each other (see section 7.2). In the following chapters, we will examine the strategies that the moderator can adopt to enhance the performance of this task as a means to spread a sense of belonging to the same group among the participants (see section 9.1).

However, even sharing a common purpose is not enough to spread feelings of mutual trust among the participants, nor to the formation of a social group. Indeed, it is necessary to consider that the common purpose is established by an exogenous source – the moderator – and is limited to the time of the discussion. Furthermore, the short duration of the meeting reduces the importance that the members of the group will be able to attach to this task.

Other elements that can favour the formation of a social group in a focus group are 'self-categorization and external recognition'. Taking the theories of Robert K. Merton (1957), Henri Tajfel (1982) and John C. Turner (1982) into consideration, a group is formed when two or more individuals perceive themselves as members of the same social group and when they are considered as such by one or more persons outside the group. In such cases, independently of everyday physical interaction, the group as such is constituted based on a cognitive process connected to identification with a common social category of belonging/reference.

Both auto-categorization and external recognition can be satisfied during the discussion of a focus group. Indeed, the participants in the discussion can belong to a common social category, favouring the subjective development of the self-definition of themselves as people belonging to the corresponding group. As a consequence, even if people who attend the discussion meet for the first time, they can perceive themselves as members of the same group according to the criterion by which they were invited/selected (e.g. because they carry out the same profession, belong to the same social class or belong to the same age group etc.). The external principle, in contrast, can be facilitated by the moderator, who refers to the participants as members belonging to the same social group (Cataldi, 2009). In this group formation process, the moderator can also play an important role, emphasizing what those present have in common and thematizing the object of the research according to the perspective – and therefore the social category of identification – starting from which the participants will have to deal with the topic of discussion (see section 7.2).

Summing up

In conclusion, in focus groups, even if all three of these conditions are manifested, the physical interaction and the sharing of a common task are generally limited at the time of the meeting. The third condition – the cognitive development of identification with a particular social group – can transcend the meeting, since it derives from belonging to the same social category. At the same time, the coexistence of the three conditions favours the establishment of a social group during a focus group. For this reason, all these conditions must still be facilitated during the discussion.

In order to facilitate the interaction and acceptance of a common task, the discussion should be articulated among people who share common interests and perceive themselves as being in an equal position. However, as we will detail later (see section 9.3), this does not necessarily imply that they also have the same opinions on the question under investigation.

Finally, in order to facilitate the process of self-categorization and external recognition of the participants as members of the same group, it is important to choose people who share similar life experiences or have the same states on the properties relevant to identifying their state of belonging to that particular social group.

5.2 The participants' characteristics

To satisfy the conditions listed above, the researcher must pay attention to the way in which he/she chooses to constitute the discussion group. In particular, two indications must be followed:

- the participants must be 'experts' on, or privileged witnesses of, the topic being studied;
- the composition of the groups must be constituted by achieving a proper balance between the degree of homogeneity and heterogeneity in relation to some properties identified as relevant to the research.

The 'experts' on the topic

It is important to invite 'experts', that is, people who have a direct experience of the research topic (Carey and Asbury, 2012: 41). They should not be 'specialists' on the topic (as in the Delphi method; see section 1.4). By 'experts', in contrast, we mean people whose point of view is developed thanks to their familiarity with the phenomenon studied, since it is part of their everyday lives and therefore they experience it at first hand (Stewart and Shamdasani, 1990: 53; Cote-Arsenault and Morrison, 1999: 281; Albanesi, 2004: 50–1). In order to facilitate this process, the participants in the discussion should have the same states on some properties relevant to identifying a particular social category of identification (e.g. referable to the profession, to the gender or to a similar experience of life) that the researcher wants to solicit in the discussion (Hogg, 2001: 61–3). During the discussion, this aspect can help the participants feel that they belong to the same social group, since they share the same characteristic or they experience similar life situations. These people will be those most suitable for talking about the phenomenon investigated, favouring the emergence of points of view and ways of categorizing the phenomenon that are similar or at least comparable (Liamputtong, 2011: 36; Acocella, 2012: 1129–30).

In the field

In research on disadvantaged families, the aim was to draw out the social conditions of women living in single-income households (where only the husband worked) in areas marked by processes of social marginalization (Meo, 2003a: 139–42). Thus married women, with children, who did not work and who lived in impoverished neighbourhoods were invited to the focus group discussions. Based on these common characteristics, the participants came to define themselves as a group and to recognize each other 'competent' to discuss the research issue: the social vulnerability of families with limited availability of economic resources.

In addition to enabling self-categorization and external recognition of group members, engaging 'experts' during a focus group discussion helps ensure that the topic is relevant to the people involved. In this way, participants will be more motivated to join the discussion and more able to thematize the topic in the short time available. This makes it possible to gather relevant and good-quality information about the object of the research (Krueger and Casey, 2000: 71; Zammuner, 2003: 109).

In relation to the phenomenon studied (unit of analysis) and the choice of the empirical cases on which the information is collected (recording unit), there are two different possibilities when it comes to involving 'experts' (see Table 5.1):

- *the focus group participants coincide with the protagonist of the specific phenomenon studied:* in this case the unit of analysis coincides with the recording unit;
- *the focus group participants do not coincide with the protagonist of the specific phenomenon studied:* in this case the unit of analysis does not coincide with the recording unit.

Some examples follow. As an example of the first case, if the unit of analysis is immigration, the empirical cases will be immigrants. Here, the research goal is to elicit immigrants' social and inter-subjective representations of the phenomenon under investigation. Therefore, even if the research topic concerns the participants' experience, the purpose of the focus group will not be to detect their autobiography or their specific life paths, but to collect the testimonies of 'experts' in their capacity as bearers of direct experience of the phenomenon investigated.

In the second case, in contrast, if the unit of analysis is immigration, the empirical cases will not be immigrants, but privileged witnesses who have direct experience of the phenomenon, although the topic does not directly concern their lives. For example, if the unit of analysis is immigration, politicians or social workers, who deal with immigration and who, for this reason, can provide information useful for the study, may be invited to the discussion. In such cases, the purpose of the focus group will be to elicit any inter-subjective representations and socially shared knowledge on the phenomenon that is disseminated among people considered 'experts' because of their profession. If the researcher decides to involve both politicians and social workers, the focus group will allow him/her to identify the common images and shared beliefs within two different social groups. The categorizations will be diverse because the experience and the way in which each group relates to the phenomenon are different.

Expert advice

To illustrate this point, we provide an example. If the intention is to study the topic of 'poverty', the researcher can conduct discussions with people living in poor families and in city areas characterized by processes of social exclusion. In this case, the research unit of analysis will coincide with the recording unit, since the empirical cases involved in the discussion have direct experience of living in a marginal social context. The purpose of the focus group could be to collect the testimony of 'experts' in order to investigate the underlying causes of vulnerability and social exclusion of poor families. Inversely, the researcher can decide to conduct the focus group on the same topic by involving social workers from public services and members of voluntary associations operating in degraded social contexts. In this case, the research unit of analysis will not coincide with the recording unit, but the empirical cases involved in the investigation will nevertheless have direct experience of the phenomenon, since they constantly relate to situations of poverty and social marginality. In this case, the purpose of the focus group could be to collect the testimony of 'experts' on the effectiveness of measures to counter the underlying causes of the vulnerability and social exclusion of poor families.

There is also a third possibility: the focus group can be used to collect the 'common sense' and the stereotypes disseminated on a given object of study. In such a case, the researcher can invite people who are not 'experts' on the phenomenon studied and the purpose of the focus group can be to bring out a form of knowledge shared by any social group that is only structured 'by hearsay' (Aronson et al., 1997; Schneider, 2004). This is the case where the research analysis unit does not coincide with the recording unit and the empirical cases involved in the discussions have only 'indirect' experience of the phenomenon under investigation.

Expert advice

In relation to the previous example aimed at studying the topic of 'poverty', the researcher could involve residents of middle-class neighbourhoods in the discussion, where the problem of poverty is not on the agenda. In this way, the research group can identify how ordinary people re-elaborate the images of the poor furnished by television, social media and newspapers, how they deal with the topic of poverty and related problems connected to conditions of social exclusion.

Table 5.1   Relationship between unit of analysis (UA) and collecting unit (CU)

UA = CU: the unit of analysis is poverty and the empirical cases are poor people	
UA ≠ CU: the unit of analysis is poverty and the empirical cases are not poor	• *Level of direct experience*: privileged witnesses who have useful information to provide due to their direct experience of the phenomenon Unit of analysis: poverty Empirical cases: politicians or social workers operating in sectors related to poverty • *Level of non-direct experience*: ordinary people who have knowledge of the phenomenon only 'by hearsay' Unit of analysis: poverty Empirical cases: people living in middle-class or residential neighbourhoods

Levels of homogeneity and heterogeneity

In any event, the groups will have to be composed in such a way as to achieve internally the correct balance between the level of homogeneity and the level of heterogeneity with reference to the sociographic features of the members (education, profession, gender etc.).

A high level of homogeneity can stimulate the conversation by creating a comfortable environment, since the perception of being peers allows people to relax and express their opinions (Morgan, 1998b: 59–60; Kelly, 2001: 171–3; Hennink, 2014: 38–9; Cyr, 2019: 21, 45). Furthermore, by perceiving others as more like themselves, the participants take less time to get to know each other and can express themselves more spontaneously (Carey and Asbury, 2012: 42).

On the other hand, a high level of heterogeneity can facilitate the emergence of a wider range of opinions and perspectives on the investigated topic, which will enrich the research results (Krueger and Casey, 2000: 71–2; Bloor et al., 2001: 36; Morgan, 2017: 416–17). Indeed, the researcher may obtain uninteresting information if all the participants in the debate have the same point of view.

Below, we indicate some criteria concerning how to choose the properties with which to define the level of homogeneity or heterogeneity of a discussion group.

Cultural level

A first property to consider is the cultural level. Involving people with different statuses on this property in the same discussion should be avoided. Indeed, it may create situations of embarrassment or friction among participants. Moreover, people with higher levels of education tend to intervene first, while those with lower cultural levels tend to conform with what was said previously, considering more cultured people as more experienced, intelligent and capable (Greenbaum, 1998: 62; Corrao, 2000: 49; Carey and Asbury, 2012: 42).

In the field

During research conducted in Ethiopia to detect opinions on HIV risk-behaviours, a series of discussions were organized with parents and teachers. The researchers decided to divide the two social groups based on a homogeneous cultural level. They chose this strategy in particular since most of the parents were illiterate and this would have made them feel uncomfortable in the discussion, leading to them assuming the same opinions as those expressed by teachers (Astatke and Serpell, 2000: 372–3).

Social position

The social position and the hierarchical level must also be considered. According to some sociometric tests, the number of communicative actions of an individual is closely related to his/her social status (Bales, 1950; Moreno, 1954; Flament, 1965). Indeed, those who enjoy more advantageous or hierarchically prestigious social positions in a group tend to perform a greater number of communicative acts, exercising a high degree of leadership over others (Bloor et al., 2001: 37; Hennink, 2014: 39).

In the field

In research on cigarette consumption among young people of different ages enrolled at the same school, the voices of some older participants sometimes overwhelmed those of the younger ones. Indeed, during the discussion the hierarchical relationships established in the school were replicated between the 'young' and the 'elderly' (Michell and Amos 1997, 1867–9).

If the social position or the hierarchical level are heterogeneous, participation in the discussion can fall within the category of 'normative' behaviours (Asch, 1951; Cooper et al., 2001). Therefore, the different social and hierarchical positions of the members will be able to influence both the temporal order and the quantity of the interventions (Cyr, 2019: 67–9). In this case, the search for consensus and compromise will dominate the discussion, and it will be usual to find situations where the participants tend to conform with the common positions in order to safeguard the cohesion of the group and avoid conflicts (Hennink, 2014: 39). In contrast, in focus group discussions, it is important to favour situations where the participation is 'consensual'. In other words, everyone should feel free to intervene when and how he/she wants.

Socio-economic level

Ensuring a certain degree of homogeneity in relation to socio-economic level is also recommended. Indeed, people with different incomes tend to have different life experiences and representations of the world that often cannot be compatible (Greenbaum, 1998: 62; Corrao, 2000: 49; Carey and Asbury, 2012: 42).

Nationality

Nationality can also create unforeseen and awkward dynamics, especially if the groups are composed of people who belong to collectives who are or perceive themselves to be in contrast with others (Bloor et al., 2001: 37). Tensions can be overcome if the social category of group identification is not the country of origin, but another property (Acocella, 2008: 98).

In the field

In research on the training of foreign students in Florence (Ceri and Ceccatelli, 2007), the focus groups were homogeneous by type of educational institution attended, but heterogeneous by nationality and gender. Despite the presence in the group of Africans, Americans, Asians and Europeans, conflicting situations did not arise because the topic of discussion was their common experience of study in Florence. This allowed the participants to feel that they belonged to the common social category of 'students', in relation to which all of them were equal. Therefore, in this case, the different origins of the participants even enriched the discussion by expressing different paths of socialization in higher education systems connected to the experiences of their countries of origin.

Anyhow, according to Anna Amelina and Thomas Faist (2012), 'naturalizing views' of ethnicity and nation should be avoided. Moreover, it is important not to emphasize ethnicity or nation as dominant categories relevant for setting up the research organization. Indeed, 'Methodological transnationalism' should encourage the researchers 'to step out of cultural traits based on belonging to one nation-state/ethnicity/race/religion. Rather, the shared characteristic for building groups could be gender or class/position in labour market, or patterns of mobility, condition of exit, legal status, age at migration, or length of stay, depending on the research question' (Frisina, 2018: 193).

Gender

In relation to gender differences, the co-presence of males and females in discussions can be a source of inhibition. This is a valid indication if the topic is closely related to gender issues (e.g. division of work in the family, care of family members, health etc.). However, according to some scholars, this is also a general indication, since males tend to speak more than females in mixed groups (Greenbaum, 1998: 35; Morrison, 1998: 204; Krueger and

Casey, 2000: 73; Bloor et al., 2001: 37). Nevertheless, this consideration should not be generalized.

In the field

In a study on adolescents' social representations of the use of soft drugs (Warner et al., 1999: 29–31), the researchers decided to define homogeneous groups of adolescents based on gender. However, drug use is not a topic that necessarily involves male and female identity or gender stereotypes. For this reason, in our view, having mixed groups could probably have been more effective in acquiring a broader variety of information.

Other problems may also arise in research involving people from peripheral, rural or world areas where patriarchal cultures still prevail, relegating women to positions of inferiority and subjection to the male figure (Knodel, 1993: 41; Corrao, 2000: 49). The same dynamics can be found when focusing on elderly people (more traditional in the ways of categorizing gender behaviour patterns). In all these cases, it may happen that it is mainly males who conduct the discussion, while women are silent or compliant with what the former claim. In these research contexts, therefore, it is advisable to set up discussion groups homogeneously composed of only males or females, 'because it remains unclear how a mixed-gender group composition [could affect] participants' contributions to the discussion' (Hennink, 2014: 38).

Age

Age is also a property to be taken into account when creating groups. Indeed, for some scholars it is advisable to reach a certain level of homogeneity on this property, since different life experiences correspond to different ages (Morrison, 1998: 204; Hennink, 2014: 38). This highlights the importance that the group shares similar everyday experiences. This is for the benefit of both the participant, because he/she can more easily identify with the social group, and the researcher, because it makes the information more comparable.

However, it frequently happens that people belonging to different generations are involved in the same focus group, especially if the unifying category of the group is not age but another more relevant category, such as, for example, type of profession or educational qualification. Indeed, in these cases, a heterogeneous composition of a group by age can favour a greater variety of information and the emergence of different points of view (Stewart and Shamdasani, 1990: 37).

In the field

In research on perceptions of alcohol consumption, groups were formed involving young and adult women habitually frequenting nightclubs, but with similar cultural levels. The aim was to detect the different representations of the phenomenon investigated (Parks et al., 1998: 704).

In contrast, in focus groups consisting of children it is appropriate to compose groups that are as homogeneous as possible, since linguistic and cognitive resources change greatly with age (Rapari, 2005: 196–8). Likewise, conducting discussions with mixed groups of young and old people is not recommended. Indeed, in this case, the participants may have overly diverse representations of the phenomenon, which risks producing a polarization in the debate (see section 9.3).

Knowledge of the phenomenon studied

It is also important to consider the type of knowledge of the phenomenon investigated that is possessed by the people who are invited to the group discussion. Involving experts and non-experts in the same discussion should be avoided. This is especially so when there is different 'technical' knowledge on the topic discussed, since the opinions expressed by the experts could influence others (Vaughn et al., 1996: 63; Cardano, 2003: 161).

In the field

In research conducted to evaluate treatments for diarrhoea in children, discussions were organized by inviting both doctors, who prescribed new therapies, and mothers, who adopted those treatments for their children (Santoso, 1996: 1164). It is natural to suppose that the mothers were conditioned by the opinions of the doctors so as not to question the certainty that their children were 'safe'.

Summing up

In conclusion, there is no procedure to be applied automatically to form a discussion group. The choice of which properties to consider and the degree of homogeneity/heterogeneity will depend on the cognitive objectives of the research.

In any event, some considerations should be borne in mind (see Table 5.2). A certain balance should be sought between homogeneity and internal heterogeneity in each discussion group. It is therefore necessary to choose some properties on which the participants will have different states, in order to avoid excessive homogeneity and to favour the emergence of multiple points of view. At the same time, it is necessary to ensure that a group is not too heterogeneous, identifying other properties on which the participants have the same status. In such a case, the internal homogeneity of the group will prevent the development of discussions that are difficult to manage due to the presence of participants with opinions that are too irreconcilable, or to the occurrence of dynamics of either inhibition or excessive conflict on the topic discussed.

Expert advice

For example, if focus groups are conducted with social workers to reflect on the topic of poverty, the level of homogeneity could be reached on the type of area of intervention (minors, families, disabilities etc.), in order to conduct a discussion starting from comparable experiences. At the same time, it is appropriate to conduct discussions involving people with a similar number of years of service. This could help to avoid situations occurring where there is inhibition related to different levels of 'seniority' or risks of compliance by social workers who have been operating for fewer years with respect to senior professionals.

In contrast, in relation to heterogeneity, for example, the participants in the discussion can work in different urban contexts according to the problems relating to the specific area of intervention of the social service. In this way, the participants in the discussion will be able to introduce different points of view on the phenomenon.

However, while guaranteeing a certain balance between the two extremes, homogeneity in the internal composition of the groups is increased when the researcher is less interested in the variety of information, but more in deepening knowledge about a certain phenomenon and some of its particular aspects (Bloor et al., 2001: 36). Indeed, in research designs that use the focus group with an analytical-in-depth function, a greater homogeneity makes it possible to thematize the topic more quickly starting from a similar perspective (see section 3.4).

On the other hand, the researcher can increase heterogeneity when he/she wants to carry out research using the exploratory-descriptive function of focus groups (Vaughn et al., 1996: 62). Indeed, a greater heterogeneity within the group makes it possible to widen knowledge about a phenomenon, rapidly acquiring a variety of information on a given phenomenon without going so far as to deepen it excessively (see section 3.3).

Table 5.2 Relationship between homogeneity and heterogeneity within the group

General criterion: to find a certain balance between homogeneity and heterogeneity in each discussion group, on the sociographic properties of the members	☐ *Level of homogeneity:* to avoid inhibition dynamics among the participants and favour the perception of being among peers ☐ *Level of heterogeneity:* to facilitate the emergence of a wider range of opinions and perspectives on the research issue
Based on the research objectives, it is possible to increase homogeneity or heterogeneity in the internal composition of each discussion group	*Increase in the level of homogeneity:* in focus groups with an analytical-in-depth function to detect more detailed information on the phenomenon by starting from a similar perspective *Increase in the level of heterogeneity:* in focus groups with exploratory descriptive functionality to detect a variety of information on the phenomenon in a short time without presuming to obtain very detailed information

Given the flexibility of research designs using focus groups, it is still possible to combine multiple strategies to choose participants during research. For example, the researcher can start by privileging the heterogeneity of the groups, in order to probe a wide range of positions, and then move on to more homogeneous groups to investigate relevant aspects that emerged during the first series of focus groups. Or the researcher can first carry out focus groups involving homogeneous groups with the aim of acquiring deeper knowledge of the phenomenon and later he/she can choose more heterogeneous groups to detect the effects of interaction on the collected information (Acocella, 2008: 102).

The researcher is not always able to establish in advance what is the best strategy to follow, or on what properties it is better to achieve a high degree of homogeneity/heterogeneity within the groups. For this reason, the research design may include a preliminary exploratory phase (see section 11.2). Otherwise, the necessary decisions will have to be taken during the research (Morgan, 1998b: 63; Frisina, 2010: 55–8).

Finally, it is necessary to specify that the choice of certain degrees of homogeneity and/or heterogeneity in a discussion group serves to identify the empirical cases on which to collect information. In the analysis, therefore, in the transformation of empirical cases into 'theoretical constructs', other homogeneity/heterogeneity criteria can be privileged (see sections 3.1 and 12.1). This is also because the researchers generally decide how to form the groups on the basis of structural characteristics (gender, educational qualifications, profession etc.) that they know. Instead the transformation of empirical cases into 'theoretical constructs' takes place on any forms of socially shared knowledge or inter-subjective representations that have emerged in the various collective debates, which will contribute in different ways to identifying, delineating and understanding the unit of analysis of the research (Ragin and Becker, 1992: 220; Walton, 1992). The process of transforming 'empirical groups' into 'theoretical groups' will be outlined in Chapter 12, where we will explore the different inferential strategies that the researcher will be able to exploit between the information detected during the field research and the formulation of the final theorizing/conceptualization, in order to identify, describe and understand the unit of analysis being studied.

5.3 Group size and number of focus groups

The criteria

The total number of participants in a focus group depends both on the number of participants in each discussion and on the number of meetings that have been scheduled. However, it is difficult to establish these figures *a priori*. Below we will indicate some general criteria that can be taken into consideration to decide the size of each group and the number of focus groups to conduct, in order to maximize the quality of the research results.

The number of participants in a group discussion

The number of participants in each focus group should facilitate the free interaction and the collection of a range of opinions adequate to fulfil the cognitive objectives.

There is no agreement among scholars on the ideal number of participants. Some scholars define a range, but opinions are conflicting on its size. According to some scholars (Morgan, 1997: 43; Morrison, 1998: 204), the number that can guarantee a good outcome of the discussion ranges from a minimum of 6 people to a maximum of 10. According to others (Dawson et al., 1993: 25), it can range from 4 to 12 participants. Richard A. Krueger and Mary A. Casey

(2000: 73) state that real focus groups are those involving a number of participants between 6 and 12, while those with 4 to 6 people are mini-focus groups. However, according to Michael Bloor, Jane Frankland, Michelle Thomas and Kate Robson (2001: 45) the optimal size should be between 6 and 8 people.

Obviously, a larger group makes it possible to obtain a wider range of positions on the research issue (Corrao, 2000: 52; Morgan, 2017: 414–15). Groups of this kind are preferred in research designs that value the exploratory-descriptive function of focus groups (Zammuner, 2003: 116–17). On the other hand, a group that is too large may make the discussion fragmented and hinder good interaction, since not everyone will have the opportunity to intervene. Moreover, it may increase both the risk of alienation of the shy or less interested people, and the probability that subgroups will form (Stewart and Shamdasani, 1990: 57; Hennink, 2014: 38).

Usually, smaller groups are preferred in research using the focus group with an analytical-in-depth function, since the aim is to conduct a more detailed study of a phenomenon. Indeed, in smaller groups, all the participants have more time to explain their thinking (Morgan, 1998b: 72–3; Corrao, 2000: 51–2). Moreover, by completing the round of interventions more quickly, more aspects of the same question can be discussed (Acocella, 2008: 104; Hennink, 2014: 38).

Small groups are also recommended in discussions with talkative people, such as the elderly (Brunelli, 2003). It is recommended to compose smaller groups, particularly when dealing with 'sensitive' and 'delicate' topics, to facilitate the establishment of a peaceful atmosphere, which may induce the participants to address the issue since they have the necessary time available (Morrison, 1998: 204; Cote-Arsenault and Morrison, 1999: 281; Barbour, 2007: 71; Carey and Asbury, 2012: 45).

Small groups are also preferred in the case of focus groups with children, since they tend to be easily distracted and need more control by the moderator (Gibson, 2007; Hennink, 2014: 38).

In the field

This strategy, for example, was used in research conducted with primary school children of different ages, in order to assess the appropriateness of a sexual abuse prevention programme. Involving a small number of children enabled the moderator to control the discussion better, being appropriately solicitous to all the attendants (Charlesworth and Rodwell, 1997: 1211).

However, it should be emphasized that too few participants can lead to rapid agreement among the various positions, resulting in a very limited range of ideas and opinions being collected (Corrao, 2000: 52; Bloor et al., 2001: 46; Cardano, 2003: 162).

It should also be borne in mind that the breadth of each group may vary from the one designed, given that often in the discussion there are fewer people than those invited. It is therefore common practice to recruit more people than expected (Greenbaum, 1998: 46; Morgan, 1998b: 104).

The number of meetings

At the beginning of research, the number of focus groups to be conducted should be decided according to the research issue. Generally, if the research pursues exploratory purposes, it is preferable to carry out several meetings to obtain a greater amount of information (Zammuner, 2003: 119). In contrast, in research that values the analytical-in-depth function of focus groups, it may be sufficient to resort to a reduced number of meetings. Indeed, in these research designs, the research issue is more focused, because the aim is generally to deepen only some aspects of a phenomenon or the adequacy of some analytical perspectives that the researcher evaluates as appreciable, as well as to develop results and knowledge obtained in previous research (see section 3.4).

In the field

A research on the use of soft drugs by adolescents had heuristic aims, so that 42 focus groups were conducted involving 232 people (Warner et al., 1999: 29). In contrast, the research on the training of foreign students in Florence (Ceri and Ceccatelli, 2007) conducted a small number of focus groups. Indeed, group discussions were used to investigate some results that emerged from the analysis of information previously collected with in-depth interviews, highlighting a few aspects to be explored in depth.

Some scholars argue that the number of meetings cannot be established in advance, even in indicative terms. As with other qualitative approaches, in order to establish the number of focus groups to be performed, these authors suggest relying on the criterion of saturation: focus groups are carried out until the information gathered becomes redundant (Breen, 2006: 466; Carlsen and Glenton, 2011; Hennink, 2014: 43). This criterion is more easily attainable in research that values the analytical-in-depth function of focus groups, since the perspective on the phenomenon investigated will be more precisely defined. Indeed, in this type of research, it is easier for information gathered at a certain point to become redundant, since the discussion outline is generally more structured, according to the aspects of the phenomenon or the analytical perspectives that the researcher wants to investigate. Moreover, the discussion outline will be similar in the various focus groups, in order to be able to compare the information that will emerge in different focus groups (see sections 3.4 and 6.1). At the same time, as discussed in the previous paragraphs, the discussion group will tend to be more homogeneous internally.

Although important, the criterion of saturation should not be overdetermined. Indeed, it seems to refer to a criterion of generalization of information typical of quantitative research (Barbour, 2007: 69). However, as anticipated, in qualitative approaches lacking an initial analysis unit, a numerical delimitation of the reference population is also missing. It is consequently not possible to establish a number of cases that would be sufficient to assess the 'statistical representativeness' of the results acquired. Therefore, the conclusions that the researcher reaches with the criterion of saturation must never be considered definitive. Indeed, the unpredictability and variety of situations relating to social phenomena do not give any guarantee that a new investigation cannot re-open the interpretative framework (Montesperelli, 1998: 89–90).

The issue of the possibility of extending the results obtained beyond the specific research carried out is not amenable to a simple solution. However, the question should not be resolved by finding the way to restore the concept of statistical representativeness in this kind of research. This is especially because, as detailed in section 3.1, the aim of research with a focus group is not to estimate the extent of a phenomenon (i.e. the breadth of its referents), but to investigate it in depth, by identifying its characteristics and the process of underlying development (Barbour, 2007: 11; Cyr, 2019: 35–40). Therefore, the object of study is not investigated extensively but intensively.

Nevertheless, to avoid a radically idiographic approach, the researcher can use other forms of generalization that can be defined in terms of extrapolation and conceptual transposition. This can be done by identifying relevant aspects to develop conceptual categories adequate to describe and understand the unit of analysis. In detail, in qualitative research, the analysis of the information that has emerged in a specific investigated empirical context aims to extrapolate and abstract concepts or conceptual structures (such as classifications and types) that transcend the particular field in which they were generated, because they are useful for understanding more processes of the reality studied. As Daniel Bertaux states (1998: 30–5), the researcher must indeed try to move 'from the particular to the general' by discovering, in the observed field, the social forms that can be present in a multiplicity of similar contexts. The plausibility of such generalizations, states Bertaux (1998: 31), lies in the discovery of 'generic mechanisms' related to configurations of social relationships, definitions of situations and logic of actions that develop in response to such situations, which aid understanding of more general social processes. With reference to these forms of generalization and conceptual abstraction, Rita Bichi (2002: 78) uses the expression 'social representativeness', understood as the reading of the socially crucial aspects of a phenomenon through the specific experience of actors/witnesses, who express orientations and behaviours that represent, therefore, ways and forms of sociality of the associated experience.

Hence, in research involving the focus group the aim is to outline conceptual categories appropriate to describe and understand the social and intersubjective representations and the socially shared knowledge disseminated in particular social groups (see section 1.2).

The conceptual category referring to the focus group analysis unit can be progressively outlined during the field research, and this influences the choice of the total number of discussions to be conducted. Indeed, given the flexibility of the focus group research designs and the circular relationship that arises between empirical observations and theorization, usually at the beginning of research, the total number of meetings can only be roughly defined and progressively specified during field research based on the results obtained that can be linked to the conceptual category that the researcher wants to outline. The field phase can be planned progressively, in order to draw out the variety in the ways of representing a social phenomenon in relation to the solicited social group or to identify some relevant features useful for outlining and understanding the conceptual category referable to the unit of analysis.

In this regard, if in the planning phase – whether starting from previous knowledge or carrying out initial investigations in the field – the phenomenon investigated turns out to be very complex and multifaceted, it may be decided to conduct a number of focus groups matching the number of 'traits' of the unit of analysis that the researcher wants to explore. Each focus group will involve a different group considered the most suitable to investigate that specific 'trait'. Comparison between the different focus groups will thus be useful to reflect on the various aspects of the chosen unit of analysis.

Similarly, during the gradual phases of planning, it is also possible to identify some relevant characteristics or combinations of characteristics that the researcher evaluates as suitable for delineating the conceptual category related to the research question. If so, he/she can decide to conduct several focus groups in similar groups, in order to identify whether these characteristics occur in a similar way, as well as in different groups, in order to determine whether these characteristics manifest themselves differently. The discussions will proceed until the collection of an amount of information and the achievement of a level of knowledge that the researcher judges useful to provide adequate interpretations regarding the phenomenon.

Therefore, the purpose of the planning strategy of how many focus groups to organize is to reflect diversity, not to achieve representativeness. The issue is not the relationship between number of participants and the population of reference, but rather the achievement of adequate knowledge on 'dimensions that are likely to be relevant in terms of giving rise to differing perceptions or experiences' (Barbour, 2007: 69). The planning strategy is iterative, and can evolve during the research process: while theory increases, the researcher can discover new dimensions that may influence different perspectives on the research issues (Hennink, 2014: 42).

Moreover, from the reported, albeit different, examples the 'comparison' can be highlighted as fundamental in this type of investigation. 'The [same] question of how many focus groups to hold is determined by the comparisons that the researcher wishes to make' (Frisina, 2018: 193). Indeed, through comparisons between items of information gathered from different sources – in this case different empirical groups – 'a model of how it happens' is progressively outlined in the researcher's mind. At the outset this model may be inaccurate and loaded with the inevitable prejudices, but it can become gradually more precise and full of sociological information (Bertaux, 1998: 105).

The decision to carry out further focus groups can also arise in the analysis because the information gathered is not satisfactory or not sufficient to interpret unexpected results. Focus groups may also be repeated because those conducted so far have not produced quality information (Morgan, 1997: 44). In any event, Sabrina Corrao (2000: 64) pragmatically notes that the actual number of focus groups often depends on the material resources available to the researcher and on the timing of the research.

5.4 Recruiting the participants

Random extraction of participants

As underlined above, a criterion for generalization of statistical information is not pursued in research using the focus group. Likewise, probabilistic case extraction procedures are generally not adopted (Barbour, 2007: 69). Indeed, since the unit of analysis is usually outlined only in generic terms at the beginning, in the planning phase of the research it is not possible to know the reference population, which is a requisite for being able to proceed to the extraction of random cases.

However, sometimes, according to the requirements chosen by the researcher for the composition of the groups, it is possible to identify a reference population. Indeed, these choices take place on socio-demographic properties in relation to which it is possible to find lists of complete and updated names (Krueger and Casey, 2000: 75). In this regard, Mario Cardano (2011: 224–5) uses the expression 'qualified lists of names'. What qualifies these lists is that the people listed there share exactly the characteristic that identifies the type of person that the researcher would like to involve in the discussion: the list of students of a faculty, if the researcher is interested in discussing universities; the members list of a film club, if the researcher is interested in discussing cinema novelties. If a research group can access a qualified list of names, it is still important to check that it contains all the information related to the characteristics of the individuals considered relevant to the research. In particular, it is advisable to find those characteristics on which the researcher wants to obtain a certain degree of homogeneity and heterogeneity for each discussion group. In this case, it is possible to proceed to a probabilistic extraction of the cases and, therefore, of the participants in the group discussion.

In the field

An example of research that used a probabilistic sampling procedure concerned the career aspirations of young women enrolled at university. The discussion groups were shaped by randomly extracting participants from among all the students at a large Canadian university (Erwin and Stewart, 1997: 211–12).

In any event, the adoption of probabilistic case extraction procedures should not serve the need to obtain a 'representative sample', since this transcends the purposes of research using the focus group (Stewart and Shamdasani, 1990: 16–18). Therefore, this strategy should be followed only because random extraction offers the advantage of eliminating distortions (selection bias), such as the tendency to include only people who know each other or are more easily reachable (Morgan, 1998b: 57; Cardano, 2003: 164).

Nevertheless, the disadvantage of adopting probabilistic case extraction procedures is that, often, during the implementation of a focus group, a sort of self-selection of the participants takes place, for several reasons. For example, the busiest people are unlikely to participate because of the time required for the group discussion. Indeed, it is difficult to find a day and hour for the appointment that is good for everyone; at the same time, the discussion takes place in a specific location, which sometimes differs from a person's home/office or places on a daily basis. Another consideration should be considered: the frequency of rejections/denials (Zammuner, 2003: 131). Indeed, it often happens that a person does not accept the invitation, or he/she makes the commitment to participate in the discussion but does not show up (Stewart and Shamdasani, 1990: 53). Furthermore, it is important also to consider the willingness of the participants to interact with other people. Sabrina Corrao (2000: 66–7) argues that, for a successful focus group, instead of randomly choosing group members from a sample list, it may be appropriate to invite people interested in the topic and who can therefore make a greater contribution to the researcher's discussion and analysis. This also allows the researcher to involve more motivated people, reducing the various risks of self-selection and denial.

In the field

In research on HIV risk-behaviours in heterosexual relationships involving women over 30 years old, the participants were recruited by means of flyers. Given the delicacy of the topic, the research group wanted to ensure the involvement of people motivated to share their experience with other women (Maxwell and Boyle, 1995: 279–80).

Furthermore, as detailed before (see section 5.3), the purpose of focus group research is 'not to infer but to understand, not to generalize but determine the range, and not to make statements about the population but to provide insights about how people in the groups perceive a situation' (Krueger and Casey, 2000: 76–7). For this reason, participants are chosen through a 'purposive sampling strategy', because they have specific characteristics or experience that can best inform the research issues, rather than selecting them randomly (Barbour, 2007: 67–70; Cyr, 2019: 35–40). Moreover, 'focus group research seeks not only normative views but often actively seeks the perspectives of "outliers" or deviant behaviour to enable the full range of behaviours or perceptions on the research issues to be captured. [...] People with the required characteristics are unlikely be evenly distributed in the population and likely to be missed if random selection was used' (Hennink, 2014: 41–2).

Recruitment through 'key figures'

To recruit people for a group discussion, the researcher can rely on the network of acquaintances of the possible participants using 'key figures'. For example, local community leaders in the research community can be used, as well as schools, associations and organizations operating in the area concerned (Vaughn et al., 1996: 65; Corrao, 2000: 66).

There are several variants of the key figure in the literature (Liamputtong, 2011: 52–3; Hennink, 2014: 44–5). In community studies, frequent recourse is made to the cultural mediator. The figure of the mediator has the distinctive feature of belonging simultaneously to both the society of origin of the researcher and the community under study. In research practice, the cultural mediator is usually the person who will present the researcher to the community under analysis and will try to reassure people about the seriousness of the investigation.

Another key figure to be used for recruitment is the key informant. Unlike the cultural mediator, the key informant is a member of the culture under study. The informant can occupy two different positions within the community of belonging: an institutional role, having the task of controlling the flow of information in and out; and a non-institutional role, guided by a more spontaneous cooperation based on interpersonal relationships.

Finally, there is the possibility of using a qualified witness. He/she is a person who can be consulted in the preliminary phase of the investigation because he/she is considered an expert on some specific aspects of the research issue. Sometimes, a qualified witness is also a privileged witness, according to the centrality and prestige of the social position occupied in a particular group or community, and thus able to influence the other members. Both the qualified witness and the privileged witness should have as a specific characteristic the ability to reflect and observe the topic under study. This ability can help the researcher in identifying and recruiting the persons to be invited to the group discussion.

Using a key figure can facilitate the involvement of people who have characteristics relevant to the research and who, at the same time, are more interested and willing to participate. However, the key figure may tend to choose a specific kind of person and systematically avoid others (Bloor et al., 2001: 52); this may privilege some members of the population to the detriment of others. To avoid this problem, Richard A. Krueger and Mary A. Casey (2000: 76–7) suggest using different types of key figures and asking them to compile a list of people with the features required and then proceed, on the basis of this list, to a random draw. In any event, the use of key figures seems to be the best strategy when the research concerns populations that are difficult to reach in other ways or those who, because of culture or social conditions, are reluctant to participate in a discussion of this kind (Bloor et al., 2001: 55–6).

In the field

In an investigation conducted in America to explore the perception of crime among women belonging to the Hispanic minority (Madriz, 1998),

(Continued)

the research group encountered numerous obstacles to contacting a sufficient number of women. Indeed, many women were afraid to expose themselves too much, since they were illegal immigrants or did undeclared work. The researchers remedied this difficulty by making contact with leading members of the Hispanic community and explaining to them the importance of involving women of their community for the research. In this way, it was possible to approach the community members and gain their trust by recruiting a sufficient number of participants.

Avalanche recruitment

Another widespread procedure is 'avalanche' or 'snowball' recruitment, which makes use of the social network of the possible participants (Cardano, 2011: 224). It consists of asking people who are already participating in a focus group to indicate new names for subsequent discussions (Liamputtong, 2011: 51).

However, some distortions can be introduced with this procedure, because people who have a greater number of relationships are more likely to be recruited. Moreover, using the social network of the people involved in the first focus groups, some portions of the population may be unintentionally privileged instead of others, since it is easier for individuals to have relations with people similar by gender, age, profession, place of residence and so on (Montesperelli, 1998: 88).

Sometimes, the avalanche technique is used to form the same discussion group by asking the first people contacted to bring friends, relatives or acquaintances who live in the same condition and might be interested in discussing it. This variant is considered appropriate for dealing with sensitive topics because it is thought that people are more likely to talk about these topics in the presence of acquaintances (Cote-Arsenault and Morrison, 1999: 281; Zammuner, 2003: 125). Nevertheless, this variant does not consider the limits, mentioned above, concerning the involvement of acquaintances in the same discussion (Barbour, 2007: 74–5). Indeed, negative dynamics can compromise the quality of the results.

Another way to intercept the people to be invited to a focus group discussion is to go directly to the places that they frequent (parks, hospitals etc.), or to associate the group discussion with other initiatives (such as conferences or seminars). Both procedures enable recruitment of individuals interested in the research topic. The second also makes it possible to reach categories of people that are usually difficult to reach, such as professionals, managers and so on (Stewart and Shamdasani, 1990: 58; Corrao, 2000: 66; Krueger and Casey, 2000: 75–6).

In the field

A strategy of this kind was adopted in research on forms of marginalization among elderly people. Focus groups were organized involving seniors participating in activities designed for them and attending facilities, organizations or associations, holding the discussion in that same place (Brunelli, 2003).

However, even this kind of recruitment is likely to involve people who have everyday relationships with each other. Therefore, also when using recruitment strategies of this type, various risks can be incurred.

Summing up

There is no optimal strategy. Ultimately, it is necessary to evaluate the best route on the basis of the research objectives and the characteristics of the potential cases that could be involved (Hennink, 2014: 43–5).

Regardless of the procedure adopted to recruit them, it is always necessary to check that the persons contacted have the requisites established for the purposes of the research and have not participated, at least in the last six months, in another focus group discussion (Bellenger et al., 1976: 9; Morgan, 1998b: 88). A person, who has already taken part in a focus group knows the functioning of this technique and should be more willing to interact with others (Zammuner, 2003: 124). However, at the same time, it is also possible that he/she acts as a leader towards the other participants, flaunting his/her experience and perhaps anticipating the moves of the moderator (Greenbaum, 1998: 37).

5.5 Fix the appointment: logistics and context

Contact management

After planning how the groups should be composed and recruiting the participants, the next step is to make an appointment.

To do this, it will be useful to have the help of a person in charge of organizing the meeting: the manager. He/she contacts the participants first by letter/email and then by telephone. Usually there are three telephone contacts:

- the first is used to check people's availability and what day is preferred;
- the second is used to communicate when the discussion will take place;

- the third, a few days before the group discussion, is used to remind participants about the appointment.

The manager also engages in finding possible participants who can replace those who cancel or who do not agree to participate in the research. However, the moderator or observer often performs the manager's functions.

Context of discussion

The context in which the group meeting takes place plays a fundamental role in influencing the disposition of the people to speak freely and to interact with others without worries. The voluntary and motivational nature of the participation must therefore be encouraged and made as pleasant as possible with some indispensable measures.

For example, the place where the discussion takes place should be 'neutral', that is, a place that does not convey specific meanings or does not belong to institutions that can somehow embarrass or cause a negative reaction in participants (Liamputtong, 2011: 57–8). It is necessary to avoid a place full of tensions (due to cultural, ethical, religious or political reasons etc.) for the groups involved, since the discussion may be compromised if there is a high degree of conflict and hostility. Likewise, the option for a context associated with the control, oppression or limitation of free expression of ideas must be discouraged, as it would arouse strong feelings of inhibition among the participants. Choosing a non-neutral location can also discourage participation in the meeting.

Expert advice

There are obviously situations where it is not possible to choose a 'neutral' location. This is especially true when research is carried out in so-called 'total institutions' such as prisons or military barracks. For example, in focus groups with prisoners the researcher should have the foresight to look for a dedicated room. It is also important to ask to have prison guards outside the room rather than within during the discussion to avoid inhibitions and have the possibility of favouring the free expression of opinion.

Some authors suggest choosing 'natural' places that are usually frequented by the participants, in order to reduce the artificiality of the focus group discussion (given that a group discussion is always only apparently natural – see section 1.1). However, this choice should be carefully evaluated. Indeed, the choice of a natural place does not always facilitate communication among participants. For example, in research with students if the researcher decides to hold the focus groups in a school, during the discussion pupils could tend to behave as in a lesson. They therefore attribute the role of the teacher to the moderator and perceive the meeting as aimed at maintaining control over the situation, rather than collecting their opinions (Bloor et al., 2001: 62; Green and Hart, 2001: 26–9).

Appointment

Also, the contextual factors more specifically connected to the meeting are fundamental for creating a relaxed atmosphere. In this sense, the participants' selection, contact, recruitment and invitation phases are an integral part of the group discussion, because they contribute to defining the relationships on which the information construction draws. In these moments, the researcher will have to take particular care both in proposing the group discussion, explaining broadly the objectives, the methods of implementation and the actors involved, and in trying to understand the individual needs related to the possibility of reconciling personal commitments with an eventual appointment (Liamputtong, 2011: 59). These aspects contribute to creating in the people who will participate in the meeting an initial perception of the importance of the research and the seriousness of the work group.

Meeting the needs of the person contacted is one of the fundamental precautions required for the success of the discussion group. A very important factor concerns the choice of the time and place of the appointment. In the focus group, this is the real first challenge for a researcher. It can be said that once this first challenge has been overcome, the moderator is already halfway there. As is well known, it is very difficult to reconcile all the needs, and this is even more true when the groups are large and composed of individuals who have very different rhythms and lifestyles. All the logistical aspects must therefore be considered, concerning both the temporal dimension and the physical-spatial dimension of the meeting (Puchta and Potter, 2004; Barbour, 2007).

Regarding the temporal dimension, it is necessary to identify a time slot that is good for all the participants. Often the best choice is the late afternoon. Indeed, it is usually difficult to organize a focus group during the morning, especially for workers (unless the discussion is held in the workplace). It can also be difficult to obtain an appointment at the weekend, because, although it is freer from work, it is always considered unsuitable for a public commitment (as a group discussion may be perceived). Moreover, some requirements of the collection technique should be considered. For example, it is not recommended to hold the meeting in the evening, when people's attention normally tends to diminish and they feel the fatigue of the whole day. Furthermore, a minimum duration of the discussion must be taken into account. It varies approximately between an hour and a half and two hours, so the researcher should ask participants to devote this amount of time to the discussion, concentrate and avoid distractions and/or interruptions in the meantime. Concerning this last point, in the invitation the duration of the meeting could be rounded up, in order to take account of the inevitable lateness of some participants and to create a first moment of informal conversation and refreshment.

The choice of the meeting place is also important from a logistical point of view. Indeed, the logistical position assumed by the site and its accessibility for the guests must be considered (Cyr, 2019: 72). To this end, many manuals propose finding a location well served by public transport, which has ample parking and is located in a built-up area (Liamputtong, 2011: 59; Hennink, 2014: 80–2).

The moderator and the researcher should also pay attention to the internal characteristics of the adopted site. It should be particularly silent, and it should allow the group debate to be conducted without interruption or interference. At the same time, it should be able to protect the privacy of the participants, which means for example that the doors should be closed and outside viewers should be excluded.

The venue of the debate should also be large enough to hold the desired number of participants, with a central table around which to sit and with a special corner used for refreshments. On this point, David W. Stewart and Prem N. Shamdasani (1990) highlight the importance of considering the ways in which people relate to the surrounding physical environment, which are also indicative of the type of relationships that can be established among multiple actors. Thus, the participants will read the circle arrangement requested by the moderator as a signal of the style that can be adopted during performance of the task, which is basically democratic and participatory (Hennink, 2014: 80–2). Moreover, the circle positioning of participants makes it possible to maintain direct control over verbal and non-verbal behaviours through an 'eye to eye' perspective that will facilitate interactions among the participants. At the same time, a circular table has the advantage of avoiding the establishment of preconceived hierarchies due to the position occupied, as can happen around a rectangular table (Bloor et al., 2001: 60).

For the purposes of collecting information, it is also useful to find a room that is well equipped for recording the debate, using audio-magnetic or audio-visual supports that are not too intrusive.

In conclusion, from the participants' point of view the room should be comfortable and offer the opportunity to feel at ease. From the research staff's point of view, it should be functional and facilitate optimal information collection.

Logistics in online focus groups

An online tool can help to solve logistical problems affecting the recruitment of participants. A key limitation of focus group research is that it tends to be bound in time and space by the need to identify, recruit and assemble a group in a single place for the purposes of discussion (Cher Ping and Seng Chee, 2001: 54). On a practical level, it is always difficult to gather all participants at the same time and place. Technology can help to remove this limitation, making it possible to use focus groups more broadly in an internet-enabled world. Thus the use of online tools can eliminate the problem of scheduling a common site for participants who are based in different geographical locations, which often results in exclusion of certain participants for logistical reasons (Stewart and Shamdasani, 2017: 49; Matthews et al., 2018: 1622).

The flexibility associated with online focus groups allows respondents from all over the world to assemble, meet and discuss electronically. Moreover, it creates opportunities to expand the pool of potential participants and to conduct group discussions with people with whom it would otherwise be difficult, if not impossible, to gather together in a specific place for a face-to-face group meeting. This is especially so if they are busy professionals based in different geographical areas and/or immobile people for physical or economic reasons, and/or people who are unavailable at the same time (Cher Ping and Seng Chee, 2001: 51). In other words, the main advantage of online focus group is eliminating the logistical problem, allowing the possibility to gather individuals who it would otherwise be difficult to schedule to participate in a focus group at a fixed physical location.

However, it is necessary to bear in mind that the focus group works when the participants feel themselves part of a group. Therefore, overcoming the logistical difficulties to get people from different countries and places to meet, if these people have nothing in common, does not help at all for a focus group. Also, language skills are important. Hence, choosing to conduct a focus group in English for people who are not native-speakers can be a limitation. Furthermore, since the synchronicity plays an important role for the interaction (see section 1.3), in online focus groups identifying a time slot that is good for all the participants could be difficult. On the other hand, when the participants come from different parts of the world, there may be an extra difficulty due to the time zone. In other words, the time schedule should be borne in mind to facilitate the presence of participants from different geographical areas.

Finally, another advantage of online focus groups is that they reduce travel costs: interacting over the web can avoid a significant amount of expense. Online focus groups enable the researchers to overcome various challenges revolving around cost and location (Stewart and Shamdasani, 2017: 49).

137

However, indirect costs for technology should be considered, such as the cost of access to a focus group management platform, internet and connection costs and so on.

Further reading

Kitzinger, J. (1994) 'The methodology of focus groups: the importance of interaction between research participants', *Sociology of Health & Illness*, 16 (1): 103–21.

This article explores how homogeneity and heterogeneity within each discussion group can be an advantage or a disadvantage for interaction.

Krueger, R.A. and Casey, M.A. (2000) *Focus Groups: A Practical Guide for Applied Research* (3rd edn). Thousand Oaks, CA: Sage.

This updated edition of the best-selling book by Richard A. Krueger and Mary A. Casey offers numerous theoretical and practical strategies for finding and selecting participants.

Exercises

1. You would like to conduct research on urban security. How do you put together discussion groups with reference to the criterion of the level of direct or indirect experience of the participants on the research issue?

2. You are conducting research where the risk of bringing together a discussion group with people who know each other is realistic. What strategy do you adopt to reduce this risk?

6

Designing Focus Group Tools

The term 'focus group' refers to the overall technique. The tools at the service of this technique are the discussion outline and all the strategies by which the moderator – the person who leads the collective debate (see Chapter 7) – supports the discussion and the interaction.

In this chapter, we will consider these tools. In detail, we will examine the discussion outline, identifying its main characteristics, and the probing techniques, distinguishing between them among strategies to stimulate discussion, strategies to clarify information provided by participants, and strategies to facilitate interaction.

―――――――――― **Chapter goals** ――――――――――

- *Knowledge*: tools for supporting focus group discussion.
- *Applying knowledge and understanding*: how to draft the focus group outline and the probing techniques used by the moderator to support discussion and interaction.
- *Making judgements*: developing adequate knowledge on the criteria to be followed to construct an effective outline and on the strategies to stimulate discussion, clarify the information provided by participants and facilitate the interaction.

6.1 The discussion outline

General features

During a focus group, the discussion outline is the main tool available to the moderator to support and re-launch the discussion.

As in the case of other qualitative techniques, in the focus group, the properties that refer to the unit of analysis that the researcher wants to detect are not structured in predefined questions, which also provide for alternative answers. Indeed, when designing the focus group outline, the researcher uses 'sensitizing concepts' constituting a 'map of the concepts', which will guide the discussion and will be submitted to the attention of the participants.

Some scholars denote this tool of the focus group using the term 'guide' rather than 'outline' (Corrao, 2000). To clarify the relationship between the two concepts, it can be said that the guide is a macro-instrument made up of a complex set of components; the outline is only one of the components of the complex. Indeed, the guide includes, in addition to the outline, all the instructions that the moderator can follow during the discussion, such as how to present the theme and the research group, the rules that the participants must follow during the discussion and so on (Barbour, 2007). In contrast, the focus group outline refers specifically to the topics that will be discussed during group discussion and the various probing techniques that the moderator will use to support the discussion and interaction (see section 7.2).

To develop an outline of a focus group, the researcher tries to obtain more information about the studied object through the media, past research and interviews with key informants. The aim is to identify the most relevant themes and dimensions. This information will be used to formulate the focus group outline.

The outline of a focus group must be organized according to four properties:

- the structuring level of the group discussion framework;
- the complexity level of the topics studied;
- the salience level of the topics investigated;
- the preparation of the questions for a group.

The structuring level of the group discussion framework

The structuring level of the outline tool is the detail in which the dimensions of the unit of analysis to be investigated are defined and specified (Bichi, 2002: 19–20).

This property varies along a continuum. At one extreme is an unstructured outline of a focus group. This type of outline provides only some general issues to be explored and it is used when the researcher wants to highlight the perspectives of the investigated population and not how the latter reacts/responds to the debate's proposed framework. Therefore, in the group discussions conducted with unstructured outlines, agendas (the relevant aspects and their order), timing and contents are dictated by the flow of debate and the group interaction (Puchta and Potter, 2004: 87–98; Frisina, 2010: 40). The participants will orient the discussion in one way or another. Discussions with less structured outlines require the moderator to be more skilled in preventing the participants from straying too far from the main themes and determining whether a topic has been dealt with adequately (Acocella, 2008: 120; Carey and Asbury, 2012: 59–63).

At the opposite extreme is a structured outline of a focus group. In this case, the discussion's outline is highly detailed, providing the dimensions and the aspects of the analysis unit to be explored according to analytical approaches of the research group. Hence, in group discussions conducted with structured outlines, the participants will follow this identified framework to discuss the phenomenon, even if the form and order of the proposed dimensions/aspects may change (Krueger and Casey, 2000: 39–43). In this type of focus group, therefore, the discussion will mainly be aimed at gathering information on topics established, starting from the cognitive interests of the research group (Corrao, 2000: 56; Cardano, 2003: 168–9; Albanesi, 2004: 75).

The structuring level of the focus group outline is related to the extent of the research group's knowledge on the topic (Morgan, 1998a: 48). The greater the researcher's knowledge of the object of study, the more he/she can envisage in advance what dimensions and aspects to take into account. Indeed, very structured outlines are usually employed in research designs with analytical-in-depth or experimental purposes, when the research group already has knowledge about the phenomenon and wants to obtain more detailed information or wants to evaluate the adequacy of some analytical frameworks. Therefore, the focus group outline's level of structuring will be higher, since the topics and analytical perspectives on the investigated phenomenon that the research group wants to bring to the attention of the participants increase (Morrison-Beedy et al., 2001: 48; Cyr, 2019: 50–61). In these cases, an important role is played by the theory. Indeed, to interpret a phenomenon, there will probably be several reference theories, with their own explanatory structure of relevant or influential factors on the studied phenomenon. Often, the researcher selects a theory not only in pragmatic manner (by considering its explanatory effectiveness) but also on the basis of his/her theoretical reference school or membership of a scientific community.

In the field

A highly structured outline was used in research conducted to clarify some results of a survey on the perception of deviant behaviour (Cataldi, 2016). At the beginning of the sessions, participants individually answered questions taken from the questionnaire given in the survey concerning the level of admissibility and severity of some deviant behaviours and the role attributed to social rules as a deterrent to them. Later, the moderator, reading the answers, urged the comparison of opinions on these topics.

In contrast, the structuring level of a focus group outline is usually low in research designs with an exploratory-descriptive function, since the aim of the research is to investigate a phenomenon that is still relatively unknown to the researcher or on which there is little reference literature. Indeed, when the topic is not known by the research group, it is impossible to articulate and structure the focus group outline from the beginning of the research. Regardless of the degree of knowledge on the topic investigated, less structured outlines are also adopted when the research group wants to enhance the insiders' point of view on the topic investigated.

In the field

In a research project concerning opinions on biotechnologies, since the results of previous surveys and pilot interviews had provided little useful information to the research group, the research staff drafted an unstructured outline: only a few keywords were provided, indicative of the relevant themes and topics (Wagner, 2001). This strategy made it possible to improve knowledge on the topic and to draw up a questionnaire to be administered to a larger number of people, starting from the results obtained (Wagner et al., 2002: 329).

The structuring level of a focus group outline can also vary in inverse proportion to the level of knowledge of the participants on the topic studied: it may be low if the participants are 'experts' on the phenomenon, but will necessarily increase as the level of experience decreases, because the participants' knowledge about the object of study may be limited. Indeed, usually, as said (see section 5.2), 'non-expert' people are invited to the discussion when the aim is to detect stereotypes and common sense representations. For this reason, it is advisable to provide a more structured outline and a good themed topic to prevent the debate from going off topic too much or focusing on non-central issues for research purposes (Barbour, 2007: 87–8).

As detailed in section 3.1, the degree of structuring influences the focus group discussion agenda and, therefore, the role of the researcher and the research group in the production of the results. Indeed, the discussion outline consists of the set of conceptual, terminological and analytical categories in which the information referring to the research analysis unit is found.

Focus group discussions articulated on very structured outlines will favour the 'etic' categories of the researcher, while focus group discussions based on unstructured outlines will favour the 'emic' categories of the insider. However, in the former case, the use of overly structured conceptual, terminological and analytical categories by the research group may limit the focus group's effectiveness in bringing out other aspects or perspectives. Vice versa, in the latter case, the absence of a structure can drag the discussion into the common sense of the participants, without an adequate level of problematization of the theme being investigated.

Obviously, the 'emic' nature of qualitative research approaches – where the purpose of operationalizing the properties included in the survey tool is not pursued, as happens, for example, in surveys using a questionnaire – allows achievement of a balance between the cognitive interests of the research group on the object of study and the analytical perspectives that arise spontaneously from group discussion. Indeed, the task of the moderator during the group debate will always be twofold:

- to propose the general themes, which have been appropriately chosen according to the objectives of the research;
- 'listening to the field', that is, the insiders who will provide their own interpretation of the phenomenon, relaunching, supporting and directing the discussion according to narrative frameworks developed by the interaction of the participants.

Therefore, even in more structured focus groups, it is possible to adapt the outline to the various meetings and to the specificity of the different interactive contexts, as well as to dealing with unexpected dimensions and aspects that emerge spontaneously in the discussion, if they are interesting for the object of study (Puchta and Potter, 2004: 2939). In the same way, in less structured focus groups, in the case of excessive digression, it is possible to lead participants to the topics related to the research topic, as well as to introduce some dimensions and aspects related to the analysis unit that emerged in previous discussions if the interactive context allows it (Acocella, 2008: 122).

Ultimately, it is always necessary to find a balance between the researcher's reference frameworks and those that emerge from the context, enhancing both of them. Indeed, on the one hand, the research group takes a 'perspective from the inside' (insider perspective), entering into the world of the social actors studied to generate an account through the evidences found empirically. On the other hand, the research group also takes an 'external perspective' (outsider perspective), theoretically interpreting what has emerged in the various discussions and highlighting aspects unknown even to the actors themselves.

To enhance the 'emic' nature of the focus group, it is also common to adopt a 'spiral' approach (Cyr, 2019: 10, 56–7): at the beginning an unstructured outline is prepared with general aspects to be treated that nevertheless allow some movement in several directions in carrying out the field research. Based on information collected in the first group discussions, it is possible to increase the articulation of the themes and dimensions to be addressed, leading in this way to increasingly focused and detailed discussion on the topic of research (Stewart and Shamdasani, 1990: 62–3; Frisina, 2010: 55–8).

The complexity level of studied topics

The outline of a focus group should be built by taking into account the level of attention of the participants, which is usually low initially, grows after the start of the group discussion, reaches a maximum on which it stabilizes for some time in the middle of the discussion, and then decreases rapidly due to fatigue (Fideli and Marradi, 1996). For this reason, it may be useful to prepare an initial part of the outline with some 'opening questions' intended to create a comfortable environment, highlighting the characteristics that the participants have in common. They are very general questions and mainly used for 'ice breaking' (Bloor et al., 2001: 70–3), overcoming initial embarrassments and facilitating the establishment of a friendly atmosphere among the participants (Breen, 2006: 468). It may be useful to prepare also some 'introductory questions' for the purpose of presenting the topic of study and encouraging the participants to express 'how they see or understand the issue, service, or product under investigation' (Krueger and Casey, 2000: 44–5).

At this point, it is possible to proceed with the most substantial part of the group discussion, starting to address the main topic and identify the information necessary to respond to the cognitive objectives set (Cyr, 2019: 57–66). However, also in this case, it may be useful to deal with the topic of discussion by progressively increasing the level of complexity of the aspects to be submitted to the attention of the participants. This strategy enables the participants to progressively focus their attention on the central theme, reducing, at the same time, their cognitive effort. For this reason, when designing focus group outlines, the research group often follows a 'funnel' strategy that allows the moderator to deal with the research issues gradually, starting from the more general dimensions and then specifying some aspects of the studied phenomenon (Stewart and Shamdasani, 1990: 79; Zammuner, 2003: 177; Hennink, 2014: 50–1).

Moreover, since in social sciences the concepts of properties are often very complex and multidimensional, it is necessary to specify and to detect the various dimensions in an independent way. For this reason, the 'funnel' strategy to specify the aspects of the research issue progressively will be repeated for each new dimension that is chosen to investigate.

Expert advice

If the focus group topic is the integration of immigrants, it may be useful to introduce the discussion by asking for a generic definition of integration. Then it is possible to articulate the debate on various dimensions of the phenomenon (economic, social, cultural etc.) and, for each of these, examine some more detailed aspects (e.g. for the economic dimension, investigate the aspects related to the job, the relationship with local services, local policies etc.).

Regardless of the degree of structuring of the discussion outline chosen by the research group, following a 'funnel' discussion planning strategy makes it possible to ascertain whether the aspects relevant to the researchers are also interesting for the participants. Indeed, if the moderator must continually direct the group members to the themes and perspectives foreseen in the outline, this could be a sign that there is too much separation between the points of view of the participants and those of the researcher (Stewart and Shamdasani, 1990: 75; Morgan, 1998a: 49–51).

Moreover, regardless of the level of structuring expected for the discussion by the research group, it is advisable to avoid, when possible, inserting specific questions in the focus group outline, but simply predict some general themes – and for each of them some more specific aspects – in order to deal with the phenomenon with participants (Cyr, 2019: 55–7). This will reduce the risk for the moderator of stating the investigated object in a too directive way or by using the same questions in different group discussions, instead of adapting the focus group outline to the various interactive contexts. At the same time, in this way it will be possible to limit the conditioning due to the presence of the moderator and to an excessive imposition of the conceptual, linguistic and analytics categories of the research group. As we will elaborate (see section 7.2), the use of probing techniques can also limit the risks of conditioning, manipulation and control over debate and interaction among the participants.

Richard A. Krueger and Mary A. Casey (2000: 45–6) argue that it is also useful to provide a final part of the focus group outline aimed at closing the debate. In detail, they propose three possible closing strategies:

- *All-things-considered questions*. The participants are asked to reflect on the various aspects that have emerged and to indicate the most important topic, in order to identify both the definitive position of the group and some important areas of the phenomenon investigated.
- *Summary questions*. The moderator summarizes what has emerged from the discussion and asks the participants for their opinion on the adequacy of his/her summary.
- *Final questions*. The moderator asks the participants if everything has been said on the topic and if there are points not addressed, especially in view of a better planning of the discussion in the subsequent information collections.

Since the focus group outline is composed of several parts and probably will also contain several topics to be discussed, it may be useful to set in advance a maximum time to be granted to the various sessions of the discussion according to a level of importance conferred to each part. This will allow the moderator to balance the debate better without the risk of overshooting some parts of the outline and hastily dealing with others due to lack of time.

The salience level of investigated topics

According to the principle of salience, a focus group outline should include only the aspects of the phenomenon studied that are considered most relevant for the cognitive objectives. Otherwise, there is the risk of constructing a prolific and cumbersome tool, which will require energy of both the moderator and the participants in dealing with the topic, some aspects of which will be discussed in a marginal way. Therefore, a discussion based on a few salient questions allows all the participants to reflect on each argument and express their opinions in an appropriate manner in the short time available.

Compliance with this requirement is important for the development of the outline of a focus group, more so than in other qualitative techniques, since the discussion is articulated in a short time among many people and without a precise order in the shifts (Hennink, 2014: 81–2). By contrast, during an in-depth interview, for example, the interaction is articulated only between the interviewer and the interviewee, focusing mainly on what the latter will say. Although the requirement of saliency remains valid in this case, it is therefore possible to prepare more detailed and longer outlines, making it possible, in the same duration of the interaction, to address a number of topics greater than those that can be dealt with in a focus group (Bichi, 2002).

In order to guarantee the criterion of salience, when designing a focus group outline, it may also be useful to identify, *a priori*, aspects of the phenomenon under study that do not need to be discussed. This could help the participants to focus on the object of study and the moderator to lead the discussion (Acocella, 2008: 126).

The preparation of the questions for a group

In a focus group outline the questions must be prepared keeping a collective in mind (Smithson, 2000: 105). Therefore questions addressed to individuals rather than the whole group are to be avoided, as well as questions aimed at collecting personal motivations and experiences, rather than widespread inter-subjective representations and socially shared knowledge. Indeed, questions of this kind would not stimulate interaction in group discussion, or the dissemination among the participants of a feeling of mutual belonging (Barbour, 2007: 20; Hennink, 2014: 26–7).

Instead, when examining the outline of published focus groups there are sometimes questions formulated using the 'second person singular' rather than the 'second person plural'. Obviously, when the moderator deems it appropriate, he/she can exceptionally address questions to individuals (e.g. to ask for clarification, to encourage a person who is not very talkative, to moderate a person who talks too much etc.). This kind of question is valuable for the collection of useful information. However, except in these cases, the formulation of a question using the third person singular should be avoided (Cardano, 2011: 214).

Furthermore, with reference to the topic dealt with during the focus group, the questions must be formulated in such a way as to underline that the participants were invited not as mere individuals but as members of an 'expert' group capable of giving relevant information on the topics investigated (see section 5.2). If 'non-expert' people have been invited to the discussion, the questions should be formulated in such a way as to encourage interaction among the participants and the comparison of their opinions, to allow the emergence of inter-subjective representations derived from the negotiation of positions and from the contribution of all the points made.

On the other hand, if the focus group is used to detect individual attitudes or personal experiences, the outline will induce the members of the group to provide individual reflections or to describe biographical experiences that do not promote group formation and the sharing of meanings. In this way, time will be taken away from group discussion (Corrao, 2000: 16; Smithson, 2000: 105; Frisina, 2018: 190), no real debate will be elicited among the participants, and their perception of all being members of the same group will not be stimulated.

Nevertheless, the tendency to underline life paths and to formulate individual responses has been found in various outlines, in which many questions have been formulated as if it were a group interview rather than a group discussion.

147

In the field

A focus group outline for a research study on child mistreatment included questions such as 'What are the biggest concerns for you and your family?' (Abramczyk, 1995: 140–2). This question is formulated incorrectly, since the answer involves drawing up a list of these concerns on the part of each participant, who mainly interacted with the moderator.

In the field

In a focus group outline used to identify the life conditions of elderly people, the first question was: 'Please tell us about the last time you got really frustrated trying to use something?' (Rogers et al., 1998: 112–13). This question is formulated incorrectly, since the elderly person's story will focus on his/her average day and daily difficulties, preventing direct confrontation with others in relation to the discussed themes.

Often, researchers choose to structure the focus group outline in this way only because it makes it possible to interview many people in a short time (Parker and Tritter, 2006: 25–6). This is a hybrid form between focus group and individual interview, that loses the strengths attributed to both the focus group technique (the effect of multiplication of information following interaction between individuals) and the interview technique (such as granting a person the possibility to autonomously construct his/her own argumentation following his/her narrative subjectivity). For this reason, we discourage the use of this hybrid form.

Expert advice

To better understand how to structure an in-depth interview outline and a focus group outline properly, it may be useful to give an example starting from the same object of study. For example, if the goal is to investigate university choices, in an interview the topic can be posed by asking: 'What were the reasons that led you to choose this university course?', 'Starting from this choice, what are your professional expectations for the future?'. In a focus group conducted with university students, the theme could instead be posed in the following way: 'You can indicate the strengths or weaknesses of the educational objectives of several university courses', 'You can try to outline the professional profiles attributable to these university courses.'

6.2 Probing techniques

General features

The focus group is a 'reactive' information-gathering technique because it always involves active intervention by the moderator. However, in his/her functions the moderator can resort to probing strategies aimed at supporting the debate and the interaction among the participants. Compared to a direct question, these probing strategies can produce a less direct and structured stimulus on the topic under study. Indeed, probing strategies consist of tasks that the moderator asks the participants to perform, individually or collectively, in order to make the debate more participatory and interactive, allowing him/her, at the same time, to assume a more marginal role (Barbour, 2007: 84–6). Through these strategies, therefore, the moderator seeks to reduce the level of intrusiveness of his/her presence, trying to limit the risks of overly controlling the interaction among the participants or imposing the research group's conceptual and linguistics categories on the topic studied. At the same time, these strategies may favour the development of the dialogic and interactive process that underlies the formation of the social representation and the shared social knowledge (Marková et al., 2007: 48).

Such strategies have different purposes: sometimes they are aimed at focusing the participants' attention on the central theme or at clarifying some information emerged in the discussion; at other times they are more focused on management of the interactive context (see Appendix 2).

We can therefore divide them among:

- strategies to stimulate discussion;
- strategies to clarify the information provided by the participants;
- strategies of interaction facilitation.

Strategies to stimulate discussion

Discussion stimulus strategies are intended to focus the attention of the participants on aspects relevant to the cognitive objectives of the research group. For this reason, many authors also call them 'focusing exercises' (Vaughn et al., 1996: 86; Albanesi, 2004: 93). These activities are, therefore, strategies to avoid excessive digressions from the topics relevant to the discussion, which the moderator puts in place without assuming too intrusive a role.

During a focus group, the moderator's strategies to stimulate discussion are:

- the ranking of items exercise proposed by the research group;
- the use of cards with items chosen by the research group;
- comment on/completion of a story;

- the interpretation of a thematic vignette;
- the pause of reflection on discussion topics.

The ranking of items exercise

During the discussion, the moderator can submit to the participants a list of dimensions/aspects related to the analysis unit prepared by the research group, asking them to identify an order of importance during the collective debate (Krueger, 1998: 29: Hennink, 2014: 64). This can primarily serve to direct the attention of the participants to the dimensions and aspects of the topic that are most relevant to the research (Zammuner, 2003: 162). Second, this exercise can help to understand which dimensions and aspects are most interesting for the participants and, therefore, should be explored in the current or future discussion (Bloor et al., 2001: 67; Colucci, 2007: 1425).

In the field

This strategy was adopted in research conducted by Jenny Kitzinger (1998) on the opinion about the messages conveyed by the mass media on HIV/AIDS. In the various discussions, the moderator presented the participants with sheets containing the description of some categories of people (homosexuals, people who have heterosexual relationships with occasional partners, blood donors, doctors and nurses who treat people with AIDS, drug addicts etc.), asking them to grade these groups according to a level of illness risk. The aim was to identify the representations and assumptions regarding the different categories of people.

Cards with items chosen by the research group

During focus group discussion, to introduce some points of view on the object being studied the moderator can also present the participants with cards containing items/sentences that refer to the unit of analysis, chosen on the basis of the research group's cognitive interests or defined on the basis of the results of previous investigations. This will help to conduct the discussion on those issues (Frisina, 2010: 57). The use of these cards can also introduce a variety of different dimensions, making it possible to broaden the stimuli posed to participants and thus increase the variability of the information yielded by the discussion. The aim is to encourage a variety of viewpoints, in order to favour the emergence of diverse voices, as well as of the multiple meanings that people attribute to social representations (Smithson, 2000: 111; Puchta and Potter, 2004: 126–30; Marková et al., 2007: 48).

Comment on/completion of a story

The moderator can also choose to introduce some theoretical or analytical dimensions related to the unit of analysis by presenting a story and asking participants to comment on it or to conclude it (Stewart and Shamdasani, 1990: 90). Besides focusing attention on certain dimensions/aspects, the comment made on the story or its completion helps to bring out the logic of argumentation or social representations that can prevail among participants concerning a given phenomenon (Colucci, 2007: 1427; Cardano, 2011: 214–15).

Compared to the first two strategies, the use of a story is a less reactive probing strategy. Indeed, in a story, conceptual, linguistic and analytical categories can be more subtle, and the complexity of the story can hide the real purpose of the interrogative stimulus to the participants, even if the research group maintains a certain awareness of the meaning that will be given to a large part of the group responses.

In the field

This exercise was proposed in research on the social representations of poverty among people who, by profession or vocation, routinely deal with the phenomenon (Cardano et al., 2003). The story was: 'Let us now reflect on an episode related to a family living in conditions of social exclusion, for example the White family. In a municipality office, there are two social workers discussing the White case. Mr White is unemployed, his wife is a housewife and his daughter is nine years old. The Whites have been receiving social benefits for six months and the two social workers are discussing what to do: "After six months, the situation of the Whites has not changed. I would confirm the benefit for another six months, so that they can afford ordinary household expenses. Without our social monetary contribution they cannot do it". "I do not agree, I think it is better to suspend the benefit; Mr White has not done much to find a job. Let's have him attend a training course, so he will finally get a move on".' The conversation continues but we stop here. In your opinion, what happened? What decision did the two social workers take?

Thematic vignettes

An even less reactive strategy for stimulating discussion is the use of thematic vignettes (Barbour, 2007: 87–8). With thematic vignettes, hypothetical representations of situations or scenarios with vague outlines are presented to the participants, asking them how they would behave in similar circumstances

(Banks, 2008). This exercise, like a story, can also serve to draw out widespread beliefs about a certain phenomenon under investigation.

A variation of this strategy is the 'game of the news bulletin' (Bloor et al., 2001: 70). This consists of the distribution of photographs (related to the topic studied) to the participants, asking them to prepare a news bulletin together. This strategy allows group members to focus the attention on some aspects (through the photos), bringing out their logic of argumentation or their main representations of the discussion topic (Liamputtong, 2011: 66–7; Hennink, 2014: 64–5).

In the field

A similar exercise was proposed by Rosaline Barbour (2007: 85) in a study of discrimination against immigrants in Scotland. Indeed, in the focus groups, the moderator showed the participants images of the national advertising campaign 'One Scotland. Many cultures' to start the discussion on racism and the most effective public policies to overcome it.

Pause for reflection on discussion topics

A completely non-reactive strategy of stimulating discussion is the request for a pause of reflection on what has emerged from the discussion. Indeed, at some moments of the discussion, the moderator can invite the participants to take a break to give them time to evaluate if they have said everything on research topics (Krueger and Casey, 2000: 110; Puchta and Potter, 2004: 89).

Strategies for clarifying the information

The moderator's strategies for clarifying the information provided by the participants are designed to reduce the risks of 'semantic dispersion'. This is linked to the lack of a rigid connection between concepts and terms, which makes linguistic codes not fully shared and communication imperfect (Marradi, 2007: 30–40). The only time to clarify the content of the group discussion is during the information collection in the field. To satisfy this need, therefore, the moderator can resort to various strategies aimed at eliciting clarifications and in-depth analysis directly from the participants. Although such strategies may be more or less intrusive, these exercises reduce the influence of the research group's conceptual, analytical and linguistic categories, since they prevent the moderator/researcher from giving a personal interpretation to ambiguous statements collected during field research. At the same time, these strategies may encourage a 'reticular' interaction and the synergy among participants, allowing them to define their position better and gain greater awareness of their ideas (Hennink, 2014: 30–1).

During a focus group, the moderator's strategies to clarify the information provided by the participants are:

- the 'emic' definition of key concepts;
- classifying the items proposed by participants;
- ranking the items proposed by participants.

The 'emic' definition of key concepts

During a group discussion, there is no guarantee that the participants will give the same meaning to the same term. For this reason, a very useful strategy is to ask participants to define (even in writing) the most relevant key concepts related to the research object. This strategy enables the moderator to clarify the content of the discussion, as well as to use the different meanings attributed to the same concept in order to support the collective debate and foster confrontation among the participants on the topics discussed (Barbour, 2007: 149; Duchesne, 2017: 377–8).

Classifying items

In a classification exercise, the participants are invited to divide into different classes the aspects that emerged during the discussion of a particular topic, giving them verbal labels. The negotiation of the items' positions and the attribution of a label to each class can facilitate explanation of the meanings attributed by the participants to the various terms/expressions used during the group discussion.

In the field

This strategy was adopted in research conducted by Chiara Salvadori (2006) on solidarity and forms of social participation. Indeed, during the group discussion, three participants had provided different meanings of 'solidarity': the first stated that 'solidarity is being able to understand the people we encounter and try to help'; the second that 'solidarity is emotion ... the ability to feel'; the third that 'solidarity is the union of many

(Continued)

---

people for a purpose useful for the common good of society'. The moderator then asked the participants to compare the three meanings of 'solidarity' in order to determine whether there were different classification criteria under these different definitions. In this way, the conceptual categories of the participants could be better explained.

Ranking items

Carrying out an ordering exercise on the items proposed by participants makes it possible to clarify which aspects arising during the discussion are considered more important by the members of the group. This will determine whether the discussed items occupy a central or peripheral position in the participants' life experiences and then, during the analysis, to attribute different 'weights' to the various topics discussed (Krueger and Casey, 2000: 49–50; Frisina, 2018: 195).

In the field

This kind of strategy was used in a research study aimed at specifying the criteria used to assess foster care in a family (Moro et al., 2005). The group discussion involved social workers, psychologists and magistrates. In particular, during the various sessions, the moderator asked the participants to identify the strengths or weaknesses of adoption processes and then to order these elements by importance, with reference to the success/failure of foster care in a family.

The ranking exercise can therefore be adopted as a strategy both to stimulate the group discussion and to clarify the information that emerged during a debate (Barbour, 2007: 87–8). The difference in the use of this strategy is that, in the former case, the elements to be ordered are proposed by the research group in order to focus the attention of participants on these, while in the latter case the elements to be ordered have emerged in the discussion spontaneously from the interaction among the participants. Hence, the exercise of ordering for clarification purposes is less intrusive than the use of this exercise for stimulating purposes. Indeed, when the elements to be ordered are not suggested by the moderator there is a lower risk that the research group impose its conceptual, analytical and linguistic categories on participants during the collective debate.

The strategies of interaction facilitation

The moderator's strategies of interaction facilitation are aimed at fostering a confidential atmosphere among the participants and the continuous comparison of their opinions on discussion topics. Indeed, the mere presence of other people can exert an inhibitory action, thus influencing the way in which each participant will formulate his/her own judgements or evaluate the adequacy of a response to be given. Moreover, during a focus group, different group dynamics (leadership, conformism, shyness etc.) can develop among the participants, which may limit the participants' freedom of expression or the fidelity of their responses (Liamputtong, 2011: 80–2; Carey and Asbury, 2012: 28; Cyr, 2019: 79–81).

During a focus group, the moderators' strategies for interaction facilitation are:

- the breaking of conformist cognitive schemes;
- the moderation of leaders;
- role-playing;
- a 'round-table' discussion on a specific research issue.

Breaking conformist cognitive schemes

The strategy of breaking conformist cognitive schemes aims to limit the risk of participants' answers being based on acquiescence or social conformism (Forsyth, 2014: 204–7). Indeed, it is possible that the participants, intimidated by the public interaction of the collective debate, adapt (at least publicly) their opinion to the most widespread positions or to those judged socially more acceptable (Kidd and Parshall, 2000: 294–5; Hennink, 2014: 30–3). To overcome the pressure exerted by such social conventions, the moderator can resort to several strategies. For example, he/she can question the legitimacy and unanimity of social consent, introducing different points of view on the investigated topic, as well as reducing pressure on the single participant by shifting the attention to possible behaviours adopted by 'third persons' instead of the people present (Moser and Kalton, 1977: 327; Colucci, 2007: 1428).

Expert advice

If you want to investigate a sensitive topic such as the use of soft drugs, you could introduce the theme in this form: 'Many people smoke marijuana.

(Continued)

155

Could you tell me why you think they do it?' The purpose is to reassure those present that the meeting is not aimed at assessing their possible behaviour, thus allowing them to feel free to express their opinion as to why soft drugs are generally used.

To reduce the risks of social conformity, the moderator can also support minority positions and thus increase the variety of topics of the discussion. Indeed, several authors suggest that the creation of a minority is useful to increase the originality of the information produced, as it presents to the group the same issues from a different perspective (Nemeth and Wachtler, 1983; Turner and Pratkanis, 1997).

Strategies for moderating leaders

The moderator should moderate over-talkative people, who tend to impose themselves and influence the group's opinions to an excessive extent (Smithson, 2000: 107–8). Also, in this case he/she can adopt several strategies. For example, the moderator can decide to stop short the collective debate and list all the positions discussed so far, asking participants to comment on them or to indicate, for each, the strengths and weaknesses. In this way, the moderator brings all positions to the same level of importance and gives more space to different points of view on the discussion, supporting a minority position and reducing, at the same time, the position imposed by the leader (Nemeth and Wachtler, 1983; Acocella, 2012; Cyr, 2019: 79–81).

In extreme cases, the moderator can also oppose first-hand those who are monopolizing the debate too much. Obviously, this tactic is more intrusive than the previous one and can greatly affect group discussion. Therefore, the moderator should choose this strategy only when other paths have been followed without success and the discussion is coming to a standstill.

Role-playing

Role-playing is a strategy of soliciting interaction aimed at increasing the level of involvement of participants in discussion, rather than moderating particular negative group dynamics. Provided with an imaginary theme or scenario, the moderator asks the participants to stage a performance during which each person can assume a role and a part (Wooten, 2017: 256–62). The hypothesis is that the way in which people participate in the role play reproduces some social representations and the socially shared knowledge associated with a social role, as well as some models of action related to them. In this way, role-playing can elicit stereotypical and simplified representations connected to particular social categorization processes (Colucci, 2007: 1427–8; Liamputtong, 2011: 67).

In the field

The strategy of role-playing has been adopted in a research study focused on social workers' stereotypes about political refugees (Acocella and Turchi, 2020). In the group discussions, the moderator asked some of the participants to play the role of immigrants and others to play the role of various professional figures involved in reception practices. During the role play, the moderator was able to observe the prevalence of particular stereotyped representations of migrants by social workers, such as, for example, the idea that all refugees are mostly interested or willing to perform unqualified jobs.

Role-playing games are often used in group discussions involving children (Rapari, 2005: 204; Liamputtong, 2011: 118), who tend to interact if questioned but then mainly only with the moderator.

'Round-table' discussion on specific issues

Finally, the moderator can ask participants to take a 'round-table' in order to tell personal anecdotes about the matter dealt with (Stewart and Shamdasani, 1990: 93). This strategy works only if it is adopted in a limited way on specific topics and/or in particular situations. For example, this tactic is useful to encourage the most shy or reluctant to speak: when their turn arrives, silence would create an embarrassing situation, attracting the attention of the other participants.

This strategy apparently contradicts the moderator's role of facilitator, since it encourages interaction mainly between him/her and the single participants. However, although generally discouraged, this style of conduct may be assumed for a short time in order to increase the involvement of a participant who has more difficulty interacting in groups or entering the discussion. Once they have been encouraged, the moderator should reactivate the usual interaction of a group discussion, where there is no pre-established turn for taking the floor.

Further reading

Forsyth, D.R. (2014) *Group Dynamics* (6th edn). Belmont, CA: Wadsworth Cengage Learning.

This book offers a broad overview of group dynamics, drawing on examples from a range of disciplines including psychology, law, education, sociology and political science.

Barbour, R. (2007) *Doing Focus Groups*. London: Sage.

Within this recommended book on focus groups in action research, Chapter 6 presents numerous practical ideas (including various exercise and visual materials) for planning effective discussions.

Exercises

1. You are conducting a research on the well-being of the human body. How would you introduce this topic in group discussion in order to facilitate interaction among the participants, rather than the expression of personal experiences by each participant?

2. In drafting a discussion outline on the attitudes toward recycling and separate collection, you decide to preview some probing strategies to stimulate discussion. Try to achieve this goal using three different tactics.

Part III

CONDUCTING

7

Moderating the Focus Group

The moderator introduces the object of study and leads the group discussion during the focus group. In this chapter, we will focus on this figure, outlining his/her characteristics and functions. Considering the rise of the Web 2.0, we will also discuss in the chapter how the role of the moderator can change if a focus group is conducted face-to-face or virtually. Finally, we will dedicate a part of the chapter to the moderator's 'notes from the field', which collect his/her impressions and considerations of the overall progress of the group discussion.

Chapter goals

- *Knowledge*: the role and functions of the moderator in both face-to-face and online focus groups.
- *Applying knowledge and understanding*: how to choose the moderation styles of discussion, and how to record the information and take notes.
- *Making judgements*: how to maximize the moderator's tasks, both the instrumental, aimed at obtaining information, and the relational, aimed at managing the interactions.

7.1 The moderation styles of discussion

The focus group is a 'reactive' information-gathering technique because it always involves active intervention by the moderator. A 'reactive' method is defined as a technique in which the researcher does not limit himself/herself to observing events or behaviours in natural contexts, but rather asks questions of the social actors involved in field research in order to detect their opinion and representations about a phenomenon studied (Webb et al., 1981; Lee, 2000). The researcher who uses a reactive technique, therefore, intentionally proposes stimuli to 'provoke' a response from the subjects participating in the research. Participants are 'extracted' from their everyday routines and guided to better 'problematize' the object of the research in order to provide useful information on the phenomenon studied.

In the focus group, this task of gathering information in the field is carried out by the moderator, who guides, supports and re-launches the discussion according to an outline (see section 6.1) designed on the basis of the research purposes and adapted to the various participants involved.

The relationship between the moderator and the participants

Therefore, the moderator is actively part of the interactive context that produces knowledge about the phenomenon under study in the research. Indeed, even if the information capacity of the focus group resides in the interaction between the participants, the discussion context is also the product of verbal and non-verbal interactions between the moderator leading the debate and the participants who respond to the stimuli received.

It can be argued that the interaction between the moderator and the participants is asymmetric, since the former poses the topics to be discussed and the latter respond (Carey and Asbury, 2012: 29). The greater power of the moderator – perceived and real – can over-determine his/her role and actions in the group. A negative assessment, too direct an intervention or excessively active participation can all heavily influence the participants in the discussion. Even in the absence of such conspicuous signs, participants may form a certain idea of the moderator and adapt their answers consequently (Krueger, 1998: 70–3; Barbour, 2007: 51).

This concern leads many researchers to adopt less intrusive roles as the moderator so as to prevent his/her actions from influencing the group discussion (Zammuner, 2003: 174). However, if exaggerated, this concern risks not appreciating adequately that the whole set-up of the group discussion is 'artificial' and the mere presence of the moderator can influence the attitudes of the participants.

This brings into focus the relational and contextual nature of group discussion. As already detailed (see section 1.3), focus groups may be regarded as socially situated interactions, where opinions (as well as attitudes and evaluations in general) cannot be meaningfully separated from participants' interactions or from the production context (Puchta and Potter, 2004: 67–87). This means that the setting created during the information gathering inevitably involves the establishment of roles also between those who collect and those who provide information. In other words, the information collected does not exist prior to the investigation, but is in fact the outcome of the interactions and contradictions produced during the debate.

Concepts and Theories

To say that the information collected does not exist prior to the investigation is to overcome the legacy of behaviourism. Developed in psychology at the beginning of the 20th century, the school of behaviourism has had among its greatest exponents the psychologists John B. Watson (1914), Edward C. Tolman (1932) and Burrhus F. Skinner (1957), and the political scientist Arthur Bentley (1908). In investigations for research purposes, the respondent is considered to be a 'database formulating answers', while the stimulus provider is 'a machine collecting such data'. Beyond the school of thought, even today the practice of gathering information can be affected by ideas inherited from behaviourism, leading interviewers and moderators to be affected by a lack of sensitivity to the interactive nature of the data production context and to the cognitive states of respondents (Hedström and Ylikoski, 2010).

In the interactive context, the moderator is a strategic figure. Indeed, in leading group discussion, the moderator has to adapt the conduction style appropriately to the cognitive objectives of the research group and the specificity of the interactive dynamics produced in every discussion session (Smithson, 2000: 110–11).

In particular, in order to transform the asymmetry of his/her position in the group into a resource for interactive dynamics, the moderator should promote a conducting style which enhances active listening. Indeed, to moderate means to manage, not guide, the discussion. The real protagonists are the participants and the researcher's aim is to learn from them (Vaughn et al., 1996: 88).

The moderator should therefore 'listen', showing interest, curiosity, respectfulness and attention to what emerges during the group discussion, and he/she should emphasize the role of the participants as 'information holders' responding to the research objectives (Frisina, 2010: 91). In this way, the moderator can also develop empathy with the participants, trying to assume their perspective on reality, their language and their way of categorizing the phenomenon (Hennink, 2014: 74; Cyr, 2019: 56, 61).

At the same time, however, the moderator should take an 'active role' in the discussion, helping the participants to 'problematize' the object of the research (Wooten, 2017: 255). Indeed, even if the topic of the discussion is relevant to the experiences of the participants, it is probable they take for granted many of its aspects, owing to their prevalence in everyday life (Montesperelli, 2014: 261–5). Socially shared knowledge in its different forms is usually immersed in daily activities, which people habitually perform without consciously engaging their minds (Moscovici, 2000: 147–8). Focus group discussions may provide a space for questioning points of view and experiences that are usually taken for granted, generating processes of 'consciousness raising' and transforming personal troubles into public issues (Barbour, 2007: 150). At the same time, the moderator's interest is to extrapolate aspects of the study phenomenon that may be relevant for research purposes, since group discussion is conducted to achieve a specific cognitive objective. In problematizing the research matter, therefore, the moderator should also help the participants to focus their attention on the aspects considered most important to the research question (Zammuner, 2003: 13).

The level of directivity of conduction

In the position of 'active listening', the moderator can choose among different ways to intervene in the discussion. He/she can take a less active role in the discussion, providing maximum 'neutral' stimuli, or he/she can participate in a more active way, choosing to intervene whenever he/she considers it appropriate.

Generally, the level of 'directivity' adopted during information gathering influences the moderator's conducting style. The level of directivity of the conduction indicates the degree of freedom given to the moderator to decide how to conduct the discussion. If the directivity is high, the moderator indicates the discussion topics, introducing specific aspects of the investigated phenomenon or particular analytical perspectives to follow, in order to focus participants' attention (Frey and Fontana, 1993: 27; Cyr, 2019: 50–61).

There are different stances on the level of directivity in a focus group. For example, according to Robert K. Merton and Patricia L. Kendall (1946: 545–6), the focus group discussion should be conducted without any directivity by the moderator, because it is interesting to note what people freely think and feel. Indeed, too directive a discussion would impose the moderator's frame of reference. In contrast, according to Thomas Greenbaum (1998: 73–4), the discussion must always be very directive in order to focus group members' attention on the cognitive objectives of the research group. Indeed, this scholar compares the moderator to 'an orchestra conductor'.

Neither position should be taken to the extreme. The degree of directivity varies mainly according to the cognitive objectives and, therefore, to the functions attributed to the focus group. Usually, the following principles are valid:

- a lower level of directivity is ideal in exploratory-descriptive research designs, in order to uncover aspects of a little known phenomenon or one not previously considered (Stewart and Shamdasani, 1990: 89; Barbour, 2007: 102–3);
- a higher level of directivity can be adopted in analytical-in-depth designs, to deepen the knowledge of a phenomenon or to evaluate the adequacy of an analytical perspective considered significant by the researcher (Morgan, 1997: 54; Cardano, 2003: 158).

At other times the group dynamics among the participants, rather than the research objectives, influence the level of directivity of the conduction. Indeed, the moderator can take a more directive conduction style if during the discussion he/she finds group dynamics compromising the quality and reliability of the answers. The level of directivity is also influenced by the characteristics of the participants. For example, with older people (who tend to be less concise) and with children (who are easily distracted) a higher level of directivity is required to prevent the discussion from wandering.

As already noted with regard to the level of structuring of the discussion outline (see section 6.1), as the level of directivity increases, the focus of the discussion moves progressively from the participants' reference frameworks to those of the research group and the level of the moderator's influence increases (Morgan, 1997: 46–54; Morrison-Beedy et al., 2001: 48).

Moreover, the flexibility of qualitative research with focus groups allows the researcher to vary the level of directivity during the various steps of the field research. Indeed, the moderator can adopt a less directive conduction style in the first focus groups and decide how to focus the perspective on the theme in the following discussions. This conduction strategy may better safeguard the 'emic' nature of the group discussion context, aimed at bringing out participants' perspectives on the phenomenon studied (Stewart and Shamdasani, 1990: 62–3; Barbour, 2007: 26; Cyr, 2019: 10).

However, focus group discussions will never be totally without directivity. Indeed, these discussions are always conducted to respond to a cognitive research goal. Conduction that is too passive on the part of the moderator may even compromise the quality of the focus group results.

Leading a group does not mean over-determining the questions, directing participants towards one type of response at the expense of others. Indeed, a focus group, being inherently dialogical, should always give the participants scope for relatively free communication of ideas. If we see focus groups as communicative activities, even in discussions conducted with a higher level of directivity, the moderator should not compromise the capacity of the participants to collaborate and jointly produce new knowledge (Puchta and Potter, 2004: 29–39). In order to explore a particular problem, the moderator should continually find a balance between temporary fixation and freezing his/her perspective with respect to a specific issue, in order to enhance interactions among participants and their viewpoint on the study object (Marková et al., 2007: 202–3; Hennink, 2014: 50–1). Therefore, after the researcher presents the aspects and analytical perspectives that he/she wants to explore, participants must feel free to evaluate them, expressing their points of view without any conditioning.

In the field

An example of a very directive discussion with overdetermined questions might be the research on adolescents' perception of smoking, promoted by the Roy Castle Lung Cancer Foundation (Porcellato et al., 2002). In this research, the moderator often asked questions that conveyed a negative message about smoking, thus directing the opinions of the adolescents on the positions of the research client. Consider, for example, the following question: 'What activities would you like to do in the classroom to make sure that you do not start to smoke when you grow up?' (2002: 320).

The non-standardization of stimuli

A higher level of directivity does not necessarily imply a higher level of standardization, in terms of uniformity in form and presentation of the stimuli offered (Bichi, 2002). As already detailed (see section 1.1), there is a clear incompatibility between the 'emic' nature of focus group research and the standardization of information collected during the discussion.

However, this point is not uncontested. Some scholars, for example Vanda Zammuner (2003: 174), argues that a high degree of standardization favours the full comparability of the information obtained in different focus groups. However, there is no guarantee that a question posed in the same form will be interpreted in the same way by all members of the group or by individuals in different groups. For this reason, other scholars – such as William Goode and Paul Hatt (1952) – assign to the researcher the task of standardizing the transmitted meanings, rather than the forms used to transmit them, adapting questions to the needs of those who respond. To communicate the same concept to different participants the researcher should therefore adapt the way in which he/she asks a question to the specificity of each individual.

In the specific case of the focus group, if the research group chooses to investigate the same dimensions and analytical perspectives in different discussions, the moderator's task is to adapt them to the specificity of the different interactive contexts and draw out the meaning given to these dimensions and analytical perspectives by the participants (Greenbaum, 1998). Likewise, rather than asking the same questions in all meetings, he/she will try to express the same concepts using different terms or expressions, in order to adapt them to the characteristics of the participants, as well as to their communicative and cognitive skills (Marková et al., 2007). In this way, even in the most directed focus groups, the moderator will be able to safeguard the conceptual, analytical and linguistic categories of the group members (Cyr, 2019: 54–7).

In the field

In a study researching a programme to prevent childhood sexual abuse (Charlesworth and Rodwell, 1997), the moderator chose to form internally homogeneous groups by age. With young children, the discussion of sexual abuse was introduced through a simulation (with puppets), followed by the question 'Did you think the play told a happy story or a sad story?'. The moderator then asked more specific questions, like 'Can you tell me what you think "secret touch" is?'.

Also widespread is the belief that high standardization of the data collection guarantees the replicability of the information produced. However, repeating the focus group with the same discussion outline, involving the same people and the same moderator, does not guarantee obtaining equivalent information. On the contrary, the particular group dynamics developed in each discussion can activate different reasoning or connection among ideas.

7.2 The function of the moderator

The role of the moderator therefore oscillates between two tasks (see Appendix 3): an instrumental one, aimed at obtaining information pertinent to cognitive objectives; and a relational one, aimed at managing the interactions of the participants during the discussion (Stewart and Shamdasani, 1990: 70–1; Kidd and Parshall, 2000: 293–5).

To better understand the figure of the moderator, it is possible to divide his/her functions into three sets:

- clarification and regulation of the discussion;
- support for the production of information;
- facilitation of interaction.

Clarify and regulate the discussion

The clarification and regulation functions of the discussion are aimed at explaining to the participants the purpose of the meeting, the tasks to be performed and giving rules to follow during the conversation (see Figure 7.1).

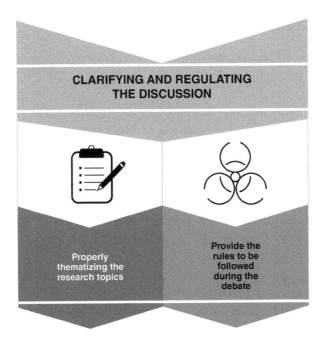

Figure 7.1   Moderator's task: clarifying and regulating the discussion

The first purpose that the moderator should pursue while performing his/her functions of clarification and regulation of the discussion is *to thematize the discussion topics appropriately*, according to the objectives of the research and the people who have been invited to the debate (Barbour, 2007: 138).

As detailed in section 1.2, the focus group is used when the concern is to identify the inter-subjective representations and the socially shared knowledge disseminated in particular social groups ('citizens', 'politicians', 'women', 'young people', 'social workers' etc.). During the group discussion, the moderator has the task of dealing with the object studied, by trying to bring out the social category that the participants are called upon to represent on that specific occasion and which identifies their membership of a particular community. Hence 'helping to thematize' means bringing out the social category of identification from which the research group wants participants to discuss the topic of discussion, because it is interested in that particular 'point of view' on the phenomenon (therefore, the point of view of 'citizens', 'politicians', 'women', 'young people', 'social workers', etc.).

Each member of the group belongs to a different social sphere, and the way a phenomenon is described will vary according to the point of view he/she adopts (Marková et al., 2007: 67–8). A policeman who, for instance, is also a father, will conceptualize public security in different ways according to whether he looks at it from his professional (policeman) or private (father) perspective. By thematizing the discussion, the moderator will also clarify the goal of the meeting and the reasons why exactly those people have been invited (Krueger and Casey, 2000: 107–8).

In the field

An example of a good thematization of the object of study can be found in research on foreign students conducted in Florence (Ceri and Ceccatelli, 2007). The moderator introduced the topic by emphasizing the need to collect the testimonies of the foreign students involved in the discussions to try to 'look at Florence through the eyes of a person from another country who has come to study in this city'.

The task of thematizing the discussion topics is more difficult when the participants are people who are not 'experts' on the phenomenon studied. As detailed in section 5.2, the purpose of these focus groups is to draw out a form of knowledge shared by a social group that is structured on 'hearsay'. In such a case, the thematizing will consist of a more detailed definition of the research object. At the same time, it will be good to adopt a more directive style of moderation and a more structured focus group outline to prevent the discussions from wandering too much or focusing on marginal issues.

The second purpose that the moderator should pursue while performing his/her functions of clarification and regulation of the discussion is *to provide rules to be followed during the debate* (Cardano, 2011: 219). For example, at the beginning of the discussion, the moderator can explain what a focus group is, as well as clarify that he/she intervenes only to introduce the themes or to facilitate the comparison of opinions. This introduction to the technique can help to make participants understand how the technique works and to clarify that the discussion must proceed freely among themselves without too much interference by the moderator (Krueger and Casey, 2000: 107–8). In this way, the moderator can motivate participants to take charge of the discussion without waiting to be invited.

169

For the same reason, it may be useful for the moderator to indicate the duration of the meeting and provide some rules to follow during the discussion (Krueger, 1998: 22–3). For example:

- everyone should speak audibly and one at a time to facilitate registration;
- everyone must listen to and respect the opinions of others since there are no right or wrong answers (Vaughn et al., 1996: 80; Albanesi, 2004: 90–1);
- no one should be afraid to express an opinion even if it is contrary to what has been said by someone else (Stewart and Shamdasani, 1990: 92–3); indeed, we do not want everyone to agree and different points of view are therefore welcome on the same topic (Morgan, 1997: 185);
- there is no intervention order; everyone is free to intervene when and how often they deem appropriate (Vaughn et al., 1996: 84);
- it is preferable to keep discussion relevant to the topics to be discussed;
- it is permissible to change one's opinion without fear of appearing inconsistent.

It may also be useful to stress – from the beginning – which aspects of the investigated phenomenon are of interest and which are considered marginal, in order to focus participants' attention.

Supporting the production of information

The functions supporting the production of information are designed to animate the discussion and obtain information relevant to the research purpose (see Figure 7.2).

The first purpose the moderator should pursue while performing his/her functions of supporting the production of information is *to stimulate the discussion adequately.*

The moderator stimulates the discussion during the entire session; he/she gradually introduces the themes and leads the participants back to them in the event of excessive digression (Vaughn et al., 1996: 82–3; Cyr, 2019: 55–7); re-proposes the arguments not adequately detailed; avoids going back to aspects already discussed successfully; revives the debate if it reaches deadlock. If unforeseen topics or aspects emerge during the discussion, he/she should be able to assess whether they are interesting for cognitive purposes and if it is appropriate to deepen them (Stewart and Shamdasani, 1990: 78–82; Puchta and Potter, 2004: 52–62). Dwelling on marginal aspects is to be avoided. The meeting session should be used to obtain a great deal of information that is as pertinent as possible, because once finished there will not be another opportunity (Acocella, 2008: 64).

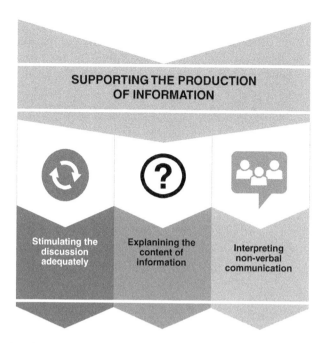

Figure 7.2 Moderator's task: supporting the production of information

For this reason, the moderator should have sufficient knowledge of the object of study to allow him/her to provide appropriate stimuli. Indeed, he/she should be able to evaluate the adequacy of the information, making continuous connections between events, actors, facts that emerge during the debate (therefore, during the meeting session and not only during the analysis). Thus, the moderator can re-launch and deepen the discussion in light of the research cognitive objectives or of information already gathered (Krueger and Casey, 2000: 99). However, the moderator should exhibit only partial knowledge of the topic (Vaughn et al., 1996: 85–6) to avoid excessively influencing the participants with his/her own conceptual, linguistic or argumentative perceptions of the study phenomenon.

To minimize the moderator's intrusiveness, it is useful to resort to indirect reactive probing strategies (see section 6.2).

These strategies (see Table 7.1) enhance a less directive style of conducting and favour a more discursive approach to the debate, while still allowing the moderator to focus the participants' attention on the main topics related to the object of study.

The moderator also performs a further highly important task: *explaining the content of the information*, clarifying the meaning attributed by the participants to the terms and expressions used during the discussion. Indeed, since the connection between concepts and terms is not rigid, communication is never

Table 7.1   Strategies to stimulate the discussion

Ranking exercise of items proposed by the research group	Introducing different items, asking participants to identify an order of importance
Use of cards with items chosen by the research group	Introducing different points of view on the research issues, in order to focus participants' attention
Comment/completion of a story	Asking participants to comment/complete a story, in order to bring out their logic of argumentation or their representations about a given phenomenon
Interpretation of a thematic vignette	Bringing out widespread beliefs about a given phenomenon with a less reactive strategy
Pause of reflection on discussion topics	Giving participants time to evaluate if they have said everything on topic discussed

perfect (Marradi, 2007: 30–40). This is a cognitive problem that can emerge during the response elaboration process and involves polysemic or semantic dispersion. During focus group discussions, this problem can multiply according to the number and type of participants. However, in research with focus groups, the polysemic/semantic dispersion of the language can also be an opportunity, allowing a social scientist to discover, at least partly, the extent to which social knowledge is actually shared or only taken-as-shared (Marková et al., 2007: 18–19, 25; Acocella, 2012: 1131).

For this reason, the moderator should take a maieutic role, encouraging participants to clarify their statements, deepening any controversial aspects and resolving any ambiguities. The meeting itself is a unique opportunity to ask for explanations or clarify the content of the debate. A timely intervention by the moderator reduces the risk of having to eliminate unclear information or producing incorrect interpretations during analysis.

To reduce the risk of excessive conditioning, the moderator can resort to indirect reactive probing strategies (see section 6.2).

With these strategies (see Table 7.2), 'the moderator can encourage participants, if necessary, to explain themselves the meaning of the terms and expressions they use, rather than providing definitions' (Acocella, 2012: 1131). Continuous interaction allows the participants to clarify their individual opinions and to compare their positions according to a sharing and comparing process (Morgan, 1998a) that leads to a definition and to an elucidation of the

Table 7.2   Strategies to clarify the information provided by the participants

'Emic' definition of the definition of key-concepts	Asking participants to define (even writing) the most relevant key-concepts related to the research object
Classification exercise of the items proposed by participants	Inviting participants to divide the items provided by the group into different classes and to label them
Ranking exercise of the items proposed by participants	Asking participants to attribute different 'weights' to the various topics provided by the group

subjective meanings. This is useful to collect different nuances that hide behind the same term, and to encourage comparison among the participants on the discussed topics (Barbour, 2007: 138; Hennink, 2014: 30–1).

Finally, another fundamental task of the moderator is *to interpret non-verbal communication*. Therefore, he/she should be able to evaluate bodily gestures, facial expressions or tone of voice. Sometimes he/she can also exploit non-verbal behaviour of participants to encourage them to talk: 'Peter, I noticed you turned away when Jorge talked about full inclusion. What is your opinion on full inclusion?' (Vaughn et al., 1996: 85). Participants' gestures are rich in information and they can become integral parts of the analysis (Cyr, 2019: 94). Furthermore, gestures can be useful to evaluate the quality and the reliability of answers (see sections 8.3, 10.1 and 11.1). The moderator should also know how to consider the different meanings of silences (Bloor et al., 2001: 77–8; Frisina, 2018: 196). However, when the moderator is supported by an observer, this task can be shared and at the end of the focus group the moderator can reflect on all these aspects with the observer's help (Acocella, 2008: 69–87).

In the field

In a study evaluating the quality of dental services conducted by Kate Robson (1999), the moderator came to understand that the silence of some invited dentists was due to reluctance to 'break ranks' in the presence of other colleagues. Indeed, giving a critical evaluation of colleagues' work indirectly involved a presumption of disloyalty to their professional group.

Facilitate the interaction

In order to facilitate the interaction, the moderator should aim for internal group cohesion and the comparison of opinions among the participants (see Figure 7.3). In particular, the moderator should pay specific attention to the dialogical nature of the focus group, emphasizing the collective rather than the individual.

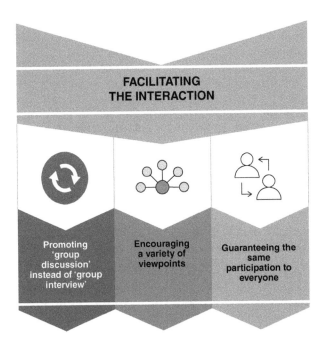

Figure 7.3 Moderator's task: facilitating the interaction

Concepts and Theories

'If we say that socially shared knowledge has a dialogical nature, it implies that it is formed and maintained in and through dialogical thinking and communication. This does not mean to deny that individuals have the capacity of individual reasoning and thinking. This means, however, that the Ego and Alter jointly co-constitute and transform forms of conceptual knowledge' (Marková et al., 2007: 17). Hence, a dialogical approach to socially shared knowledge allows considering the focus group as a method to study communication in interaction. 'Since focus groups are dialogues, they appear to be a particularly suitable means of exploring forms of socially shared knowledge, opinions and beliefs in their dynamics. At the same time, because dialogue is not a transmission of neutral information or of facts from speaker to listener, the contents of what participants say and the forms, in which these contents circulate, cannot be meaningfully separated from participants' interactions. [Therefore,] focus groups are situated communication activities in which we can examine language, thinking and knowledge in action and so they provide manifold research opportunities for taking a dynamic research perspective' (Marková et al., 2007: 202).

According to Claudia Puchta and Jonathan Potter (2004), there are three practices to be implemented to facilitate group discussion: to promote group interaction; to encourage a variety of viewpoints; and to generate informality.

Therefore, in order to facilitate the interaction, the first goal of the moderator should be *soliciting a 'group discussion' rather than creating a 'group interview'* (Corrao, 2000: 16; Parker and Tritter, 2006: 25–6; Barbour, 2007: 2–3). Indeed, focus groups' hallmark is their interactive nature (Kitzinger, 1995: 299; Hennink, 2014: 26–7; Frisina, 2018: 190).

Figure 7.4 compares the typical conduction of an 'interview in a group' (model A) with that of a 'group discussion' (model B). Model A does not encourage interaction among participants, since the conversation is articulated

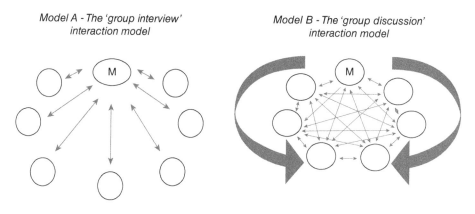

Model A - The 'group interview' interaction model

Model B - The 'group discussion' interaction model

Group interviews excel at eliciting 'private' accounts

Group discussions excel at eliciting the interactional context in which the accounts are produced

Figure 7.4 The interaction model between the moderator and the participants

Source: Elaboration from Acocella, 2008: 61-2

between the moderator, who asks the questions, and each participant, who answers in turn. Hence, the importance of the group as an overarching dynamic entity, rather than its individual parts, risks being suffocated by the role of the conductor, who becomes the main interlocutor of each participant (Acocella, 2008: 61–2).

During a focus group, the moderator should therefore choose a type of interaction among the participants like model B. Following this style, rather than addressing questions to individual participants, the moderator launches a discussion topic (represented in the figure by large curved arrows), leaving the participants free to interact (Hennink, 2014: 72–3).

Second, to stimulate a group discussion rather than a group interview, the moderator must prepare the stimuli that guide the debate keeping a community in mind. So, for example, he/she should avoid asking questions aimed at gathering information about individual motivations and personal experiences. This kind of question does not stimulate interaction between participants and does not engender a feeling of reciprocal belonging, but it pushes the group members to interact mainly with the moderator to make individual reflections (Meo, 2003b: 282). As detailed in section 6.1, questions should instead be formulated so as to encourage group formation and meanings sharing, in order to draw out intersubjective representations derived from the negotiation of positions and the contribution of all participants (Cardano, 2011: 21; Liamputtong, 2011: 16–18; Halkier, 2017: 406–7).

Concepts and Theories

Whereas in the 'group interview' an 'external interaction' prevails, where single individuals are considered as independent entities, the 'group discussion' encourages an 'internal interaction', developing dialogical relations among participants, which become 'a constellation of interdependent constituents'. 'The constellation defines its elements; and, vice versa, the elements define the unit in question [...]. The participants are in a complementary dialogical engagement in communication and [...], in and through communication they undergo both simultaneous and sequential changes' (Marková et al., 2007: 9–10). In this way, the collective construction of an argument emerges as a collaborative procedure, rather than as an individual's view.

To promote group participation the moderator should also *encourage a variety of viewpoints*, soliciting contributions from the participants in order to bring out the similarities and differences between opinions and to explain the strengths and weaknesses of various positions (Puchta and Potter, 2004: 126–30). Therefore, even though the focus group is a method to study socially shared knowledge, the notion of social representation cannot be conceived of as a set of homogeneous, static and decontextualized 'ideas' that a person (or a group of subjects) has on a given topic. Socially shared knowledge is by its nature characterized by tensions, contradictions, vagueness and ambiguities, as well as by regularities and recurrent themes (Marková et al., 2007: 48). The focus group is a method, then, to highlight the emergence of diverse voices, as well as the multiple meanings that people attribute to social representations (Smithson, 2000: 111; Hennink, 2014: 26–7; Cyr, 2019: 110).

In this way, the focus group allows the researcher to identify how the macrostructures of society (e.g. social norms and socially produced categorization processes) influence the microstructures of everyday life. However, it is also possible to investigate the acts of resistance (pushes towards change) against certain rules (Kitzinger, 2004). 'The focus group, therefore, appears to be not only a valuable method for investigating how the social order is maintained throughout, but also to study the cracks, tension, ambivalence created by the discursive practices of daily resistance against various sources of normativity' (Frisina, 2018: 204).

Furthermore, the group expresses or, better, generates opinions for the researcher (Myers, 2004). Thus, the participants act as if their purpose was to generate opinions (Puchta and Potter, 2004: 67–8). Therefore, unlike in everyday life, in the focus group, disagreement can be encouraged and legitimized by the moderator, displaying the manifold heterogeneity of social representations or tensions against normative assumptions. The debate should understand the process of creating consensus and dissent via interaction, allowing the moderator to investigate how people interpret and reconstruct social phenomena, change their meanings and create new meanings.

However, interaction and group dynamics do not always unfold consistently (Carey and Asbury, 2012: 28).

Concepts and Theories

In a focus group the study of socially shared knowledge has to absorb emotional and relational problems that are expressed through a variety of symbolic means. For example, participants may have a fear of losing face

(Continued)

or other kinds of socially induced fears, they may express antagonism against others, and they can also employ indirect communicative strategies hiding oppositional attitudes towards others (Marková et al., 2007: 48). At same time, even if the focus group encourages the formulation of ideas, reticular interaction does not always allow all participants to express their points of view. While listening to what is said, each individual is stimulated to formulate ideas in response. Yet not everyone can express ideas once the opportunity to speak presents itself, and sometimes participants cannot remember all the thoughts that the previous discussion raised. Likewise, the speed of the interaction does not always allow participants to go through every topic in detail, especially if it presents many aspects to deal with. Indeed, the interaction develops by means of the association of ideas. This flow can cause a change of topic along the lines of an intervention. Some topics that have only briefly emerged can be quickly abandoned, while others can be dwelt upon in detail even if they are not strictly relevant to the purpose of the research (Acocella, 2012: 1131–3).

For this reason, the moderator should also *ensure equal participation for everyone*. During the discussion, he/she should observe the interaction of the group members, identifying the presence of leadership relationships, subjection or complicity among the participants and trying to lead the discussion in order to overcome them (Stewart and Shamdasani, 1990: 89; Corrao, 2000: 60).

Importantly, the task is to facilitate, not supervise, the participants, as too rigid a level of control can be damaging to the success of the research (Bloor et al., 2001: 75). It is recommended, therefore, that the moderator alternates direct and indirect reactive probing strategies (see section 6.2) in order to reduce the risk of conditioning, manipulating or over-controlling interaction among the participants (see Table 7.3).

Table 7.3 The strategies of interaction facilitation

Breaking of conformist cognitive schemes	Introducing different points of view; shifting the attention to participants' behaviours adopted by 'third persons'; supporting minority positions
Moderation of leaders	Bringing all positions to the same level of importance and giving more space to different points of view

Role-playing	Staging a performance in order to increase the level of involvement of participants
'Round-table' discussion on a specific research issue	Encouraging the most shy or reluctant people to speak

With these strategies, the moderator can encourage more equal participation, helping participants to adapt to the situation and trying to minimize the influence of the group on individual perceptions. At the same time, the moderator can solicit comparisons between different opinions to prevent participants from reaching agreement too quickly and adopting conformist opinions. In this way, the moderator can also keep the level of conflict under control, in order to avoid excessive friction or intractable differences of opinion. As we will explore further (in Chapter 8), the observer can support the moderator in these tasks.

7.3 Conducting an online focus group

The online application

Focus groups, in both face-to-face and virtual contexts, involve, by definition, a discussion of a topic under the direction of a skilled moderator. The online focus group involves a moderator who invites pre-screened, qualified respondents who represent the target of interest to log on to conferencing software at a pre-arranged time and take part in an online focus group. The moderator guides the discussion. In the best discussions, as with face-to-face groups, respondents interact with each other as well as with the moderator in real time to generate deeper insights about the topic.

Interaction issues

Interaction with a moderator is sufficiently important that it can be considered one of the distinctive aspects of the focus group, even in online applications.

For this reason, in our opinion, group discussions with automated moderation should be excluded from the focus group family. This novel technique involves participants but no human moderator. Hence, this online variant lacks a key element of the interaction, namely that between participants and moderator. In our view, this application therefore more properly belongs to the family of group interviews.

One of the prerequisites for success in an online focus group is active facilitation by a skilled moderator. Facilitation of productive face-to-face focus group discussions requires a skilled moderator, and the skill of the moderator of online focus groups is no less important – indeed, it may even be greater in the online context (Abrams and Gaiser, 2017: 436; Matthews et al., 2018: 1622).

Distinctive features

One key difference compared with the moderation of a face-to-face focus group concerns the initial phase. While face-to-face focus groups begin with the arrival and welcoming of the participants to the facility, 'in the online world is the online research site where participants go to register for the group in which they will participate. It is crucial that the online research site includes a welcome message along with an overview of the process for first-time users' (Stewart and Shamdasani, 2017: 56).

An introduction exercise is useful for helping the group to bond. 'In the face-to-face focus group there are various techniques to break the ice. Then there will often be the possibility of offering food and beverage for an initial informal contact. In the case of the online focus group it may be important to do an introduction exercise in order to enable trust and to set participants at ease so they feel relaxed and motivated in participating in the focus group' (Abrams and Gaiser, 2017: 437–8).

A further aspect to consider is the capacity for control of the interaction by the moderator. The online moderator should maintain even greater control of the situation than the face-to-face moderator, to deal with the absence of face-to-face interaction and non-verbal communication (Liamputtong, 2011: 157–62). Non-verbal communication is often crucial for determining when further questioning or probing will be useful, and it is often an important source of interplay among group members. 'In face-to-face group discussions the moderator and group participants rely on a wide range of visual and other nonverbal cues to manage the discussion. Lacking visual and verbal cues such as nods, smiles and vocal acknowledgements may leave participants confused about what they are supposed to do' (Abrams and Gaiser, 2017: 438). This means that the moderator must be especially proactive in moving the discussion along, by probing and following up answers to questions with requests for additional information or for clarification (Lobe, 2017: 236–40).

For this reason, some researchers stress the need for the online focus group to be prepared beforehand and with great care (Stewart and Williams, 2005). Moderating online is difficult and demands a great deal of reflection. Particular care is therefore required in order to prevent a chaotic group discussion.

Supporting tools

Conversely, the online environment can provide tools to assist the online moderator that are not generally available to moderators of face-to-face groups (Cher Ping and Seng Chee, 2001: 56). 'These tools include time-tracking monitors that inform the moderator about which group participants have contributed, how long each participant has talked, and the time since a participant's last contribution. They also include the feature of allowing respondents to raise their hands to be recognized' (Stewart and Shamdasani, 2017: 60). The majority of online platforms offer the option to share contemporaneous scripts and conversations. Scripts are mainly available as chat rooms, and for the moderator they are useful for directing the attention of the group to the main question or keywords, or to give technical instructions and administrative information. At the same time, they require twofold attention. Indeed, controlling scripts and conversations simultaneously is 'often more complex and interweaving because participants can speak and/or type simultaneously' (Abrams and Gaiser, 2017: 438). The moderator can also use a private chat to engage a participant who is isolated and not contributing to the group discussion (Abrams and Gaiser, 2017: 438). As in the face-to-face focus group, the moderator in an online focus group can use different response elicitation techniques designed to deepen responses to questions. In particular, whiteboard exercises and the ability to mark-up concepts or other visual stimuli simulate many of the characteristics of in-person groups.

Finally, some online platforms provide customizable meeting rooms, sophisticated user permissions management, and audio and videoconferencing (Stewart and Shamdasani, 2017: 56).

7.4 The recording of the discussion and the notes 'from the field'

It may also be useful to consider the recording tools for group discussion at the service of the moderator.

Recording the discussion

The group discussion is generally recorded. Taking notes during the group discussion is very difficult. Furthermore, it would distract the moderator from his/her main role: obtaining information relevant to the cognitive objectives and supporting the interaction of the participants.

In general, the presence of recording tools does not disturb participants. To reassure them, it is sufficient to explain that the discussion will be recorded in order to facilitate the work of gathering information and to improve the quality of the analysis (Bloor et al., 2001: 66). Experience shows that the participants pay attention to the recorder only at the beginning of the discussion, forgetting it during the debate (Albanesi, 2004: 90). After all, recording is a guarantee that the content of the discussion has been collected in a reliable way. Indeed, if the moderator limits himself/herself to taking notes, he/she could transcribe the interventions in a partial and imprecise manner and/or incorrectly interpret what the participants say, not least because of the speed of interaction (Colella, 2011: 54).

In all situations, the anonymity of the participants must be ensured. Thus, the moderator can reassure them that the transcription of the discussion will be made only for research purposes and that if the researcher reports excerpts of discussion in the analysis report, the names of the participants will be changed and all identifying information will be eliminated (Cyr, 2019: 74). To reassure the participants, the moderator can also allow them to participate in the group discussion using fictitious names.

Usually the discussion is recorded, but not videotaped. Video camera can create increased inhibition, especially if it is operated by a cameraman. If instead it is fixed, several authors claim that its influence is equivalent to that of a simple audio recorder (Krueger and Casey, 2000). However, this claim is disputed, since the presence of a camera reduces the guarantee of anonymity as well as being more conspicuous. In the event that the moderator does decide to videotape the discussion, it may be useful to use two cameras in order to record all of the participants, who are typically arranged in a circle. Compared with audio recording alone, the camera also records non-verbal behaviours, which can supplement and reinforce analysis of the verbal information collected during the discussion (Hennink, 2014: 85).

Notes from the 'field'

Usually the moderator takes notes during the group discussion. Furthermore, it may be useful to write – at the end of each meeting – some notes 'from the field' concerning the overall progress of the discussion (Liamputtong, 2011: 63). There is no specific consensus about this tool among focus group literature. Some references to 'notes from the field' can be found among discussion of the interview (Bichi, 2002). In any event, it may be interesting to reflect on the appropriateness of collecting such annotations from the moderator (see Table 7.4).

Notes 'from the field' can be means to make considerations and evaluations as to the overall progress of the research. They can help the moderator to become familiar with the topic studied and to articulate his/her progressive knowledge on the object, in order to monitor and specify the various phases of the research during the gathering of information in the field (Hammersley and Atkinson, 1983; Liamputtong, 2011: 63; Hennink, 2014: 83–4).

Given the multiplicity of possibilities, it is also possible to formulate a hypothesis about the collection of different types of 'from the field' notes.

Although it was thought in the field of ethnographic research, it may be interesting to adopt the distinction drawn by Giampietro Gobo (2001: 132) between 'descriptive notes' and 'interpretative notes', to discern the activities related to the description of empirical materials collected from the interpretation of these materials.

In 'descriptive notes', for example, the moderator can report some verbal and non-verbal behaviours of the participants observed, describing them in their 'factual essence' – states Gobo (2001: 134) – for example not using qualifying adjectives which, in a sense, already give them an interpretation. In these notes, the moderator can also value the 'natural languages' of the participants, noting some 'emic' words of the natural dialogues.

In 'interpretative notes', instead, the moderator can report the ideas, hypotheses and interpretations suggested by the conversations and the interactive dynamics that emerged during the group discussion. They include, therefore, the preliminary questions that are posed, the hypotheses that are to be developed and monitored, the issues that have emerged thus far and the concepts to be explored in subsequent phases of field research. All these components form the nucleus of the subsequent analysis of the information, the conclusive ones. These notes are also written in a language different from the descriptive one, often starting from the researcher's 'etic' categories.

The effort to distinguish between 'descriptive notes' and 'interpretative notes' allows the moderator to analyse the object of study, further safeguarding the 'emic' nature of the focus group context of gathering information. Indeed, they can help the moderator to distinguish his/her conceptual, linguistic and analytical frame from what emerges following the perspective of the various group discussions. He/she will also be able to identify with greater clarity how his/her knowledge and perception of the phenomenon changes, identifying, for example, new 'etic' categories founded in an 'emic' way: interpretative categories formulated by enhancing the conceptual, linguistic and analytical frame of the subjects involved in the research (Liamputtong, 2011: 63; Hennink, 2014: 83–4).

Besides 'descriptive notes' and 'interpretative notes', it may also be interesting to collect 'methodological notes' (Schatzman and Strauss, 1973: 99–101; Greenbaum, 2000: 119). In these notes, the moderator can register his/her methodological considerations in relation to the group discussion and information production. For example, the moderator can point out the parts of the discussion outline that he/she has focused on most or which he/she has not been able to investigate. At same time, he/she can identify if topics have been added or explored in a different way in some group discussions. Likewise, the moderator can record the conduction style adopted to solicit debate from and interaction between participants.

In these notes, the moderator can also report any difficulties encountered and how they could be overcome in subsequent phases of field research. In this way, he/she can better define the design of the research, with reference to the choice of cases or to the discussion outline. For example, the moderator can assess whether some topics have been adequately detailed, focusing on other aspects in subsequent discussions. Likewise, the moderator can evaluate whether it is appropriate to introduce new themes in the focus group outline or change the composition of the discussion group to introduce new perspectives.

Finally, it may also be useful for the moderator to collect 'personal notes' or 'emotional notes' (Corsaro, 1985: 295). Remember that the moderator is an integral part of the interactive context that occurs during a focus group. In these notes, therefore, the moderator can report feelings experienced during the group discussion, any moments of discomfort or embarrassment, the personal feelings (of sympathy, dislike, affinity etc.) elicited by the participants, and the feelings and reactions arising from what he/she has heard. In this way, the moderator will be able to recognize and define as clearly as possible everything that may have influenced his/her moderation style. These notes can help the researcher to explain any prejudices or stereotypes invoked by the participants or by topics in the group discussion. They can also be useful to find a certain degree of distance from the studied phenomenon. Emotional notes are therefore a way to signal and recognize implicitly that the moderator is not a mere 'collector' of information, nor an impassive machine (Greenbaum, 2000: 119; Cigliuti, 2014: 103).

A final important point is the encounter between moderator and observer. Indeed, the field notes can be the result of a debriefing with the observer that can take place immediately after the group discussion. A comparison of the different points of view can help make the field notes more intersubjective and richer in detailed information.

Table 7.4 The field notes by the moderator: types and examples

Descriptive notes	☐ Non-verbal behaviours of the participants (e.g. nodding, shaking head)
	☐ Factual behaviours (e.g. raising from the chair, sitting posture)
	☐ Verbal 'emic' words of the natural dialogues (e.g. keywords, typical expressions)

Interpretative notes	☐	Concepts emerged from the fields (e.g. key concepts emerged from the discussion)
	☐	Ideas on the topic of investigation (e.g. novelty emerged from a discussion; interpretative points to be deepened)
	☐	Hypothesis of interpretation (e.g. advancements in knowledge and interpretation)
Methodological notes	☐	Notes on the moderation style (e.g. aspects to be improved)
	☐	Notes on the group interaction (e.g. dynamics to prevent)
	☐	Notes on the focus group outline or the tools (e.g. aspects to be improved)
	☐	Notes on the logistics (e.g. aspects to be improved)
Personal notes	☐	Emotions linked to the role (comfort/discomfort)
	☐	Emotions linked to the interaction (e.g. relational climate)
	☐	Emotions linked to the context (e.g. the logistics, the technical equipment)

In the various forms listed (see Table 7.4), notes 'from the field' will provide materials that also feed into the analysis, reconstructing, explaining and evaluating all the phases of the research and the choices made in the field. This allows the research group to 'check' and 'make transparent' the entire process of gathering information and producing knowledge. The way in which the information is produced and the choices that underlie this process will guide the research in one direction or another (see section 3.2). Therefore, it is important to keep track of this process and bear it in mind during the analysis, in order to evaluate and adequately deal with the available empirical materials.

Further reading

Krueger, R.A. (1997) *Moderating Focus Groups*. Thousand Oaks, CA: Sage.

Based on years of experience in moderating and training, the author offers an easy-to-read overview of various approaches and strategies for guiding a group discussion and managing difficult situations.

Greenbaum, T.L. (2000) *Moderating Focus Groups: A Practical Guide for Group Facilitation*. Thousand Oaks, CA: Sage.

This book proposes a wide range of techniques for managing group dynamics and energizing a tired group.

Exercises

1. You are conducting research on social vulnerability. In the research design, you have planned to conduct some focus groups involving unemployed men. How would you introduce the discussion topic in such a way as to solicit a 'group discussion' and not a 'group interview'?

2. During a group discussion, a topic provokes conflict among the participants. Some members of the group get angry and others stop talking. After the discussion, what do you include in the 'descriptive notes' and in the 'interpretative notes' with reference to the specific group interaction?

8

Observing the Focus Group

To carry out a good focus group, we recommend that, alongside the moderator, there is also an observer attending the discussion session. We know that in some focus groups the presence of an observer is not planned, often due to a lack of available human resources. In other focus groups, there is a person who accompanies the moderator, but is only seen as an assistant for the logistical aspects.

In this chapter, we will show that having an observer is fundamental for taking notes on both the contents of the discussion and interactions among the participants. We will then describe his/her tasks and also the tools that he/she may use, taking into account that: part of his/her work can be carried out live during the group discussion; another part of the work will be carried out after the discussion in order to build the corpus of the texts, sheets and notes that will be submitted to the analysis; and a third part of the work will be conducted during the analysis processing.

--- **Chapter goals** ---

- *Knowledge*: the usefulness, the role and the functions of the observer in the focus group.
- *Applying knowledge and understanding*: what to observe in, and how to observe, a focus group discussion.
- *Making judgements*: how to maximize the observer's tasks: the instrumental task aimed at obtaining information, and the relational task aimed at observing the interactions.

8.1 Not only an assistant

The moderator's assistant carries out an important role, both during the collective discussion and in the analysis phase (Zammuner, 2003: 206–8; Ellis, 2016: 58; Remenyi, 2017: 197). He/she must be an integral part of the research group, participating in the entire investigation process.

The assistant's role

In focus group guidance and in the research designs that use the focus group, the assistant is mainly assigned an ancillary role as support for the moderator in carrying out the logistical activities. Indeed, the assistant primarily has the task of preparing the setting for the discussion. He/she attends to the arrangement of the room and the chairs, prepares the place cards, organizes the refreshment, checks the recording equipment (video or audio), and provides all the tools needed to support the debate (photos, paper, blackboard etc.).

Second, the assistant can supervise the participants in filling out a questionnaire, either at the beginning or at the end of the discussion, check possession of the requirements of the sampling criteria, or collect sociographic information (age, qualification, profession etc.) which can be useful in analysing information.

During the discussion, the assistant may also be asked to take notes on:

- *Turn taking.* This activity is very important because it helps when transcribing the discussion to recognize correctly the participants as and when they intervene, which is not always possible by simply listening to the recorded voices (Krueger, 1998: 76–80).
- *Key topics and key concepts.* His/her task in this case is to take notes that transcribe as literally as possible the order of the themes that have emerged and the most significant sentences (Albanesi, 2004, 97). These notes can also be useful in the case of recorder malfunction.
- *Quotes.* The most significant citations that have emerged from the conversation (Krueger, 1998: 76–80).

Moreover, if the moderator agrees, the assistant can ask questions to stimulate the discussion or resume issues not adequately addressed (Krueger and Casey, 2000: 101), and summarize, at the end of the debate, what has emerged, underlining the central themes, key ideas, the various points of view put forward and the argumentative strength of some topics.

The observer's role

However, limiting the functions of the assistant to those listed above is reductive. Indeed, it is possible to assign greater autonomy and centrality to this figure. During the discussion, while the moderator is busy keeping the discussion alive and leading it on the topics, the assistant can:

- gather information on the type of interaction that is established among the participants, also detecting non-verbal behaviours (Trobia, 2005: 57; Remenyi, 2017);
- observe how the various topics are treated and the possible production of particular group dynamics which could influence the results (Albanesi, 2004: 97–8).

The observation of the interaction among the participants requires continuous attention, which the moderator – engaged in other tasks – cannot guarantee. For this reason, present during each meeting must be a person who devotes himself/herself exclusively (or at least predominantly) to this activity. To do so properly, he/she must have a profound knowledge of group dynamics.

Interactions are an integral part of the process of information building. Therefore, interpretation of the information on a focus group cannot omit analysis of the dynamics that develop among the participants during the discussion. This is for two reasons (Acocella, 2008: 71–3): the unit of analysis (i.e. the object of the research) is not the individual participant, but the group in its entirety; the information produced by the group is not simply the sum of the single answers, rather the effect of synergy among participants' ideas and opinions. Therefore, the analysis of the interaction can serve to examine the way in which the information was produced and the role played by the participants and by the moderator in this production.

The assistant is therefore a central figure in research with a focus group. Nevertheless, his/her importance has not yet been sufficiently recognized. In literature, the references to his/her role are always marginal and in the practice of research little attention is paid to the assistant's training and identification of his/her characteristics and tasks.

In our view, the assistant can play an even more fundamental role by being completely dedicated to the detection and analysis of interactions. In particular, his/her task may be observing what happens during the discussion through a non-reactive observation (Bruschi, 1999: 329). For this reason it seems appropriate to denote this figure with the term 'observer', given that the generic term 'assistant' seems to confine him/her to an ancillary role.

The observation will be aimed at two main purposes:

- *Evaluate whether the information has been invalidated by particular group dynamics*. During a focus group, dynamics of conformism and attitudes of acquiescence can arise, as well as subjugation or extreme conflict. These dynamics may strongly influence the discussion, and compromise the degree of fidelity of the answers provided.

189

- *Give different degrees of importance to the topics dealt with.* The various participants will not address in the same way and with the same intensity all themes. Since the focus group unit of analysis is not the individual participants but rather the group as a whole, every single intervention cannot be extrapolated from the general group discourse. Indeed, the purpose is to acquire full meaning in the general framework of a collective signification.

In order to carry out these activities the observer will base his/her investigation on the observation of both verbal and non-verbal behaviours. Although this work can also be done at the end through textual analysis, in reality we cannot overlook the advantages of the presence of someone who directly observes how this information is produced and which group dynamics are developed. This kind of information collected during the discussion can also be integrated immediately afterwards, with the collaboration of the moderator, or in the analysis phase through the replay and/or transcription of the recording (see sections 7.4, 10.1 and 11.1). If there is a pause during the discussion, the information that the assistant collects can be useful for suggesting to the moderator any behaviour to be corrected or adopted upon resumption of the focus group (Albanesi, 2004: 98). However, the main purpose of observing the interaction and non-verbal behaviour is to integrate and reinforce the analysis of the verbal information gathered during the discussion.

Summing up, it is important to bear in mind that, if the research involves an observer, as recommended by us, this person will have an important role and will be able to intervene in different phases of the research:

- In the planning phase, because many of the collection tools to be used will have to be discussed in the research group.
- During the group discussion phase, mainly in order to observe the interactions, control the reliability of the information, and evaluate the weight that the different themes have been given, and the bias of non-verbal behaviour.
- After the discussion, in building the corpus of the texts. In this case, he/she will share the observations with the moderator and will define the field notes, which will constitute the corpus of the texts to be analysed. The observer will also help with transcription of the discussion, providing the transcriptionist with useful information on, for example, the relational climate of the focus group, turn taking and so on.
- Finally, in the course of the information processing phase, especially for the relational analysis.

When there is no observer

In the event that, for practical reasons, the research design does not envisage the presence of an observer (a choice not recommended), the moderator should:

- Take note – even in an unstructured form – of the main interaction mechanisms indicated below, paying particular attention to compiling a more structured observational note immediately after the conclusion of the focus group.
- Have the discussion session video-recorded, so as to observe non-verbal behaviour and interactions after the session (see section 7.4). Although a video camera can create more inhibitions, especially if it is managed by a cameraman, several authors claim that its influence is equivalent to that of a simple recorder (Krueger and Casey, 2000). In any event, if the research staff decides to videotape the discussion, it may be useful to use two cameras, in order to record all the participants seated in a circle.

8.2 The control of information reliability

General features

To gather information on the type of interaction that develops among the actors and to control how this affects the quality of the results of the research, the observer can carry out a series of activities both during the group discussion and subsequently (immediately after the meeting or during the transcription and analysis of information). As detailed in section 1.2, social representations are 'thoughts in movement'. For this reason, paying attention to group dynamics allows the dialogic and interactive process that underlies the formation of the shared social knowledge to be explored (Puchta and Potter, 2004: 9–20; Barbour, 2007: 35; Carey and Asbury, 2012: 28; Halkier, 2017: 394–8).

The position of the participants

First of all, at the beginning of the discussion, he/she can draw a map of the positions occupied by the moderator (M), by himself/herself (O), and by the various participants (Krueger, 1998: 77). This can be used to remember in the analysis their arrangement in the circle and to check if this influenced the way in which, during the discussion, those present intervened or interacted with the other members of the group. Moreover, the moderator could administer to participants a questionnaire to collect their socio-demographic information.

In the field

The observer can take a very simple note at the beginning of each focus group, which identifies the various participants seated at the table. The numbering usually starts from the moderator's right.

(Continued)

191

Participants:

1. male, 23 years old, lives in Florence as a transfer student, a university student of medicine;

2. female, 25 years old, lives in Florence as a transfer student, a university student in economics;

3. male, 22 years old, has lived in Florence for some years with his family of origin, a university student of literature;

4. male, 25 years old, lives in Florence with his family of origin, a university student of physiotherapy;

5. male, 24 years old, has always lived in Florence with his family of origin, a university student of psychology;

6. female, 25 years old, lives in Florence as a transfer student, a university student of physics.

The adjacencies

Second, the observer should take into account not only what is said but also how it is said, for whom it is said, and in which communicative activity types. 'In the focus group, indeed, the discourse is always addressed to somebody but that it also can be considered as a response to previous discourse, which has occurred before and elsewhere. This […] means that the observer should consider the way in which discourse is constructed: how participants interpret each other's discourse, how they link their own discourse with the discourse of the other participants, how they create new and original ways of putting a certain argument into words, how they bring certain topics to the floor, develop and transform them in the course of their discussion, how they come to agree or disagree with certain topics, etc.' (Marková et al., 2007: 49).

To reconstruct the flow of interaction, the observer can resort to an adjacency matrix (Trobia, 2005: 57), which shows in each cell the number of times each participant has spoken to one of the other group members or has reacted to his/her intervention. Table 8.1 provides a hypothetical example. The observer could not compile this type of matrix instantaneously during the discussion. However, during the discussion, the observer can start tracing it, filling in a simpler matrix in which the number of times a participant talks to another are counted with a cross. In the analysis, the table will be filled in in more detail.

Table 8.1 Adjacency matrix

	Participant 1	Participant 2	Participant 3	Participant 4	Participant 5	Participant 6	Participant 7	Total
Participant 1		2	0	0	0	0	0	2
Participant 2	4		0	12	0	3	1	20
Participant 3	1	3		0	0	0	3	7
Participant 4	1	11	0		0	7	6	25
Participant 5	2	0	0	0		1	0	3
Participant 6	0	4	0	8	2		2	16
Participant 7	0	0	3	8	0	0		11
Total	8	20	3	28	2	11	12	84

Source: Elaboration from Trobia, 2005: 57

In this matrix (see Table 8.1), initiators of a communication are in the rows and the recipients/reagents are in the columns: the table shows that Participant 2 talked 4 times to Participant 1, while Participant 1 talked to Participant 2 only 2 times. The matrix marginals provide the number of times a participant intervened to contact another (marginal in the column), or a participant intervened because he/she was stimulated by another (marginal in the row).

This matrix could be further elaborated and have some variants. For example, the researcher could consider direct acts of people to themselves (e.g. shame or self-talk), thus filling the diagonal cells as well (Trobia, 2005: 57–8).

Another useful approach is to include the moderator as an actor of the focus group to show the number of times he/she has addressed a participant or one of those present has reacted to his/her stimulus.

Starting from the above adjacency matrix, the observer can produce a graphic representation of the interactions during a discussion (e.g. using a sociogram – see section 11.1), in order to characterize the forms of interaction established among the members of the group, and the direction and density of interactions between two participants. In this way, it is possible to identify the structure of the interactions, as well as the position of each individual in the group. A table matrix can summarize the entire discussion, or it can refer to a single section of the focus group (in which case it could be repeated several times during the same discussion). Indeed, the relationships between the participants may take different forms on the basis of the topic dealt with (Acocella, 2008: 74–5).

We will discuss this later in the book in the chapter on analysis (see section 11.1). Here, suffice it to say that the role of the observer does not concern only the specific moment of the session. Indeed, as detailed (see section 8.1), the observer should already be involved in the research design phase to develop the appropriate observation tools to be used during the discussion. He/she should also be involved at the end of the group discussion in finalizing the documentary material that will be used for the transcription, sharing observations and field notes with the moderator. Finally, the observer should be involved in the analysis of empirical material collected to process information related to the relational dimension.

The participants' interactive profiles

However, to identify the characteristics of the participants it is not sufficient to rely on interactive dynamics. Indeed, from the information gathered by the adjacency matrix, we can only state that participants 2, 4 and 6 often interacted with each other. For this reason, the observer can also enrich and clarify the profiles of the participants by observing their non-verbal behaviour and the way in which they deal with the various topics. 'The participants are heterogeneous subjects: they adopt different positions and change them.

In doing so they use different forms of socially shared knowledge. The positions from which a participant speaks affects relationships with other participants in various ways' (Marková et al., 2007: 49).

For this purpose, the observer can use a table prepared before the discussion, which indicates various possible interactive profiles that can emerge in the discussion and classify them (see Table 8.2).

Table 8.2 Types of interactive profile

Type	Participant
A: Leader	4 and 6
B: Disinterested	5
C: Cultured	7
D: Curious	
E: Expert	2
F: Hurried	
G: Shy	1
H: Alleged expert	
I: Excluded	3

Source: Elaboration from Acocella, 2008: 77

Like the adjacency table matrix (see Table 8.1), the description of the participants' interactive profiles can also summarize the progress of the entire meeting or refer to individual parts (therefore, it can be repeated several times during the same discussion). Indeed, the way in which participants behave can change during the discussion in relation to the topic treated or to the behaviours assumed by the other members of the group. Roles and profiles are not fixed characteristics of the people but are on the contrary negotiated throughout a focus group discussion (Smithson, 2000: 109; Liamputtong, 2011: 16–18; Hennink, 2014: 26–7). In other words, the interactive profiles can be considered as discursive roles, since they are the result of contingent dynamics.

It is also to be considered that the observer's opinion on the profiles is personal: there is no 'objective' criterion with which to attribute to a participant the qualification of leader or expert. To reduce the impact of subjectivity, sharing opinions with the moderator at the end of the meeting is appropriate (see section 7.4). This activity will also be useful for joint evaluation of how the moderator behaved in managing the various personalities, taking into account the intrapersonal dynamics and the relational risks that will be illustrated in the next chapters (see section 11.1).

Group dynamics

The information collected so far is useful in providing information on the amount, intensity and form of the interaction. To enrich the characteristics of the type of interaction and understand the way in which they influence the discussion, the observer can point out other useful elements on group dynamics, in order to identify eventual reliability problems in the formation of participants' judgements (Hogg and Tindale, 2001; Forsyth, 2014). The observer can facilitate this task by using also in this case a table prepared before the discussion, which identifies various possible communicative and cognitive risks of a group interaction (see Table 8.3).

Table 8.3 Legend of group dynamics (example of research on immigration integration)

Type	Among participants	On the topic
Subordination	From 4 to 1	Always
Conflict	Between 4 and 7	On risky behaviour
Subgroup formation	5	On the definition of the concept of integration of immigrants
Agreement	Between 6 and 4	On the issue of immigrants
Acquiescence (towards the moderator)	5	
Displacement of the conflict		
Disagreement	4	Always
Theorization		
Conformity with social norms	6 and 2	On the question of life in the neighbourhood
Role confusion (towards the moderator)		

Source: Elaboration from Acocella, 2008: 78

In Table 8.3, space may be provided to indicate the various participants involved in the particular dynamics and under what circumstances this occurred. Also in this case, in the table it is appropriate to provide some blank rows to include dynamics and interactions not foreseen during the tuning of the instruments and which emerged during the discussion.

In the field

As an example of the main dynamics being traced by an observer, we can mention a research on stereotypes in the dress code of young Western women and young Muslim women (Guizzardi, 2009). The discussion was aimed at deepening the cultural conditioning or freedom of young people, in the construction of their own image.

Table 8.4 Legend of group dynamics (vocational secondary school)

Dynamics	Involved participants	Topic of the interaction
Agreement	1, 4, 6, 8	Members of Western societies are much freer than those of non-Western societies
	4, 5, 6, 7, 8	For us it is a personal choice whether to let ourselves be influenced or not; they are forced by their parents and by the State
Subgroup formation	Two subgroups	In our society imitation counts more than compulsion
Coupling	8, 1	Different constraints (we have social constraints that are not life-threatening, while they have more dangerous constraints)
Displacement of the conflict	8	The veil from a constriction becomes a habit
	1, 4, 6, 8	The veil is worn for the culture
Conformity to social norms	All participants	In many Islamic populations there are so many problems (hunger, wars, dictatorships etc.), so that maybe people don't even think about the veil

Source: Elaboration from Acocella, 2009: 80

As Table 8.4 shows, students attending vocational schools agreed on the stereotype that members of Western societies are much freer than those of non-Western societies (see Agreement). But in any event a subgroup was formed on the fact that, in Western culture, imitation

(Continued)

prevails rather than compulsion (see Subgroup formation). There was also strong agreement on the fact that while in the West a person can choose to be influenced or not by others, in Islamic countries women are forced to make a specific choice by parents and the State (see Agreement). There was an attempt by a student to point out that, at the end, the veil can transform from constriction to a simple habit; however, in the discussion this attempt did not find success among other participants, who stressed the importance of cultural conditioning (see Displacement of the conflict). Finally, common sense prevailed in a conformist way on the consideration that Islamic populations face so many problems (hunger, wars, dictatorships, etc.), that 'maybe people don't even think about the veil' (see Conformity to social norms). In contrast, two students argued that in the West it is easier to escape social constraints because people do not 'risk their life', while in Islamic countries people have more dangerous constraints (see Coupling).

Table 8.5 Legend of group dynamics (secondary school of humanities)

Dynamics	Involved participants	Topic of the interaction
Agreement	2, 3, 6 and 7	The social conditioning/personal freedom binomial is also valid in the West
	2, 6, 7	In Italy women have fought for their freedom, but today some TV programmes have returned to using the image of women instrumentally
Subgroup formation	Females vs Males	In the West, prevails the social conditioning
Conformity to social norms	2 and 7	Even in the West there are strong constraints due to fashion, the influence of peer groups and cultural traditions
Disagreement	2 and 5 vs 6	The burka is the XS size of Western women

Source: Elaboration from Acocella, 2009: 80

As shown in Table 8.5, the theme was approached differently by the students of humanities schools. Agreement was reached on the fact that the binomial social conditioning/personal freedom applies even in the West in the construction of one's own image (see Agreement). In some moments, women were opposed to men, arguing that the social conditioning prevails in Western societies (see Subgroup formation). Three female students also argued that, although in Italy women have struggled for their freedom, today some TV programmes have returned to using the image of women instrumentally (see Agreement). One student also stated 'The burka is the XS size of Western women', but on this point two other students have expressed strong disagreement (see Disagreement). The debate also revealed the agreement of two students, a man and a woman, on the fact that even in the West there are strong constraints due to fashion, the influence of peer groups and cultural traditions (Acocella, 2009: 66–7).

The example provided gives an effective picture of how the analysis of group dynamics can be an integral part of the analysis of the content of a focus group. In particular it allows the research group to recover synergy in the formulation of ideas, evaluating whether and how the interactions contribute to structure of the emerged information (Halkier, 2017: 406–7; Frisina, 2018: 190). In other words, the observing activity should consider 'phenomena of agreement-disagreement, as well as all the discursive means that are used to reach states of mutual understanding' (Marková et al., 2007: 49).

Indeed, interactions between the participants form both a means of generating information as well as a focus of analysis. As Sheila Kitzinger (1994b: 112–17) outlines, talking of group effects in general is impossible and one should rather examine the composition of the groups and how the characteristics of any particular group may influence what is said. Instead of disregarding the information gathered from group settings, we need to acknowledge the different types of discourses that may be expressed in the 'public' arena (Cyr, 2019: 79–80).

The moderator's strategies

So far, only the interaction among group members participating in the discussion has been considered. However, the moderator also plays an important role in the discussion, and therefore in the process of producing the results. As detailed in section 7.2, he/she performs many functions in fostering discussion and interaction or clarifying participants' statements. Hence, it would be appropriate to consider as well the role played by this actor to highlight if and how it affects the results.

To this end, the observer can gather information on the moderator's mode of conduct and on the strategies that he/she has adopted to perform his/her functions. Also, to facilitate his/her work, the observer can prepare in advance a table in which to report when and with whom the moderator has used these strategies (see Table 8.6).

Table 8.6 Observation of the strategies adopted by the moderator (example of research on immigration integration)

Strategies		On the topic	Towards whom
Strategies for stimulating the discussion	Exercise of sentence ordering proposed by the researcher/ moderator	At the beginning	All participants
	Articulation of the discussion starting from cards containing phrases proposed by the researcher/ moderator	At the beginning	All participants
	Projective tools (thematic vignettes)	For the reconstruction of risky behaviour	All participants
	Request for a pause for reflection on what has emerged from the discussion		
	Reminder requests for the discussion	For all the topics	4
	Opaque tools (comment on stories)		
Strategies for clarifying information	Questions for clarification	For social life in the neighbourhood	7
	Questions for interpretation		
	Questions for further information		

Strategies		On the topic	Towards whom
	Give incorrect interpretations	For the expression 'integration of immigrants'	7 and 5
	Request to classify the answers		
	Request to order the answers	For the expression 'integration of immigrants'	All participants
	Observe (or solicit) interaction among participants to clarify obscure meanings		
Strategies to foster interaction	Interaction request questions		
	'Round-table'	To express their opinion on social life in the neighbourhood	1
	Directive leadership	For all the topics	4
	Probing for expert		
	Probing to moderate a leader		
	Probing for alleged expert	To express their opinion on immigrants	5

Source: Elaboration from Acocella, 2008: 79

8.3 Weighting the topics covered

Why weight up a theme?

The collection and analysis of information on the type of interaction that is established among the participants has as its second purpose the attribution of different 'weights' to the various topics covered. Not all the participants will intervene on all the themes or with the same intensity.

The general tendency is instead to provide the results obtained through a focus group without taking into account the fact that they were produced in a group discussion. Indeed, a list of themes that emerged during the meeting is often presented, flanked by extracts isolated from the collective debate – which therefore lose the complexity, dynamism and interactivity of the context in which they were produced. For this reason, Sheila Kitzinger notes that 'reading some such reports it is hard to believe that there was ever more than one person in the room at the same time' (1994b: 104).

However, in the course of the analysis or presentation of the results, a topic addressed only by a few people or hinted at and then immediately abandoned cannot be considered and reported in the same way as another that was agreed by all members of the group, perhaps even with a certain fervour.

Keeping these aspects in mind during the gathering and analysis of information, as well as in the final report, should not lead us to believe that the aims of those using this technique are being betrayed. Indeed, a more statistical use of information is justified by the fact that when the focus group is used, it is important to note what the group has said and how, and not the individual opinions that have emerged. Ultimately, it should always be recalled that the focus group unit of analysis is not the individual participants, but the group as a whole.

Therefore, when the results of a focus group are presented, the framework negotiated by the participants and the interactive context in which the responses were produced should be taken into account. In this sense, no single intervention can be extrapolated from the general group discourse, since it will acquire full meaning only in the general framework of a collective signification.

In order to attribute a different 'weight' to the various themes that emerged during the discussion and to highlight the group dimension of the various opinions, the observer can determine:

1. the extent of a theme (or its appearance);
2. the frequency with which a theme (or its appearance) was treated;
3. who launched a theme (or its appearance) and how it was launched.

The extent of a theme

Richard A. Krueger and Mary A. Casey clarify that 'extensiveness is how many different people said something' (2000: 136). The observer can detect the extensiveness of both a theme and some aspects of it; the first type of detection is more immediate (even if it will not provide information on how a topic is dealt with) and can be easily performed during the discussion.

The observer can prepare a table (see Table 8.7) in which the topics included in the track are listed in the rows and the names of the participants in the columns. As soon as the discussion begins, the observer marks the names of the participants in the cell at the top of each column; during the debate, he/she marks with an X the cell situated at the intersection of the column of the intervening participant and the row of the covered topic.

Table 8.7 Extensiveness of a theme (example of research on immigration integration)

	Participant 1	Participant 2	Participant 3	Participant 4	Participant 5	Participant 6	Participant 7
Definition of 'integration of immigrants'		X	X	X	X	X	X
Fear of immigrants		X	X	X		X	X
Distrust of the police	X	X		X		X	
Difficulty in life in the neighbourhood	X		X	X			
Relationships with social workers *		XX			X	X	

Note: * Unexpected topic

Source: Elaboration from Acocella, 2008: 81

It is important to be ready to recognize and report new aspects not foreseen by the researcher and spontaneously raised by the participants (Dawson et al., 1993: 42; Puchta and Potter, 2004: 111–14; Hennink, 2014: 196). In this regard, it is useful to provide blank rows in the table in order to insert new topics not previously previewed and emerged during the group discussion, signalling with a particular mark the cell corresponding to the intersection between the new theme and the person who proposed it (see Table 8.7).

During the analysis, through replay of the discussion and reading of the transcripts, the observer can follow the same procedure in relation to the various aspects that emerged on each theme.

This kind of analysis makes it possible to highlight the extent to which a given theme or aspect is considered important by the group, taking the minority positions or opinions into consideration as well. Obviously, when interpreting information, the way in which a theme has been treated and the overall process of formulating the judgement of group members (see section 11.1) must also be taken into consideration. In this way, it will be possible to highlight if particular dynamics (such as conformism or compliance) have occurred that may have compromised the quality of the information.

The frequency of a theme

According to Richard A. Krueger and Marie A. Casey, 'frequency is how many times something is said' (2000: 136), which is certainly a property to be taken into account when establishing the subjects to which the group gives more importance. Obviously, when calculating the frequency of a theme (or its appearance), its extensiveness should also be taken into consideration. Indeed, if 'we have had groups in which one person kept returning to the same theme, [...] although the theme was mentioned a fair amount, it was brought up by only one person' (Krueger and Casey, 2000: 136).

The observer can better interpret the value of this property by bearing in mind the type of interaction and the dynamics produced in the group during the discussion. Indeed, it may happen that some aspects do not emerge during the discussion because the participants do not want to talk about them or because they have not been adequately stimulated, not because they do not consider them important (Corrao, 2000: 60). It may therefore be appropriate also to consider what did not emerge, even though it was expected.

The observer can signal the frequency of a theme or some of its aspects using a sheet like Table 8.8.

Table 8.8   Frequency of a theme

Neighbourhood problems	Frequency
Traffic	12
Immigrants	10
Drug dealing	5
Aggression	3
Police	3
Robberies	1

Source: Elaboration from Acocella, 2008: 84

The source of a theme

In order to attribute weight to the various themes, it should be noted whether they were elicited by the moderator or spontaneously emerged during the discussion. In the latter case, the frame of reference of the participants and the issues that occupy a more central position in their daily lives emerge with greater clarity and can therefore be considered more relevant for the group.

However, the observer must also try to keep the group dynamics and the influences derived from particular interactions under control. Unlike the fidelity checks highlighted in the previous paragraph, which necessarily pertain to every single discussion, when the observer tries to attribute different 'weights' to the topics discussed, he/she can use this information in order to have an overall picture of all the focus groups conducted. Indeed, the extensiveness, the frequency and the source of a theme (or one of its aspects) that emerged from a group discussion can be compared with what has emerged from other discussions, so that this information can give an overview of the most cited topics in the research.

8.4 Non-verbal communication

One kind of information that can only be collected during the discussion (and therefore only by the observer) is that relating to non-verbal behaviour: pauses, mood changes, enthusiasm, distraction, spontaneity and so on. It is to these that the observer must pay the utmost attention during the discussion (Krueger, 1998: 73; Zammuner, 2003: 208; Frisina, 2010: 83).

In the following chapters, we will go further into how non-verbal communication conveys interaction and group relationships (see section 11.1). In this chapter, we will focus on the notes that the observer can take on these behaviours, explaining what types of acts should be observed and how to classify them.

This task is crucial and should be carried out with care because non-verbal behaviours convey a great deal of information that cannot be lost (Hennink, 2014: 75; Cyr, 2019: 94). This is especially true if – as in most cases – the focus group is not videotaped.

Non-verbal behaviours have four components (Gorden, 1980; Acocella, 2008):

- proxemic;
- chronemic;
- kinesic;
- paralinguistic.

The proxemic

The proxemic component refers to the use of interpersonal space to communicate. It can signal the degree of attention, interest and embarrassment of the participants: for example, bending forward while listening to another participant is a sign of interest; moving away from the table and looking away while others speak may indicate little interest and so on.

The chronemic

The chronemic component is about the pauses and the silences that are more or less long and can signal embarrassment or moments of reflection: for example, stopping for a moment while talking can signal the need to reflect and find words to communicate in the best way what one is thinking; a long silence can indicate a moment of embarrassment and so on.

The kinesic

The kinesic component mainly affects the movements of the face or body and can communicate the emotions and accompany the words: for example, redness of the face can indicate embarrassment or anger at what is being said or heard; shifting in one's chair or nervously moving hands and legs while talking can signal nervousness and so on.

The paralinguistic

The paralinguistic component concerns the tone of the voice, the emphasis of an affirmation and so on. It can help to establish the degree of involvement and intensity of an affirmation: for example raising the voice can indicate that the person speaking is very involved, whilst lowering of the voice can signal a moment of shame.

How to record non-verbal behaviours

All these non-verbal behavioural components can constitute signals, usually unconsciously emitted, relating to the mood of the participants. It is not possible to assign them an absolute value, but the observer can try to understand their meaning starting from the particular communicative context in which they took place (Matoesian and Coldren, 2002: 484).

Non-verbal communication is therefore strictly connected to verbal communication. As the type of interaction established during the discussion, this also helps to explain the motivations underlying each communication act, facilitating their understanding since different phrases can assume different meanings according to the non-verbal codes adopted (Diana and Montesperelli, 2005: 24–5; Forsyth, 2014: 415–16). Moreover, they can give indications on the degree of fidelity of an answer (e.g. in relation to the level of sincerity, attention etc.). Finally, non-verbal communication can be used for the attribution of different 'weights' to the various topics covered, since it can highlight the degree of embarrassment, strength, fervour and so on of the various participants in relation to the various opinions expressed.

To take note of non-verbal behaviour during the meeting, the observer can use a table such as Table 8.9. Moreover, in the transcription of the discussion, these non-verbal behaviours will be reported by an appropriate symbology, which will be examined in depth later (see section 10.1).

Table 8.9 Observation sheet for non-verbal behavioural components (example of research on immigration integration)

Component of non-verbal behaviour	Classification of various non-verbal behaviours	Participant	On the topic
Proxemics	Move away from the table and look elsewhere	5	On the topic: risky behaviour
	Shift on the chair		
	Approach the table	3	For social life in the neighbourhood: 'When I lived in Torpignattara [He approaches the table]'
	Other:		

(Continued)

Table 8.9 (Continued)

Component of non-verbal behaviour	Classification of various non-verbal behaviours	Participant	On the topic
Chronemics	Long break		
	Pause	2	For social life in the neighbourhood: '... life was not easy in the neighbourhood'
	Silence	All participants	For the expression 'integration of immigrants'
	Accelerated	4	While expressing a judgement on immigrants: 'you have to limit the number' [accelerated]
	Slowed down		
	Other:		
Kinesics	Embarrassment		
	Anger	5	While expressing a judgement on immigrants: '[anger] I'm afraid to walk at night alone in the neighbourhood because there are too many immigrants'
	Confusion		
	Other:		
	Showing agreement without speaking	5 and 7	For the expression 'integration of immigrants': Participant 7: 'For me integration means sharing everything ... even culture'. Participant 5: Nodding

Component of non-verbal behaviour	Classification of various non-verbal behaviours	Participant	On the topic
	Showing disagreement without speaking	1	While expressing a judgement on immigrants: Participant 2: 'I believe that immigrants serve our country'. Participant 1: Shakes his head
	Other:		
Paralinguistics	Emphasis		
	High voice	6	For life in the neighbourhood: 'I feel good in Torpignattara!!!'
	Low voice	4	For the topic on immigrants: 'Yes, but they are too many'
	Overlap	5 and 7	On immigrant criminality: Participant 7: 'I have a lot of friends who are immigrants'. Participant 5: (at the same time) 'Yes, but immigrants are too many!'
	Other:		

Source: Elaboration from Acocella (2008: 86–7)

Further reading

Hogg, M.A. and Tindale, S. (eds) (2001) *Blackwell Handbook of Social Psychology: Group Processes.* Oxford: Blackwell.

This handbook of social psychology provides a comprehensive overview of theory and research at the intra-individual, interpersonal, intergroup, and group levels.

Pennington, D.C. (2014) *The Social Psychology of Behaviour in Small Groups.* New York: Taylor & Francis.

The book is an accessible text suitable for undergraduates studying social psychology. A specific area is devoted to observation of behaviours in the group and the main issues to be considered when planning observation.

Exercises

1. You are conducting a focus group in which the participants talk in fits and starts and continuously interrupt each other. What kind of group dynamics would you attribute to these forms of interactions?

2. In planning a focus group, the research staff decides to use some vignettes to stimulate the discussion on a sensitive topic. What tool do you plan to use during the focus group to observe the moderator's behaviour in the use of the vignettes and the effect of this probing on participants?

9

Running the Focus Group

After detailing the role of the moderator and the observer, we now focus on what happens within the group in a collective discussion session. Indeed, each session develops in a unique way: even if the same people were called to meet again and discuss the same topics, without memory of the previous occasion, the session would almost certainly develop differently. This factor must be taken into consideration because it is precisely the group dynamics that influence the information produced during a focus group.

In the chapter, therefore, we will examine how, during group discussion by a focus group, a new collective identity is affirmed, which is at the same time the product and the condition of what each participant does and says in a session. After discussing the strategies that, during the group discussion, lead the participants to move from a subjective identity to a specific member of the group, we will describe the intrapersonal and interpersonal group dynamics that can influence the content produced during a focus group meeting, highlighting the advantages and disadvantages of the interaction. Finally, we will analyse the power dynamics within the groups.

--------- Chapter goals ---------

- *Knowledge*: group dynamics operating in a focus group session.
- *Applying knowledge and understanding*: how intrapersonal and interpersonal group dynamics work.
- *Making judgements*: being aware of the cognitive and communicative risks connected to interaction and the power dynamics that operate in the groups.

9.1 Becoming a group: the focus group rules and tasks

When a focus group is effective, during a discussion session, the participants should not act as independent entities but as part of the same social group (see sections 5.1 and 7.2). In other words, a group identity should prevail over individual identities. Therefore, a 'socially structured constellations of participants, who adopt different roles with a social [...] distribution of responsibilities' (Marková et al., 2007: 101) should be formed.

The formation of a social group

At this point, we can try to answer this question: how can a group be formed?

The moderator plays a very important role in this process. Indeed, his/her presence not only contributes to the establishment of a friendly atmosphere, but above all is involved in the assignment of certain tasks and norms that should be respected throughout the discussion. The acceptance of these norms and tasks commonly represents for the participants the transition from a subjective identity to a group identity as a member. Therefore, this is a crucial step in which, as detailed in see section 5.1, a participant: on the one hand sees himself/herself hetero-categorized from the outside (i.e. at least by the moderator and the observer) as a member of the group; and on the other hand self-categorizes as a group member.

The new categorization influences the individual self-esteem and the behaviour of the participants, who will be oriented both to studying others and to being accepted as members of the group.

Group formation at the beginning of the focus group

The formation of the group therefore takes place from the first minutes of the meeting and becomes clear even then in the spatial arrangement of the participants. The moderator suggests that the subjects involved should sit in a circle or around a table. In the initial phase of the meeting, the moderator also offers light refreshments and carries out an initial warming-up phase, asking the participants to introduce themselves (see section 5.5). This phase allows an attentive but relaxed atmosphere to be created, which will be the reference frame for the entire debate (Bloor et al., 2001: 60).

The initial presentation also allows participants to understand that their presence in the discussion is not random. Indeed, it is probable that – even with the moderator's help – the characteristics that the participants have in common will immediately emerge, identifying the social category that they represent in that focus group (see section 5.1).

Expert advice

Offering refreshments at the beginning of the meeting is important in order to 'break the ice' and 'warm up' the environment. Indeed, during the refreshment, the guests will begin to familiarize with each other and with the moderator. The moderator can also use this moment to develop a first impression of the individual participants (Krueger, 1988: 19–20).

The rules of the group

A second important moment is the moderator's introduction of the topic of discussion and of the basic rules of the debate. This moment is crucial for the success of the whole session. Indeed, this introduction depends on both the understanding and interiorization of the fundamental debate rules, and the acquisition and elaboration by the group of the objectives of the meeting (Greenbaum, 2000: 35–7).

The basic rule of focused discussion is founded on the principle of free expression and can be summarized in the recommendation and commitment to leave space for everyone's communication (see section 7.2).

Another important rule concerns time management. In a more or less explicit way, the moderator must give space to all the participants and then divide the available time, which will be limited, according to the criterion of fairness.

In the field

The following excerpt exemplifies both contestation and defence of the 'rules of the game' during a focus group conducted by Rachel Ayrton (2019). Some participants had previously challenged Participant 1 (P1) about the length of his contributions, which they considered to be inequitable given the parameters of time.

P1: I haven't finished. You want me to finish, or that is okay?

Moderator: Oh, yeah, if you want to say something [particularly about that image …].

P1: Because I was never allowed to finish … my contribution.

(Continued)

> P2: I'm sorry – it's because we have a limited time, you know?
>
> P1: It's not about the time you are talking, it is about how much can you give as a good contribution to this research ... when you talk more it means you have more information. And if you talk less it means you are satisfied with the few information that you give. (Ayrton, 2019: 327)

Other general norms, such as those related to cordiality and kindness, will remain implicit. For example, the rule that it is impolite for a participant to turn his/her back on others or to leave prematurely without warning will be taken for granted.

In general, it could be argued that if these norms help the group to regulate the interactions and to coordinate collective activities, they also provide a way of judging the ability of the individuals involved to be among other people in a civilized way. For these reasons, those who transgress them will be considered rude or accused of deviance by other participants (Cooper et al., 2001: 261).

The task of the group

The assignment of a common task is also fundamental to helping the formation of the group (Kerr and Park, 2001). Indeed, for the participants in the focus group, the sharing of a common purpose is one of the elements that can encourage the transition from a subjective identity to another specific identity as a group member (see section 5.1).

The main task of the group is to talk profitably on the topic of investigation by expressing their ideas and opinions.

Following the typology proposed by Rupert Brown (1988), in general we can state that the task required of the focus group is:

- *Unitary (i.e. not divisible).* It does not require subdivision into sub-tasks, since it is necessary that the entire discussion group pays attention to the topic of investigation and expresses its impressions and experiences according to a mechanism of concatenation.
- *Optimizing.* The participants are not asked to achieve the goals of the meeting in the shortest possible time, but rather to express their thoughts in detail, elaborating in both a private and and a collective way.
- *Subjunctive and additive together.* The task must be carried out and completed by each participant, expressing his/her own ideas. The individual

contributions, however, will have a synergistic effect on subsequent interventions, suggesting ideas or memories that lead to the formation of new positions and ideas stimulated by the collective debate.

The phases of the task

The articulation of the task assigned to the discussion group will follow three phases:

- first, orientation to the problem of investigation and to the rules of discussion;
- second, and centrally, where the theme is treated in a more profound way;
- third, a control phase, in which the moderator tries to summarize the main ideas that have emerged, being helped by the participants in a sort of feedback process.

Instrumental dimension and socio-emotional dimension

The task assigned to the group also includes two closely interrelated components:

- the instrumental dimension, related to the understanding of the topic of discussion and the return of useful information;
- the socio-emotional dimension, concerning behaviours aimed at dissolving internal tensions and increasing interpersonal relationships.

According to the theory of Robert Freed Bales (1950), each group tries to develop the two components, so that the instrumental activities will tend to be compensated by the socio-emotional ones. In this way, the deepening of the topic of discussion will proceed simultaneously with the development of social relations. We will discuss this in more detail in Chapter 11. Here, it should be pointed out only that, in the focus group, the discussion of the topic of discussion is never independent of the interaction, and the expression of emotions can be more or less instrumental in carrying out this task (Kelly, 2001: 168–9).

9.2 Intrapersonal dynamics

The group is constituted on reciprocal relationships among different people. The group, therefore, is not independent of the individual subjects that compose it. However, the same individual members are influenced by their own perceptions as members (Asch, 1951; Festinger, 1957; Hogg and Tindale, 2001; Forsyth, 2014). In this sense, in the group there may be a change in the conception of the self of individuals, such that the identity of each can be considered to be characterized by a personal and a social matrix. According to John Charles Turner (1982):

- the personal matrix is linked to the individual or idiosyncratic characteristics of the people who interact with each other;
- the social matrix is connected to the group to which the individual belongs, since each person will tend to consider himself/herself, in a certain sense, interchangeable with respect to the other members of the group.

For this reason, the personal characteristics of individuals will assume a particular social value, creating elementary and complex dynamics of attraction and repulsion within the group. In this section, we focus on the intrapersonal dimensions of the focus group discussion, mainly examining how the personal characteristics of individual participants can influence group formation and dynamics.

Socio-demographic characteristics

Several scholars have focused on the importance of some basic properties as regards their influence on group interaction processes, such as age, gender, cultural level and social position (Kelly, 2001: 171–3). As detailed in section 5.2, even in focus group sessions the internal heterogeneity among the participants of a group could lead to inhibiting effects on debate and the free expression of ideas (Liamputtong, 2011: 80–2; Carey and Asbury, 2012: 28; Hennink, 2014: 30–3).

In the field

In the course of research on juvenile delinquency (Cataldi, 2016), in a focus group session, there was a young lawyer participant who, as he was elegantly dressed and self-confident, presented himself as a successful person. Another young participant, an aspiring lawyer, felt attracted to this figure and during the first part of the focus group identified himself with this participant, considering him a model and thus providing very similar answers.

Thus socio-demographic characteristics can influence the intrapersonal dynamics that develop during group discussion, since participants who perceive themselves or are perceived by other participants as in a stronger position can trigger mechanisms of supremacy or subordination (Kerr and Park, 2001: 126; Cyr, 2019: 69–70).

In the composition of the group, the researcher can assess the possible impact of some socio-demographic characteristics of participants on group dynamics. However, despite these precautions, in the design of the focus group, it is impossible to foresee all the interpersonal dynamics that will develop in the discussion. Therefore, it is the moderator's task to find the most appropriate ways to intervene in such situations, evaluating how they can produce effects of inhibition or excessive identification (see sections 7.2 and 8.2).

Types of personality

Intrapersonal dynamics are also influenced by the personality of the people interacting. Psychologists identify various criteria for classifying personality types. Among these, the following aspects seem relevant to our purposes:

- interpersonal orientation;
- social sensitivity;
- the tendency towards supremacy or dependence;
- emotional stability.

By 'interpersonal orientation' we mean the way in which people act in the presence of other individuals (Shaw, 1981; Cooper et al., 2001; Vogt and Colvin, 2003). Based on this criterion, for example, we can label a participant as 'conformist', 'authoritarian', 'condescending', and so on.

The 'social sensitivity' of a person depends on the ability to perceive the needs, emotions and preferences of other people. Based on this criterion, for example, we can distinguish between 'empathic', 'sociable', 'independent', and so on.

The 'tendency towards supremacy' concerns the intensity with which an individual tends to affirm himself/herself. Some examples are the propensity to assertiveness, domination, individual predominance and superiority.

Finally, the 'emotional stability' of a person refers to his/her ability to control feelings in specific situations.

In a focus group, these traits will tend to emerge and may influence the level of interaction among the participants.

Moreover, various problems can arise due to the incompatibility among some individuals. In the literature there are several suggestions in this regard, which also describe in caricatured terms some characteristics of more problematic personalities. For example, Richard A. Krueger and Mary A. Casey (2000: 111–15) describe four types of personality that may jeopardize the outcome of the group discussion:

- the shy;
- the expert;
- the dominant talker;
- the rambler.

'Shy' individuals, for example, are characterized by their tendency not to intervene during the debate and to be very reserved. Attempts to reassure a shy person may have the opposite effect, making him/her even more reticent.

The 'expert' is someone who knows everything (or thinks he/she knows everything) and tends to intervene on any topic. Within the group, such a person can inhibit the free expression of the other participants, who may feel less informed on some topics.

Expert advice

The presence of a single person with a high level of expertise on the topic hampers the discussion, especially if the other participants do not have the same level of knowledge. It may also happen that, even if he/she presents her/himself as such, the person is not truly expert. The presence of such a person is even more detrimental to interactions, with the risk of misleading the group discussion.

The 'dominant talker' is instead someone chatty who tends to monopolize the collective discussion. It is a figure that we can find in almost all sessions: he/she tends not to let someone else speak, hindering the plurality of ideas and voices.

Finally, Richard A. Krueger and Mary A. Casey (2000: 115) also use the term 'rambler' to denote a person who never reaches the central core of the issue and her/his interventions are characterized by many digressions relating to personal events or marginal themes. This behaviour makes the discussion boring and unfocused, so that other participants lose interest and concentration.

To this gallery of typical characters we can add the figure of the 'hostile' (Cyr, 2019: 79–81), that is, the person who always tends to contradict what has been stated by others. The impact of such a personality can be very negative if it creates internal tensions and the debate ceases to be a pleasant exchange of ideas.

Unlike the socio-demographic characteristics, the personality of the participants can hardly ever be considered *ex-ante* in the composition of the group, since the researcher generally does not know the people before the meeting or otherwise has little information on these characteristics. Moreover, he/she cannot predict what character traits will prevail during group interaction. As a result, the conduct of the moderator is fundamental to the success of the debate: he/she will have to intervene when he/she considers that such intrapersonal dynamics are excessively influencing the group discussion. By adopting the various probing strategies available (see sections 6.2 and 7.2), the moderator will therefore encourage the most reluctant to intervene and curb those who monopolize the discussion.

9.3 Interpersonal dynamics

Interpersonal dynamics are connected to the community dimension of the group. While in intrapersonal dynamics the more personal aspect of participants tends to emerge, in interpersonal relational processes the affirmation of a new collective identity emerges instead, which is simultaneously the product of and the stimulus for individual action.

In the section below, using some tools furnished by social psychology, we will deepen the examination of the group cohesion and relational interdependence that can be produced during a focus group.

Group cohesion

During a focus group, the tools adopted by the moderator to support interaction among participants and group formation are aimed at encouraging internal group cohesion and the comparison of opinions (see section 7.2).

Within a focus group session, group cohesion can be categorized into two interrelated processes:

- the first is triggered by the individual and depends on the extent to which a person is attracted to the group;
- the second starts from the group and depends on the extent to which a group is able to attract a person.

Obviously, in reality, these two processes cannot be separated, but we keep them distinct for expository purposes. Indeed, the first process depends above all on the level of individual motivation to perform the task and tends to vary according to the degree of interest that the proposed topic arouses among the participants. In the second process, cohesion will stem from the group's ability to attract the individual: a passionate debate, for example, is much more likely to induce even the most reluctant persons to talk about themselves, giving them also a sense of security.

The more the topic of the discussion approaches the world of people's lives, the more the group's motivation will increase. In a focus group, this effect is encouraged by the fact that people with a certain familiarity with the investigated phenomenon are invited to the discussion (see section 5.2). This will increase the ability of the participants to discuss and examine the research issue in an appropriate manner in the short time available, encouraging the collection of in-depth, relevant and quality information. Otherwise, they are more likely to be less active, to reason by stereotyping, to give short answers and to remain silent, with the risk that their intervention will not make a significant contribution to the research (Cote-Arsenault and Morrison, 1999: 281; Albanesi, 2004: 50–1).

In the same way, in order to avoid ambiguities due to views that are too distant or irreconcilable, it is helpful that the experiences that participants have had of the object of study are in some way similar or comparable. In a focus group, this is facilitated by the fact that participants share some relevant properties, which identify them as belonging to the same 'social group' (see section 5.2). In this way, even if the discussion takes place among people who meet each other for the first time, they will feel that they have had been in similar situations before because they have experienced a similar professional or social context (Stewart and Shamdasani, 1990: 53; Lorenzi-Cioldi and Clémence, 2001: 320–5). Obviously, in the transition from mere agglomeration to the formation of a community, the moderator also plays an important role: he/she underlines what the participants have in common, thus allowing them to identify the point of view from which they are asked to address the phenomenon (Barbour, 2007: 138).

Finally, the choice of a specific study object based on the criterion of salience also facilitates conversation (see section 6.1), making it more likely that all the research topics can be addressed in depth in the short time available (generally, between one and a half hours and two hours). Indeed, in focus group discussions, interaction often proceeds by associating ideas, which causes constant changes of topics. Newly emerged themes may be abandoned, while others may be explored only in a marginal way. The fact that the discussion is focused on salient aspects therefore increases the possibility that the time available to the participants will be enough for them to reflect and express their opinions on each theme in an appropriate manner (Hennink, 2014: 81–2).

The social/interactive character of emerging information

Various research studies show that in everyday life individual attitudes are affected by the interaction with others (Baldwin, 1895; Mead, 1934; Lazarsfeld et al., 1948; Vygotsky, 1979). Similarly, using the focus group technique, the exchange of ideas and the synergy among individual contributions makes it possible to support the social/interactive nature of emerging information appropriately. Indeed, the information content of the focus group is the result of a 'collective construction' (Smithson, 2000: 109), in which the personal guidelines are also defined *in itinere*, shared and negotiated among all the participants. In other words, in focus groups the opinions are constructed collectively.

As discussed in section 7.2, by developing dialogic relationships, focus group discussion encourages 'internal interaction' rather than 'external interaction' in order to enhance the participants' communicative activities within the group, where forms of socially shared knowledge (e.g. opinions, attitudes, social representations etc.) circulate and are elaborated. An 'internal interaction' can define the communicative interdependence among the participants in terms of their mutual engagement. However, this activity can take different forms. Indeed, as in everyday life, in group discussions, social actors use different forms of socially shared knowledge in the conversation (Barbour, 2007: 35; Frisina, 2018: 204). Moreover, human dialogue can never be reduced to mere transmission of information, because it is always characterized by an open and heterogeneous interplay of multiple meanings and voices in continuous tension.

Concepts and Theories

In a focus group, even if participants establish intersubjective and close relations and even if they share a great deal of knowledge, different tensions may characterize the dialogue. 'There is tension between antinomic but mutually interdependent tendencies in talk; there is tension between the positions of the self and other, between relatively established knowledge and new knowledge, and so on. [In this way], dialogues maintain existing social realities and involve thinking about, imagining and creating new social realities' (Marková et al., 2007: 25–6).

For this reason, we can state that a focus group is a situated communication activity in which it is possible to examine the dialogical nature of socially shared knowledge. Even though discussions involve a homogeneous membership, the group and its members will show heterogeneities of thinking and talking (Liamputtong, 2011: 16–18; Hennink, 2014: 26–7). Furthermore, it is not a discussion context in which individual contributions simply display some pre-established mental states, since the circulation of ideas is closely intertwined with the way in which the participants manage relationships, negotiate their 'positioning' and are emotionally involved in the topic under discussion (Lorenzi-Cioldi and Clémence, 2001: 312).

221

'If the interaction among participants develops smoothly and without excessively directive behaviour by the moderator, the information generated by the discussion can multiply. The group synergy can favour the production of a plurality of positions and stimulate participants to remember forgotten or unconsidered details. Moreover, group discussions often proceed by means of association of ideas. In these cases, a sort of chain effect is created as one intervention paves the way to the next and encourages the formulation of different interpretations on the topic investigated' (Acocella, 2012: 1132). Hence, the individual contributions are transformed in a dialogical process, providing insight into the formation and change of social representations, beliefs and knowledge that circulate in societies (Smithson, 2000: 109; Halkier, 2017: 406–7). Given these assumptions, the focus group technique is particularly suited to obtaining new and unexpected opinions, thereby stimulating researchers' interpretative imaginations.

The cognitive and communicative risks related to the interaction

However, as detailed in section 7.2, interaction and group dynamics do not always unfold consistently. Indeed, several cognitive and communicative risks can emerge during a focus group discussion. In particular, during the response elaboration process, in the formulation of a judgement, 'participants can also activate defensive strategies to protect themselves from the anxiety deriving from being in a group, as well as other strategies aimed at evaluating the advantages or disadvantages of letting themselves freely interact with other people. In these situations, the fear of being judged, to disappoint expectations or to get lost is also quite common' (Acocella, 2012: 1133).

For this reason, some mechanisms are activated that can inhibit the production of diversified ideas during a debate session, which risk limiting the reliability of the information, as well as the quality of the final result. They are:

- conformism and groupthink;
- internalization;
- narrativization;
- polarization of ideas.

Conformism and groupthink

In general, conformism refers to a person's propensity to abide by the group's expectation or that of the majority of the group (Asch, 1951; Campbell et al., 1986; Hogg, 2001). This hampers the creativity and spontaneity of the group, so that expected responses tend to be generated, with the inevitable result of diminishing the usefulness of the focus group and its capacity for involvement.

Conformism usually derives from the fear of being judged. Even if the discussion takes place freely, during a focus group these cognitive mechanisms can lead participants to conform (at least publicly) with the most common opinions in the group, because they are considered socially accepted (Mackie, 1987: 50; Kidd and Parshall, 2000: 294–5). In this way, fear of disapproval enhances majority influence but inhibits minority influence. This will induce the participants to conform with the situation of the discussion and, therefore, their answers will be the product of the opinions expressed by the majority of participants and of the interactions produced by that discussion (Martin and Hewstone, 2001: 226).

At other times, conformism can result from the pressure of social conventions (Marwell and Schmitt, 1967; Bickman, 1974; Hogg, 2001), leading participants to provide more socially desirable and stereotypical answers. Therefore, in these cases, participants try to present themselves in the way that is the most socially acceptable (Liamputtong, 2011: 108; Cyr, 2019: 34–5). This tendency most often acts in an unconscious way and can be triggered both when delicate topics are treated (attitudes and behaviours that violate generally recognized norms, sanctioned or not by the law), and in the presence of tacit norms of the reference group.

In the field

Some desirability mechanisms occurred in research on stereotypes related to the 'social construction of the body' (Acocella, 2009). In a group discussion, some students felt some inhibition in dealing with issues related to one's own behavioural patterns, conforming to the implicit norms of the group or opinions deemed to be more standard. The most conformist responses were found in relation to issues such as the conditioning of fashion, the media and the unwritten rules of society on the way young people build their own social image.

At the extreme of conformism there is groupthink: 'a mode of thinking that people engage in when they are deeply involved in a cohesive in-group, when the members' strivings for unanimity override their motivation to realistically appraise alternative courses of action' (Janis, 1982: 9). Groupthink may produce phenomena such as absolute conformity and the illusion of unanimity, as well as the blocking of new ideas and the formation of negative stereotypes towards outgroup people (Turner and Pratkanis, 1997; Marques et al., 2001; Cyr, 2019: 79–80).

These processes can contaminate the discussion, as they tend to produce a convergence of positions that will inevitably hinder the diversification of opinions. However, social psychologists have demonstrated that conformism and groupthink drastically decrease when a cognitive dissonance arises in the group (Turner and Pratkanis, 1997), such as when a minority presents the same issues to the group from a different point of view or with a wider range of alternatives. According to the 'conversion theory' of Serge Moscovici (1980), both the majority and minority can be a source of social influence if people engage in a bilateral comparison process. In detail, this 'theory predicts that a majority should encourage individuals to focus their attention on the relationship between themselves and members of the majority (interpersonal focus), while a minority should lead to greater attention being focused on the content of the minority's message (message focus)' (Martin and Hewstone, 2001: 214).

On the basis of these principles, where an extremely conformist situation arises in a focus group discussion, the moderator may prefer to value the diversity of positions and support the opinions proposed by the minority of participants to ensure a wider range of information. In this task, he/she can use appropriate probing tools or specific strategies (see section 6.2). For example, with the aim of enriching the level of message processing, the moderator can use the thought-listing technique, in order to enhance the quantity and the quality of divergent thinking.

Other studies have demonstrated that conformism and groupthink increase in ambiguous situations, where participants are more inclined to trust other people's opinions (Allen, 1965; Allen and Levine, 1969; Kerr and Park, 2001: 121–3). Many participants may perceive the context produced by a focus group as ambiguous, since it is unusual and new to them. This is why this defensive strategy is likely to be adopted. The level of ambiguity increases when the topics are of little interest to the participants (McKennell, 1974: 226; Kerr and Park, 2001: 112–16). This is another reason why it is relevant to invite people who are familiar with the topic of discussion.

Internalization

Another influence mechanism is internalization (Maass and Clark, 1983; Albrecht et al., 1993: 56–7). This process is different from compliance. 'Compliance can be said to occur when an individual accepts influence because he hopes to achieve a favourable reaction from another person or group. […] [Instead,] internalization can be said to occur when an individual accepts influence because the content of the induced behaviour – the ideas and actions of which it is composed – is intrinsically rewarding. He adopts the induced behaviour because it is […] useful for the solution of a problem or finds it congenial to his needs' (Kelman, 1958: 53). In 'compliance', the influencing agent's power is based on means-control, while, in 'internaliza-tion', the induced response depends on the credibility of the influencing agent.

During a discussion, this process can introduce some bias when there are different levels of knowledge in the group of the phenomenon under study, inducing some participants to follow the opinions of people considered more experienced. This becomes evident especially when participants lose their creativity and tend to repeat what has already been proposed by the other participants (Albrecht et al., 1993: 56–7).

To avoid this problem occurring, the moderator has several options. First of all, he/she can ask the participants before starting the discussion to write their opinions (as in the nominal group technique and the Delphi method), and then invite them to discuss their ideas publicly. In this way, it will be possible to identify how everyone's opinion, however well-formed, finds continuous reformulation in the group debate and tends to change, adapting to the dynamics of sharing. However, this bias often occurs during the discussion. In these cases, the moderator can use some probing strategies in order to intro-duce different points of view, and thus increase the variability of the informa-tion yielded by the discussion (see section 6.2).

The narrativization of meanings

Some authors also speak of another phenomenon that can occur in focus groups: the narrativization of meanings. This dynamic is based on the tendency to justify the opinions expressed on the basis of social contexts of conflict and consensus that are defined *ad hoc*. Thus, for example, in the formation of ideas on the world and in the narration/interpretation of conflicts a fundamental role is played by the imagination, which can be observed in the common use of fairytale schemata, such as the contrast between good and evil, between the strong and the weak, and so on.

In the field

In research on active Catholics and politics (Di Giammaria et al., 2015), the group of politicians was labelled as 'they' and linked to adjectives such as 'dirty', 'spurious' and 'wheeler-dealer', while the group of citizens was labelled as 'we' and linked to adjectives such as 'honest', 'workers' and 'coherent'. This narrative did not allow the researcher to gather opinions in depth, restricting the discussion to a superficial level of collective rhetoric. This is why the mod-erator gradually introduced new questions not provided for in the focus group guide, soliciting the collection of concrete examples related to the topic.

225

Obviously, in order to prevent this problem, it is necessary to pay attention to the discussion outline by providing *ex-ante* stimuli that prevent narrativization of the meanings. However, there are arguments that convey highly polarized social imaginaries. Consider the theme of the reception of migrants or current political issues. What the researcher should do in designing the focus group outline and the moderator should take into consideration is that the questions that are asked should allow answers that go beyond stereotypes and clichés. An effective way is to involve participants through personal experiences and not through hearsay.

The polarization of ideas

Finally, there is the possibility that the focus group will become an arena of heated debate. The polarization of opinions is another mechanism that can occur during group interaction, potentially causing unreliable responses. It results in people adopting positions that are more extreme than they would adopt in their ordinary daily life (Myers and Lamm, 1976; Isenberg, 1986).

Various theories help explain group polarization. According to one theory, one-upmanship and pluralistic balance are two important mechanisms that generate group polarization (Fromkin, 1970; Pruitt, 1971). One-upmanship, by definition, is the practice of trying to one-up, or outdo, an opponent. In a group setting, one-upmanship refers to the situation when two individuals hold similar positions during a group discussion and one seeks to outdo the other by moving his/her thinking towards the more socially desirable value. Pluralistic balance, on the other hand, refers to the 'compromise' that people attempt to achieve, considering the trade-off between their own preference and the preferences of other people. Another theory is based on persuasion and considers informational influence (Kaplan, 1977). According to this view, novelty and validity are two determinants of persuasiveness. Therefore, an individual's opinions are determined by how he/she weighs the pro and con arguments considered to be 'persuasive' (Forsyth, 2014: 383).

In focus groups, this phenomenon can develop for various reasons. For instance, the interaction can provide the individual with a range of elements supporting his/her initial suppositions not considered previously, thus strengthening his/her initial convictions (Burnstein, 1982; Hinsz and Davis, 1984). However, these positions may also become stronger because they may be considered prototypical of one's group of reference (solicited in that particular discussion) and used to differentiate from groups perceived as very distant (Zuber et al., 1992; Cooper et al., 2001: 267–70; Hogg, 2001: 64).

The advice is therefore to keep polarization processes under control. It will be the task of the observer to monitor and note the changes of both individual and group opinion. Furthermore, the moderator can solicit a plurality of intermediate and different positions with respect to the polarized conceptions (Puchta and Potter, 2004: 126–30; Acocella, 2012: 1134–5). For this purpose, activity-oriented questions are particularly useful, where participants are asked to 'do' something. The benefit of these strategies is that they provide a different way to elicit answers and promote discussion. Moreover, they have the advantage of engaging participants and preventing the contrast. For example, one way to minimize conflict or polarization is when participants are asked to list all elements of a domain putting forward their ideas. In the meantime, the moderator records the ideas on a flip chart or whiteboard, and he/she solicits the discussion asking to compare each element. This strategy could help to inhibit the crystallization of dissenting viewpoints.

In the field

In research on euthanasia among young people (Cataldi, 2016), a strong ethical polarization emerged between those who were in favour and those who were morally opposed to euthanasia. Participants were asked to think about the reasons in favour and/or against the euthanasia. They were provided with small pieces of paper. The various responses were collected and were then read by the moderator. This strategy inhibited polarization.

9.4 Dynamics of power and leadership

Although the theme of leadership in focus groups has a fundamental role in the understanding of group dynamics, it has been little studied by researchers, who have mostly emphasized the participatory and, so to speak, 'democratic' aspect of the technique.

Leadership in focus groups

In reality, talking about power relations within discussion groups does not mean questioning their typical forms of involvement and sharing skills. Instead, it simply means that within a group, in connection with the assignment of tasks, there is a natural division of roles, which, although not well defined and provisional, performs the function of regulating activities and relationships (Hogg, 2001: 72; Marková et al., 2007: 173; Cyr, 2019: 61–9).

Concepts and Theories

As Daniel Bertaux states (1998: 44), taking into account the power relations in our societies, that we can expect the 'social world' to be the product of regulated activities and interactions among categories of agents/
actors placed in different positions. These positions will be characterized
by formal and informal rules, resources for action and intersubjective relationships of alliance and opposition. All features vary considerably based
on the position occupied. We must, therefore, expect that the agents/
actors have not only different experiences of social relations based on
their structural position (and their life courses), but also different (sometimes even opposite) visions of the same social realities. On these assumptions, Bourdieu (1989: 16) uses the concept of 'field' to describe this set
of invisible relations underlying social space.

Therefore, the processes of taking and recognition of power are linked to
relational flows of mutual influence and control among the members of a
society, as well as among the participants of a focus group.

Concepts and Theories

A focus group can also be considered a 'field', that is, a social space
organized as an ensemble of invisible relations, which constitute a space
of positions (Bourdieu, 1989: 16). Indeed, in a focus group 'the sampling
criteria postulate shared characteristics between the participants which
are commensurate with their positioning within a specific field, of which
the focus group is a sub-field. [...] Depending on their own positionality
in relation to the research focus, [even] the researcher-facilitator may
be positioned within, at the margins of, or outside this field' (Ayrton,
2019: 333).

Within a discussion group, two specific forms of power can be identified
(Carey and Asbury, 2012: 29):

- power exercised by the moderator;
- power exercised by some participants.

In both cases, it is very difficult to distinguish the perceptive dimension from that of real possession. Hence, it would be difficult to determine whether the person in question really has the ability to influence others, or whether it is simply assumed.

Moderator leadership

In the case of the moderator, however, his/her institutionalized task requires precisely the exercise of a certain type of power in leading the discussion (Barbour, 2007: 51). For this reason, David W. Stewart and Prem N. Shamdasani (1990) use the expression 'nominal leader' to designate this role, because by definition the moderator gives directives, is motivated, tries to motivate others and sets a good example for the group. This role is determined by the very nature of the technique. What is necessary is that the other participants should recognize this privileged position, so that the role of leader changes from nominal to being effective. The moderator's position occupying a central seat from which he/she can control everyone's gaze will tend to favour the process of acquiring and approving power.

However, some personal qualities will be indispensable for facilitating the exercise of such a role. For example, some authors believe that three types of skill are needed (Greenbaum, 2000: 29–40):

- *Facilitating group goals.* This category includes all the skills that enable the leader to help the group fulfil its goals, such as intelligence, cunning and knowledge of the methodologies suitable for achieving the objectives.
- *Group sociability.* This includes all the skills related to working in a group, cooperation and popularity.
- *Individual prominence.* This category comprises all skills related to the person's desire to be recognized within the group, such as sense of initiative, self-confidence and persistence.

In particular, as detailed in section 7.1, the moderator can adopt different styles of leadership. Depending on the situation, one type of leadership or another will be more appropriate. Indeed, the moderator should know how to move from one style of leadership to another, according to the different discussion contexts, which can range from the need to be synthetic due to time constraints to the need to involve and motivate some participants (Cyr, 2019: 57–60). The style also depends on the research objectives and the focus group outline: an unstructured guide, for example, is more in keeping with a participatory style because it is more suitable for generating new ideas (Morgan, 1997: 54; Puchta and Potter, 2004: 118–20; Marková et al., 2007: 87). Finally, the style should be evaluated according to the size of the group: while in larger groups it is more difficult to maintain control, smaller groups will have to be encouraged to be creative (Acocella, 2008: 103–4).

The moderator can therefore oscillate between two poles: the instrumental one linked to the task, and the socio-emotional one linked to relationships. A fair balance between these components makes the coordinator the appropriate person to moderate the focus group (Stewart and Shamdasani, 1990: 70–1; Kidd and Parshall, 2000: 298–9; Smithson, 2000). In particular, when the moderator opts for a supportive leadership, he/she will have to worry about the general well-being of the group, paying particular attention to shy participants and to the personal needs of individual members (Barbour, 2007: 26).

Expert advice

A supportive leadership style will adapt more to those situations in which participants address 'sensitive' issues, in order to create a friendly climate of discussion in which all people feel as comfortable as possible.

In other cases, the moderator can opt for a directive leadership. The moderator's task will therefore be oriented to offering guidance and direction to the debate and will mostly follow the steps foreseen by the discussion scheme (Morgan, 1997: 54; Cardano, 2003: 158). It will also provide clear and more precise rules to be followed during group discussion.

Expert advice

A directive leadership style will be more effective when:

- there is a greater risk of losing concentration, turning the meeting into a mere entertainment;
- the topic of discussion is more foreign to the participants, with the risk that the discussion will wander or focus on aspects marginal to the research purposes.

In other situations, the moderator can also opt for participatory leadership (Frisina, 2018: 192). The coordinator will be able to take advantage of a participatory leadership above all when he/she wants to amplify the role of the participants in order to make them the main protagonists of the discussion (Hennink, 2014: 74). In such a case, the moderator will ask the participants to take an active role of intervention also in relation to the structuring of the session, which will therefore tend to follow much less rigid guidelines.

Expert advice

Participatory leadership could be especially useful in the following cases:

- when it is wanted to enhance exploratory purposes aimed at investigating topics not well known by the research group;
- when it is wanted to assign specific tasks to the group, such as during a final summary of the discussion, in which the moderator can ask the participants for substantial help in identifying the most important positions and reporting any additional elements not previously expressed.

Moreover, there are situations in which a leadership oriented to success is useful. This type of leadership is focused on achieving the objectives of the debate. Hence, this type of leadership will be aimed at improving group performance and giving advice on how to conduct the debate.

Expert advice

Successful leadership is especially useful when participants need to feel supported in their task. The moderator should therefore praise the members who are committed to achieving the objectives.

Obviously, it is not only the skills and moderation style of the facilitator that define the logics of power within the 'field' (Bourdieu, 1989) of a focus group. Other features of the moderator also contribute. The first is the possibility of being perceived as an insider or an outsider to the group. This is why gender, ethnicity and also the facilitator's credentials play an important role (Zammuner, 2003: 190–2). These elements contribute to a diverse perception of the moderator, attributing to her/him a greater or lesser power, as well as a greater capacity for attraction or repulsion on the part of the group. In particular, 'where there is a particularly steep power gradient between participants and the facilitator, such as across majority/minority world difference, this can override the researcher/facilitator's attempts to reposition [his/herself]' (Ayrton, 2019: 335).

231

In the field

During research on the South Sudanese diaspora in the UK, the moderator recognized that a significant weight was assigned to her 'position as an indigenous British woman', through naming the racial-cultural and migratory boundaries of the field (Ayrton, 2019: 335).

Leadership among the participants

Furthermore, there may emerge in the group stronger personalities which tend to monopolize attention and influence others through their behaviour. Mechanisms of this type are very common and should not distress the moderator, who with a participatory style will also encourage others present to intervene and express themselves.

Generally, the guidelines on the conduct of focus groups treat power as a procedural problem to be minimized and mitigated. However, power is an inevitable aspect of social life and the micro-dynamics of groups (Marková et al., 2007: 101). In the process of forming public opinion, some people always influence the attitudes or actions of others in a formal or informal way (Hogg, 2001: 69–70). Therefore, during a focus group discussion the dynamics of power also give important information regarding the way the opinions on the phenomenon under study are formed. Since the purpose of the focus group is to bring out the inter-subjective representations and the socially shared knowledge disseminated in particular social groups, the dynamics of power cannot be neglected or defined *a priori* as negative (Cyr, 2019: 61). Moreover, eliminating them completely can elicit an investigative array which is very distant from everyday life, and this can be a barrier to the understanding of a phenomenon.

Concepts and Theories

In Rachel Ayrton's opinion, the way that these processes play out is important for understanding the kind of information that focus groups produce, providing 'valuable insights into the relational significance of the substantive topic that is the focus of discussions' (2019: 336). Therefore, taken to the extreme, the strategies adopted by the moderator to minimize the dynamics of power in the focus group would produce a heavily 'sanitised' discussion, keeping participants' performances separate from 'everyday forms of communication'. In this sense, Ayrton suggests that the skill of facilitation can be to leave 'as much space for a variety of forms of interaction as possible, whilst maintaining ethical parameters. In searching for this balance, [...] rather than dismissing some participants' behaviour as "problematic," "dominant" or "unruly," it is more informative to attend to the different sources of "rules" that participants follow and to acknowledge these as worthy of interest' (2019: 330).

In a focus group, the dynamics manifest themselves under the careful monitoring of the moderator, who should avoid the occurrence of inhibitory effects. Obviously, the assessment of when a certain type of influence by a leader is 'negative' (or not) will change from context to context. In any event, this evaluation is one of the moderator's tasks and will depend on his/her experience or empathic ability.

The processes of acquisition and recognition of leadership by one or more participants take place following the typical phases of adjustment, accreditation and affirmation identified by Edwin P. Hollander (1958):

- first, the 'potential' leader will tend to adapt to the group, agreeing to the rules and following them very carefully;
- step by step, he/she will try to build a certain credibility with regard to others and the moderator, in order to prepare the ground for asserting his/her legitimacy;
- only later will the subject succeed in affirming her/himself as leader, influencing the group with engaging and charming proposals.

Leadership affirmation is connected to social-cognitive processes of attributions and perceptions. The effective leaders will tend to show themselves more loyal regarding the group's objectives. Indeed, 'effective leaders project an image of competency and trustworthiness. The trustworthiness encourages followers to perceive the validity of the mission, and the competence creates the expectation that success is possible. Leadership involves a relationship in which leaders motivate followers to give their best, by providing challenges and support for [...] their efforts' (Chemers, 2001: 393). During a focus group discussion, the role of such leaders will be to motivate the group and direct it towards the task, proving to be more of a help than an obstacle to the moderator in the information construction phase.

At other times, during a focus group, the various dynamics of power can be ascribed to different characteristics of the people involved (Kelly, 2001: 171–3).

233

This is because the participants of a focus group are 'both members of the group in which they are currently involved and social actors who have various social statuses and roles in their everyday life' (Marková et al., 2007: 66).

Concepts and Theories

In the focus group discursive processes, the moderator should consider the participants to be members of various social groups historically situated, who share a great deal of social knowledge and participate in social life on the basis of implicit schemes and routines. Not considering this aspect leads to not recognizing the differences in status and power in the interactions, as if everyone had the same rights, both in conversations and in society (Wodak, 2004: 187). Furthermore, it ignores the cultural and historical context. On the other hand, keeping this aspect in mind allows one to clearly appreciate the knowledge and memory of social practices, as well as social inequalities. Thus the discursive practices allow the researcher to take into consideration the social context and the organizational structures in which the interactions take place, reproducing them in the focus group conversations (Frisina, 2010: 74–6).

For example, mechanisms of subjection can be triggered towards participants with very different characteristics. Indeed, we have already investigated how people with higher status may consciously or unconsciously exercise a sort of restraint on other individuals, towards whom they will enjoy a more or less legitimized power of reward and sanction (Bloor et al., 2001: 37; Carey and Asbury, 2012: 42). Similarly, some participants will be influenced by the opinions of other group members deemed more competent or generically 'acculturated', or who exercise the so-called 'expert power' (French and Raven, 1959) deriving from their additional knowledge (or presumed such).

In this sense, the recommendation that group participants should be homogenous, in order to reduce any 'interference' due to power differences, is valid (Hennink, 2014: 39). At the same time, it is important that the moderator endeavours to curb subordination and/or acceptance dynamics, which can reduce the freedom of expression by participants. However, it is not certain that the socio-demographic characteristics of the participants necessarily influence their opinions.

Also, other dynamics of power or leadership need to be moderated during a focus group discussion. For example, sometimes participants impose their opinion not because they take a leadership position in the group, but simply because they have a more aggressive personality that threatens to stifle the participation of others present (Cyr, 2019: 79–80). At other times, situations can be found in which a participant tries to take on a substitute role to that of the moderator, wanting to impose his/her imprint on the group discussion (Acocella, 2008: 136). All these situations are detrimental to the discussion. In such cases, failure by the moderator to intervene could even compromise the success of the focus group.

Further reading

Marková, I., Linell, P., Grossen M. and Salazar-Orvig, A. (2007) *Dialogue in Focus Groups: Exploring Socially Shared Knowledge*. London: Equinox.

The specificity of this book is the adoption of a dialogical perspective which emphasizes the self–others interdependence. From this starting point, the whole book is dedicated to understanding how to analyse interactions and forms of socially shared knowledge as they are expressed in focus groups.

Acocella, I. (2012) 'The focus groups in social research: advantages and disadvantages', *Quality & Quantity*, 46 (4): 1125–36.

The goal of this paper is to evaluate the nature of the focus group, analysing its advantages and disadvantages. In particular, the article individuates the cognitive and communicative risks that can emerge during a group discussion and their possible solutions.

Exercises

1. During a group discussion that you are moderating you find a person who monopolizes the dialogue and does not let the other participants speak. How do you behave?

2. Make a list of social norms (also called rules) that guide a group discussion.

Part IV

ANALYSING AND WRITING UP

10

Transcribing and Analysing the Focus Group Content

After conducting a focus group, the researcher has a great deal of material available: the field notes, the sheets filled in by the observer, the socio-demographic information of the participants and the audio or video recording of the discussion sessions conducted. What is to be done with this material? In this chapter we will discuss how to analyse the content of the focus group empirical materials.

The first step is to make a good transcript and prepare the material for analysis, bearing in mind that all the documentation available becomes part of the *data corpus*. The second step is to consider what kind of strategy to adopt in analysing the material.

In this regard, there are two options:

- the first is a manual analysis, which comprises different strategies and techniques, such as the qualitative content encoding analysis and its variants, and the narrative analysis;
- the second is computerized analysis, which comprises both qualitative strategies for bottom-up text coding, and quantitative strategies based on a statistical-textual logic.

Chapter goals

- *Knowledge*: deepening of the different strategies and techniques for transcription and analysis of focus groups.
- *Applying knowledge and understanding*: knowing how to build up the empirical corpus for the analysis and how to use the main qualitative and quantitative analysis techniques.
- *Making judgements*: being aware of the research objectives and the resources available to choose the most appropriate strategy of analysis.

10.1 Transcription

In social research, an integral or complete transcription of group discussions is highly recommended. It is important that the transcription is as faithful as possible even in reporting the silences, local dialect expressions, inflections and idioms typical of the spoken language.

This mode of transcription is the basis that ensures the highest degree of rigour in the subsequent analysis (Stewart and Shamdasani, 1990; Bloor et al., 2001). It can therefore be considered the prerequisite for good research.

The advantages of an integral transcription

The main advantage of integral transcription is unquestionably the completeness of the information and the wealth of detail. These elements are useful in identifying how focus group content is produced. In particular, an integral transcription of group discussions is essential in the following cases (Corrao, 2000: 70–2):

- when a detailed content analysis is performed;
- when the researcher is interested in detailed comparison between the different categories of social group involved;
- when the intention is to use the group debate for analysing the interaction between the participants.

To enable accurate recollection of the sessions, during the discussions significant non-verbal behaviours must also be noted in the text of the transcription. For example, gestures, facial expressions and tone of voice of participants should be inserted and indicated differently from the spoken words by means of appropriate 'markers', such as square brackets or the use of a different font (Cardano, 2011: 248–53; Carey and Asbury, 2012: 81).

The building of a 'data corpus'

It is important that the transcription work be done shortly after the group meetings so as not to lose impressions and vivid memories of the progress of the discussion. Immediately after each focus group, or at least before conducting the next group, the material collected should be arranged and subjected to a first elaboration.

This means that the notes taken during the discussion should be integrated, the audio recordings transcribed, and any video recording inspected in order to identify the non-verbal behaviours of the participants during the meeting. In addition, all the field notes and the sheets filled in by the observer constitute the *data corpus*. In the absence of a video recording, the notes by the observer will be used to provide information about non-verbal behaviours. Thus, important information such as that about the group dynamics and the mood of the discussion will not be lost (Dawson et al., 1993: 37–8, 45; Greenbaum, 1998: 51–2, 76; Krueger and Morgan, 1998: 134–5; Litosseliti, 2003: 81; Ellis, 2016: 58).

The procedure

The transcription takes a fairly significant amount of time. It should be borne in mind that two hours of recording normally require at least seven to eight hours of work and that the resulting transcription will be about 50–70 pages in length. The complete transcription of the discussions can be particularly complex, especially in situations where there are continuous overlaps of voices and reciprocal interruptions (Liamputtong, 2011: 166).

Precisely for these reasons, transcription is a delicate and not mechanical process. To obtain an integral and accurate report, the research team must necessarily take into account that it is a shift between two different communication codes. Therefore, it can also be considered a moment of interpretation and creation, in which the scholar uses the scientific skills established during the research experience and those acquired during the discussion sessions to transpose the various linguistic codes that characterize a focus group session.

Tips

There are strategies for producing good transcriptions. First, it is advisable to include in the header of the transcription the number of participants, their personal data, the arrangement around the debate table, the specification of the place and time of the meeting. In addition, each participant must be assigned a recognition number (see section 8.2).

In order to report every part of the conversation faithfully, it is essential to recover, where possible, the physical and non-verbal characteristics that accompanied the interaction, indicating pauses, laughter, silences, embarrassment and so on. Using the observation sheets and the notes filled in by the observer, it is possible to use a symbology (see Table 10.1) for transcribing the components of non-verbal behaviour, which we consider very useful (Puchta and Potter, 2004: 164–6; Acocella, 2008: 86–7; Liamputtong, 2011: 166–70).

Table 10.1   Symbols for the components of non-verbal behaviour

Chronemics	'.......'	Long pause
	'...'	Pause
	....	Silence
Kinesics	[Including notes]	For various reactions, for example: redness, embarrassment, anger etc.
	????	For people who show their disagreement without speaking
	Yes!yes!	For people who show their agreement without speaking
Paralinguistics	Underscore	Emphasis
	Uppercase	High voice
	Smaller size word font	Low voice

Source: Elaboration from Acocella, 2008: 86–7

Finally, the transcription can also contain notes written by the researcher immediately after the session (Corrao, 2000: 71). These notes (see Table 10.2 for an example) concern general observations about the participants, the relationships established, the tone of the group discussion, the way the required task was performed – both in terms of the participants and of the moderator – the most interesting points that have emerged, and finally the suggestions to keep in mind for the development of the subsequent groups (see section 7.4).

Table 10.2   Example of notes included in the transcription of a focus group on the perception of deviant behaviours by young people

NOTES

☐ **PARTICIPANTS**: Participant 1 was very active in the first part, in the second he showed tiredness, he was distracted, and he listened less to what others said.

☐ **TONE**: At the beginning the participants were agitated, worried and curious about the task required of them. Then, the discussion warmed up.

☐ **PARTICIPANTS' TASKS**: After an initial phase of adjustment and round-table debate, the interaction methods and the questions were well understood.

☐ **MODERATOR TASK**: I felt at ease. I tried to be more directive. I tried to express in my own words what I understood from the individual interventions, in order to broaden the concepts. Aspect to be improved: do not pedantically follow the focus group outline.

☐ **INTERESTING POINTS**: Criterion expressed by number 1 on not harming others was taken up by number 3. Number 4 instead expressed the criterion that freedom of choice is complete if individual actions do not involve others. In the end, number 1 also stated the principle of doing to others what a person would like to be done to oneself.

☐ **CHANGES OF IDEA**: Number 2 changed his mind several times during the discussion, following the idea of number 1 on the topics of drugs and of norms.

☐ **KEEP IN MIND**: To deepen the selection criteria.

Source: Elaboration from Cataldi, 2009

Several authors (Vaughn et al., 1996; Krueger and Casey, 2000; Liamputtong, 2011) agree that there are elements that are necessary to consider in this regard:

- *Find the big ideas.* Every discussion group is the bearer of positions and meanings. Hence, it is advisable that the moderator notes, in a schematic way and immediately after the session, the ideas that the group has expressed.
- *Consider the choice and the meaning of words.* The researcher must remember that the use of one word rather than another has great significance. Therefore, it will be useful to write down the recurring term and then discover, even later, the nuanced meaning attributed to it.
- *Consider the context and always keep the interaction in mind.* The opinions collected are not individual, but the result of interaction. For this reason, it will be useful to point out in the commentary cases of suspected courtesy bias or changes of opinion.

10.2 Analysis of the empirical material collected

After having transcribed the group discussions, the researcher will face the crucial question of his/her research: what emerged from the focus group?

To answer that, it is necessary to analyse the empirical material collected. This analysis is focused on the content of the communication flow of the group discussions, in order to clarify, classify and synthesize the main topics that emerged. This is a transformative task, involving selection and systematization of the oral material collected and recorded. The analysis requires codification and comparison of the information obtained both from a single discussion group and between different ones.

To analyse the outputs of a focus group critically, the analyser should ask himself/herself (Krueger and Casey, 2000: 125–9):

- Based on initial cognitive needs, how much information has been obtained?
- At what level of depth have the topics of interest been identified?
- What conclusions can be drawn from the outputs?

To answer these questions, two options can be followed:

- the first is a manual option, which comprises different strategies and techniques, such as the qualitative content encoding analysis and its variants and narrative analysis;
- the second is a computerized option, which comprises both qualitative strategies for bottom-up text coding, and quantitative techniques based on a statistical-textual logic.

Figure 10.1 illustrates the process of analysing the content of a focus group.

Below, we will go deeper into these analysis strategies and examine how the researcher can integrate a hermeneutic approach to the text with computerized analysis.

In particular, we will show how, at times, focus group analysis can be aimed at identifying useful categories of text recoding to summarize and interpret the main themes that emerged in the group discussions. Alternatively, the analysis of the focus group can follow a narrative approach, which may be more appropriate when the aim is to explore how participants co-construct understandings and meanings.

Finally, we will show how computer-based analysis can help the researcher in his/her analysis and explore different techniques of computerized analysis. The first is the computerized analysis of text encoding, with the purpose of creating theories using an inductive approach and a comparative method. The second is computerized analysis with statistical-textual logic, with the purpose of reorganizing the texts through quantification of key concepts or lexicometric parameters.

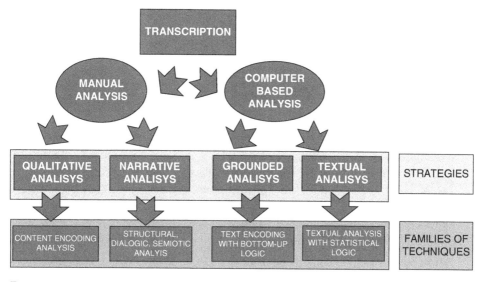

Figure 10.1 How to analyse the content of focus groups

10.3 Content encoding analysis

Having been immersed in the information gathered, on reading the transcripts it is possible to identify the various topics addressed by the discussions and the range of opinions that emerged (Dawson et al., 1993; Morgan, 1997). This information can be summarized and analysed in a variety of different ways (e.g. Bertrand et al., 1992; Krueger and Casey, 2000), but the literature agrees on the usefulness of encoding the information collected, in order to identify some appropriate categories for systematization (Knodel, 1993; Barbour, 2007; Carey and Asbury, 2012).

General characteristics

The goal of the content encoding analysis is to identify patterns in the texts that are relevant or interesting. This is much more than simply summarizing the information gathered; a good analysis interprets them and gives them meaning (Maguire and Delahunt, 2017: 3353).

The content encoding analysis is guided by the key concepts that emerge from the collected empirical materials. Indeed, the choice of which passages of the group discussion to include in the analysis and which to neglect depends strictly on the objectives of the research. In this regard, Richard A. Krueger advises: 'The selection should be influenced by the purpose of the study' (1988: 131).

Furthermore, the wide freedom of selection that can be attributed to the researcher must always take into account the systematic approach followed during the entire research, and therefore on the choices made to proceed in a 'controlled' and 'transparent' way during the field research. As discussed in section 3.1, the 'professional knowing' (Barbour, 2007: 140–1) should lead a researcher in these choices, because it has the advantage of being more inter-subjective. Conversely such choices risk becoming self-referential.

When applied to the focus group, it is always necessary to remember that this technique does not allow extrapolation of individual positions; the context in which these positions have emerged (i.e. the group) must be also considered (Liamputtong, 2011: 173; Carey and Asbury, 2012: 96–7). Indeed, the unit of analysis of research is not the single participant, but the group as a whole. Moreover, the information that emerges is not the sum of the answers of single participants but the product of the synergy that developed during the group discussion (Kitzinger, 1994a). What interests the researcher are the inter-subjective representations and the socially shared knowledge of the social group that the participants were called upon to represent (Marková et al., 2007; Hennink, 2014: 26–7; Halkier, 2017: 406–7).

The phases

To perform this analysis, it is possible to move through the following steps:

- become familiar with the text and take free notes;
- encoding;
- draft a grid;
- identify macro-themes and sub-themes;
- refine the themes;
- draw up a thematic map.

These steps are very important to distinguish the simple description of infor-mation that emerged during a focus group from the interpretation that the researcher will provide of such information, in order to give a theoretical depth by formulating meaning models within which the information appears intelligible.

These are not distinct or successive phases. Instead, they occur in an iterative and recursive manner, making flexible the analysis procedures and remaining open to empirical material. Furthermore, some phases can be skipped (e.g. the researcher can choose not to plot the thematic map and use only the grid); others can be carried out simultaneously.

Becoming familiar with the text and taking free notes

The first step in any analysis is reading and re-reading the transcripts. It is important to become familiar with the entire empirical materials collected (i.e. all the focus group transcripts, the field notes, the sheets filled in by the observer, the socio-demographic information of the participants and the audio or video recordings of the discussion sessions conducted). This is necessary before one goes any further. At this phase, it is useful to make notes and jot down early impressions.

In the field

An example of familiarization with the information collected is provided in a study on the ways in which students make sense of the 'feedback' they have received over the course of their studies (Maguire and Delahunt, 2017). A first reading of the eight focus groups led to this note that we report as an example: 'The students do seem to think that feedback is important but don't always find it useful. There is a sense that the whole assessment process, including feedback, can be seen as threatening and is not always understood. The students are very clear that they want very specific feedback that tells them how to improve in a personalized way. They want to be able to discuss their work on a one-to-one basis with lecturers, as this is more personal and also private. The emotional impact of feedback is important'.

The impressions that are written by the researchers following a first reading of the corpus must not have the task of anticipating the analysis that will be carried out. However, becoming familiar with the corpus helps to organize work in the later stages and be guided by the texts in the analysis work. Furthermore, it should be borne in mind that a common pitfall is the outline of the researcher's analytic framework (Clarke and Braun, 2013). Therefore, this phase is fundamental: not only should the researcher put questions to the information collected, but the same empirical material should put questions to the researcher.

The encoding

After becoming familiar with the information collected and the transcripts, the researcher can start by generating initial codes. This phase makes it possible to organize the gathered information in a meaningful and systematic way. Coding reduces a great deal of information into small 'scraps' of meaning. The technique therefore involves a preparation of the text that will be broken down into micro-units, codifying the various statements – also called 'speech acts'. After this work of fragmentation and segmentation, the text will be recomposed through large groupings of meaning (Knodel, 1993: 46–7; Barbour, 2007: 129–30; Liamputtong, 2011: 173).

There are different ways to code, and the method will be determined by the researcher's perspective and the investigation's questions.

In particular, there is a more deductive or theoretical way, which processes the information collected starting from research questions. In such a case, the process builds on a pre-organized list or open template of themes. It is necessary to go systematically through the entire empirical material gathered and identify a specific code for any perceived patterns or themes. If the researcher proceeds in this way, it is not necessary to codify everything that is found in the text of the transcripts, but only what it is possible to code (Corrao, 2000: 72–3; Krueger and Casey, 2000: 132–7; Cardano, 2011: 266–8).

In contrast, there is a more inductive approach, which aims to identify the main codes starting with the collected materials. This approach is inspired by grounded theory – developed by Barney Glaser and Anselm Strauss (1967) – according to which the 'theory' must arise from the information found during field research. If the researcher proceeds in a more inductive manner, it is advisable to code every piece of text, through categorizations that enhance the conceptual, linguistic and analytical frame of the participants (Barbour, 2007: 158–9; Hennink, 2014: 179, 186–7). In such a case, the researcher can use line-by-line coding, in order to code every single line (Carey and Asbury, 2012: 81).

In other words, the researcher can opt for two possibilities:

- the first starts from a pre-existing base which tries to capture pre-configured themes or thematic aspects in the text of the transcripts;
- the second is based on open coding, which means that the researcher does not have a preset template, but rather the codes are developed and modified through the text analysis process.

In any event, the researcher must always take the text into account and follow adjustments and changes in a flexible manner.

The deductive approach and the coding process, which starts from a pre-existing basis of already pre-configured thematic aspects, generally prevail in research designs that enhance the analytical-in-depth function of the focus group (see section 3.4). Indeed, in these cases, the main aim is to identify more relevant features or deepen analytical perspectives that the researcher identifies as significant.

In the field

As an example of deductive coding, we report the analysis strategy in a study on stereotypes in the dress code of young Western women and young Muslim women (Guizzardi, 2009). Focus groups were conducted to clarify some interpretations derived from the analysis of data from 900 questionnaires administered to young students. The coding was conducted bringing the information collected in the discussions back to the various items in the questionnaire. For example, the sentences 'Muslim women tend to hide their femininity especially after moving to Italy, because Italian males are too intrusive' or 'Muslim men push women to cover their body to defend themselves from the malevolent eyes of Italian males' were linked to the item of the questionnaire 'Some girls of Muslim culture wear veils, because they wish to present themselves as girls from a good family', allowing an enrichment of its meaning through qualitative analysis (Acocella, 2009: 72–5).

Instead, inductive coding strategies or those that follow progressive coding procedures are more widespread in research designs that enhance the exploratory-descriptive functions of focus groups (see section 3.3). Indeed, in these cases, the main aim is to discover aspects not previously considered and offering new analytical perspectives on the phenomenon.

In the field

An example of inductive and open coding is provided by a consultation exercise on childcare on a university campus (Cormack et al., 2018). The participants talked a great deal about practical considerations, such as transportation and so on. The research group noticed that there was more than one instance of logistical concern in transcripts. Before wondering how it fitted into the overall analysis, or whether it merited being labelled as a theme or sub-theme, the research group simply annotated it with the code 'SL' (sensitivity to logistics).

Whichever approach is chosen, it should be considered that the analytical-in-depth and the exploratory-descriptive research designs are ideal-typical research designs, and that hybrid forms are more common during field research. For this reason, our suggestion is to adopt a mixed approach. On the one hand, then, the researcher can mark and code in the information collected everything that concerns the answers to research questions, according to a pre-organized list or open template of themes. On the other hand, he/she can highlight all the aspects that seem relevant in the body of texts and then re-read to make sense of them on the basis of a new possible categorization. Thus, the researcher continues to be surprised by the empirical material collected without remaining too anchored to his/her analytic framework.

Finally, it is important to consider the intersubjective dimension of coding operations within a research group. Indeed, coding can be carried out collectively in a group work session by the research staff or, after an initial agreement, by individual researchers who can code on their own and then discuss the assigned codes with others (Corrao, 2000: 69; Sargent et al., 2016). This allows for greater accuracy in the process.

In the field

In one research study for evaluating a treatment programme aimed at training and employment opportunities for individuals with substance use disorders (Davis and Brolin, 2014), the authors coded in two stages. First, a research team reviewed the transcript and attached codes using a Word document programme. Then, another research team read the transcript with the codes and noted quotes that they thought should be coded differently. In discussing the interpretations together, they had the opportunity to compare the different points of view. Sometimes these discussions ended with a quote having two codes (2014: 6–7).

Draft a grid

In order to codify and organize the material systematically, it is very useful to construct a reading grid. It allows the researcher to sort all the information that emerged during group discussions, keeping the aims and questions of the research in mind (Knodel, 1993: 43; Corrao, 2000: 72–3; Barbour, 2007: 134–4; Frisina, 2010: 113–14). For this reason, the interaction between grid and texts must be continuous because the researcher will have to change the tool whenever the analysis highlights new themes.

This grid is particularly useful both for identifying the main thematic issues that emerged in group discussions and for reconstructing the development of the debates around them (Frisina, 2010: 108–9; Cardano, 2011: 265–6).

The grid can spring from analysis of the single discussion, as well as from comparison of the materials that emerged in different discussions (see Table 10.3). The comparison between the various discussion groups will thus make it possible to highlight convergences and divergences on the same theme.

In the field

Table 10.3 Example of a reading grid on focus groups euthanasia: focus on the position of admissibility (Cataldi, 2016)

EUTHANASIA – ADMISSIBILITY

1. **Conception of the choice:** compliance with the decision	F2_3: [...] Yes, because if I love a person, I have to accept his choice. It's not like I can keep trying to keep him alive anyway. If he asks me to pull the plug out, why don't I do it? F5_1: With an extreme illness, I say, I have definitely the right to choose.
2. **Vital conception:** the dying person is no longer a human being	F1_5: I would do it, not for fear of suffering, but because in any case I think that in those conditions there is nothing else that brings you closer to a human being. F4_1: No, I can't tolerate that my life, as I'm, should be reduced to that of a vegetable, forced to live thanks to a machine, to something artificial. I reject a life that doesn't exist for me. For me that is not a life.
3. **Self-affirmation conception:** affirmation of one's identity	F4_2: I don't passively suffer, but I can affirm my personality, deciding that dying is the last decision of my life. Dying's my last way of affirming my soul, my identity, my ultimate personal gesture.
4. **Altruistic conception toward the suffering person:** it avoids pain, it is an act of love	F1_5: Yes, but by not [pulling the plug] you are also an instrument of suffering. Therefore, euthanasia prevents suffering. F1_3: For me it is an act of love when the disease causes physical pain to the patient. If the person has pain it is an act of love; murder is another thing.
5. **Altruistic conception toward the care giver:** respect for the care giver	F2_3: I am in favour. I have a grandmother who is very sick and beyond all help ... my mom, while caring for my grandmother, dies too. F2_3: If I were sick, I'd also hope to have the lucidity to think that I don't want to make even those close to me suffer, in the sense that a family that lives with a terminally ill person, has no life.

At the same time, if we compare groups formed on different categories of identification/belonging (see sections 5.1 and 5.2), the grid will allow the researcher to evaluate how different social groups present different ways of categorizing and representing the same phenomenon (Knodel, 1993: 42–3 and 49; Barbour, 2007: 135–7).

Ultimately, the grid will allow the researcher to summarize the main issues that emerged during the field research, evaluating their consistency with the initial objectives of the research, in how many group discussions these topics have been treated and the different way in which each topic has been discussed.

Macro-themes and sub-themes

The reading grid allows the researcher to recode the text again, giving it a new form. To this end, it is possible to group the various positions identified into macro-units that correspond to the themes or sub-themes. It is thus possible to explore how and whether the codes can be grouped thematically. There are no rigid and fast rules for determining whether a theme is significant and interesting (Braun and Clarke, 2006). 'Themes are different from codes in that they are more about grouping repeating elements of the data – searching for patterns rather than isolating individual categories' (Cormack et al., 2018: 5). Therefore, a theme is a pattern that captures something significant or interesting about the research issues and the information gathered.

Authors refer to this re-coding phase with different expressions. John Knodel, for example, speaks about 'code mapping' (1993: 45). For Knodel, indeed, the procedure involves the segmentation of the original manuscript into analytically distinct elements, the coding and grouping of individual sentences into macro-entries. Richard A. Krueger speaks of 'axial coding' (1988: 128), referring to a reassembly of the information gathered according to an order of importance of the single parts of the text. In any event, this phase will require a process of code-and-retrieve on the text that will have to be adequately argued and explained by the researcher when presenting the results.

In the field

In the research into childcare on a university campus, the research group realized that all of the information coded under SL (sensitivity to logistics), PC (an awareness of political context) or U (awareness of potential discomfort) could be considered a form of sensitivity to participants' feelings. This gave rise to the theme 'emotional sensitivity' (Cormack et al., 2018: 6).

Refine the themes

The labels used for the themes or the categories should be coherent, and they should be distinct from each other. Hence, a final refinement of the themes is necessary. To do this, it is important to ask oneself the following questions:

- Does the label (theme) make sense?
- Does the empirical material gathered support the label?
- Am I trying to fit too much into a label?
- If the labels overlap, are they really separate labels?
- Are there other themes within the information collected?

Naturally, the researcher must be ready to readjust the labels as the analysis proceeds whenever changes are needed: there will therefore be a continuous iteration process between the text and the themes identified (Corrao, 2000: 72). Additionally, a good strategy is to widen the intersubjective basis: the analysts can divide the material and separately construct the grids and then compare them to obtain a single scheme of information reading and classification (Morgan, 1997).

Furthermore, all the typical techniques of classification, construction of a typology and, although rarely, a taxonomy can be used. As regards classification, it is sufficient to recall that there are some indispensable requirements for it to be effective (Marradi, 1984):

- the uniqueness of the *fundamentum divisionis*, according to which the attribution of cases to categories of the same classification must be based on a single logical foundation;
- the mutual exclusiveness of the categories, so that each case must be assigned to only one category;
- completeness, according to which each case must be attributable to at least one category.

Typologies and taxonomies differ from simple classification in that they resort to more *fundamenta divisionis*, in the former case jointly, in the latter case sequentially (Marradi, 1993).

Regarding analysis of the content, it will be necessary to consider two other criteria for the creation of macro-themes and sub-themes (Losito, 1993): the 'homogeneity' of the classification units inserted in each category (e.g. if the researcher chooses to identify the interactive interventions in the discussion as a classification unit, it will not be possible to include individual statements of a participant in the category); the 'relevance' of the categories, according to which the classification should be in line with both the objectives of the research and the discussion results.

The thematic map

At the end of this phase, the researcher needs to identify 'the "essence" of what each theme is about' (Braun and Clarke, 2006: 92). For this purpose, the researcher can ask himself/herself some key questions (Maguire and Delahunt, 2017: 3359):

- What is the theme saying?
- If there are subthemes, how do they interact and relate to the main theme?
- How do the themes relate to each other?

To answer these questions, a useful approach is to draw a thematic map. This is a visual representation of themes and sub-themes. A thematic map is produced in relation to the way in which the information collected responds to the main study questions.

In the field

Figure 10.2 is an extract from a final thematic map of research on 'What students want from feedback' (Maguire and Delahunt, 2017: 3359). The map indicates the relationship between the central themes and the sub-themes that emerged from the focus groups. In particular, the results show that for students, feedback is rooted in the following challenges: understanding assessment criteria, judging their own work, needing more specific guidance, and perceiving feedback as potentially threatening.

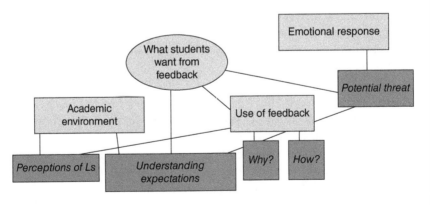

Figure 10.2 Example of a thematic map on a research on students' opinions on teachers' feedback (Maguire and Delahunt, 2017: 3359)

Note: Perception of Ls means the Perceptions of Lecturers

The operations of comparison, convergence, divergence and cataloguing of the information will be conducted on the material collected in each discussion and subsequently compared with each other in order to arrive at the final report (see section 12.2).

10.4 Narrative analysis

General features

Focus groups are a rich source of narrative dialogues. Taking a narrative approach to analysing focus groups is particularly useful if the researcher wants to examine how participants co-construct understandings and meanings (Marková et al., 2007: 72). Moreover, this approach makes it possible to identify a framework that is helpful for understanding a phenomenon within different settings.

According to Catherine Kohler Riessman (2008: 11), narrative analysis refers to a 'family of methods for interpreting texts that have in common a storied form'. The approach is very adaptable, and there are many different ways in which it can be used.

To carry out this analysis, a researcher usually proceeds as follows (Lyndon, 2018):

- becoming familiar with the text and taking free notes;
- analysing the stories told by the participants and noting their structure;
- noting down the resulting ideas and anchoring the research questions;
- compiling a grid/map.

Also, in this case the steps will be recursive and not ordered. Indeed, the researcher usually has to return to earlier stages. This forwards-and-backwards process is represented by the double-edged arrow in Figure 10.3.

The central phase that distinguishes this analysis from other families of techniques is the reconstruction of a story (Cardano, 2011: 258–9; Carey and Asbury, 2012: 85).

To make this stage more manageable, the researcher can divide the focus group into units of analysis which he/she can loosely term 'stories'. As Sandra Lyndon (2018: 7) says: 'These are not stories in the traditional sense of Labov and Waletzky (1967), which have a clear structure and temporal sequence. Instead they are based on Gee's (1991, 2008) idea of units of analysis, which divides narratives into stanzas or units of meaning'.

This part of the process is complex, but can be guided by key questions such as the following (Lyndon, 2018):

- What story are focus group participants telling?
- How do stories get interrupted or diverted?
- How are characters constructed?

As with other qualitative approaches, there are several inflections to narrative inquiry (Clandinin and Connelly, 2000; Alvermann, 2002). Here we present some that are well suited to focus groups.

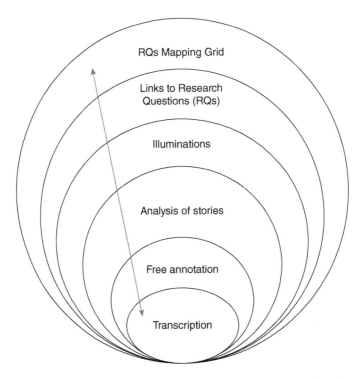

Figure 10.3 Using a narrative approach to analyse focus groups (Lyndon, 2018: 6)

Structural analysis

Structural analysis is a very useful tool with which to organize the information collected. It allows the researcher to go into depth on the oral storytelling of the focus group participants. In particular, in structural analysis, how a teller communicates the story – the form it takes – is examined. The temporal ordering of events in a story is a necessary condition for the emergence of that story. The events in the sequence must be bound together by some principles of logical coherence (Franzosi, 1998: 521). Narratives have a sequential and/or temporal ordering describing some kind of tension or unexpected action that requires a reaction and/or adjustment (Riessman, 2008; Cardano, 2011: 258–9).

Structural analysis is sometimes facilitated by the way in which the research group sets up the focus group discussion. Indeed, the research group can make use of probing techniques such as commenting on/completing a story or a thematic vignette in order to provide participants with a basic narrative frame in which to discuss the topic being studied (see section 6.2).

Focus groups conducted in this way encourage the collection of information that allows a narrative approach to be adopted in the analysis, at the same time bringing out widespread beliefs and intersubjective representations on a given phenomenon (Marková et al., 2007: 72, 151–4).

Starting from this base, the structural analysis technique can identify some elements that make up the narrative structure within the focus group discussion. They are:

- scene setting: narrative introduction/background;
- dilemma: a complicating factor;
- turning point: event(s) important in heightening/resolving the dilemma(s);
- resolution: the dilemma's resolution;
- justification: explanations or rationalizations;
- outcome: the final outcome;
- reflections: further thoughts;
- coda: a short restatement.

The presence of these elements makes it possible to identify patterns or narrative profiles shared by participants.

In the field

In 'Qualitative election study of Britain', Kristi Winters (2019) used narrative analysis to systematize and compare the structure of voters' stories about electoral choice. Narrative analysis enabled Winters to determine a pattern in the information collected which evidenced different types of voters, including ones with a long-term partisan identification who reported psychological obstacles to voting for a different party.

Dialogical analysis

Another tool is dialogical analysis. Catherine Kohler Riessman (2008: 105) describes it as 'a broad and varied interpretative approach' which 'interrogates how talk among speakers is interactively (dialogically) produced and performed as narrative'. This analysis makes it possible to focus on the context and view narratives as being multi-voiced and co-constructed. For this reason, dialogical analysis is a method suitable for analysing studies that involve focus groups.

Dialogical analysis draws on Erving Goffman's (1969) theory of performance of identity and how this is constructed in relation to the audience (Marková et al., 2007: 71–4). Riessman (2008) suggests that dialogue that is formed during the focus group is 'plurivocal', because all the participants co-participate, adopting various roles and positions, and repositioning themselves in a common framework. Equally, the analyst and reader represent further voices through their engagement with the narrative bringing their own positions and interpretations.

In particular, this approach facilitates the interconnection of two contexts (Lyndon, 2018):

- *the local context*: that is, the co-production of stories between the participants and the researcher;
- *the broader context*: that is, how culture and socially shared knowledge are reproduced within the narrative.

In the field

Sandra Lyndon's (2018) research project analysed the information collected in six focus groups on understandings of child poverty. The dialogical analytical approach made it possible to examine how participants co-constructed narratives of poverty within the setting, as well as links to broader political discourses of poverty.

This analytical approach therefore enhances communication among the participants in a focus group. Communication is a social and relational activity. It is based on processes of exchange and plea bargaining among communicating people: each communicative act has effects on the sequence of exchanges within a process of reciprocal influence, thus contributing to giving shape to the interaction in progress. It also has a cultural matrix and a conventional nature, since it is an outcome of agreements and conventions culturally established within a given community. Hence, dialogical analysis takes advantage of the interaction and debate typical of the focus group as a means to encourage the emergence of inter-subjective representations and socially shared knowledge disseminated within the social group, which the participants are called to represent (Marková et al., 2007: 22; Liamputtong, 2011: 16–18; Hennink, 2014: 26–7; Halkier, 2017: 406–7).

In the field

An analytical strategy was also used in the research mentioned above on stereotypes in the dress code of young Western women and young Muslim women (Guizzardi, 2009). The students involved belonged to two types of high school: vocational on the one hand and humanities on the other. The analysis of the interaction produced among the students of the two differ-ent schools showed different social narrations on the phenomenon. Indeed, among the students of vocational schools more sociological cate-gories prevailed, leading the discussion to be structured around the role assumed by the binomial 'social conditioning/free choice' in the construc-tion of one's own image. Therefore, the debate focused on the contrast between 'wanting to feel part of a group' or 'the approval of the fashion market', on the one hand, and the 'will to affirm one's individuality or one's own difference with respect to others' on the other. In contrast, among the students of the humanities schools more philosophical categories pre-vailed, leading the discussion to be structured around the binomial 'to be/appear'. In this case, the debate focused on arguing that a young person can choose to project outside, with a greater or lesser awareness, a certain image of self that does not necessarily coincide with what is his/her deep-est personality. Hence, in this representation, a young man/woman can be one way and choose to appear as another (Acocella, 2009: 58–60).

Dialogical analysis allows differences to emerge by using the synergy of the discussion group to make explicit the cognitive processes – even implicit and taken for granted – influenced by feelings of belonging to 'social groups of reference/identification' (see section 1.2). These cognitive processes intervene in the structuring of social identity and, in turn, influence the individuals' modes of categorizing reality and acting in everyday life (Tajfel, 1974; Turner, 1982: Tajfel and Turner, 1986).

Semiotic analysis

Finally, a further means to analyse the focus group, which can accompany nar-rative analysis, is semiotic analysis (Corrao, 2000: 74–5; Barbour, 2007: 158–9). This is an approach that draws on the theories of linguistics and philosophy, primarily those of Algirdas Julien Greimas (1970, 1983) and Umberto Eco (1984).

This analysis technique starts from the fundamental concept of semiotics, which is the discipline that studies signs and the way these make sense (signification process). Therefore, semiotic analysis focuses on the relationship between a signifier and a meaning, between the sign and its content.

Given that the sign is in general something that refers to something else, the signification process means any relationship that binds something 'materially present' to something else 'absent' (e.g. the red on a traffic light means/stands for 'stop'). Semiotic analysis focuses on the study of signification within the group, considering the discussion as a process by which expressions (acoustic, visual, written etc.) take on the value of a sign. In other words, semiotic analysis considers the object of discussion as a sign – that is, something that gives rise to a relationship between two elements, where the first is of an empirical type and the second of a conceptual nature (Morris, 1938: 32).

In the field of marketing, such signs can be, for example, an advertising message, a prototype, a package (pack), a slogan, a symbol, an image, a logo etc. They can be presented and discussed among the participants as potential targets of the product, in order to capture their signification processes.

The tools used for this purpose are the analysis of the linguistic registers, the reconstruction of the reading and decoding paths of the message and the cognitive investigation underlying the signification processes.

In the field

Semiotic analysis was used in research on an advertisement for a cold tea drink (Gobo, 2005). The jingle of the advertisement was based on the double-sense sentence 'Produced with Real water', where 'Real' was also the name of the brand. However, group discussion showed that the brand was not adequately recognized. For example, a participant asked: 'Does it mean that it is real mineral water, that is, truly mineral water, genuine, pure?' (2005: 85).

Semiotic analysis is therefore useful for analysing the information gathered in a focus group, because it enables an explicit process of signification during which the members of the group assign specific meanings to the terms and expressions used in the discussion. Indeed, during a focus group the interaction can clarify the content of the discussion, allowing those present to make explicit their conceptual, linguistic and argumentative schemes, according to a sharing and comparing procedure that leads to the definition of subjective meanings up to the creation of new areas of mutual understanding (Smithson, 2000: 111; Carey and Asbury, 2012: 28). The moderator plays a strategic role in expressing the content of the information that emerged during the debate (see sections 6.2 and 7.2).

Semiotic analysis is aimed at gathering and systematizing these processes of signification, in order to bring out both the different meanings that can emerge in relation to the same term/expression used during the group discussion, and the convergences of meanings that lead to assigning and sharing a common definition of this term/expression (Barbour, 2007: 158–9).

Semiotic analysis is therefore an important strategy with which to bring out the meanings that can emerge during a group discussion. It can highlight the categorization processes associated with the social group evoked in the focus group, and also the manner in which the same interaction can produce new meanings and sharing, thanks to the comparison of ideas, the negotiation of individual positions and the contribution of all participants (Marková et al., 2007: 46–7; Carey and Asbury, 2012: 28).

10.5 Computer-based analysis

Computer-based analysis can help the researcher in his/her evaluation. Indeed, it has the fundamental purpose of reducing the great variety of information contained in focus group texts to a smaller and interpretable corpus.

The different techniques

The analysis of textual material carried out with specific IT packages is called CAQDAS (Computer Aided Qualitative Data Analysis), which can be distinguished into families of techniques that follow different logics and approaches. The choice of one technique rather than another produces, of course, different research paths and results. For this reason, each responds to specific analysis objectives and requires texts with different characteristics (Weitzman and Miles, 1995; Venturini, 2002; Grbich, 2007; Giuliano and La Rocca, 2008).

Within computer-based analysis, there are families of techniques that enhance procedures for recoding information in themes and macro-themes in a similar way to the content encoding analysis described above (see section 10.3). The various packages are differentiated by the possibilities offered to the analyst: coding, search and retrieval of information, registration of side notes, presentation of networks among the information collected, and representation of conceptual networks. Thus, these techniques are only a support to the researcher. The advantages of this strategy must be read in terms of the systematic nature of the analysis and the ability to manage material. Indeed, especially when the texts to be analysed are very long, the use of IT assistance can be of great help, although it requires preparatory work of no small importance.

Other families of techniques use statistical-textual logic that reorganize information gathered through quantification of key concepts or lexicometric criteria. Therefore, in these analysis processes, the information contained in the texts is expressed in the form of quantitative data, for the purpose of generating the frequency distributions (in relation to recurrent words or themes) or models of association among variables.

A sort of 'horror *numeri*'

As regards this second family of analysis techniques, several authors are sceptical of the automated procedures applied to focus groups, outlining some of the common risks:

- the mystification of the element (e.g. the frequency of recurrence of a given word) to the detriment of an overall view concerning the progress of the discussions and the key concepts;
- the sacrifice of the depth and richness of the material collected, in favour of statistical analysis: that is to say, favouring analysis on the metric dimension to the detriment of the 'theory oriented' analysis;
- the affirmation of a positivist view that tends to consider the results of focus groups as data with statistical significance, from which inferences can be made with regard to a population.

In some of these positions, we can see a sort of 'horror *numeri*' (fear of numbers), supported by the fact that the focus groups do not have the objective of producing data frequency distributions (Stewart and Shamdasani, 1990: 16–18; Krueger and Casey, 2000: 76–7; Barbour, 2007: 69). In others, the belief is that the researcher should look for results that resemble reference patterns rather than numbers (Liamputtong, 2011: 173; Hennink, 2014: 175; Cyr, 2019: 35–40).

In our opinion, computer techniques can be used for the analysis of focus group information collected provided that the risks are taken into account and that operations that pertain exclusively to the researcher are not delegated to them. In this sense, the use of statistical techniques of text analysis must take a calculation of costs and benefits into account: the price paid to analyse these empirical materials with cardinal techniques should be compensated by benefits in terms of synthesis and concision of the results produced.

At the same time, a strength of quantitative analysis is its ability to elicit those concepts that, although never in the foreground, are a constant element of the landscape. Interpretative or qualitative analysis risks neglecting some important elements disseminated within the text. The analyst is inclined to perceive the various comments selectively, tending to isolate only those that confirm a particular point of view, and avoiding treatment of information that causes cognitive dissonance. Software can reduce this problem, constituting a valid aid in an analysis that proceeds by looking for clues, cues for interpretation and unexpected elements (Astolfi and Fazzi, 2005). In this regard, 'the analysis process is like detective work. One looks for clues, but in this case the clues are trends and patterns that reappear among various focus groups' (Krueger, 1988: 152).

Another strength of the statistical technique is that it can highlight the 'halo effect' (Montesperelli, 1998) – or the tendency to extrapolate interpretations of the words of a single participant to the entire group or to the whole series of focus sessions. The use of IT tools can help the researcher to identify the occurrences of a given topic and therefore to resize or enhance a given position.

Below, we will discuss two kinds of computer-based analysis:

- computerized analysis of text encoding that has the purpose of generating theories and uses an inductive approach and a comparative method;
- computerized analysis with statistical-textual logic that has the purpose of reorganizing the texts through a quantification of key concepts or lexicometric parameters.

10.6 Computerized analysis of text encoding

As discussed in section 10.3, the researcher can choose to bring out the meaning of a text by using an inductive approach typical of grounded theory (Glaser and Strauss, 1967). In particular, this approach adopts an analysis strategy that aims to construct 'theories' from below, from the 'ground', and, therefore, from the information found during field research (Glaser and Strauss, 1967: 21; Liamputtong, 2011: 173; Carvalho and Winters, 2014).

A key feature of grounded theory is the comparative method. Indeed, generation of theories occurs above all by using the comparative method and through a triple form of coding (Corbin and Strauss, 2015):

- *Open coding*: the analytical process whereby categories capable of summarizing textual information are identified, named and classified. Therefore, open coding consists in creating labels in order to to synthesize the 'fragments' of meaning that emerge from the transcripts;
- *Axial coding*: consists of identifying relationships among the open codes. The main question addressed in this phase is: What are the connections among the codes?
- *Selective coding*: the phase in which a 'core category' is identified and is chosen to be the pivot of the interpretation.

Besides the possibility of manual analysis, among the software currently on the market (see Appendix 4) there are several that adopt this logic, for example ATLAS.ti. Moreover, a logic of this kind has also been incorporated by the two subsequent software programs, NUD*IST, N6 and NVivo.

The procedure

If the researcher decides to use these techniques, the procedure requires performance of some preliminary operations: the creation of an analysis unit, the assignment of the primary document to the unit and the opening of the file.

After this, the researcher can proceed with the text encoding. The first operation is the 'open code'. This is the step whereby a comprehensive and detailed interrogation of the information collected is undertaken in order to highlight the general 'open codes' (Carvalho and Winters, 2014).

In the field

If the researcher uses ATLAS.ti, to prepare the focus group transcript, one simply needs to make sure that each speaker is clearly indicated by their name, pseudonym or some abbreviation, followed by a colon (:). The program will automatically code the focus group texts by searching for any colons in the transcript. It is also possible to use auto-coding to quickly and easily identify keywords throughout the empirical material collected. More than one open code can be entered for each speaker/unit of speech by writing the code names separated by a semicolon (;). The researcher can also revise the new encodings in the codes and quotations managers, from which it is also possible to export reports of one's coded quotations (www.atlasti.com).

Then 'axial coding' can be performed. This process identifies the links among open codes in order to identify 'code notes' and reorganize the materials at a more general level (Giuliano and La Rocca, 2008). There are different types of relationships (e.g. ATLAS.ti identifies symmetric, causal, transitive and contradictory relationships). However, in general, the relationships are based on two main criteria:

- semantic network, which makes it possible to create a list of nodes according to semantic connections;
- causal relationships, which makes it possible to create a list of nodes according to causal dependency connections.

> ### In the field
>
> An example of semantic axial coding using the software NVivo is provided by the analysis of people's perceptions of party leaders during the 2010 British General Election (Carvalho and Winters, 2014). First, the researchers tried to classify the words and phrases that participants used when looking at a photograph of a party leader. For example, they coded the following expressions: 'honest', 'idealist', 'open-minded', 'looks like he/she empathizes'. Then, the researchers decided to group together codes that described the 'positive', 'negative' and 'neutral' characteristics on a semantic level.

On this basis it is possible to carry out selective coding, which consists of identifying the 'core category', which can be considered the main category of interpretation. The idea is to develop a single storyline around which everything else is draped. There is a belief that such a core concept always exists.

> ### In the field
>
> An example of such an analysis was conducted in the medical research field, with the aim of exploring the topic of 'end-of-life' in different ethnic groups (Shrank et al., 2005). The analysis of empirical materials was implemented using ATLAS.ti software. Each code was discussed by two evaluators until a consensus was reached. A total of 141 open codes were generated, feeding into 19 axial codes. Then, the 19 axial codes were reduced to two core categories: 'the structure of end-of-life conversations' and 'the underlying values to these conversations'. For core categories, the comparison between different ethnic groups was conducted. For example, regarding 'the structure of end-of-life conversations', in comparison to the African-American group, the non-Hispanic white groups were more exclusive when selecting which family members could participate, were more interested in consultation from specialists, and were less interested in spiritual guidance.

10.7 Computerized analysis with statistical-textual logic

General features

A cluster of tools pertaining to the statistical-textual logic strategy is the content analysis group of techniques. First propounded in the field of political communication by the American Harold D. Laswell (1927) and then enriched by the works of Paul F. Lazarsfeld, Bernard Berelson and Hazel Gaudet (1948), Jean-Paul Benzècri (1992) and Klaus Krippendorff (2004), this strategy aims to analyse (through statistical tools) textual or audiovisual materials, even very large ones (Gobo, 2005; Allen, 2017). An available software program is, for example, HAMLET, which enables manual text processing.

Another cluster of procedures based on the statistical-textual logic enables the processing and analysis of a set of texts according to a logic of lexicometric type. This group of techniques works on the corpus with statistical tools and uses computer tools such as TaLTaC and Lexico, which allow automatic processing of the text. SPAD and T-LAB are also used for analysis of lexical correspondences.

Objectives

With reference to the focus groups, both the quantitative analysis of the content and the lexicometric analysis have the following objectives in common (della Ratta-Rinaldi, 2000: 103):

- identify the main topics through the extraction of the distinctive language that characterizes the focus group discussions, analysing the indicative frequency of words and extracting the factors;
- identify the most significant portions of text that can be associated with certain words, to be understood as keywords of the discussion;
- identify the language differences between the moderator and the participants and, possibly, among the latter in the same discussion;
- characterize the tone of the discussion through the extraction of positive and negative terminology or other relevant semantic characteristics.

The preparation of the text

What are the steps necessary to carry out a textual statistical analysis of focus groups?

First of all, it is appropriate to constitute the body of the text so that it is ready for textual analysis. Indeed, in the focus group transcript the discussion group is considered to be a single text produced by interpersonal comparison. The analysis can then be advanced to include the whole focus group to be analysed in a single text.

To reflect the variety of the interaction, it is nevertheless appropriate to proceed with the partition of the text, marking the beginning of each fragment/corpus. The text of the focus groups, indeed, is characterized by a separation between the interventions of the moderator and those of each participant: the coding system will be able to take these distinctions into account, tracing the partitions within the text to the interventions of the various actors. To this end, it will be useful to include the codes referring to the authors of the individual interventions in the transcription of the text.

At this point, the preparatory operations for normalization, lemmatization and disambiguation of the text will have to be performed (Di Franco, 1997, 2007; Allen, 2017). Normalization consists of the elimination of irrelevant capital letters and the uniformity of the spellings in the text. Lemmatization is the complex of operations that lead to reuniting all the forms of lexical inflections used under the respective lemma (the root of the word): for example, considered under the same lemma will be a verb with its different endings. The purpose of disambiguation is to give each word or phrase its meaning, distinguishing it from other terms with different meanings.

Identification of keywords and key segments

It will also be necessary to break down the textual corpus to be examined into units of analysis, such as single words, complete sentences or key phrases, which make it possible to have simple constitutive elements on which to make subsequent elaborations.

In particular, it is necessary to carry out:

- vocabulary analysis aimed at identifying word-themes, or those words that appear most frequently;
- analysis of keywords that are over-used, identifying the interaction contexts in which they are uttered or associated with other keywords;
- counting of repeated segments, that is, the sequences of words that are repeated at least twice in the same segments, which may have fewer semantic uncertainties with respect to the single graphic forms.

At the same time, the manuscript can be subdivided according to so-called 'thematic categories' (Losito, 1993: 45). This work will be easier for more structured focus groups, in which the discussion outline is subdivided by specific topics. In contrast, it will be more complex for non-structured groups, in which the thematic nodes emerged in the course of the debate in a more spontaneous way (see section 6.1).

Analysis of concordances

Once the most relevant words, keywords and repeated segments have been identified, it is possible to return to the original text and, by means of analysis of the concordances, 'specify the areas of meaning to which the main words refer' (della Ratta-Rinaldi, 2000: 111). Concordance analysis studies the meaningful contexts of interaction in which a given word is inserted (Bolasco, 1999). In this way, the analysis of concordances is useful for bringing out the 'latent intentions' of the discourse, allowing the researcher to highlight, for example, the associations of positive or negative adjectives to a specific term (Astolfi and Fazzi, 2005; Allen, 2017).

In the field

In a focus group study on values, the researchers can conduct an analysis of concordances with the T-LAB software in order to associate the words/adjectives used to describe a central theme. The result of the analysis of concordances is illustrated in Figure 10.4. The radar chart represents the co-occurrences of the word 'family' with other words/adjectives. The words/adjectives placed closest to the centre such as 'health', 'good', 'happiness', 'home' and 'work' are the words most associated with the term 'family'.

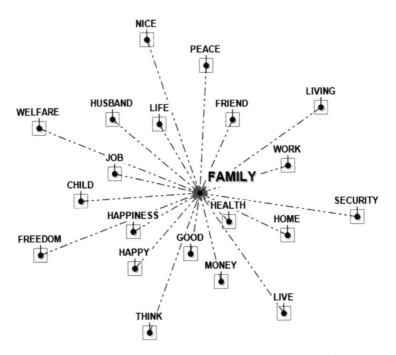

Figure 10.4 Radar chart representing the co-occurrences of the word 'family' in focus group research on values

The analysis of correspondences

It is also possible to conduct a study of the different partitions into which the text is divided, comparing them with each other and trying, through an analysis of lexical correspondences (ACL), to obtain a background view of the relations existing among the information collected (Di Franco, 1997: 73). With ACL, indeed, it is possible to graphically represent the associations between the lexical forms and the texts distributed on a factorial level. This can be achieved by constructing a text matrix in which, for example, rows represent words, columns represent the text and the value in each cell equates to the number of times a particular word appears in the corpus and/or in the partition of the text.

In the field

In an illustrative example of a focus group study on values, the researchers can conduct a multiple correspondence analysis with T-LAB software. As active variables, they can use the same criteria for the formation of discussion groups: the age (X axis) and the education level (Y axis). With regard to the themes (most common headings), the graph plane (Figure 10.5 below) shows the family is a value and a topic across all groups. However, whereas young people tend to place more emphasis on expressive themes, such as personal and emotional fulfilment, middle-aged participants are very attentive to the issues of safety and work.

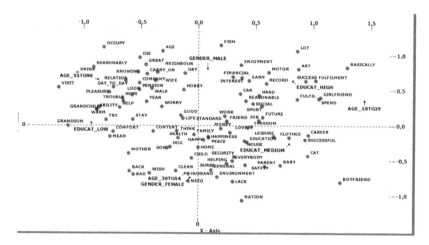

Figure 10.5   Multiple correspondence graph plane in focus group research on values

---

In conclusion, it is possible to argue that the choice of the analysis strategy depends on the research objectives and the progress of the field research. In any event, it should be borne in mind also that in computerized analysis:

- Each type of analysis requires a circularity in the construction between theory and research.
- Every analysis technique and hence every software program is an expression of a particular approach to research. Knowing the underlying logic and the features of the software program helps the researcher to choose the software that best suits his/her needs.
- No software program is self-sufficient and even automatic ones (such as TaLTaC and Lexico) always require the researcher's guidance.

Further reading

Krippendorff, K. (2004) *Content Analysis: An Introduction to its Methodology* (2nd edn). Thousand Oaks, CA: Sage.

The second edition of this classic text is the best introduction to content analysis. The book suggests different ways to analyse meaning in empirical materials such as texts, images or voices.

Corbin, J. and Strauss A. (2015) *Basics of Qualitative Research Techniques and Procedures for Developing Grounded Theory* (4th edn). Thousand Oaks, CA: Sage.

This book can be considered a landmark study of qualitative methods developing grounded theory.

Exercises

1. Conduct a focus group with 12 participants and make an audio recording only. What strategies do you use to make an integral transcription as faithful as possible to the group discussion?

2. You have conducted six focus groups on the use of the Snapchat app by teenagers for sharing photos. During the sessions you asked participants to show examples of images that they had shared in the last few days before the group discussion and to comment on them. You then acquired these images. How do you plan to integrate the images you have available in the corpus of information collected? How do you plan to analyse the images? If you choose to perform a content analysis with the help of an IT package, what software would you choose and why?

11

Analysing the Focus Group Relational and Technical Dimensions

Usually, the analysis of focus groups concerns the content of group discussions. However, if the researcher conducts only this kind of analysis, he/she may underestimate a very substantial part of the information gathered.

Indeed, the focus group furnishes additional information in two dimensions:

- The first dimension consists of the relationships that are established during a group discussion. The relational component comprises the specific information of the focus group. In this chapter, we will therefore propose some tools that help in analysing and enhancing the relational component of the focus group.
- The second dimension is a technical-operational one. The focus group can indeed give reflective stimuli on the research path carried out and/or even contribute to assessing the adequacy of a technique for collecting information on the basis of how they are perceived and used by the participants. In the second part of this chapter, therefore, some proposals will be made on how to use the technical-operational analysis with focus group to support other quantitative and qualitative research techniques.

Chapter goals

- *Knowledge*: knowing how relationships contribute to building information in a focus group and knowing how to evaluate other techniques for collecting information by means of focus groups.
- *Applying knowledge and understanding*: knowing how to use tools for the analysis of the relational and technical-operational dimensions of focus groups.
- *Making judgements*: being aware that the information gathered results from the continual negotiation among the participants and that focus groups can offer reflexive stimuli for improving research tools.

11.1 Relational analysis

More than with any other type of technique, in the case of a focus group, no information exists before the collection takes place. The empirical material gathered derives from the continual negotiation among the participants. Indeed, ideas and opinions emerging during a group discussion are never just individual; rather, they arise in the conversation, they can change and be formulated thanks to the interaction with the other members of the group (Kitzinger, 1994a; Puchta and Potter, 2004: 9–20; Farnsworth and Bronwyn, 2010: 606; Liamputtong, 2011: 16–18; Halkier, 2017: 394–8). For this reason, it is possible to argue that the relational component constitutes the specific information of the focus group (see section 1.2).

The relational nature of focus group information

An analysis aimed at investigating the relationships therefore serves precisely this purpose: to enhance the information specificity of focus groups by focusing on the nature of the relationships established within the sessions. It aims to identify the mechanisms by which the opinions are formed, shared and crystallized during a discussion, analysing group members' behaviours and relationships, including those between the moderator and the other participants.

The literature pays little attention to this component, although it is essential for the production of information. Moreover, when analysis of the relational component is discussed, it is rarely specified which instrument can be more suitable for the analysis. Precisely for this reason, in this paragraph we intend to put forward some concrete proposals about conducting relational analysis. In particular, we will use two tools:

- interaction process analysis (IPA);
- sociograms.

By means of these tools, it is possible to analyse:

- the efficiency and effectiveness of focus groups;
- the relationships within individual groups;
- the interactive profiles of the participants;
- the moderation styles adopted.

Analysis of the efficiency and effectiveness of focus groups

The IPA tool

A useful tool for reading the relationships established during a group discussion is interaction process analysis (IPA), formulated by Robert Freed Bales in 1950. IPA is a tool that illustrates the dynamics of task implementation and of maintaining relationships, central processes in small group interactions.

Concepts and Theories

Bales's thought was developed in a stimulating cultural context along with studies by Kurt Lewin, Morton Deutch, Leon Festinger and Stanley Schachter. According to Bales's theory (1950), if the main function of every small group is to achieve a specific objective, the behaviour of the individual members is principally geared to fulfilment of common objectives and shared activities. From this perspective, the emotional manifestations of the participants have a task that should not be underestimated: within a small group, emotional behaviours can contribute to consolidate relationships, to build interactions or to hinder them.

The IPA tool developed by Bales is well suited to analysis of the relationships within focus groups because the social interactions are characterized by the same logic as that of small groups. From the relational point of view, the focus group consists of a small group of people selected and convened by the researcher with the aim of performing a specific task: contributing to the research through a group discussion (see section 5.1).

The Bales diagram is very useful for understanding the types of interaction that are established not only generically in small groups, but also in the course of a focus group session. In particular the IPA tool acts to detect the expressions of social interactions, dividing them into two fundamental areas: the

Table 11.1 Interaction process analysis (IPA)

SOCIO-EMOTIONAL AREA

Function	A - Positive reactions		B - Negative reactions	
Process	1. Shows solidarity, raises other's status, gives help, rewards	2. Shows tension release, jokes, laughs, shows satisfaction	3. Agrees, shows passive acceptance, understands, concurs, complies	10. Disagrees, shows passive rejection, formality, withholds help	11. Shows tension, asks for help, withdraws from field	12. Shows antagonism. Deflates other's status, defends self, asserts self
Problem at group level	Integration	Tension-management	Decision	Decision	Tension-management	Integration

TASK AREA

Function	C - Attempted Answers		D - Questions	
Process	4. Gives suggestions, directions, implying autonomy for others	5. Gives opinion, evaluation, analysis, expresses feelings, wishes	6. Gives orientation, information, repeats, clarifies, confirms	7. Asks for orientation, information, repetition, confirmation	8. Asks for opinion, evaluation, analysis, expression of feeling	9. Asks for suggestions, directions, possible actions
Problem at group level	Control	Evaluation	Orientation	Orientation	Evaluation	Control

Source: Elaboration from Bales, 1950: 35

instrumental area of the task and the socio-emotional area. Indeed, in a focus group the achievement of the objectives by carrying out the collection of information is essential, especially because this task is strictly connected with the cognitive goal of the research. However, it is equally important to motivate and stimulate the production of information by maintaining relations and activating the socio-emotional area.

In particular, the Bales diagram considers two pairs of behavioural areas, which include positive and negative reactions (A and B) and attempted answers and questions (C and D), relative to both the social–emotional (A and B) and instrumental–adaptive (C and D) components (see Table 11.1). Furthermore, each area is subdivided into three observation categories, which refer to any problems that the group may have to deal with during the discussion.

The subdivision of the text into acts

How to use this tool in practice? First, it is necessary to start from the full transcripts of the focus groups. The first operation is to read each group discussion (FG) and divide it into minimum conative acts. Starting from the definition that the act corresponds to the smallest significant and identifiable behaviour that an observer can perceive (Brown, 1988), in the transcripts of focus groups the researcher can consider as minimal acts all individual verbal and non-verbal interventions produced by the participant/moderator, and by the participant/participant, provided with an independent sense.

In the field

Consider the following extract from a conversation (Cataldi, 2014: 9):

> *Moderator*: First of all, I would like to thank you for coming [ACT 1]. (She smiles [ACT 2]). I am very grateful that you have decided to participate in such an important research project [ACT 3]. As you know, the topic of the group discussion is the political orientations of catholic people [ACT 4]. I would ask you to speak one at a time [ACT 5].

In this excerpt of focus groups, five conative acts have been identified. All of them belong to the moderator; the majority are verbal acts and one is a non-verbal communication act. Smiling is a non-verbal act, but it plays an important role in group interactions. To identify the acts, it is important that all behaviours, including those recorded by the observer, are included in the transcription.

The coding of the acts

After doing this, each act should be labelled and codified in accordance with the behavioural areas, as reported in Bales' IPA (see Table 11.1).

In the field

In the same research there is an example of codification (Cataldi, 2014: 9):

FG L5_M: First of all, I would like to thank you for coming [A1]. (He smiles [A2]). I am very grateful that you have decided to participate in such an important research project [A1]. As you know, the topic of the focus group is your political orientations [B6]. I would ask you to speak one at a time [B4].

Coding serves to distinguish socio-emotional acts from task-oriented ones and also to identify the right conative category.

It is advisable that the coding be carried out by at least two different researchers separately. Furthermore, it is necessary that the attributions of the codes be compared, and that a discussion follows on the reasons for the choice of the codes on which there is no agreement. An idea is to set up a group of experts for coding and resolving disputes on the allocation of IPA codes.

The counting and construction of the matrices

Starting from the assigned codes, it is possible to analyse how different focus group sessions went. This can be done by inserting the assigned codes into small data matrices (micro-matrixes) having as rows the minimum acts identified in a focus group and as columns the following variables:

- the variable that records the phase of the discussion and the specific question posed by the moderator in relation to which the verbal or non-verbal act occurs ('time');
- the variable that records the performer of the act (actor);
- the variable that keeps track of the main participant referred to by the action line (related);
- the variable that records the type of act coded according to Bales' IPA (behaviour).

It is then possible to proceed with overall analysis of behavioural codes adopted by individuals (the moderator and the participants) through the calculation of the percentages of the behavioural group sessions, of the average and the standard deviation of the acts.

In the end, it is possible to construct the final matrices (focus groups separated for total acts and acts only of the moderator), having in rows the single focus groups and in columns the percentage of the coded behavioural acts and the other variables. Some variables can be expressly dichotomized in order to facilitate the analysis; other variables are cardinal.

In the field

In a pilot study on relational analysis (Cataldi, 2018), the final matrix had 30 focus groups in the rows and the following variables in the columns: % of positive socio-emotional behaviours, % of negative socio-emotional behaviours, % of adaptive instrumental behaviours questions and % of instrumental-adaptive behaviours answers. Then, there were other cardinal variables, such as the number of participants in the focus group and other dichotomous variables, such as gender of the moderator, gender of the participants (dichotomized in two modes: mixed or uniform), age of the participants (divided into: young people and adults). The presence of these additional variables enabled the conduct of multivariate analyses, which made it possible to assess which of the various factors was most influential in the structuring of group dynamics.

The structuring of the components

What results can this analysis provide? First, this analysis can highlight how the various components of behaviour were structured within each session. Each focus group will indeed have a specific percentage of socio-emotional behaviours and another percentage of instrumental-adaptive behaviours. This emerges from a simple frequency analysis, which can be applied systematically to each discussion group.

Normally, since focus groups are formed precisely by virtue of a precise task – gathering information on a specific theme suggested by the moderator through group discussion – the speech acts geared towards performing the task stand at around 75.0%, while the speech acts made up of social-emotional behaviours are around 25.0%. However, the researcher need not worry if the focus group yields a different structuring of the components. Indeed, this also depends very much on the purpose of the focus group and on the structuring of the discussion outline. For example, a focus group conducted with an exploratory-descriptive function will generally have a more open discussion outline and will give more space to the expression of the relational dimension, compared to a focus group conducted with an (quasi) experimental function. Moreover, the choice of the topic will also contribute to the structuring of the components because the discussion of a sensitive topic may require a greater investment in relations. Discussion on politics, for example, may be divisive and can give rise to a considerable presence of negative emotional reactions.

Comparison between different sessions

The structuring of the components can therefore be considered as the basis for a comparative analysis between the different focus groups carried out. In this way, the analysis allows identifying the focus groups that have been more efficient and more effective in terms of information gathered and less productive because, for example, discussions have been excessively conflictual and controversial.

In the field

As shown in Table 11.2, in an investigation into the acceptance of deviant behaviours among young people (Cataldi, 2014), it emerged that the first focus group, whose initial function was to sound out the topic and to test the tool, was the least efficient in instrumental terms in carrying out the task. In the fourth group the presence of negative social-emotional behaviours was due to the discussion on abortion, which triggered a heated argument between two of the participants. Furthermore, in the eighth focus group, the affinity in religious orientation and the young age of the participants favoured the formation of strong consensus expressed through positive social-emotional behaviours.

Table 11.2 Consistency of the social-emotional component (positive and negative) per 8 focus group sessions

Focus group	% Positive social-emotional behaviour	% Negative social-emotional behaviour	% Total social-emotional behaviour
Group 1	20.8	13.2	34.0
Group 2	19.0	5.6	24.6
Group 3	23.9	2.8	26.7
Group 4	20.9	13.6	34.5
Group 5	17.9	6.2	24.1

Focus group	% Positive social-emotional behaviour	% Negative social-emotional behaviour	% Total social-emotional behaviour
Group 6	16.7	9.1	25.8
Group 7	16.0	8.9	24.9
Group 8	26.9	3.2	30.1

Source: Cataldi, 2014: 7

For example, usually in research the first focus group – which has the initial role of probing the tool – is the least efficient in terms of performance of the task and more inclined to bring out the relational aspect of support and discussion among the participants. Other important factors in the structuring of the components may be the leadership style of the moderator, which is usually strictly connected to the homogeneity/heterogeneity of groups in terms of age, gender, social conditions, knowledge of the discussed topic and so on (Cataldi, 2018: 298–300).

Comparison between the sections

The counting of behaviours can also be carried out in relation to the individual sections of the group discussion meetings. In this case, the counting is done by 'comparing the variable that identifies the different phases of information gathering ("moments"), with the variable for labelling the interventions ("behaviours"), in relation to the participants involved in the specific sections. This makes it possible to distinguish in each session the most efficient moments in terms of information emerged, from those that have less efficiency' (Cataldi, 2014: 12) due to the emergence of particular group dynamics (e.g. vigorous antagonism or extreme conformity among the participants).

For this reason, it is possible to find the matching with all instrumental phases identified by Bales can be recognized in a focus group (1950). For example, there is an 'initial orientation phase, in which participants tend to seek information on the task and to move towards the problem. This phase corresponds to the warming-up stage. It includes the introduction of the research, the presentation of the task and the first round-table discussions – often ordered by the position of the participants – which have ice-breaking as their main purpose' (Cataldi, 2018: 301). Normally, this phase is characterized by a preponderance of the adaptive instrumental component of the task, aimed at obtaining information relating to guidance and explanation.

Then there is a central phase in which the participants exchange ideas and opinions within the debate. This phase aims to collect information interactively (Stewart and Shamdasani, 1990: 79; Hennink, 2014: 50–1; Cyr, 2019: 57–66). In this phase, the components can be distributed differently depending on the type of interaction established and the ability of the debate to offer information consistent with the purposes of the research. Then there is a final phase in which the synthesis of the collected opinions takes place followed by the conclusion and final thanks. If the interaction among participants was positive, in this phase there will be a preponderance of the positive socio-emotional component.

The patterns of relationships within individual groups

Sociograms

The sociogram is another useful tool for analysing the relational dimension in focus group. While the IPA is focused on participants' behaviours, the sociogram can help the researcher to visualize the type of relationships that are configured within a group. This can be useful for analysing the mechanisms of opinion-formation and consensus building during a discussion.

The sociogram is a tool elaborated in the social network analysis. It illustrates the links among different people/objects. Jacob Levi Moreno (1954) elaborated this tool in order to develop a method to study the structure of groups' interpersonal relationships. Indeed, the sociogram is based on a sociometric logic and it is a graphical representation of the interpersonal social links.

In relation to focus groups, a sociogram is therefore a diagram made up of two fundamental elements:

- points (illustrated by circles or squares and labelled with numbers or initials), which represent the participants;
- lines and arrows connecting or separating the points, which represent the agreements/disagreements, the choices/refusals and their direction.

Sociograms therefore allow the identification of cliques, also known as 'maximal connected subgraphs', which are the most connected or mutually connected subjects within a network. Therefore, depending on the types of relationship that are established, it is possible to identify a greater or smaller social distance among the units in a small group, as well as the different positions of the members in the communications flow, or the different arrangement of connections within the group. In this way, the sociogram permits a simple graphical visualization of the interaction established in a network (chains, polygons, networks), the position of each member within the group (peripheral, excluded, popular or leader subjects) and the sociometric structure of the network (cliques and subgroups).

Visualizing the structure of the interpersonal relationships within a focus group is really useful for understanding how opinions are stabilized or shift, as well as the positioning/repositioning of each member in thegroup (Barbour, 2007: 164; Marková et al., 2007: 49; Acocella, 2008: 74–5; Liamputtong, 2011: 173).

The procedure

This analysis can be based on the calculation of the frequency of the interventions by each group member. Furthermore, to identify the direction, the recipient or recipients of each intervention can also be registered.

The observer plays an important role in detecting group interactions and dynamics during a focus group. As detailed (see section 8.2), to reconstruct the type of interaction, he/she can resort to an adjacency matrix (Trobia, 2005: 57), which shows in each cell the number of times each participant has spoken to one of the other participants or reacted to his/her intervention. The matrix is produced during the meeting to collect immediate impressions of the discussion and support the moderator in his/her functions, but it is generally perfected in the analysis.

In this way it is possible to recognize the participants who intervened the most and those who intervened the least in the discussion. Moreover, from the crosstabs of the two rows (participants * participants), it is possible to obtain a graphic representation of the interaction among the members of the group. Starting from the frequencies of the interventions, it is also possible to understand the relational position of each participant in the group, detecting if he/she has a central or marginal position, if there are conversational subgroups, if preferential treatment is shown among certain members, and so on.

Therefore, the interactive dynamics developing in a focus group contribute to give different forms to a sociogram structure. There may be different geometric shapes, which can be more symmetrical or unbalanced. This depends on the number of speech/relational acts addressed to other members and the reciprocity in verbal and non-verbal communication.

In the field

Figure 11.1 shows the structures of the sociogram that emerged in the course of the investigation into the acceptance of deviant behaviour among young people (Cataldi, 2014). In Focus group A, the structure of the relations is similar to that of a star inscribed in a rectangle. This structure is characterized not only by the transitivity of many

(Continued)

---

bonds, but also by the centrality of a participant, who assumed a privileged position in communication and a role of mediator, often making himself the bearer of the group's requests to the moderator. In Focus group B, a very different interactive structure is instead configured. In a case like this, the broken relationships are multiple and represent the particularly fragmented and not very interactive pattern of the discussion group. The difficulty consisted especially in the shyness and the young age of the female participants.

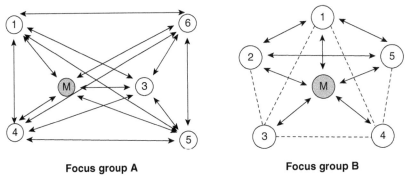

Focus group A   **Focus group B**

Figure 11.1   Sociograms of the links established in two focus groups

Source: Cataldi, 2014: 3

This analysis can be carried out by hand or also with the support of social network analysis (SNA). SNA adopts a quantitative-relational approach that is based on relational data, such as the interactions that characterize a group of people or a set of more or less complex organizations (families, associations, companies, nations etc.). Interactions are represented by exchanges of various kinds (communication or material exchange). The potentials of this type of analysis are essentially two: the application of graph theory to relational data and, consequently, the description of the structure of interactions through various indices derived from matrix algebra (Wasserman and Faust, 1994). To this end, SNA provides various types of analysis aimed at the study of the following structural characteristics: density, inclusion, connectivity, structural equivalence, centrality and centralization, cohesion. The results are given by a series of indicators (indexes) that furnish a quantitative representation of the properties analysed and that can refer to the group as a whole (e.g. centralization) or to its individual members (e.g. centrality). These indices are calculated by applying complex mathematical algorithms thanks to the support of special software such as UCINET and E-Net.

Analysis of interactive profiles

However, to identify the role played by the various participants, it is not enough to count only the frequencies of the interactive relationships. Indeed, starting from these all that can be identified is that some participants interacted more and others remained more on the margins, as well as if some participants were more at the centre of attention. To refine the analysis, in a focus group it is fundamental to use again the information gathered by the observer, who during the debate outlines the interactive profiles by observing the way in which each member of the group dealt with the various topics and the non-verbal behaviours (see section 8.2). Only in this way is it possible to specify whether, for example, a more central participant in the discussion has been a leader or an expert, as well as whether a more marginal participant is shy or uninterested.

Even if there is no 'objective' criterion for qualifying a participant, this evaluation is necessary to determine the real impact of the interactions on the information produced in a focus group. This analysis can be supported by discussion with the moderator, replay of the recording and careful reading of the debate. It is also important to consider that many factors influence the structuring of relationships in small discussion groups. These are, for example: the physical arrangement of the participants around the debate table, the socio-demographic characteristics, and the personal attitudes of the participants, or the style of moderation (Smithson, 2000: 109; Liamputtong, 2011: 16–18).

In the field

In a piece of research on stereotypes in the dress code of young Western women and young Muslim women (Guizzardi, 2009), one participant had put himself forward as an expert on Islamic countries. However, following some statements and some precise stimuli on the part of the moderator, it was clear that this participant was not well informed about the topic. The observer therefore qualified this participant as a 'fake' expert. In the same discussion, a person who intervened following a direct prompt from the moderator instead showed herself to be very attentive to the discussion and with ideas that were innovative in relation to those that had emerged previously. Hence, the observer qualified this participant as 'shy' and 'innovative'. During the analysis, it was possible to assess the impact that the two participants had on the discussion as a whole and to reach a better interpretation of the information (Acocella, 2009: 66–7).

Analysis of the group dynamics

Interpersonal dynamics

Interpersonal dynamics are both the product of and the condition for individual action, so much so that if what tends to emerge in interpersonal dynamics is the personalistic aspect of interaction among the participants, in interpersonal relational processes there is instead affirmation of a new collective identity. For this reason, in order to enhance the interactive nature of the information gathered in a focus group, it is also necessary to analyse the impact of group dynamics on individual participants (Kitzinger, 1994a).

For example, one aspect to be explored is the dynamics of power and the eventual affirmation of a leader (see section 9.4). As detailed in section 5.2, the participants in the discussion are chosen on the basis of certain characteristics aimed at enhancing the perception of being among 'equals'. However, stronger personalities can sometimes emerge during sessions, who try to lead or monopolize the discussion.

The relational centrality of a participant is not sufficient to be able to consider him/her a leader. It is important to relate the frequency of interventions and the number of communications made by/to the participant, as well as the intransitivity of the relationships and the collective recognition of the privileged role that the subject holds with respect to the rest of the group.

It is interesting to explore the dynamics of power and leadership also to identify any potential influence that the leader has on other group members. Indeed, some participants may find themselves being controlled by the judgement and constrained by the leader's opinion (Carey and Asbury, 2012: 28; Hennink, 2014: 30–3; Cyr, 2019: 79–80).

In the analysis of group interactions and dynamics it is also interesting to evaluate the vivacity of the debate or if the discussion tends to focus on only a few points.

The moderation style analysis

Relational analysis can also be useful to outline the role of the moderator in a group discussion better. Indeed, the institutionalized task of the moderator requires him/her to exercise a certain type of power in guiding the discussion (see section 9.4). The moderator has a key role in the focus group because his/her primary task is to keep the group 'focused' and to generate a lively and productive discussion (Barbour, 2007: 51; Carey and Asbury, 2012: 29).

Regarding moderation styles, by means of relationship analysis it is possible to distinguish a session that is characterized by a more participatory approach in comparison to another session where the style is more directive (Stewart and Shamdasani, 1990: 89; Morgan, 1997: 54; Cardano, 2003: 158).

In the field

Table 11.3 shows the moderator's acts in the eight focus groups conducted in research on the perception of deviant behaviour by young people (Cataldi, 2014). The Table shows, for example, that in the eighth group there were numerous interventions by the moderator falling within the categories of question C7 and C8 of the instrumental-adaptive area. This responds to the increasing need of the moderator to acquire information, clarifications and specifications, in the continuous attempt to deepen and understand the reasons underlying certain considerations.

Table 11.3   Moderator's behaviours in eight focus groups: % acts based on the IPA scheme

	Group 1	Group 2	Group 3	Group 4	Group 5	Group 6	Group 7	Group 8
1. Shows solidarity, raises others' status, gives help, reward	2.0	1.8	2.8	1.6	4.6	5.9	1.0	0.7
2. Shows tension release, jokes, laughs, shows satisfaction	2.0	2.7	4.7	0.8	0.8	1.0	/	6.0
3. Agrees, shows passive acceptance, understands, concurs, complies	2.0	1.8	1.8	26.2	2.3	/	13.3	22.4
4. Gives suggestions, directions, implying autonomy for other	17.2	6.3	13.1	11.9	9.9	15.7	10.2	9.0
5. Gives opinions, evaluation, analysis, expresses feeling, wish	8.1	14.4	0.9	0.8	/	1.0	1.0	/

(Continued)

Table 11.3 (Continued)

	Group 1	Group 2	Group 3	Group 4	Group 5	Group 6	Group 7	Group 8
6. Gives orientation, information, repeats, clarifies, confirms	26.3	5.4	7.5	1.6	4.6	11.8	5.1	2.2
7. Asks for orientation, information repetition, confirmation	21.2	46.8	49.5	38.8	50.3	42.0	40.8	32.8
8. Asks for opinions, evaluation, analysis, expression of feeling	21.2	20.8	19.7	18.3	27.5	21.6	28.6	26.9
9. Asks for suggestions, directions, possible action	/	/	/	/	/	/	/	/
10. Disagrees, shows passive rejection, formality, withholds help	/	/	/	/	/	1.0	/	/
TOTAL	100	100	100	100	100	100	100	100

Source: Cataldi, 2014: 6

However, it is also necessary to analyse whether and how the presence of the moderator excessively influences group dynamics.

In the field

In research on the effects of violence shown on television (Morrison, 1998: 185) the researchers found that the participants' responses assumed stronger tones if the moderator was a man, especially if of robust physique.

On the other hand, violent behaviour on television was never justified if the moderator was a woman or a thin man. These results are an interesting example of the influence that the moderator's characteristics can have on the group. At the same time, the relationships developed within the focus group are useful to reflect generally on the way in which social relations may influence social representations on a phenomenon.

11.2 The technical-operational analysis

Technical-operational analysis examines the tools to be used or which have been used during a piece of research, especially in relation to how they are perceived and employed by respondents. In relation to these aspects, in this section we will discuss the use of the focus group to assess the adequacy of a technique for collecting information and to suggest any changes/precautions when designing it. In this type of analysis, the focus group can be useful to support both quantitative and qualitative techniques.

Supporting scaling techniques

We have already investigated the usefulness of using the focus group in mixed methods research designs (see Chapter 4), both in the orientation phase (*ex-ante* role) and in the analytical-interpretative phase (*ex-post* role). In what follows, we will explore how the technical-operational analysis of a focus group can be useful for the formulation of the main scales used in a survey.

Scaling techniques are very common in the formulation of survey question-naires. In particular, these techniques are used to detect attitudes, that is, mental states that exert a directive influence on the individual's response in a situation with which he/she involves (Pavsic and Pitrone, 2003).

The detection of attitudes is characterized by problematic elements:

* difficulties in operationalization (reduction of the concept to variables);
* non-direct observation;
* high risk of distortion (as the effect produced by social desirability of the respondent).

Therefore, scaling techniques are a set of methodological procedures designed to detect the opinions of the interviewees on a specific topic, in order to draw out their attitude (not directly observable).

287

In relation to scaling techniques, the focus group can be useful for formulating a wide range of scaling tools. In this section, we will focus on two of the most common ones: the Likert scale and the self-anchoring scale.

Supporting the Likert scale

The Likert scale consists in a certain number of statements (termed 'items') that express a positive and negative attitude with respect to a specific topic (Likert, 1932). For each item, there is a scale of agreement/disagreement, generally in 5 or 7 modes. The respondent can therefore express a score from 1 (minimum agreement) to 7 (maximum agreement) on each item. The sum of these judgements will show the attitude of the respondent towards the research object in a reasonably precise manner. The simplest way to attribute the final score to each respondent is as follows: the researcher can distinguish favourable items from unfavourable ones; the scores of the unfavourable items are inverted to add them up with the favourable ones; the scores that the respondent gave to each item are added up. The total score on the scale expresses its (supposed) status on the general property that the scale claims to measure (summated ratings).

The use of the focus group may therefore be useful to:

- *Identify salient items for the research target.* The focus group discussions will allow exploring the vital context of the people to whom the survey is addressed. This will allow the researcher to select items most relevant according to the frame of reference of the respondent to the survey.
- *Identify possible causes of distortion and bias that may occur at the time of administration.* For example, a type of distortion typical of Likert scales is the social desirability mechanism that induces the interviewee to choose the alternative that seems to offer the best self-image. In this regard, a focus group can be useful for identifying the items that most likely produce this bias, in order to eliminate them.

Another purpose of the technical-operational analysis with a focus group is to evaluate the meaning attributed to the items used on the Likert scale. Indeed, the focus group can identify the difficulties related to the understanding of an item and its polysemic features. In particular:

- *The vagueness of the item.* During group discussions, requests for examples may emerge regarding a particular item. This may be symptomatic of the use of a sentence that is too general.
- *The ambiguity of the item.* The group discussion can bring out different understandings of the same sentence.

- *The use of a terminology that is not suited to the target audience.* The focus groups can help identify the degree of appropriateness of the language used in drafting the items.

Supporting self-anchoring scales

The family of self-anchoring scales is characterized by a continuum delimited by two extreme categories, the only ones with meaning and labelling. Hence, the researcher establishes a minimum figure (usually zero) and a maximum, and the interviewee is only informed of the interpretation that he/she must give to the boxes that are at the two extremes. These techniques can be defined as 'self-anchoring' because it is the interviewee himself/herself who self-evaluates, anchoring his/her state semantically to the two extremes of the scale (one of which represents the worst possible state, and the other the best state). With reference to the object to be evaluated, sometimes the extreme categories are constituted by single terms/expressions (e.g. 'minimum trust' – 'maximum trust', as in the *Cantril scale*); other times by adjectives (e.g. 'dishonest' – 'honest', as in the *Differential semantic*); other times again by complete but opposite sentences (e.g. 'Italy must be one and indivisible' – 'Italy must be a confederation of independent states', as in the *Forced choice scale*).

However, there are different causes of infidelity of the data produced by these techniques. Indeed, as Alberto Marradi (2007) argues, an interviewee may:

- conceive the property on which he/she is asked to self-evaluate his/her state in a different way from the researcher;
- understand differently from the researcher the score corresponding to his/her status on that given property and, therefore, express a different assessment;
- voluntarily express a wrong assessment of his/her own state, to give a better self-image (social desirability effect);
- misunderstand the functioning of the self-anchoring scale;
- understand the functioning of the self-anchoring scale but tend to use it in a systematically distorted way (e.g. by attributing all high or low scores to the objects to be evaluated, as well as to always locate himself/herself only in the central areas).

The use of the focus group to support the formulation of a self-anchoring scale can help the researcher to reduce some of these risks, by providing information on the possible mechanisms for assigning and anchoring the scores by the interviewees. In this way, the researcher will be able to formulate more effective scales to be included in the questionnaire. Focus groups can also help to make explicit the meanings tacitly given by the respondent to scale scores.

In the field

In research on deviance (Cataldi, 2016), for example, concerning the 0 score of minimum gravity attributed to soft drugs, one participant stated:

> F4_1: So, I wrote smoking marijuana 0, but not because it's not serious, but because it didn't even deserve an evaluation. It would be more correct to put 'not classified', exactly: it is not valid, it is such idiotic behaviour that it is not even worth the bother, so I put 0.

The 0, in this case, does not assume the value of the lowest possible state (i.e. minimum gravity) but of the insignificance, of the nonsense of the behaviour, which is such as not to merit even evaluation. Clearly, this is a line of interpretation transversal with respect to the continuum assumed by the researcher of extreme gravity/non-gravity.

Supporting qualitative techniques

Mixed methods research designs can also include focus groups in combination with other qualitative techniques in order to analyse the same object of study from different perspectives (see section 4.5). In such cases, the technical-operational analysis of focus groups can provide a support for improving the effectiveness of the different qualitative techniques included in the research design.

In the orientation phase

In particular, in a qualitative mixed method design, focus groups are usually combined with:

- in-depth interviews;
- diary-interviews;
- biographical interviews.

The technical-operational analysis of the results emerging from focus groups can be useful in the orientation phase of a qualitative mixed methods research, in order to better define the objectives of the research, identify the case studies and determine the best ways to use these techniques.

Technical-operational analysis with focus group can also help in identifying how different qualitative detection procedures influence the people involved in the field research. Some studies that are interesting in this regard have been conducted on the different influence that the focus group or in-depth inter-view can have on the same categories of subjects in relation to the same object of study.

In the field

To expand this point we can refer to research conducted to investigate how some adolescent males relate to their peers (Wight, 1994). In this research, the focus groups and individual interviews were conducted with the same people on the same topics. In some cases, the interviews pre-ceded the focus groups; in others, they followed them. When the boys were first interviewed individually and then later participated in the col-lective discussions, they provided different information: in the individual interviews, they showed a much greater propensity to listen and a more marked sensitivity to the female point of view, while in the focus group discussions they tended to express 'macho' opinions. When, conversely, the boys were first involved in the focus groups and then interviewed, 'macho' answers constantly emerged. In this research, the use of the focus group made it possible to detect the opinion component deriving from the influence of the reference group. The use of individual inter-views, instead, brought out the most private component derived from personal re-elaboration of and resistance to the norms and values of the group itself. The quasi-experimental design conducted by Wight also prompts another consideration. The focus group did in both cases draw out the opinions most influenced by the norms of the reference group (in this case the peer group), and the influence, in relation to this topic and with participants of this type, seems to have been so decisive as to remain even in interviews when they followed the group discussion. The teenag-ers involved in the experimental research, indeed, remained consistent with the regulatory system of their reference group that the focus group had revealed more clearly.

Technical-operational analysis conducted in support of other qualitative techniques can also help identify the most suitable technique with which to investigate specific topics or how to design a differentiated use of the two techniques in order to maximize the effectiveness of both. To clarify this point, we show an example on the use of focus groups and biographical interviews in relation to sensitive topics. Indeed, in the literature, there is much discussion about which of two techniques is best suited to investigate these issues. There is no single solution in relation to sensitive issues.

However, technical-operational analysis conducted with focus groups can help in developing a better research design. For example, it can allow the researcher to identify how to enhance the use of the individual interview to reconstruct the biography of a person who has experienced a difficult situation, as well as the subjection-subjectivation processes derived from this experience. At the same time, the same analysis can help identify how to structure focus group discussions that involve people who have experienced the same difficult situation, in order to investigate social representations on this topic. In this regard, technical-operational analysis can be used to clarify the perspective to be enhanced to address the issue, in order to use the accounts of the focus group participants to bring out inter-subjective representations rather than their personal experiences.

In the field

To clarify the point, we can consider a hypothetical research design on poverty, which combines focus group and biographical interviews. The technical-operational analysis, with reference to individual interviews, may be useful to identify some indicators of social exclusion (e.g. the relationship with labour market or with services etc.), and how to conduct the interview to highlight subjection-subjectivation processes (e.g. helping interviewee to recount how he/she reacted to a 'biographical challenge' such as the job loss or an eviction). However, with reference to focus groups, this analysis can help to identify a more inter-subjective perspective on the issue of poverty (e.g. the exogenous factors that may prevent the risk of poverty), as well as to prepare probing techniques that may reduce the risk of dealing with personal experiences (such as stories on poverty that highlight different factors of exclusion or social reintegration).

Technical-operational analysis conducted in support of other qualitative techniques also allows the researcher to identify which people can be involved in the field research. For example, in a group discussion, a situation can arise where interaction favours only the emergence of shared information. Instead, other information which is not common among the participants and which however could be useful for cognitive purposes may not emerge in the sharing process. The group identity, indeed, may induce the participants to highlight the similarities and not the differences. Similar situations can be avoided if technical-operational analysis is used.

Expert advice

In the above example, if the researcher decides to conduct focus groups with vulnerable or socially marginalized people, the technical-operational analysis can help to identify relevant properties to ensure a certain degree of homogeneity internal to the groups. The aim is to involve people with similar experiences in order to encourage the emergence of comparable intersubjective representations.

Receiving feedback on the research

In some cases, the technical-operational analysis can be carried out with reflective purposes in order to acquire complete feedback on the research. This will be an ongoing self-assessment of the investigation that can be carried out after each discussion session in order to:

- improve the inputs used by the moderator;
- take stock of the information reached by the researcher on the specific topics of investigation;
- analyse the validity and reliability of information;
- evaluate how discussion tools were perceived and used by members of group discussions.

At the same time, a research feedback strategy can be 'group discussion about the group discussion', whose purpose is to explore in more depth the interaction paths among the actors to bring out the information construction methods. Specifically, this strategy allows the researcher to focus on the cognitive and emotional processes of the participants in the act of responding to a stimulus of debate, thus making it possible not only to obtain additional information on the individual topics of investigation, but also to analyse the possible impact that these arguments have on the respondents.

The reflective technique therefore helps to:

- identify the conceptual frameworks of the participants related to the definition of the object of study;
- assess the adequacy and complexity of the stimuli used during the discussion, depending on the characteristics of the participants;
- explore the reasons for the answers given by the participants to a given topic;
- obtain further information on the topic of investigation and on some unexpected aspects that emerged during the discussions.

293

Furthermore, the more complex and articulated the discussion outline is, the more technical analysis will be appropriate. This is especially the case when the moderator stimulates discussion by using subsidiary probing techniques such as thematic vignettes, cards with items, stories to complete and so on. Precisely in relation to these aspects, the technical-operational analysis aims at clarification and suggests possible modifications/precautions.

Further reading

Cataldi, S. (2018) 'A proposal for the analysis of the relational dimension in the interview techniques: a pilot study on in-depth interviews and focus groups', *Quality and Quantity*, 52 (1): 295–312.

The aim of this pilot study is to identify the relational characteristics of two specific interrogation techniques, considering them as forms of social interaction: the focus group and the in-depth interview.

Scott, J. and Carringhton, P.J. (eds) (2011) *The SAGE Handbook of Social Network Analysis*. Thousand Oaks, CA: Sage.

This handbook provides a systematic review on social network analysis.

Exercises

1. Use the sociogram to analyse the interaction produced in a focus group. The sociogram places a participant at the centre of the debate. How do you decide if this person is a leader, an expert or an alleged expert?

2. You are conducting mixed methods research to evaluate the degree course in sociology, and you decide to use a focus group to support the construction of a questionnaire with a Likert scale. What technical-operational analysis would you perform? Explain the procedure in detail.

12

Interpreting and Reporting the Focus Group Results

Having analysed the information, the researcher has to draw conclusions and present the results of his/her research. The questions that may arise are different. For example, the researcher can ask himself/herself: What consequences can I draw from my research? Can the results of my research be generalized, or are they considered valid for similar cases as well? Also, how can I write a research report? How can I make the results of my research understandable?

In this chapter, we address these questions. In the first part, we will try to understand how the results of the focus group analysis are interpreted, examining the logics of inference and the ways in which the researcher moves from empirical cases to theoretical cases. In the second part, we will describe how to write a report on an investigation conducted with focus groups. Finally, we will go further and examine how to write a scientific article.

─────────────── **Chapter goals** ───────────────

- *Knowledge*: knowing how to interpret information, reach conclusions and present the results of research conducted by means of focus groups.

(Continued)

- *Applying knowledge and understanding*: knowing how to use different inference logics and report focus group information.
- *Making judgements*: being aware of the public and replicable nature of the research conducted through focus groups.

12.1 Interpreting the results

Building an interpretative framework

After the information analysis, some questions arise spontaneously; they concern how to interpret the information analysed and how to construct a theory from focus group results.

In reality, in research with focus groups the interpretation of results does not always lead to the construction of a true structured theory. Rather, we can talk about the definition of an interpretative framework. In any event, the interpretation should allow the researcher to read the empirical materials within a broader framework and to extend the research outputs even beyond the individual group discussions carried out.

There are two fundamental steps in interpreting the results of the analysis:

- outlining the conceptual category referable to the analysis unit;
- moving from the empirical case to the theoretical case.

Outlining the conceptual category referable to the unit of analysis

We know that in research with focus groups, the relationship between empirical observations and theorization is circular and that, after field research, qualitative analysis generally aims to define the characteristics of the unit of analysis (the research object). This means that in the investigation there is always the need to bring the information collected empirically to a higher level of theoretical generality (see section 3.1).

The inferential process is crucial for this purpose. In other words, it is fundamental to find the logical reasoning that allows the researcher to read the empirical material correctly and to produce a final interpretation. In particular, it is necessary to choose which inferential process makes it possible to connote the unit of analysis, outlining a conceptual category of reference (Cardano, 2020: 45–9).

This obviously depends on the type of research design and the purpose of the investigation.

In research with analytical-in-depth or experimental functions

When the researcher chooses to use focus groups for analytical purposes (therefore in research designs with analytical-in-depth or experimental functions), since the aim is to enhance the homogeneity of information, the group discussions conducted are not considered independent of each other. This type of research design is therefore characterized by a more defined research plan from the initial phases, with a more structured tool to detect information and a choice of empirical cases in which to enhance internal homogeneity in a single discussion group and external heterogeneity among the discussion groups (see sections 3.4 and 3.5).

In these research designs, therefore, the inferential strategy that the researcher can exploit is induction. This consists of discovering a regularity and formulating a generalization through successive empirical tests (Vicsek, 2010). In particular, inductive reasoning is used to identify aspects relevant to developing the conceptual category related to the unit of analysis. The conceptual category is produced by starting from the analysis of the empirical materials collected. Its adequacy is tested by comparison between the groups. Therefore, the comparison is fundamental for identifying the general properties considered useful for understanding the phenomenon studied.

In the context of inductive reasoning, however, two types of inference can be distinguished: enumerative induction and analytical induction.

Enumerative induction or numerical saturation

'Enumerative' induction refers to the criterion of 'saturation' of information. According to the logic of this inferential strategy, it is necessary to compare a number of homogeneous cases until the information becomes redundant (see section 5.3). The force of this argument, indeed, depends on the accumulation of the observations made: the higher the number of observations that give the same result, the greater is the argumentative force of the rule found (Carlsen and Glenton, 2011; Hennink, 2014: 43). This inference is therefore based on the principle that the corroborative force of the cases decreases during work.

Expert advice

The enumerative induction consists in discovering a regularity and in formulating a generalization in the following way:

(Continued)

297

p1 ∧ p2 ∧ ... pn (CASE)

q1 ∧ q2 ∧ ... qn (RESULT)

----

p → q (RULE)

An example applied to social sciences could be the following one:

- long period of unemployment (p1) ∧ long period of unemployment (p1) ∧ ... long period of unemployment (p1)
- condition of social exclusion (q1) ∧ condition of social exclusion (q2) ∧ ... condition of social exclusion (qn)
- long periods of unemployment (p) therefore (→) condition of social exclusion (q) until proven otherwise.

For example, if, while comparing several group discussions with social workers on the theme of vulnerability, the researcher more than once finds that, in the collective representations of this social group, a long period of unemployment is connected to a condition of social exclusion, he/she can consider 'long-period unemployment' to be a relevant aspect (and therefore a valid indicator) for defining the conceptual category of 'social exclusion'.

In this case, the researcher will write the number of conducted observations in his/her report, highlighting the association found. In reference to each relevant feature of conceptual category, the identified characteristic will be accompanied by excerpts from group discussions used to bring it out.

However, in qualitative approaches the criterion of 'saturation' should not be overestimated, since it seems to refer to a criterion of generalization of information typical of quantitative research (Barbour, 2007: 69). The problem underlying this inferential strategy is that, in qualitative research lacking a numerical delimitation of the reference population, it is not possible to define how many cases to observe in order to establish the degree of relevance of the identified rule with certainty (Montesperelli, 1998: 89–90).

Analytical induction or the semantic coverage of the conceptual category

A different type of induction, used in social sciences, is 'analytical' induction. In detail, analytical induction tries to identify some combinations of characteristics related to the intension of the conceptual analysis unit that the researcher is trying to define. These combining characteristics also allow the constitutive process of the phenomenon observed to be explained (Lindesmith, 1947; Robinson, 1951; Becker, 1998; Hennink, 2014: 182–3).

The distinctive feature of this form of inference concerns the inductive origin of the hypothesis of configuration of the conceptual category (Lindesmith, 1947). Indeed, this hypothesis is formulated starting from analysis of the empirical materials collected, and its adequacy is progressively evaluated during the comparison of all the observed cases. In this way, the researcher identifies and selects a combination of characteristics – common to all the cases – considered useful to capture the phenomenon investigated and therefore to define the conceptual category related to the unit of analysis (Robinson, 1951).

Expert advice

Analytical induction consists in discovering a regularity and formulating a generalization in the following way: $(a \land b \land c) \rightarrow S$.

In analytical induction, $(a \land b \land c) \rightarrow S$ relates to the relationship between the properties observed and their attribution to the conceptual category that the researcher is trying to determine. It is therefore a matter of the relationship between *definiens* and *definiendum*: before the $\rightarrow$ there are the characteristics that have been isolated because they are common to the empirical cases observed to define the conceptual category; after the $\rightarrow$ there is the definition of the category identified.

Returning to the previous example regarding social exclusion, as the researcher compares several group discussions with social workers, he/she finds that, in the collective representations of this social group, a combination of characteristics is common to all discussions – such as (a) 'a long period of unemployment', (b) 'a high number of different jobs performed' and (c) 'a low age on first employment' – and associated with a condition of social exclusion. Hence, the researcher can isolate these characteristics and consider them relevant to defining the conceptual category 'social exclusion' (S). The combination of these characteristics enables the researcher also to explain the constitutive process of the observed phenomenon. Indeed, if the characteristics describe the phenomenon to which the unit of analysis refers (in short, if they are valid indicators of the conceptual category 'social exclusion'), the way in which these features are combined also allows the researcher to give a possible interpretation regarding the constitutive process of the phenomenon (therefore, the process underlying the 'development of a condition of social exclusion').

In this inferential strategy, particular attention is devoted to deviant cases that contradict the provisional hypothesis and hence to those cases which – while presenting the characteristics of the identified conceptual category – do not adapt to the phenomenon as outlined up to that moment (Hennink, 2014: 182–3). In such circumstances, therefore, it is necessary to specify the hypothesis further, since the characteristics identified hitherto are not sufficient to connote the phenomenon under study adequately, nor to clearly discriminate the cases to which this phenomenon may refer. This specification takes place by identifying a new characteristic that justifies the exclusion of the deviant case, but at the same time is adequate for all the cases previously considered. Indeed, it is a property on which the deviant case does not have a positive state (namely, it is not a property that characterizes it), while it is present in all the other cases analysed up to that point. The new feature is then added to the other attributes previously identified. Starting from this new configuration, the comparison with the other cases detected in the investigation continues, until the next deviant case that will require a further specification of the hypothesis (Becker, 1998: 246).

Expert advice

Returning to the previous example, while continuing the comparison with other group discussions, the researcher finds a new characteristic: a high level of commitment in seeking employment. Social workers consider this an important element with which to evaluate the responsiveness in terms of problem solving and contrast to social exclusion factors.

For this reason, this characteristic is different from the others that characterize those who live in a condition of social exclusion. Indeed, it seems to refer to people who, while experiencing a condition of social marginalization, still have proactive attitudes that motivate them to improve their condition. Therefore, the level of commitment in seeking employment can discriminate the status of those who experience 'vulnerability' compared to those who experience more definitive forms of social exclusion. Once this new characteristic is identified, the researcher can analyse the cases previously observed again and investigate how this tendency 'to react' was dealt with in previous discussions. If the researcher finds similarities, he/she can better specify the conceptual category by adding a new property: 'a low level of commitment in the job search' (d).

Hence, he/she has a new configuration: $(a \wedge b \wedge c \wedge d) \rightarrow S1$.

While S referred to a generic definition of 'condition of social exclusion', S1 identifies a new, more specific conceptual category that can be defined

---

as 'a chronic condition of social exclusion'. Following on from the identification of the new property (the level of commitment in the job search), the researcher can try to configure another conceptual category related to the 'condition of social vulnerability' by making a new comparison among the various focus groups conducted.

Analytical induction therefore makes it possible to remedy the shortcoming of simple induction, which – based on the principle of enumerative saturation – leads the researcher to compare a number of homogeneous cases until redundancy of the information is reached (considering this to be an indication of having traced some relevant properties). Instead, regardless of the number of observed cases, analytical induction compares and reorganizes the observed empirical materials in order to identify interesting attribute combinations – among the characteristics common to more observed cases – thus dividing the empirical cases into groups corresponding to the various configurations outlined. The argumentative force stems from the fact that the researcher uses this attribute configuration to specify and define the conceptual category; indeed, the relevance of these features lies in the fact that they are combined in the same way in all cases included in that conceptual category. Furthermore, the features relevant to delineating the conceptual category are continuously redefined starting from the cases included or excluded (because they are deviants).

Using this inferential strategy, in the research report the researcher will not only have to specify the number of observations carried out, highlighting the association found, but he/she will also have to report the various combinations of attributes identified for the different conceptual configurations outlined. For each conceptual category, the configuration of attributes will be accompanied by excerpts from group discussions used to specify and clarify that conceptual category.

In research with exploratory-descriptive functions

Such inferential strategies can also be exploited in research designs with exploratory-descriptive functions. Indeed, even if the collection plan is less defined at the beginning in this kind of research, it is nonetheless possible that the researcher, by comparing similar or different cases, can identify some common characteristics.

However, since in such research designs each focus group can be treated independently, different aspects of the analysis unit may also emerge from one discussion to another (see section 3.3). Rather than deepening, in these research designs the aim is to draw out the variability of the analytical aspects and perspectives that will emerge during the group discussions. For this reason, in such cases, the type of inference that can be exploited is not based on the search for recurrences among the collected materials, but rather on enhancing the differences, albeit from a comparative terms perspective, in order to produce an interpretative unification hypothesis.

Therefore, the 'comparison' between different groups is fundamental in this type of investigation, in order to bring out 'dimensions that are likely to be relevant in terms of giving rise to differing perceptions or experiences' (Barbour, 2007: 69). Furthermore, through the comparison between different empirical groups, in the researcher's mind a model of 'how it happens' in reference to the phenomenon investigated is progressively delineated (Bertaux, 1998: 105).

This inferential strategy is more frequent in research designs with exploratory-descriptive purposes. This is because of the flexible research planning used throughout the information collection process, with the continuous remodelling of the choice of empirical cases to be observed and of the aspects to be investigated in light of theory that gradually emerges from field collection (Hennink, 2014: 42).

In any event, as detailed in sections 3.1 and 3.3, in such cases the final conceptualization referable to the unit of analysis is not a simple reflected reproduction of the reality of the facts found, but the result of choices that the researcher will make, assessing situation by situation. By making these choices, the researcher will orient himself/herself through categories and analytical perspectives deriving from his/her professional background (Barbour, 2007: 140–1), which have the advantage of being more intersubjective.

Expert advice

Taking up the previous illustration on social exclusion, if the researcher finds during the investigation that a long period of unemployment is associated with situations of vulnerability or social exclusion, he/she will look for cases that have different states on this property: for example, short periods of unemployment or intermittent situations in relation to labour market entry. Hence, in such cases, from time to time, the various empirical cases will refer to 'different traits' of the unit of analysis, yielding a large quantity of indicators related to it. This will also allow reflection in comparative terms on what is the most plausible explanation that makes the information gathered intelligible and consistent.

In research reports, in such a case, the researcher will state the variety of the elements detected, even if they are presented within a theoretical framework that takes everything together, making clear the choices made in relation to the various aspects that emerged. He/she will therefore emphasize: (a) the elements emerging in a discussion group which make that specific empirical case relevant to his/her unit of analysis (on which aspects, for what perspective); and (b) which characteristics and perspectives on the phenomenon that emerged in the various discussions should be emphasized and which should be ignored. The presentation of the results will be accompanied by excerpts from group discussions relevant to the various characteristics of the unit of analysis, enhancing theoretical fruitfulness of each single focus group.

Moving from 'empirical groups' to 'theoretical groups'

Therefore, the main interpretative challenge that the researcher faces is to relate the results achieved to a conceptual macro-category that aids understanding of the characteristics of the phenomenon under investigation. However, it does not concern only the identification of interesting features to be attributed to the conceptual category referable to the research analysis unit. Indeed, this challenge also includes the transformation of the individual 'empirical groups' involved in the discussion into 'theoretical groups', enhancing the particular perspective through which each group categorizes the object of investigation.

We know that in qualitative research approaches, not only is the unit of analysis defined *ex-post*, but the same 'empirical cases' can be redefined *ex-post* as specific theoretical constructs (see section 3.1). The characteristics identified to delineate the conceptual category related to the unit of analysis can be useful in this process of transforming an 'empirical case' into a 'theoretical construct' (Ragin and Becker, 1992: 220).

In other words, the empirical cases should be considered on the basis of their theoretical fruitfulness or based on their ability to provide information useful for identifying, delineating or understanding the unit of analysis (Macnaghten and Myers, 2004: 67; Barbour, 2007: 69). Therefore, in light of conceptual re-elaborations, the 'empirical cases' will be reinterpreted, in various ways, as different types of 'theoretical cases' or 'specific theoretical constructs' that will contribute differently to identifying, delineating or understanding the unit of research analysis or a part thereof (Walton, 1992).

In research with analytical-in-depth or experimental functions

In research designs with analytical-in-depth or experimental functions, this transformation process takes place through the strategy of choosing cases that will be homogeneous internally – namely, referable to the same 'trait' of the unit of analysis – and heterogeneous among themselves – namely, referable to different 'traits' of the unit of analysis (see section 3.4). The comparison of homogeneous cases will allow the perspective of the same social group to be deepened and, therefore, the outlining of specific 'theoretical cases'. Instead, the comparison among different cases will allow highlighting of the points of view on the phenomenon that link to the different theoretical cases identified (Bloor et al., 2001: 36; Carey and Asbury, 2012: 41–3; Hennink, 2014: 112–13).

In the field

In the research on the political opinions of active Italian Catholics (Di Giammaria et al., 2015), the focus groups comprised participants belonging to 12 Catholic associations. Thus, the discussion groups were homogeneous internally based on the mission of the association. Bearing in mind that there is no longer a Catholic political party in Italy, the discussion showed that the associations have to deal with a 'cognitive dissonance' between political orientation and Catholic orientation. The main result highlights the fact that the different strategies adopted by participants to fill the cognitive dissonance are associated with the different missions of the religious groups, allowing the researcher to identify different 'theoretical cases' (see Table 12.1).

Table 12.1 Strategies adopted by groups and participants in focus groups to fill the cognitive dissonance between political orientation and Catholic orientation

Type of strategy	Sample excerpts from focus groups	Prevailing characteristics of groups (F = Focus group)
Hierarchization of the norms	F5_M3: I put life and family first, I bet on this, at least we all agree on this, because these are the two points. Everything else doesn't interest us and it's much less relevant.	Groups of cultural engagement (F7)
Re-interpretation of the norms	F3_F1: I'm thinking of our community, for example: we have never done major anti-abortion campaigns, but I think we do a lot of work in the suburbs to support families.	Groups of spiritual renewal (F1, F5, F6, F10, F12)

Type of strategy	Sample excerpts from focus groups	Prevailing characteristics of groups (F = Focus group)
Unmasking of instrumental strategies	F8_F3: He who speaks of the sense of family, but then is divorced and does not respect these rules first. Well, this is really a fool.	Groups of spiritual (F2, F9) and spiritual-social (F3) commitment
Attributions of removal	F4_M1: Yes, but we must be careful about this issue of non-negotiable values, because many times they are the alibi for not looking at other things, which are however connected.	Groups of socio-cultural (F4) and social (F8) commitment
Free will and removal of authority	F11_M1: I see this in a very personal way because I can't afford to judge a person who decides to abort.	Groups of socio-cultural commitment (F4)

Source: Elaboration from Di Giammaria et al., 2015: 122

In research with exploratory-descriptive functions

In exploratory research designs, groups may be more heterogeneous both internally and externally in order to increase the variety of information collected (Bloor et al., 2001: 36; Zammuner, 2003: 116–17). Hence, in this case, it is not certain that all discussion groups fall into the same theoretical construct, since each group will be able to take very different positions on the phenomenon (see section 3.1). In these cases, as detailed in section 5.3, it is important to enhance an external heterogeneity among the discussion groups aimed at exploring different dimensions on the phenomenon investigated (Barbour, 2007: 69; Hennink, 2014: 42). Therefore, the formation of the various 'theoretical groups' will take place starting from these differences, since they will be considered expressions of different perspectives on the research analysis unit.

In the field

An example is provided by a piece of research on the discursive cons-truction of national identity of Austrians (Wodak et al., 2009).

(Continued)

> The discussion groups were very heterogeneous. From the comparison of focus groups, two main discursive strategies emerged, influenced by the political leanings and the different regional contexts: 1) Conservative strategies of the construction of national identity; 2) Transformative strategies in the construction of national identity. These differences allowed the researcher to identify two 'theoretical groups'.

In the example given, the 'empirical groups' were included in the two identified 'theoretical groups'. However, at other times, due to the variety and flexibility of the exploratory drawings, it may even happen that within the same discussion several perspectives are delineated by different subgroups. In these cases, therefore, in a focus group discussion it will be possible to identify different theoretical constructs corresponding to the various subgroups.

12.2 Writing the research report

The writing experience

Writing is always an art. Writing is a creative and even artistic act. Indeed, it is a generative action. For this reason, writing a research report can be simultaneously a difficult and exciting experience.

At the same time, writing a research report has some specific characteristics, which circumscribe the creativity of writing with certain precise constraints. Knowing these constraints can be of great help to a researcher preparing to write a report for the first time. In what follows we identify some important factors.

The recipients of the report

The first important factor concerns the recipients of the report. When writing, it is always important to keep the target of one's research in mind. In the field of qualitative research this aspect is even more important. Indeed, writing is not just a form of reporting but becomes part of the whole research experience because it gives shape to a new social relationship which puts the researcher in contact with other social actors. Writing a research report should therefore be considered a social action that relates the researcher (or the research group) to the recipients (Krueger and Casey, 2000: 146–7; Frisina, 2010: 125–32).

Usually, there are three recipients of a report:

- the client, who may be the manager of the company or of the public or private entity that commissioned the research, but also the research coordinator or the supervisor of the thesis;
- the research participants, or those who have been directly or indirectly involved in the focus groups;
- a common reader, who can be anyone who reads, but also a colleague or a member of the scientific community.

Taking into account the categories of recipients and readers of the report is very important. In most cases the research report will be aimed at all three of these targets together. This means that a research report must be clear enough for everyone to understand. In some cases, the report will be intended only for a specific target among these. Writing should consider the recipient in choosing the appropriate language and considering the social expectations of the target audience.

However, as some cultural anthropologists point out (Dwyer, 1977; Tedlock, 1979; Clifford, 1986), writing reports always inherently has both an ethical dimension and a political dimension. This means that the researcher must be very attentive to research participants and to the protection of privacy and anonymity (see sections 2.3 and 2.8). At the same time, a research report is also a knowledge tool that can have a significant impact on the people studied. Indeed, research through reports can play an important role. It can do so, for example, by bringing to light a social malaise, in giving voice to those who have no voice, dealing with new or little-explored issues, raising public awareness of a problem, orienting public policies or the choices of a company and so on. This potential must be kept in mind when writing research reports (Barbour, 2007: 17–18).

Concepts and Theories

In the introduction of a classical book of cultural anthropology, James Geertz Clifford (1986) explains that research reports are always conditioned by various factors:

- the centrality of the context;
- the prominent role of rhetoric;
- the relationship with the institutions;
- the political dimension;
- the historical dimension.

The illustration and motivation of the choices

In addition to 'ethnographic sensitivity', a good report should take into account the public nature of social research. A good report must reconstruct, explain and evaluate all the phases of the field research in order to 'make transparent' the entire process of gathering information and producing knowledge about the phenomenon studied (see section 3.1). This means that all the steps and choices made by the research group must be explicit and motivated in the report (Bowen, 2006: 14; Hennink, 2014: 180).

Therefore, it is necessary:

- to explain why the research group chose to use the focus group method, what the reasons were for using this technique, and its limitations;
- to describe how the analysis unit was identified and, consequently, the planning of the discussions, the structuring of the concept map, the choice of cases and the formation of the groups;
- to illustrate how the focus groups were moderated and observed;
- to indicate how the planning of the research changed and was specified in the course of work, each time enhancing the results obtained;
- to clarify the method of analysis chosen by the researcher.

Often the explanation of these steps is condensed into a few lines relating to the method. However, we recommend giving more space to this part and to the reconstruction and justification of the choices made. This means accompanying the reader and making the construction of the empirical base transparent. Remember that in this reconstruction the researcher can take advantage of the 'notes from the field' collected by the moderator at the end of each group discussion (see section 7.4).

Focusing the report

A significant feature of the focus group research report is focusing. The focus group produces a great deal of information. Despite this, the researcher will always have to keep the research topic in mind during the analysis, in order not to provide an ill-defined and unfocused report (Krueger, 1988: 131).

To this end, besides taking new and unexpected aspects emerging from the field into account, the researcher will always have to bear in mind the key questions that drove the research design and the information-gathering phase. In particular, to carry out good clarification work, it is advisable to bear the following questions in mind:

- What did you know about the topic before doing this research and what was confirmed or disproved in light of what was found?

- What sensitizing concepts did you use to conduct the research?
- What expected and unexpected results did you obtain?
- What implications do these new results have for the topic in question?

Sensitizing concepts and results

These questions reveal a very important distinction between sensitizing concepts (see section 3.1) and research results.

According to Herbert Blumer (1954), sensitizing concepts should give the researcher a general sense of reference and guidance in approaching empirical instances. 'Definitive concepts provide prescriptions of what to see, sensitizing concepts merely suggest directions along which to look' (Blumer, 1954: 7). They are conceptual constructs that have to be used as analytical tools, often taken from the researcher's professional encyclopaedia, in order to provide possible lines of inquiry (Barbour, 2007: 140–1).

In other words, sensitizing concepts are used by researchers to orientate himself/herself in the field research. They can be used both in the definition of the research design and in the construction of information collection tools. Furthermore, their purpose is to provide an analytical approach to the object of study, both during the analysis for the classification and coding operations, and in order to formulate the models and theories within which the information collected will be intelligible. For this reason, they cannot coincide with the research results, that instead derive from the collection and analysis of new information (Baxter and Jack, 2008: 553).

In the field

To clarify the difference between sensitizing concepts and empirical results, we can refer to the research on stereotypes in the dress code of young Western women and young Muslim women (Guizzardi, 2009). In discussions, only very general dimensions were envisaged as 'sensitizing concepts', which can be summarized as 'social conditioning/free choice'. After the analysis, the sensitive concept of 'social conditioning' was articulated by 'consumerism', 'influence of the fashion market', 'gregariousness' and 'need to feel part of a group of reference'. 'Free choice', however, was articulated by 'will to affirm one's individuality and personality' and 'to affirm one's own difference from others even within a group' (Acocella, 2009: 58–60).

The level of articulation and specification of sensitizing concepts varies in different research designs according to the cognitive objectives and the function attributed to the use of the focus group. For example, in exploratory-descriptive designs, sensitizing concepts are usually more generic and used in a flexible way, while in research with analytical-in-depth or experimental purposes sensitizing concepts usually have a higher level of detail specification and articulation (see section 3.1).

In a report, the researcher should clarify the state of the art before the start of the research, the framework within which the research team carried out the investigation with the support of sensitizing concepts, and the research results. Obviously, these three levels are closely linked, but confusion among them should be avoided.

Furthermore, the report should illustrate the research results at two different levels: description of the empirical materials collected, and theoretical interpretation of these empirical materials based on the cognitive objectives of the investigation.

There is also often some confusion in research reports. Distinguishing the 'description' and 'interpretation' makes it possible to differentiate the initial conceptual, linguistic and analytical frame of the researcher from those deriving from the information gathered in the discussion groups. In other words, this distinction makes it possible to identify more clearly both how the knowledge and perception of the phenomenon has changed following the research, and how the categories of interpretation of the phenomenon have been formulated.

Description of the results

Therefore, the research results should first be presented in descriptive terms, reporting some of the participants' verbal and non-verbal behaviours, especially emphasizing the 'natural languages' of the group discussions.

The level of detail depends on the purposes of the research and the report. If the research has an exploratory-descriptive design, it is very important to describe in detail and in depth the results achieved and the differences that emerge, giving reasons for the internal and external heterogeneity of the groups. Even when the research has an analytical-in-depth or experimental function, a description of the results is important. In such cases, the description of the content of the discussions will be more conditioned by the hypotheses formulated at the beginning of the research, but, in any event, it will allow the researcher to take advantage of the segmentation criterion with which the groups were assembled.

In the descriptive presentation of the research results, an important role is played by the inclusion in the report of quotations from utterances by the participants and/or the insertion of fragments of group discussions (Krueger and Casey, 2000: 153; Cardano, 2011: 227; Hennink, 2014: 191). This allows the report to be communicative and enhances the 'emic' character of the focus group.

When quoting the excerpts, however, it is necessary to remember to ensure the complete anonymity of the participants (see section 2.8). Thus, all names must be deleted and replaced with codes (Carey and Asbury, 2012: 86). These codes may be useful for identifying the participants' gender, age or other characteristics important for the selection of groups/participants and the focus group number. Therefore, the legend of the identification codes used can be reported.

The insertion of excerpts from discussions is fundamental for the descriptive exposition of empirical materials, but it is also the first step towards the theoretical interpretation. Indeed, to identify the excerpts from group discussions to be included in the report, the researcher will make choices. These choices will necessarily be selective and discretionary. However, it is important that the citations are not selected only on the basis of aesthetic criteria or rhetorical force, but according to systematic and controllable criteria, so that the process by which conclusions are reached is explicit and transparent (Bowen, 2006: 14; Hennink, 2014: 180).

In this process of choice, a fundamental role is played by the objectives of the investigation, the type of analysis performed, and the results that are intended to be illustrated. Sensitizing concepts also play an important role, since they help the researcher to argue why it was decided to develop one analytical perspective on the phenomenon rather than another, as well as to arrive at the final elaborations and, therefore, formulation of the analytical model best suited to interpreting the information gathered (see section 3.1).

The collective level of the analysis unit

An error frequently committed when describing the research results with focus groups is to use a level of results reporting that is individual (based on the opinions of the individual participants). However, it must be borne in mind that the focus group technique, precisely because it relies on the group, makes sense in collecting concepts and collective opinions (Barbour, 2007: 164; Liamputtong, 2011: 173; Cyr, 2019: 10–20). Therefore, the words spoken by a participant cannot be directly compared with those of another participant; rather, they should always be considered as an expression of the collective debate (Smithson, 2000: 109; Marková et al., 2007: 9–10, 202; Hennink, 2014: 26–7).

Expert advice

A common mistake in writing a focus group report is to state, for example: '4 out of 10 group participants expressed this opinion'. Unlike the survey, the focus group does not allow the gathering of individual opinions and making them comparable to each other. It is therefore wrong to count them.

Even if different opinions or positions emerge within a group, they cannot be attributed to individuals. Nor can they be counted according to a statistical method. Individual expressions must always be inserted within the group dimension. For this reason, not only must individual positions be compared, but also the positions of the group on a given topic. Furthermore, as we have specified with regard to the interpretation of results, it is very important to explain how the transition from the empirical case to the theoretical case occurred.

Group dynamics

For this reason, when describing the results, it is very important to give an account of the group dynamics. Indeed, a good report should explain what features and processes were activated during group discussions (Carey and Asbury, 2012: 96–7; Halkier, 2017: 394–8).

When possible, it will therefore be useful to support the research results with the outcomes of the relational analysis carried out, also by means of sociograms, illustration of the results of the network analysis, or IPA analysis (see section 11.1). However, if the relational analysis had not been conducted in a specific manner, it will still be useful to explain in transparent terms what intrapersonal and interpersonal dynamics have occurred among the participants and between the participants and the moderator. This will allow the reader to understand how the opinions of the participants have been defined and will make the empirical basis more accessible.

Interpretation of results

Finally, leading on from the description of the results, it will be necessary that the report also has a section devoted to interpretation. Since the information does not 'speak for itself', the conceptualizations that the researcher will produce from the empirical information collected will never be the result of a simple speculative reproduction of the reality of the detected facts (see section 3.1).

Therefore, each research report should contain and clearly present the categories of interpretation of the results. These will be the outcome of analysis of the content of the conversations, but also of the analysis of the interactive dynamics that emerged during the group discussions (see Chapters 10 and 11).

For this reason, the categories of interpretation can be considered 'etic', since they are defined by the researcher and belong to a second level of the so-called hermeneutic circle. But they will also be founded in an 'emic' way, that is, by enhancing the conceptual, linguistic and analytical frame of the people involved in research.

The interpretation will have to take account of the procedures stated above: namely, how the researcher has outlined the conceptual category referable to the unit of analysis and how he/she has moved from the empirical case to the theoretical one. It will therefore be necessary to make explicit the inferential logics used and the reasoning whereby the researcher has proceeded from the results (description) to the theoretical framework (interpretation).

In focus group research the interpretation of results does not always lead to the construction of a structured theory, but rather to an interpretative framework, which means that, depending on the purpose of the investigation, there will be different approaches to theorizing.

Even in an investigation conducted for exploratory-descriptive purposes, it is important to know how to interpret the results and give them a homogeneous meaning. There will not always be a consolidated theory available to interpret the results. However, it is possible to advance hypotheses of connection among the characteristics of the groups and the opinions that emerged.

If the research is carried out with an analytical-in-depth or experimental function, on the other hand, the research team will have at their disposal a more consolidated theoretical framework. Indeed, these types of research design start from more structured hypotheses drawn from pre-existing theoretical frameworks and previous knowledge on the study object (see sections 3.4 and 3.5). Therefore, the research group may be based on this theory for conclusions, confirming or disproving the initial hypotheses and highlighting the elements of continuity/discontinuity with the previous knowledge.

Finally, although rarely, the report should not only aim to provide interpretation, but also to discuss possible actions, especially where the aim of the research is oriented to the evaluation of policies or the planning of actions.

References and appendices

Finally, a good research report usually contains both bibliographic/site references, and attachments.

The function of the bibliographic/site references is to include the investigation within a general framework of the literature on the topic. These references are appropriate even if the report is not strictly scientific, but requested by policy makers, social actors and stakeholders in a field other than the academic one.

Similarly, the role of the attachments is to make the research path public and the empirical material inspectable. Attachments can be provided on paper or with a CD-ROM, or a link can be provided with the material.

In particular, attachments can include:

- the integral textual corpus consisting of the transcripts of the discussions;
- the moderator's field notes;

- the sheets filled in by the observer;
- graphs and analysis tables.

12.3 Writing an article for a scientific journal

The challenge

Writing an article for a peer reviewed journal is always a challenge. Indeed, the system is based on the peer review and double-blind review processes. In the case of an article that reports the results of research with focus groups, the challenge is even more interesting because it requires knowing how to combine methodological rigour with interpretative sensitivity and understanding of the context studied. Furthermore, a good article reporting the results of research with focus groups should be able to make the reader understand the participants' point of view. This means that even from the narrative point of view, a good article will contain citations of the participants' interventions and the 'tale' that emerged from the group discussion.

Choosing the journal

In order not to waste time and energies, it is advisable to focus immediately on finding the right scientific journal. Indeed, journals always have a specific interest and a preference that can be either methodological or thematic.

In the methodological area, there are world-renowned journals specialized in qualitative research. These journals could be the most suitable for papers reporting the use of focus groups in an autonomous function. Other journals are devoted to mixed methods and the combined use of qualitative and quantitative techniques.

Another possibility is to choose the journal according to the research topic. There are journals specialized in education, religion, politics and so on. One possibility is to write to the journal editor in advance to ask if the journal would be interested in receiving a paper on your topic.

Identifying the journal first helps not only in terms of knowing the editorial rules (how to insert graphics, tables, bibliographical references etc.), but also in providing the option to read similar articles that have been published in the journal, gaining insights from them.

The structure of the paper

Moreover, the author will also be able to understand what structure the journal prefers. Usually, the structure is divided into:

- title;
- abstracts and keywords;
- introduction;
- literature review;
- research and method;
- research analysis and/or results;
- conclusions and limits of the research;
- references.

In other words, in the scientific literature there is a rhetoric that is shared within the reference scientific community. For example, it may happen that after submitting a paper to a journal, the author is asked to add an introduction, if not present in the version that he/she sent. This means that there is a canonical way to present papers.

However, it is always important to keep in mind that a good-quality article must also know how to 'dare' or present the results in a creative and original way. Nevertheless, originality and creativity must have a guiding criterion: to help the reader enter the context and point of view of social actors. If this is the criterion that has prompted the author to innovate the rhetorical canons of a scientific article, he/she will see that this will be appreciated by the reviewers. This is especially so if his/her article is theoretically, methodologically and empirically founded.

Frame the research topic

Once the journal has been identified, it will be necessary to write. The first and foremost aim of a scientific report is to present a conceptually adequate description of a specific matter. The description of the latter is always a theoretical task because it requires a conceptually well-organized analysis. Therefore, to frame the theme it will be necessary to:

- identify the historical-social trends of the analysed phenomenon;
- define the concepts/terms used;
- outline study of the research topic in the reference literature;
- identify still open problems and issues.

The literature review

To do this, it is necessary to review the reference literature. Actually, background or a literature review is necessary for each section to frame the research problem and thereby highlight previous knowledge, but also to support the same results of the research.

315

The literature review is a crucial portion of the paper. Many beginner researchers have problems with the scope and structure of the literature review. Not only may a literature review generate improvements in the author's research, but reading a collection of reviews can also help him/her to develop a work scheme.

Above all, the purpose of the literature review is to frame the research topic and explain to the reader the state of the art of scientific research on that given research topic. A part of the paper should therefore be devoted to defining the terms used and illustrating the main interpretations of the phenomenon under study. A diachronic logic of research development on the topic being analysed can be followed, or a dialectical logic can be adopted whereby the different positions on a given topic are highlighted. In any event, the research questions should emerge from this section (or paragraph). We can say that a good literature review should prompt the reader to ask himself/herself the same questions that the research group asked itself at the beginning of its inquiry.

The methodology

Of great importance is description of the methodology used to obtain the information. It is necessary to clarify not only the function for which the research group has chosen to use the focus groups (autonomous or mixed methods), but also for what research design functions (exploratory-descriptive, analytical-in-depth, experimental or evaluative). Moreover, it is necessary to specify the unit of analysis, the choice of cases, the method of conducting group discussions and analysis strategies.

However, to describe the method it is not enough only to list the choices made. It is also necessary to describe the reasons and support the methodological choices with the literature. A good way for the researcher to assess the methodology section is to ask himself/herself, 'If I were challenged to justify my choice of this method, what literature would support my choice?'.

Anticipating the review

Another tip is to keep the reviewers' criteria in mind when writing. Reviewers normally base their assessments on three fundamental criteria: the originality of the paper/research; the overall impression of the research reported; evidence and examples. On this basis, reviewers provide an overall judgement on the paper (Hennink, 2014: 181).

For this reason, it is advisable to write anticipating the revisions and, therefore, keeping the following recommendations in mind:

- Make sure that the editor and the reader know what the original contribution of the paper is. The originality should be clear from the title (if possible), mentioned in the Abstract, and described in the Introduction and in the Research analysis and/or Conclusion.
- Make sure that the manuscript has a single and clear message, so that the reader follows a single narrative thread from beginning to end. This means that the information contained in the Introduction must be developed in the article. Furthermore, the points that emerged from the literature must be mentioned and analysed by the study, so that the Results and the Conclusions evidence progress with respect to previous knowledge.
- Check that the paper contains sufficient evidence, examples and references. In this regard, it is recommended that the article contain extracts from the transcripts so that the discourse comes alive with the same words used by the focus group participants. Also useful are tables summarizing the research plan (the formation of the groups, the criteria used etc.). For the results, graphs, figures and charts could be useful in order to depict the coding of the emerged opinions. If the content has been analysed by a statistical-textual computer program, it will be useful to attach at least one graph produced by the software used, with appropriate explanations of the results obtained.
- Check that the paper mentions all the sources and make sure that the manuscript ends with a complete reference list. In particular, it should be remembered that references are required for: theoretical claims, empirical findings, other perspectives to address the same topic and methodological ideas.

Review the paper

After the manuscript has been submitted to the selected journal there are two possibilities: the article can be rejected, or the article can be accepted with major or minor revisions.

Here we cannot dwell on the distorting effects that the 'publish or perish system' can have both on individuals (especially young researchers subjugated by the stress of productivity), on journals (e.g. with the proliferation of 'predatory' journals asking for a payment to publish papers and the overcrowding of proposals in other free journals), and on institutions (universities, departments, research centres). However, it is important to say that if a paper is rejected, this is not a reason for discouragement. Indeed, rejection is part of the logic of peer review, and the rejection rate is essential to maintain the high standard of contributions to a journal (Silvia, 2007).

There are two types of rejection. There is a refusal that is not accompanied by detailed explanations and that usually happens fairly quickly after the editor has only read the title and the Abstract. Usually this refusal flows from the wrong choice of journal; that is, it depends on whether the research topic or the research approach of the submitted article conforms with editorial policy choices. It is therefore necessary to reformulate the original choice before submitting the paper to another journal, to ensure that it is in line with its editorial guidelines. In rare cases, journals may also provide a suggestion of another journal focused on the topic of the research and that may be interested in the manuscript. This is greatly appreciated.

Another rejection depends on how the paper is written and its contents. This rejection is usually accompanied by an explanation of the paper's weaknesses. It is therefore important to build on these explanations in the paper. Usually the required revisions are substantial and can help the author rewrite the paper. After rewriting, it will be possible to submit the article again to the same journal or to another similar one.

Finally, there is the possibility that a paper is accepted, but it has the reviewers' and the editor's comments. The revisions may be minimal (minor) or extensive (major). In any event, the comments of the reviewer help the author to detach himself/herself from his/her own creation and to look at it from the outside, focusing on its weaknesses and strengths. It is consequently necessary that the author does not adopt a defensive position or a position of passive acceptance concerning the review. A review should not be considered an order, but rather a set of suggestions for improving the article.

Indeed, for each point that a reviewer has made an author has these three options (Lange, 2019: 2):

- rewrite the text in response to a comment;
- discuss/reject a reviewer's comment;
- combine these two options.

Incorporation of the revisions is therefore a new creative work that involves an effort to rewrite the article. The experience is that at the end careful reviewers contribute to a new development of the article, almost as if they were co-authors. In this way, the outcome will certainly be better than the first version, even if not in the form expected by the author(s).

When the revised article is finally published, it may be a contribution to the scientific field of the author. Indeed, 'only when he has published his ideas and findings has the scientist made his contribution, and only when he has thus made it part of the public domain of scholarship can he truly lay claim to it as his own. For his claim resides only in the recognition accorded by peers in the social system of science through reference to his work' (Merton, 1977: 47).

Further reading

Weaver-Hightower, M.B. (2018) *How to Write Qualitative Research*. New York: Routledge.

Using clear prose, helpful examples and lists, this book suggests step by step how writers can address those tasks in qualitative research.

Silvia, P.J. (2007) *How to Write a Lot: A Practical Guide to Productive Academic Writing*. Washington, DC: American Psychological Association.

This book is especially useful for academic authors who realize that their writing style needs improvement or who have been told that they have failed to communicate the point of their paper.

Exercises

1. What does 'deviant case' mean in analytical inference?

2. You have received a review of an article on research conducted with focus groups. The anonymous reviewer says that: 'The choice of the focus group technique seems appropriate to the purpose of the research, but this is not always sufficiently highlighted in the analysis. Indeed, the authors compare individual speech acts extracted from different focus groups as if they had been produced during an in-depth interview rather than in a group discussion. It is therefore advisable to emphasize the group level in the text'. What was the problem highlighted by the reviewer? How will you fix it to send a revised version of the paper to the editor?

Appendices – Tools

Appendix 1: Example of an informed consent form for focus group research

Informed Consent for Focus Group Research

Study Title

You are invited to participate in a research study on [PURPOSE OF STUDY].

This study is being conducted by [NAMES AND AFFILIATIONS OF RESEARCHERS].

[FUNDING SOURCE] has provided funding for this study. You are invited to participate in this study because [STATE WHY INDIVIDUAL WAS SELECTED].

Participation in this study is voluntary. [IF RELEVANT, INCLUDE: 1) WHO WILL KNOW, OR NOT KNOW, THAT THE RECIPIENTS HAVE PARTICIPATED; 2) NOT PARTICIPATING WILL NOT AFFECT ANY BENEFITS, SERVICES ETC. RECEIVED NOW OR IN THE FUTURE].

If you agree to participate in this study, you will participate in a focus group [DEFINE THIS OR USE ANOTHER TERM, E.G. GROUP DISCUSSION AS APPROPRIATE] with [WHO ELSE WILL BE IN FOCUS GROUP].

The focus group will be moderated by [FILL IN]

The topics that will be discussed during the focus group will include [FILL IN]

The focus group will last [FILL IN] minutes/hours.

The focus group will be audio-recorded in order to accurately render what is said. If you participate in the study, you may request that the recording be paused at any time. You may choose how you want to speak during the group. You may also choose to leave the focus group at any time.

[IF INCENTIVES ARE PROVIDED:] If you participate in the study, you will receive [FILL IN] for your time. You will also receive [FILL IN (E.G. INFORMATION, RESOURCE LIST, ETC.)].

Participating in this study may not benefit you directly, but it will help us learn [FILL IN]. You may find answering some of the questions upsetting, but we expect this to be no different from the kinds of things you discuss with family or friends. [ANOTHER VERSION OF THE PREVIOUS SENTENCE: We do not envision any significant risks related to participation in this study. Participants may feel some pressure to reveal feelings or experiences to the group. If participants share their experiences with colleagues and peers, they may also feel vulnerable during or after the group.]

The information that you will share with us if you participate in this study will be kept completely confidential to the full extent of the law. Participants will be asked not to use any names during the focus group discussion. Please be advised that although the researchers will take every precaution to maintain confidentiality of the data, the nature of focus groups prevents the researchers from guaranteeing confidentiality.

The researchers would recommend participants to respect the privacy of their fellow participants and not repeat what is said in the focus group to others. Reports of study findings will not include any identifying information.

Audio-recordings of the focus groups will be kept on a password-protected computer in [FACULTY NAME]'s locked office. After the focus group recording has been typed, it will be destroyed. The typed transcription will be kept on the password-protected computer and any printed copies will be kept in a locked file cabinet in Dr [NAME]'s locked office. Only [LIST NAMES OR TITLES/AFFILIATION] will be able to listen to the recording or read the typed version of the recording.

If you have any questions about this study, please contact [NAMES OF PIS (PRINCIPAL INVESTIGATORS), PHONE NUMBERS AND EMAIL ADDRESSES; RESEARCH WEBSITE AND Q&A FORUM]. If you have questions about your rights as a research participant, please contact [NAMES OF PIS, PHONE NUMBERS AND EMAIL ADDRESSES; RESEARCH WEBSITE AND Q&A FORUM].

Your signature on this consent form indicates your agreement to participate in this study. You will be given a copy of this form to keep, whether or not you agree to participate. The second signed consent form will be kept by the researcher. I have read the consent form and all of my questions about the study have been answered. I understand that the focus group will be recorded. I agree to participate in this study.

Print name: _____

Signature: _____

Date: _____

Source: Elaboration from Fordham sample Informed Consent [Focus Group Research]

Appendix 2: Example of a guide and discussion outline with related probing techniques

Focus group 'The veil and the belly button'

Below, we report a focus group outline drafted for a research study, conducted by Ivana Acocella (2009), on the stereotypes related to the 'social construction of the body'. The aim of the research was to identify the social representations widespread among Italian young people regarding female behaviour models and how such representations could be different with reference to western women or oriental women. The focus groups involved high school students of Florence.

FOCUS GROUP GUIDE

Welcome and thank you – Presentation of the research group (by the moderator).

Topic

We are conducting research in various schools to understand if and how the image that young men and women have of their body is changing. We would like to know how young people today build 'their own social image'. Today we try to deepen your representations. The information we collect will be used anonymously as is normal in scientific practice.

What is the focus group

The focus group is a group discussion in the presence of one or more moderators, which we would be. I will ask you about some general issues on which I would like to know your opinion. I will not ask questions to each of you individually but I will ask all of you as a group. Therefore, I would like the answers to my questions to arise from your own debate on the issue. There is no intervention order, but each of you is free to intervene when and how many times you want, in order to add something new to the debate or to comment on what was said before. I will only intervene to ask for clarifications or to provide you with new stimuli.

Five rules to be followed to facilitate the debate:

- everyone must speak in a LOUD VOICE and ONE AT A TIME to facilitate the recording of the discussion;
- everyone must LISTEN TO AND RESPECT the opinions of others since THERE ARE NO RIGHT OR WRONG ANSWERS;
- CHANGING ONE'S MIND IS POSSIBLE, without being worried about appearing inconsistent;
- you must not be afraid of expressing your own views even if these are in contrast with what has been said by other people; we do not want everyone to agree, so DIFFERENT POINTS OF VIEW ON THE SAME TOPIC are welcome, as well as BOTH POSITIVE AND NEGATIVE COMMENTS;
- it is good to REMAIN FOCUSED on the issues to be treated.

Organization

Our conversation will be recorded because it is difficult to remember everything that will be said, while we want to be able to consider all the opinions expressed carefully.

Duration: the discussion will last about an hour and a half.

Invitation to the participants to introduce themselves with their names.

DISCUSSION OUTLINE

First part: Concept of 'social construction of the body' (20 mins)

In sociology, the expression 'the social construction of the body' is used. What does it remind you of? Try to write your definition or to give examples that evoke this expression on the sheet of paper that we gave you.

Strategies for clarification of information provided by participants. The moderator reads aloud the definitions collected and writes them on the blackboard. He/she asks the participants if they would change something of the written definition in light of what was written by the other participants.

323

Strategies for stimulating discussion. The moderator shows some pictures (of tattoos, navel piercing, fashion, bodybuilders), asking the participants which pictures have most impressed them and what sensations they suggest in relation to the theme 'the social construction of the body'.

Strategies for clarification of information provided by participants. Ask the participants to divide the definitions into different classes, in order to establish different dimensions of the investigated concept or to find different meanings of equal terms/expressions.

Second part: Comparison with immigrants (20 mins)

Now we would like to gather your opinions on the types of body ornaments widespread among immigrants.

Strategies for stimulating discussion. We shall now read some newspaper articles on the use of the veil by Muslim women.

Reading some newspaper articles on the use of the veil by Muslim women on the following aspects:

- VEIL TO ENTER PUBLIC SPACE AND GENDER EQUALITY (Newspaper *Il Corriere* 02/02/03)

- VEIL FOR BEING A 'GOOD GIRL' AND KEEPING TEMPTATION AWAY (Newspaper *Il Corriere* 09/03/03)

- VEIL AS A PERSONAL CHOICE, EVEN ACCENTUATED IN THE CONTEXT OF IMMIGRATION (Newspaper *La Stampa* 05/11/03)

- VEIL AS A 'POLITICAL CLAIM' (Newspaper *La Repubblica* 19/12/03)

The moderator asks participants to comment on the articles and to highlight which aspects are most interesting and which sensations these aspects suggest to them in relation to the topic the 'social construction of the body'.

Strategies for clarification of information provided by participants. The moderator asks the participants to divide the definitions into different classes, in order to establish different dimensions of the investigated concept or to find different meanings of equal terms/expressions.

Third part: Comparison between Italians and immigrants (20 mins)

Comparison between Italians and foreigners. The moderator asks participants to list the differences or similarities found between Italians and foreigners from a symbolic point of view in reference to the theme 'the social construction of the body'.

Strategies for stimulating discussion. To compile this list on the differences or similarities between Italians and foreigners, it can be useful to have participants reflect on the 'free choice/social conditioning' binomial. The moderator can ask participants to define:

- 'freedom of choice' [possible aspects to deepen: affirmation of one's own individuality or difference; will to show off; desire to affirm one's freedom].
- 'social conditioning' [possible aspects to be explored: consumerism, imposition of the fashion market (for Italians); respect for a tradition/family obligation (for foreigners); gregariousness, sense of belonging to a reference group, sense of security (for all)].

Strategies for clarification of information provided by participants. Try to build a typology by following the diagram below:

	ITALIANS	FOREIGNERS
FREEDOM OF CHOICE		
SOCIAL CONDITIONING		

Appendix 3: Checklist to assist the moderator

During the gathering of information, the moderator must continuously monitor his/her style of conducting. There are some mental exercises that can help the moderator.

Some mental exercises for thematizing the discussion topics appropriately. During group discussion, the moderator can ask himself/herself:

- Is the point of view adopted by the participants consistent with the research objectives?
- Is the intervention of participant X related to the social identification category requested in this discussion?

Some mental exercises to stimulate the discussion adequately. During group discussion, the moderator can ask himself/herself:

- Has this theme been studied in depth by the group?
- Might it be useful to deepen this aspect introduced by participants, even if it is not present in the discussion outline?
- Is what the participant saying connected to the topic that emerged previously? Might it be useful to point out this link to the participants?
- Did I fully understand the meaning of the discussion on this point?
- The participants might interpret the topic of discussion differently. Might it be helpful to ask participants to specify what meanings can be associated with the term X in reference to the topic discussed?
- Is the theme discussed by participant X connected to the topic that emerged previously? Might it be useful to ask the participants directly about this?

Some mental exercises to stimulate the interaction among the participants adequately. During group discussion, the moderator can ask himself/herself:

- Has everyone spoken on this point?
- Observing participant X, it seems to me that he wanted to say something on the theme X but could not speak out. Might it be useful to solicit him directly?
- Participant X is imposing his opinion too much. Might it be helpful to support what was said by the other participants to introduce other perspectives on the topic in the discussion?
- The topic discussed is controversial. The participants are overheating. Might it be useful to temporarily move the discussion to other less controversial topics?

Appendix 4: The software programs most commonly used for focus group analysis

- **ATLAS.ti:** Widely used in the logic of grounded theory, it makes it possible to treat text in semi-automatic mode, but also images, audio and video.
- **Dedoose:** A cross-platform app with a series of workspaces which allow coding, retrieving and memoing. It encourages collaborative (even simultaneous) work.
- **Lexico:** Designed for the automatic analysis of texts, it contains all the main functions of research and statistical lexicometric analysis (frequency vocabulary, concordances etc.).
- **MAXQDA:** Designed for text and multimedia analysis, it has an easy-to-use four-screen window and a tool for embedded translation.
- **NVivo:** Representing the evolution of NUD*IST, this allows the development of semi-automatic analysis paths and is useful in handling long texts.

- **TaLTaC:** Uses both statistical and linguistic resources in an integrated manner. The text is processed automatically both lexically and textually.
- **The Ethnograph:** Manages some of the mechanical tasks of qualitative data analysis, such as identifying, coding and collecting segments, encouraging the development of code theoretical specifications.
- **T-LAB:** Comprises a set of linguistic and statistical tools that allow the exploration, analysis, comparison, graphic representation and interpretation of the contents present in the texts.

References

Abramczyk, L.W. (1995) 'I gruppi focali come strumento di ricerca e valutazione', in T. Vecchiato (ed.), *La valutazione dei servizi sociali e sanitari*. Padova: Zancan. pp. 136–48.

Abrams, M.K. and Gaiser, T.J. (2017) 'Online focus groups', in N. Fielding, R.M. Lee and G. Blank (eds), *The SAGE Handbook of Online Research Methods* (2nd edn). London: Sage. pp. 435–53.

Acocella, I. (2008) *Il focus group: teoria e tecnica*. Milan: FrancoAngeli.

Acocella, I. (2009) 'Il focus group e gli stereotipi sulla costruzione sociale del corpo', in G. Guizzardi (ed.), *Identità incorporate. Segni, immagini, differenze*. Bologna: Il Mulino. pp. 47–80.

Acocella, I. (2012) 'The focus groups in social research: advantages and disadvantages', *Quality & Quantity*, 46 (4): 1125–36. DOI: 10.1007/s11135-011-9600-4.

Acocella, I. (2013) 'Care institutions and "submerged" violence: a qualitative research design', *SAGE Research Methods Cases*. London: Sage. DOI: http://dx.doi.org/10.4135/978144627305013509353.

Acocella, I. and Turchi, M. (2020) 'The reception system for asylum seekers and refugees in Italy: a case of a new total institution?', *Annual Review of Social Work and Social Pedagogy in Austria*, 2: 73–101.

Acocella, I., Cataldi, S. and Cigliuti, K. (2016) 'Between tradition and innovation: religious practices and everyday life of second-generation Muslim women', *Fieldwork in Religion*, 11 (2): 199–216. DOI: 10.1558/firn.29964.

Adler, P.A. and Adler, P. (1994) 'Observational techniques', in N.K. Denzin and Y.S. Lincoln (eds), *Handbook of Qualitative Research*. Thousand Oaks, CA: Sage. pp. 377–92.

Albanesi, C. (2004) *I Focus Group*. Rome: Carocci.

Albrecht, T.L., Johnson, G.M. and Walther, J.B. (1993) 'Understanding communication processes in focus groups', in D.L. Morgan (ed.), *Successful Focus Groups: Advancing State of the Art*. Newbury Park, CA: Sage. pp. 51–64.

Alderson, P. and Morrow, V. (2004) *Ethics, Social Research and Consulting with Children and Young People*. London: Barnardos.

Allen, M. (2017) *SAGE Encyclopaedia of Communication Research Methods*, Vols. 1–4. Thousand Oaks, CA. Sage. DOI: 10.4135/9781483381411.

Allen, M.D. (2014) 'Telephone focus groups: strengths, challenges, and strategies for success', *Qualitative Social Work*, 13 (4): 571–83. DOI: 10.1177/1473325013499060.

Allen, V.L. (1965) 'Situation factors in conformity', in L. Berkowitz (ed.), *Advances in Experimental Social Psychology*, Vol. 2. New York: Academic Press. pp. 133–75.

Allen, V.L. and Levine, J.M. (1969) 'Consensus and conformity', *Journal of Experimental and Social Psychology*, 5 (4): 389–99. DOI: 10.1016/0022-1031(69)90032-8.

Aluwihare-Samaranayake, D. (2012) 'Ethics in qualitative research: a view of the participants' and researchers' world from a critical standpoint', *International Journal of Qualitative Methods*, 11 (2), Special Issue – Health Equity: 64–81. DOI: 10.1177/160940691201100208.

Alvermann, D.E. (2002) 'Narrative approaches', in M. Kamil, P. Mosenthal, P.D. Pearson and R. Barr (eds), *Methods of Literacy Research: The Methodology Chapters from The Handbook of Reading Research*, Vol. 3. Mahwah, NJ: Lawrence Erlbaum.

Amelina, A. and Faist, T. (2012) 'De-naturalizing the national in research methodologies: key concepts of transnational studies in migration', *Ethnic and Racial Studies*, 35 (10): 1707–24. DOI: 10.1080/01419870.2012.659273.

Aronson, E., Wilson, T.D. and Akert, R.M. (1997) *Social Psychology*. Reading, MA: Longman.

Asch, S.E. (1951) 'Effects of group pressure on the modification and distortion of judgments', in H. Guetzknow (ed.), *Groups, Leadership and Men*. Pittsburgh, PA: Carnegie Press. pp. 177–90.

Astatke, H. and Serpell, R. (2000) 'Testing the application of a western scientific theory of AIDS risk behavior among adolescents in Ethiopia', *Journal of Pediatric Psychology*, 25 (6): 367–79. DOI: 10.1093/jpepsy/25.6.367.

Astolfi, C. and Fazzi, G. (2005) 'L'analisi dei focus groups: due tecniche a confronto'. Unpublished research report.

Atkinson, P. (2014) *For Ethnography*. London: Sage.

Ayrton, R. (2019) 'The micro-dynamics of power and performance in focus groups: an example from discussions on national identity with the South Sudanese diaspora in the UK', *Qualitative Research*, 19 (3): 323–39. DOI: 10.1177/1468794118757102.

Baldwin, J.M. (1895) *Mental Development in the Child and the Race: Methods and Processes*. New York: Macmillan.

Bales, R.F. (1950) *Interaction Process Analysis: A Method for the Study of Small Groups*. Chicago, IL: Chicago University Press.

Banks, M. (2008) *Using Visual Data in Qualitative Research*. London: Sage.

Barbour, R. (2007) *Doing Focus Groups*. London: Sage.

Bartle, R.A. (2003) *Designing Virtual Worlds*. Indianapolis, IN: New Riders.

Baxter, P. and Jack, S. (2008) 'Qualitative case study methodology: study design and implementation for novice researchers', *The Qualitative Report*, 13 (4): 544–59.

Beauchamp, T.L. and Childress, J.F. (2002) *Principles of Biomedical Ethics* (5th edn). New York: Oxford University Press.

Beck, L.C., Trombetta, W.L. and Share, S. (1986) 'Using focus group sessions before decisions are made', *North Carolina Medical Journal*, 47 (2): 73–4.

Becker, H.S. (1998) *Tricks of the Trade: How to Think about Your Research While You're Doing It*. Chicago, IL: University of Chicago Press.

Bellenger, D.N., Bernhardt, K.L. and Goldstucker, J.L. (eds) (1976) *Qualitative Research in Marketing*. Chicago, IL: American Marketing Association.

Bentley, A.F. (1908) *The Process of Government: A Study of Social Pressures*. Bloomington, IN: Principia Press.

Benzècri, J-P. (1992) *Correspondence Analysis Handbook*. New York: Marcel Dekker.

Bertaux, D. (1998) *Les Récits de Vie. Perspective Éthnosociologique*. Paris: Editions Nathan.

Bertrand, J.T., Ward, V.M. and Pauc, F. (1992) 'Sexual practices among the Quiché-speaking Mayan population of Guatemala', *International Quarterly of Community Health Education*, 12 (4): 265–82.

Bezzi, C. (2001) *Il disegno della ricerca valutativa*. Milan: FrancoAngeli.

Bezzi, C. and Baldini, I. (2006) *Il Brainstorming*. Milan: FrancoAngeli.

Bichi, R. (2002) *L'intervista biografica. Una proposta metodologica*. Milan: Vitaepensiero.

Bichi, R. (2007) *La conduzione delle interviste nella ricerca sociale*. Rome: Carocci.

Bickman, L. (1974) 'The social power of a uniform', *Journal of Applied Social Psychology*, 4: 47–61.

Blaikie, N.W.H. (2000) *Designing Social Research: The Logic of Anticipation*. Cambridge: Polity Press.

Bloor, M., Frankland, J., Thomas, M. and Robson, K. (2001) *Focus Groups in Social Research*. London: Sage.

Blumer, H. (1954) 'What is wrong with social theory', *American Sociological Review*, 18: 3–10.

Blumer, H. (1969) *Symbolic Interactionism: Perspective and Methods*. Englewood Cliffs, NJ: Prentice Hall.

Bogardus, E.S. (1926) 'The group interview', *Journal of Applied Sociology*, 10: 372–82.

Bolasco, S. (1999) *Analisi multidimensionale dei dati*. Rome: Carocci.

Bourdieu, P. (1989) 'Social space and symbolic power', *Sociological Theory*, 7 (1): 14–25. DOI: 10.2307/202060.

Bowen, G.A. (2006) 'Grounded theory and sensitizing concepts', *International Journal of Qualitative Methods*, 5 (3): 12–23. DOI: 10.1177/16094069 0600500304.

Braun, V. and Clarke, V. (2006) 'Using thematic analysis in psychology', *Qualitative Research in Psychology*, 3: 77–101. DOI: http://dx.doi.org/10.1191/ 1478088706qp063oa.

Breen, R.L. (2006) 'A practical guide to focus-group research', *Journal of Geography in Higher Education*, 30 (3): 463–75. DOI: 10.1080/0309826 0600927575.

Brown, R. (1988) *Group Processes: Dynamics Within and Between Groups*. Oxford: Blackwell.

Brunelli, C. (2003) 'La qualità della vita degli anziani', PhD Dissertation.

Bruschi, A. (1999) *Metodologia delle scienze sociali*. Milan: Mondadori.

Bryman, A. (2006) 'Integrating quantitative and qualitative research: how is it done?', *Qualitative Research*, 6 (1): 97–113. DOI: 10.1177/146879 4106058877.

Buchanan, E.A. (2000) 'Ethics, qualitative research, and ethnography in virtual space', *Journal of Information Ethics*, 9 (2): 82–7.

Burnstein, E. (1982) 'Persuasion as argument processing', in H. Brandstatter, J.H. Davis and G. Stocker-Kreichgauer (eds), *Group Decision Making*. New York: Academic Press. pp. 103–24.

Caillaud, S. and Flick, U. (2017) 'Focus groups in triangulation contexts', in R. Barbour and D. Morgan (eds), *A New Era in Focus Group Research*. London: Palgrave Macmillan. pp. 155–77.

Calder, B.J. (1977) 'Focus groups and the nature of qualitative marketing research', *Journal of Marketing Research*, 14 (3): 353–64.

Calidoni, P. and Cataldi, S. (eds) (2016) *L'orientamento illusorio: marketing scolastico e persistenti disuguaglianze*. Una ricerca sul campo in Sardegna. Cagliari: CUEC.

Campbell, D.T. (1958) 'Common fate, similarity, and other indices of the status of aggregates of persons as social entities', *Behavioural Science*, 3: 14–25. DOI: 10.1002/bs.3830030103.

Campbell, D.T. and Fiske, D.W. (1959) 'Convergent and discriminant validation by the multitrait-multimethod matrix', *Psychological Bulletin*, 56 (2): 81–105.

Campbell, D.T. and Stanley, J.C. (1966) *Experimental and Quasi-Experimental Designs for Research*. Boston, MA: Houghton Mifflin.

Campbell, J.D., Tesser, A. and Fairey, P.J. (1986) 'Conformity and attention to the stimulus: Some temporal and contextual dynamics', *Journal of Personality and Social Psychology*, 51 (2): 315–24.

Campbell, M.K., Meier, A., Carr, C., Enga, Z., James, A.S., Reedy, J. and Zheng, B. (2001) 'Health behavior changes after colon cancer: a comparison of findings from face-to-face and on-line focus groups', *Family Community Health*, 24 (3): 88–103.

Campelli, E. (1991) *Da un luogo comune. Elementi di metodologia delle scienze sociali*. Rome: Carocci.

Caplan, S. (1990) 'Using focus group methodology for ergonomic design', *Ergonomics*, 33 (5): 527–33.

Cardano, M. (2003) *Tecniche di ricerca qualitativa. Percorsi di ricerca nelle scienze sociali*. Rome: Carocci.

Cardano, M. (2011) *La ricerca qualitativa*. Bologna: Il Mulino.

Cardano, M. (2020) *Defending Qualitative Research: Design, Analysis, and Textualization*. Abingdon and New York: Routledge.

Cardano, M., Meo, A., Olagnero, M. and Gruppi di ricerca Acli-Torino (2003) *Discorsi sulla povertà*. Milan: FrancoAngeli.

Carey, M.A. and Asbury, J. (2012) *Focus Group Research*. New York: Routledge.

Carlsen, B. and Glenton, C. (2011) 'What about N? A methodological study of sample-size reporting in focus group studies', *BMC Medical Research Methodology*, 11 (1): 26–35. DOI: 10.1186/1471-2288-11-26.

Carmack, H.J. and Degroot, J.M. (2014) 'Exploiting loss? Ethical considerations, boundaries, and opportunities for the study of death and grief online', *OMEGA – Journal of Death and Dying*, 68 (4): 315–35. DOI: 10.2190/OM.68.4.b.

Carvalho, E. and Winters, K. (2014) 'The grounded theory method: popular perceptions of party leaders during the 2010 British General Election', *SAGE Research Methods Cases*. London: Sage. DOI: 10.4135/978144627305013510259.

Cataldi, S. (2009) *Come si analizzano i focus group*. Milan: FrancoAngeli.

Cataldi, S. (2014) 'Relationship analysis: proposals for analysing relationship dynamics in focus groups', *SAGE Research Methods Cases*. London: Sage. DOI: 10.4135/9781446273050145528631.

Cataldi, S. (2016) 'The perception of deviant behaviours by young people: triangulating survey and focus group data', *SAGE Research Methods Cases*. London: Sage. DOI: 10.4135/9781446273050155606883.

Cataldi, S. (2018) 'A proposal for the analysis of the relational dimension in the interview techniques: a pilot study on in-depth interviews and focus groups', *Quality and Quantity*, 52 (1): 295–312. DOI 10.1007/s11135-017-0468-9.

Ceri, P. and Ceccatelli, G.G. (eds) (2007) *Studying in Florence: il sistema della formazione internazionale nell'area metropolitana fiorentina*. Florence: Plus.

Chamberlayne, P., Bormat, J. and Wengraf, T. (2000) *The Turn to Biographical Methods in Social Science: Comparative Issues and Example*. London: Routledge.

Charlesworth, W.L. and Rodwell, M.K. (1997) 'Focus group with children: a resource for sexual abuse prevention program evaluation', *Child Abuse and Neglect*, 21 (12): 1205–16.

Charmaz, K. (2000) 'Grounded theory: objectivist and constructivist methods', in N.K. Denzin and Y.S. Lincoln (eds), *Handbook of Qualitative Research*. Thousand Oaks, CA: Sage. pp. 509–35.

Charmaz, K. (2006) *Constructing Grounded Theory: A Practical Guide Through Qualitative Analysis*. London: Sage.

Chemers, M.M. (2001) 'Leadership effectiveness: an integrative review', in M.A. Hogg and S. Tindale (eds), *Blackwell Handbook of Social Psychology: Group Processes*. Oxford: Blackwell. pp. 376–99.

Cher Ping, L. and Seng Chee, T. (2001) 'Online discussion boards for focus group interviews: an exploratory study', *Journal of Educational Enquiry*, 2 (1): 50–60.

Chisnall, P.M. (2005) *Marketing Research* (3rd edn). London: McGraw-Hill.

Cigliuti, K. (2014) *Cosa sono questi 'appunti alla buona dall'aria innocente'? La costruzione delle note etnografiche*. Florence: Florence Firenze University Press.

Clandinin, D.J. and Connelly, F.M. (2000) *Narrative Inquiry Experience and Story in Qualitative Research*. San Francisco, CA: Jossey-Bass.

Clarke, V. and Braun, V. (2013) *Successful Qualitative Research: A Practical Guide for Beginners*. Thousand Oaks, CA: Sage.

Clifford, J. (1986) 'Introduction: partial truths', in J. Clifford and G.E. Marcus (eds), *Writing Culture: Poetics and Politics of Ethnography*. Berkeley, CA: University of California Press. pp. 1–26.

Cohen, M.R. and Nagel, E. (1934) *An Introduction to Logic and Scientific Method*. New York: Harcourt.

Colella, F. (2011) *Focus group. Ricerca sociale e strategie applicative*. Milan: FrancoAngeli.

Colucci, E. (2007) '"Focus groups can be fun": the use of activity-oriented questions in focus group discussions', *Qualitative Health Research*, 17 (10): 1422–33. DOI: 10.1177/1049732307308129.

Cook, T.D. and Campbell, D.T. (1979) *Quasi-Experimentation: Design and Analysis Issues for Field Settings*. Chicago, IL: Rand McNally.

Cooper, J., Kelly, K.A. and Weaver, K. (2001) 'Attitudes, norms, and social groups', in M.A. Hogg and S. Tindale (eds), *Blackwell Handbook of Social Psychology: Group Processes*. Oxford: Blackwell. pp. 259–83.

Corbin, J. and Strauss, A. (2015) *Basics of Qualitative Research Techniques and Procedures for Developing Grounded Theory* (4th edn). Thousand Oaks, CA: Sage.

Cormack, J., Postăvaru, G-I. and Basten, G. (2018) 'Analysing qualitative mini-group data using thematic analysis', *SAGE Research Methods Cases, Part 2*. London: Sage. DOI: 10.4135/9781526444875.

Corrao, S. (2000) *Il focus group*. Milan: FrancoAngeli.

Corsaro, W. (1985) *Friendship and Peer Culture in the Early Years*. Norwood, NJ: Ablex.

Cote-Arsenault, D. and Morrison, B.D. (1999) 'Practical advice for planning and conducting focus groups', *Nursing Research*, 48 (5): 280–3.

Creswell, J.W., Plano Clark, V.L., Gutmann, M.L. and Hanson, W.E. (2003) 'Advanced mixed methods research designs', in A. Tashakkori and C. Teddlie (eds), *Handbook of Mixed Methods in the Social and Behavioral Research*. Thousand Oaks, CA: Sage. pp. 209–40.

Cunningham-Burley, S., Kerr, A. and Pavis, S. (2001) 'Theorizing subjects and subject matter in focus group research', in R.S. Barbour and J. Kitzinger (eds), *Developing Focus Group Research: Politics, Theory and Practice* (2nd edn). London: Sage. pp. 186–99.

Currall, S.C. and Towler, A.J. (2003) 'Research methods in management and organizational research: toward integration of qualitative and quantitative techniques', in A. Tashakkori and C. Teddlie (eds), *Handbook of Mixed Methods in the Social and Behavioral Research*. Thousand Oaks, CA: Sage. pp. 513–26.

Cyr, J. (2019) *Focus Groups for the Social Science Researcher*. Cambridge: Cambridge University Press.

Davis, M.T. and Brolin, M. (2014) 'Focus group: evaluation of Substance Abuse Treatment Program', *SAGE Research Methods Cases*. London: Sage. DOI: 10.4135/978144627305013512924.

Dawson, S., Manderson, L., Tallo, V.L. and the International Nutrition Foundation for Developing Countries & UNDP/World Bank/WHO Special Programme for Research and Training in Tropical Diseases (1993) *A Manual for the Use of Focus Groups*. Boston, MA: International Nutrition Foundation for Developing Countries. Available at https://apps.who.int/iris/handle/10665/41795 (accessed 30 March 2020).

Dean, P. (2004) 'Nominal group technique (NGT)', in M.J. Stahl (ed.), *Encyclopaedia of Health Care Management*. Thousand Oaks, CA: Sage. pp. 389 ff.

Della Ratta-Rinaldi, F. (2000) 'L'analisi testuale: uno strumento per la ricerca sociale', *Sociologia e ricerca sociale*, 61: 102–27.

Denzin, N.K. (1989) *The Research Act: A Theoretical Introduction to Sociological Methods*. Englewood Cliffs, NJ: Prentice Hall.

Denzin, N.K. (2001) 'The reflexive interview and a performative social science', *Qualitative Research*, 1 (1): 23–46.

Deutsch, M. and Gerard, H.B. (1955) 'A study of normative and informational social influence upon individual judgment', *Journal of Abnormal and Social Psychology*, 51 (3): 629–36. DOI: 10.1037/h0046408.

Di Franco, G. (1997) *Tecniche e modelli di analisi multivariata dei dati*. Rome: Edizioni Seam.

Di Franco, G. (2007) *Corrispondenze multiple e altre tecniche multivariate per variabili categoriali*. Milan: FrancoAngeli.

Di Giammaria, L., Cataldi, S. and Di Folco, M. (2015) 'Associazionismo cattolico e politica. Tensioni valoriali e dissonanze cognitive', *Sociologia e Ricerca Sociale*, 108 (3): 113–36.

Diana, P. and Montesperelli, P. (2005) *Analizzare le interviste ermeneutiche*. Rome: Carocci.

Dingwall, R. (1997) *Context and Method in Qualitative Research*. London: Sage.

Douglas, J.D. (1976) *Investigative Social Research: Individual and Team Field Research*. Beverly Hills, CA: Sage.

Dowson, S., Manderson, L. and Tallo, V.L. (1993) *A Manual of the Use of Focus Group*. Boston, MA: International Nutrition Foundation for Developing Countries.

Duchesne, S. (2017) 'Using focus groups to study the process of (de) politicization', in R.S. Barbour and D.L. Morgan (eds), *A New Era in Focus Group Research*. London: Palgrave Macmillan. pp. 365–88.

Duhem, P. (1906) *La Théorie Physique. Son Objet, sa Structure*. Paris: Chevalier & Riviére.

Dwyer, K. (1977) 'The dialogic of anthropology', *Dialectical Anthropology*, 2: 143–51.

Eco, U. (1984) *Semiotica e filosofia del linguaggio*. Torino: Einaudi.

Ellis, P. (2016) *Understanding Research for Nursing Students* (3rd edn). Thousand Oaks, CA: Sage.

Ellison, N., Heino, R. and Gibbs, J. (2006) 'Managing impression online: self-presentation processes in the online dating environment', *Journal of Computer-Mediated Communication*, XI (2): 415–41. DOI: 10.1111/j.1083-6101.2006.00020.x.

Erwin, L. and Stewart, P. (1997) 'Gendered perspectives: a focus-group study of how undergraduate women negotiate their career aspirations', *International Journal of Qualitative Studies in Education*, 10 (2): 207–20. DOI: 10.1080/095183997237304.

European Commission, DG RTD (2018) 'Ethics in social science and humanities'. Available at http://ec.europa.eu/research/participants/data/ref/h2020/other/hi/h2020_ethics-soc-science-humanities_en.pdf (accessed 30 March 2020).

Eynon, R., Fry, J. and Schroeder, R. (2017) 'The ethics of online research', in N. Fielding, R. Lee and G. Blank (eds), *The SAGE Handbook of Online Research Methods*. London: Sage. pp. 19–37. DOI: 10.4135/9781473957992.n2.

Farnsworth, J. and Bronwyn, B. (2010) 'Analysing group dynamics within the focus group', *Qualitative Research*, 10 (5): 605–24.

Festinger, L. (1957) *A Theory of Cognitive Dissonance*. Stanford, CA: Stanford University Press.

Fideli, R. and Marradi, A. (1996) 'Intervista', in *Enciclopedia delle Scienze Sociali*, Vol. 5. Rome: Istituto della Enciclopedia Italiana. pp. 71–80.

Fielding, N.G. and Fielding, J. (1986) *Linking Data*. London: Sage.

Fiske, S.T., Cuddy, A.J.C., Glick, P. and Xu, J. (2002) 'A model of (often mixed) stereotype content: competence and warmth respectively follow from perceived status and competition', *Journal of Personality and Social Psychology*, 82 (6): 878–902.

Flament, L. (1965) *Réseaux de Communication et Structures de Groupe*. Paris: Dunod.

Flick, U. (2019) *An Introduction to Qualitative Research* (6th edn). London: Sage.

Folch-Lyon, E. and Trost, J.F. (1981) 'Conducting focus group sessions', *Studies in Family Planning*, 12: 443–9.

Fordham https://www.fordham.edu/download/downloads/id/2431/sample_informed_consent_-_focus_group_0214doc.pdf

Forsyth, D.R. (2014) *Group Dynamics* (6th edn). Belmont, CA: Wadsworth Cengage Learning.

Fox, F.E., Morris, M. and Rumsey, N. (2007) 'Doing synchronous online focus groups with young people: methodological reflections', *Qualitative Health Research*, 17 (4): 539–47.

Fox, J. and Bailenson, J.N. (2009) 'Virtual self-modeling: the effects of vicarious reinforcement and identification on exercise behaviors', *Media Psychology*, 12 (1): 1–25. DOI: 10.1080/15213260802669474.

Franzosi, R. (1998) 'Narrative analysis – or why (and how) sociologists should be interested in narrative', *Annual Review of Sociology*, 24 (1): 517–54.

Freire, P. (1968) *Pedagogia do oprimido*. Rio de Janeiro: Paz e Terra.

French, J.R.P. and Raven, B. (1959) 'The bases of social power', in D. Cartwright (ed.), *Studies in Social Power*. Ann Arbor, MI: Institute for Social Research.

Frey, J.H. and Fontana, A. (1993) 'The group interview in social research', in D.L. Morgan (ed.), *Successful Focus Group: Advancing the State of the Art*. Newbury Park, CA: Sage. pp. 20–34.

Frisina, A. (2010) *Focus group. Una guida pratica*. Bologna: Il Mulino.

Frisina, A. (2018) 'Focus groups in migration research: a forum for "public thinking"?', in R. Zapata-Barrero and E. Yalaz (eds), *Qualitative Research in European Migration Studies, IMISCOE Research Series*. Cham: Springer. pp. 189–208.

Fromkin, H. (1970) 'Effects of experimentally aroused feelings of undistinctiveness upon valuation of scarce and novel experiences', *Journal of Personality and Social Psychology*, 16 (3): 521–9.

Fuller, T., Edwards, J.N., Vorakitphokatorn, S. and Sermsri, S. (1994) 'Using focus groups to adapt survey instruments to new populations: experience from a developing country', in D.L. Morgan (ed.), *Successful Focus Groups: Advancing State of the Art*. Newbury Park, CA: Sage. pp. 89–104.

Galtung, J. (1967) *Theory and Methods of Social Research*. Oslo: Universitetsforlaget.

Gee, J.P. (1991) 'A linguistic approach to narrative', *Journal of Narrative and Life History/Narrative Inquiry*, 1: 15–39.

Gee, J.P. (2008) *An Introduction to Discourse Analysis Theory and Method*. New York: Routledge.

Geertz, C. (1975) 'Thick description: toward an interpretive theory of culture', in C. Geertz (selected essays by), *The Interpretations of Cultures*. London: Hutchinson. pp. 3–30.

Gibson, F. (2007) 'Conducting focus groups with children and young people: strategies for success', *Journal of Research in Nursing*, 12 (45): 473–83. DOI: 10.1177/1744987107079791.

Giddens, A. (1984) *The Constitution of Society: Outline of the Theory of Structuration*. Cambridge: Polity Press.

Giddens, A. (1987) *Social Theory and Modern Sociology*. Cambridge: Polity Press.

Giddings, L.S. (2006) 'Mixed methods research: positivism dressed in drag?', *Journal of Research in Nursing*, 11 (3): 195–203. DOI: 10.1177/17449 87106064635.

Gilli, G.A. (1971) *Come si fa ricerca. Guida per non specialisti*. Milan: Mondadori.

Gimbel, K. (2017) 'Respecting your participants – ethical considerations in focus groups'. Available at www.forsmarshgroup.com/knowledge/news-blog/posts/previous-years/january/respecting-your-participants-ethical-considerations-in-focus-groups/ (accessed 30 March 2020).

Giuliano, L. and La Rocca, G. (2008) *L'analisi automatica e semiautomatica dei dati testuali* (2nd edn). Milan: LED.

Glaser, B.G. and Strauss, A.L. (1967) *The Discovery of Grounded Theory: Strategies for Qualitative Research*. Chicago, IL: Aldine.

Gobo, G. (2001) *Descrivere il mondo. Teoria e pratica del metodo etnografico in sociologia*. Rome: Carocci.

Gobo, G. (2005) 'L'analisi semiotica del focus group. Il caso della comunicazione pubblicitaria', *Sociologia e Ricerca Sociale*, XXVI (76/77): 76–90.

Gobo, G. and Mauceri, S. (2014) *Constructing Survey Data: An Interactional Approach*. London: Sage.

Goffman, E. (1969) *The Presentation of Self in Everyday Life*. New York: Penguin.

Golder, S.A. and Macy, M. (2014) 'Digital footprints: opportunities and challenges for online social research', *Annual Review of Sociology*, 40 (1): 129–52. DOI: 10.1146/annurev-soc-071913-043145.

Goldman, A.E. (1962) 'The group depth interview', *Journal of Marketing*, 26 (3): 61–8.

Goode, W.J. and Hatt, P.K. (1952) *Methods in Social Research*. New York: McGraw-Hill.

Gorden, R.L. (1980) *Interviewing: Strategy, Techniques and Tactics*. Homewood, IL: Dorsey.

Grant, R.W. (2006) 'Ethics and incentives: a political approach', *The American Political Science Review*, 100 (1): 29–39.

Grbich, C. (2007) *Qualitative Data Analysis: An Introduction*. Thousand Oaks, CA: Sage.

Green, J. and Hart, L. (2001) 'The impact of context on data', in R.S. Barbour and J. Kitzinger (eds), *Developing Focus Group Research: Politics, Theory and Practice* (2nd edn). London: Sage. pp. 21–35.

Greenbaum, T.L. (1998) *The Handbook for Focus Group Research* (2nd edn). London: Sage.

Greenbaum, T.L. (2000) *Moderating Focus Groups: A Practical Guide for Group Facilitation*. Thousand Oaks, CA: Sage.

Greimas, A.J. (1970) *Du sens*. Paris: Seuil.

Greimas, A.J. (1983) *Du sens II – Essais sémiotiques*. Paris: Seuil.

Guizzardi, G. (2009) *Identità incorporate. Segni, immagini, differenze*. Bologna: Il Mulino.

Halkier, B. (2017) 'Practice theoretically inspired focus groups: socially recogniz-able performativity?', in R.S. Barbour and D.L. Morgan (eds), *A New Era in Focus Group Research*. London: Palgrave Macmillan. pp. 389–410.

Hammersley, M. and Atkinson, P. (1983) *Ethnography: Principles in Practice*. London: Tavistock.

Hansen, M.L., O'Brien, K., Meckler, G.D., Chang, A.M. and Guise, J-M. (2016) 'Understanding the value of mixed methods research: the Children's Safety Initiative – Emergency Medical Services', *Emergency Medical Journal*, 33 (7): 489–94.

Hanson, N.R. (1958) *Patterns of Discovery: An Inquiry into the Conceptual Foundations of Science*. Cambridge: Cambridge University Press.

Harris, M. (1979) *Cultural Materialism: The Struggle for a Science of Culture*. New York: Random House.

Head, E. (2009) 'The ethics and implications of paying participants in qualitative research', *International Journal of Social Research Methodology*, 12 (4): 335–44.

Hedström, P. and Ylikoski, P. (2010) 'Causal mechanisms in the social sciences', *Annual Review of Sociology*, 36: 49–67. DOI: 10.1146/annurev.soc.012809.102632.

Hennink, M.M. (2014) *Focus Group Discussions: Understanding Qualitative Research*. Oxford: Oxford University Press.

Hesse-Biber, S. (2010) 'Qualitative approaches to mixed methods practice', *Qualitative Inquiry*, 16 (6): 455–68. DOI: 10.1177/1077800410364611.

Hinsz, V.B. and Davis, J.H. (1984) 'Persuasive arguments theory, group polarization, and choice shifts', *Personality and Social Psychology Bulletin*, 10 (2): 260–8. DOI: 10.1177/0146167284102012.

Hoffman, D.L. and Novak, T.P. (2012) 'Social media strategy', in V. Shankar and G.S. Carpenter (eds), *Handbook on Marketing Strategy*. Camberley: Edward Elgar. pp. 198–216.

Hogg, M.A. (2001) 'Social categorization, depersonalization, and group behavior', in M.A. Hogg and S. Tindale (eds), *Blackwell Handbook of Social Psychology: Group Processes*. Oxford: Blackwell. pp. 56–85.

Hogg, M.A. and Tindale, S. (eds) (2001) *Blackwell Handbook of Social Psychology: Group Processes*. Oxford: Blackwell.

Hollander, E.P. (1958) 'Conformity, status and idiosyncrasy credit', *Psychological Review*, 65: 117–27.

Homans, G.C. (1950) *The Human Group*. New York: Harcourt.

Hyman, H. (1955) *Survey Design and Analysis: Principles, Cases, and Procedures*. New York: Free Press.

Im, E.O. and Chee, W. (2006) 'An online forum as a qualitative research method: practical issues', *Nursing Research*, 55 (4): 267–73.

Isenberg, D.J. (1986) 'Group polarization: a critical review and meta-analysis', *Journal of Personal and Social Psychology*, 50 (6): 1141–51.

Israel, M. (2015) *Research Ethics and Integrity for Social Scientists: Beyond Regulatory Compliance*. London: Sage.

Janis, I.L. (1982) *Groupthink* (2nd edn). Boston, MA: Houghton Mifflin.

Jevons, W.S. (1874) *The Principles of Science: A Treatise on Logic and Scientific Method*. London: Macmillan.

Jick, T.D. (1979) 'Mixing qualitative and quantitative methods: triangulation in action', *Administrative Science Quarterly*, 24 (4): 602–11.

Johnson, A.N.D. (2005) 'Self-disclosure in computer-mediated communication: the role of self-awareness and visual anonymity', *European Journal of Social Psychology*, 31: 177–92. DOI:10.1002/ejsp.36.

Johnson, B. and Turner, L.A. (2003) 'Data collection strategies in mixed methods research', in A.M. Tashakkori and C.B. Teddlie (eds), *Handbook of Mixed Methods in Social & Behavioral Research*. Thousand Oaks, CA: Sage. pp. 297–319.

Johnston, R.J., Weaver, T.F., Smith, L.A. and Swallow, S.K. (1995) 'Contingent valuation focus groups: insights from ethnographic interview techniques', *Journal of Agricultural and Resource Economics*, 24 (1): 56–69.

Kaplan, M.F. (1977) 'Discussion polarization effects in a modified jury decision paradigm: informational influences', *Sociometry*, 40 (3): 262–71.

Kaplowitz, M.D. and Hoehn, J.P. (2001) 'Do focus groups and individual interviews reveal the same information for natural resource valuation?', *Ecological Economics*, 36: 237–47.

Kelly, J.R. (2001) 'Mood and emotion in groups', in M.A. Hogg and S. Tindale (eds), *Blackwell Handbook of Social Psychology: Group Processes*. Oxford: Blackwell. pp. 164–81.

Kelly, L., Kerr, G. and Drennan, J. (2010) 'Avoidance of advertising in social networking sites: the teenage perspective', *Journal of Interactive Advertising*, 10 (2): 16–27.

Kelman, H.C. (1958) 'Compliance, identification, and internalization: three processes of attitude change', *Journal of Conflict Resolution*, 2 (1): 51–60. DOI: 10.1177/002200275800200106.

Kerr, L. and Park, E.S. (2001) 'Group performance in collaborative and social dilemma tasks: progress and prospects', in M.A. Hogg and S. Tindale (eds), *Blackwell Handbook of Social Psychology: Group Processes*. Oxford: Blackwell. pp. 107–38.

Kidd, P.S. and Parshall, M.B. (2000) 'Getting the focus and the group: enhancing analytical rigor in focus group research', *Qualitative Health Research*, 10 (3): 293–308. DOI: 10.1177/104973200129118453.

Kitzinger, C. (2004) 'Feminist approaches', in C. Seale, G. Gobo, J.F. Gubrium and D. Silverman (eds), *Qualitative Research Practice*. London: Sage. pp. 113–28.

Kitzinger, J. (1994a) 'Focus group: method or madness?', in M. Boulton (ed.), *Challenge and Innovation: Methodological Advances in Social Research on HIV/AIDS*. London: Taylor & Francis. pp. 159–75.

Kitzinger, J. (1994b) 'The methodology of focus group: the importance of interaction between research participants', *Sociology of Health & Illness*, 16 (1): 103–21. DOI: 10.1111/1467-9566.ep11347023.

Kitzinger, J. (1995) 'Qualitative research: introducing focus groups', *British Medical Journal*, 311 (7000): 299–302. DOI: 10.1136/bmj.311. 7000.299.

Kitzinger, J. (1998) 'Media impact on public beliefs about AIDS', in D. Miller, J. Kitzinger, K. Williams and P. Beharrell, *The Circuit of Mass Communication: Media Strategies, Representation and Audience Reception in the AIDS Crisis*. London: Sage. pp. 167–91. DOI: 10.4135/ 9781446279984.n8.

Knodel, J. (1993) 'The design and analysis of focus group studies: a practical approach', in D.L. Morgan (ed.), *Successful Focus Groups: Advancing State of the Art*. Newbury Park, CA: Sage. pp. 35–50.

Knodel, J., Chamratrithirong, A. and Debavalya, N. (1987) *Thailand's Reproductive Revolution: Rapid Fertility Decline in a Third-World Setting*. Madison, WI: University of Wisconsin Press.

Kravitz, D.A. and Martin, B. (1986) 'Ringelmann rediscovered: the original article', *Journal of Personality and Social Psychology*, 50 (5): 936–41. DOI: 10.1037/0022-3514.50.5.936.

Krippendorff, K. (2004) *Content Analysis: An Introduction to its Methodology* (2nd edn). Thousand Oaks, CA: Sage.

Krueger, R.A. (1988) *Focus Groups: A Practical Guide for Applied Research.* Thousand Oaks, CA: Sage.

Krueger, R.A. (1998) 'Moderating focus groups', in D.L. Morgan and R.A. Krueger (eds), *Focus Group Kit*, Vol. 4. Thousand Oaks, CA: Sage.

Krueger, R.A. and Casey, M.A. (2000) *Focus Groups. A Practical Guide for Applied Research*, 3rd edn. Thousand Oaks, CA: Sage.

Krueger, R.A. and Morgan, D.L. (1998) 'Analysing and reporting focus groups results', in D.L. Morgan and R.A. Krueger (eds), *Focus Group Kit*, Vol. 6. Thousand Oaks, CA: Sage.

Kruger, L.J., Rachel, F., Rodgers, S.J. and Long, A.L. (2018) 'Individual interviews or focus groups? Interview format and women's self-disclosure', *International Journal of Social Research Methodology*, 22 (3): 245–55. DOI: 10.1080/13645579.2018.1518857.

Kuhn, T.S. (1962) *The Structure of Scientific Revolutions*. Chicago, IL: University of Chicago Press.

Labov, W. and Waletzky, J. (1967) 'Narrative analysis: oral versions of personal experience', in J. Helm (ed.), *Essays on the Verbal and Visual Arts*. Seattle, WA: American Ethnological Society. pp. 12–44.

Lakatos, I. (1976) *Proofs and Refutations*. Cambridge: Cambridge University Press.

Lange, P. (2019) 'How to write a scientific paper for peer-reviewed journals, contribution on the website of The European Association of Science Editors (EASE)'. Available at https://ease.org.uk/publications/ease-toolkit-authors/how-to-write-a-scientific-paper-for-peer-reviewed-journals/ (accessed 30 March 2020).

Langford, D.J. and McDonagh, D. (eds) (2003) *Focus Groups: Supporting Effective Product Development*. London: Taylor & Francis.

Laswell, H.D. (1927) *Propaganda Technique in the World War*. New York: Knopf.

Latané, B., Williams, K. and Harkins, S. (1979) 'Many hands make light work: the causes and consequences of social loafing', *Journal of Personality and Social Psychology*, 37 (6): 822–32. DOI: 10.1037/0022-3514.37.6.822.

Lazarsfeld, P.F., Berelson, B. and Gaudet, H. (1948) *The People's Choice*. New York: Columbia University Press.

Lee, R. M. (2000) *Unobtrusive Methods in Social Research*. Buckingham: Open University

Leone, G. and Curigliano, G. (2005) 'L'esplorazione del senso della storia attraverso un'analisi qualitativa di focus group discussion', *Sociologia e Ricerca Sociale*, 26 (76–7): 291–310.

Lett, J. (1990) 'Emics and etics: Notes on the epistemology of anthropology', in T.N. Headland, K.L. Pike and M. Harris (eds), *Emics and Etics: The Insider/Outsider debate*. Newbury Park, CA: Sage. pp. 127–42.

Lewin, K. (1948) *Resolving Social Conflicts*. New York: Harper & Row.

Liamputtong, P. (2011) *Focus Group Methodology: Principles and Practice*. Thousand Oaks, CA: Sage.

Likert, R. (1932) 'A technique for measurement of attitudes', *Archives of Psychology*, 140 (2): 5–55.

Lindesmith, A.R. (1947) *Addiction and Opiates*. New Brunswick: Transaction.

Linstone, H.L. and Turoff, M. (eds) (2002) *The Delphi Method: Techniques and Applications*. Reading, MA: Addison-Wesley.

Litosseliti, L. (2003) *Using Focus Groups in Research*. London: Continuum.

Livingstone, S. and Lunt, P. (1994) *Talk on Television: Audience Participation and Public Debate*. London: Routledge.

Lobe, B. (2017) 'Best practices for synchronous online focus groups', in R.S. Barbour and D.L. Morgan (eds), *A New Era in Focus Group Research*. London: Palgrave Macmillan. pp. 227–50.

Lorenzi-Cioldi, F. and Clémence, A. (2001) 'Group processes and the construction of social representations', in M.A. Hogg and S. Tindale (eds), *Blackwell Handbook of Social Psychology: Group Processes*. Oxford: Blackwell. pp. 311–33.

Losito, G. (1993) *L'analisi del contenuto nella ricerca sociale*. Milan: FrancoAngeli.

Lunt, P.K. and Livingstone, S.M. (1996) 'Rethinking the focus group in media and communication research', *Journal of Communication*, 46 (2): 79–98.

Lyndon, S. (2018) 'Analysing focus groups about poverty in the early years using a narrative approach', *SAGE Research Methods Cases*. London: Sage. DOI: 10.4135/9781526445322.

Maass, A. and Clark, R.D. (1983) 'Internalization versus compliance: differential processes underlying minority influence and conformity', *European Journal of Social Psychology*, 13 (3): 197–215. DOI: 10.1002/ejsp.2420 130302.

Mackie, D.M. (1987) 'Systematic and nonsystematic processing of majority and minority persuasive communications', *Journal of Personality and Social Psychology*, 53 (1): 41–52. DOI: 10.1037/0022-3514.53.1.41.

Macnaghten, P. (2017) 'Focus groups as anticipatory methodology: a contribution from science and technology studies towards socially-resilient governance', in R.S. Barbour and D.L. Morgan (eds), *A New Era in Focus Group Research*. London: Palgrave Macmillan. pp. 343–64.

Macnaghten, P. and Myers, G. (2004) 'Focus groups', in C. Seale, G., Gobo, J.F. Gubrium and D. Silverman (eds), *Qualitative Research Practice*. London: Sage. pp. 65–79.

Madriz, E.I. (1998) 'Using focus groups with lower socioeconomic status Latina women', *Qualitative Inquiry*, 4 (1): 114–28. DOI: https://doi.org/10.1177/107780049800400107.

Magill, R.S. (1993) 'Focus groups, program evaluation, and the poor', *The Journal of Sociology & Social Welfare*, 20 (1): 103–14.

Maguire, M. and Delahunt, D. (2017) 'Doing a thematic analysis: a practical, step-by-step guide for learning and teaching scholars', *AISHE-J: The All Ireland Journal of Teaching and Learning in Higher Education*, 3: 3351–514.

Mann, C. and Stewart, F. (2000) *Internet Communication and Qualitative Research*. London: Sage. DOI: 10.4135/9781849209281.

Manovich, L. (2012) 'Trending: the promises and the challenges of big social data', in M.K. Gold (ed.), *Debates in the Digital Humanities*. Minneapolis, MN: University of Minnesota Press.

Marková, I., Linell, P., Grossen, M. and Salazar-Orvig, A. (2007) *Dialogue in Focus Groups: Exploring Socially Shared Knowledge*. London: Equinox.

Marques, J.M., Abrams, D., Páez, D. and Hogg, M.A. (2001) 'Social categorization, social identification, and rejection of deviant group members', in M.A. Hogg and S. Tindale (eds), *Blackwell Handbook of Social Psychology: Group Processes*. Oxford: Blackwell. pp. 400–24.

Marradi, A. (1984) *Concetti e metodo per la ricerca sociale*. Florence: Giuntina.

Marradi, A. (1993) 'Classificazioni, tipologie, tassonomie', in *Enciclopedia delle Scienze Sociali*, Vol. 2. Rome: Istituto della Enciclopedia Italiana. pp. 22–30.

Marradi, A. (1997) 'Esperimento, associazione, insieme non-standard', *Sociologia e Ricerca Sociale*, 53/54 (October): 53–67.

Marradi, A. (2007) *Metodologia delle scienze sociali*. Bologna: Il Mulino.

Martin, R. and Hewstone, M. (2001) 'Conformity and independence in groups: majorities and minorities', in M.A. Hogg and S. Tindale (eds), *Blackwell Handbook of Social Psychology: Group Processes*. Oxford: Blackwell. pp. 209–34.

Marwell, G. and Schmitt, D.R. (1967) 'Compliance-gaining behavior: a synthesis and model', *Sociological Quarterly*, 8 (3): 317–28. DOI: 10.1111/j.1533-8525.1967.tb01059.x.

Mason, J. (2002) *Qualitative Researching* (2nd edn). London: Sage.

Matoesian, G.M. and Coldren, J.R. (2002) 'Language and bodily conduct in focus group evaluations of legal policy', *Discourse & Society*, 13 (4): 469–93. DOI: 10.1177/0957926502013004454.

Matthews, K.L., Baird, M. and Duchesne, G. (2018) 'Using online meeting software to facilitate geographically dispersed focus groups for health workforce research', *Qualitative Health Research*, 28 (10): 1621–8. DOI: 10.1177/1049732318782167.

Maxwell, C. and Boyle, M. (1995) 'Risky heterosexual practices amongst women over 30: gender, power and long-term relationships', *Aids Care*, 7 (3): 277–93. DOI: 10.1080/09540129550126515.

McKennell, A.C. (1974) 'Surveying attitude structures: a discussion of principles and procedures', *Quality and Quantity*, 7 (2): 203–94.

McMahon, S. (2007) 'Understanding community-specific rape myths exploring student athlete culture', *Affilia: Journal of Women and Social Work*, 22 (4): 357–70. DOI: 10.1177/0886109907306331.

Mead, G. (1934) *Mind, Self and Society*. Chicago, IL: Chicago University Press.

Meo, A. (2003a) 'Arrivare a fine mese. Donne in famiglie monoreddito', in N. Bosco and N. Negri (eds), *Corsi di vita, povertà e vulnerabilità sociale*. Milan: Guerini Scientifica. pp. 139–72.

Meo, A. (2003b) 'Conversazioni e non solo. Dinamiche Relazionali e Comunicative in un focus group', *Comunicazioni Sociali*, 25 (3): 282–300. DOI: 10.1400/23900.

Merton, R.K. (1957) *Social Theory and Social Structure*. Glencoe, IL: Free Press.

Merton, R.K. (1977) *The Sociology of Science: An Episodic Memoir*. Carbondale, IL: Southern Illinois University Press.

Merton, R.K. (1987) 'The focussed interview and focus group: continuities and discontinuities', *Public Opinion Quarterly*, VI (4): 550–66.

Merton, R.K. and Kendall, P.L. (1946) 'The focused interview', *The American Journal of Sociology*, 51 (6): 541–57.

Merton, R.K., Kendall, P. and Fiske, M. (1956) *The Focused Interview: A Manual of Problems and Procedures*. New York: Free Press.

Michell, L. and Amos, A. (1997) 'Girls, pecking order and smoking', *Social Science and Medicine*, 44 (12): 1861–9. DOI: 10.1016/S0277-9536(96)00295-X.

Miles, M.B. and Huberman, A.M. (2014) *Qualitative Data Analysis: An Expanded Sourcebook* (3rd edn). Thousand Oaks, CA: Sage.

Mill, J.S. (1843) *A System of Logic Ratiocinative and Inductive*. London: Parker.

Miller, R.L. and Brewer, J.D. (2003) 'Unobtrusive measures', in R.L. Miller and J.D. Brewer (eds), *The A–Z of Social Research*. Thousand Oaks, CA: Sage. pp. 331–2.

Montesperelli, P. (1998) *L'intervista ermeneutica*. Milan: FrancoAngeli.

Montesperelli, P. (2014) *Comunicare e interpretare. Introduzione all'ermeneutica per la ricerca sociale*. Milan: Egea.

Moreno, J.L. (1954) *Fondements de la sociometrie* (translated from the American, 2nd edn, *Who Shall Survive* by H. Lesage and P-H. Maucorps). Paris: Presses Universitaires de France.

Morgan, D.L. (1997) *Focus Group as Qualitative Research* (2nd edn). London: Sage.

Morgan, D.L. (1998a) 'The focus group guidebook', in D.L. Morgan and R.A. Krueger (eds), *Focus Group Kit*, Vol. 1. Thousand Oaks, CA: Sage.

Morgan, D.L. (1998b) 'Planning focus groups', in D.L. Morgan and R.A. Krueger (eds), *Focus Group Kit*, Vol. 2. Thousand Oaks, CA: Sage. DOI: 10.4135/9781483328171.n6.

Morgan, D.L. (2017) 'A call for further innovations in focus groups', in R.S. Barbour and D.L. Morgan (eds), *A New Era in Focus Group Research*. London: Palgrave Macmillan. pp. 411–20.

Morgan, D.L. and Krueger, R.A. (1993) 'When to use focus group and why', in D.L. Morgan (ed.), *Successful Focus Group: Advancing the State of the Art*. Newbury Park, CA: Sage. pp. 3–19.

Moro, G., Cassibba, R. and Costantini, A. (2005) 'L'utilizzo del focus group per la definizione dei criteri di valutazione dell'affidamento familiare', *Sociologia e Ricerca Sociale*, 26 (76–7): 279–90.

Morris, C. (1938) *Foundations of the Theory of Signs. International Encyclopaedia of Unified Science I*, No. 2. Chicago, IL: University of Chicago Press.

Morrison, D.E. (1998) *The Search for a Method: Focus Groups and the Development of Mass Communication*. Luton: University of Luton Press.

Morrison-Beedy, D., Côté-Arsenault, D. and Feinstein, N.F. (2001) 'Maximizing results with focus groups: moderator and analysis issues', *Applied Nursing Research*, 14 (1): 48–53. DOI: 10.1053/apnr.2001.21081.

Moscovici, S. (1961) *La psychanalyse, son image et son public*. Paris: PUF.

Moscovici, S. (1980) 'Toward a theory of conversion behaviour', in L. Berkowitz (ed.), *Advances in Experimental Social Psychology*, Vol. 13. New York: Academic Press. pp. 209–39.

Moscovici, S. (2000) *Social Representations: Explorations in Social Psychology*. Cambridge: Polity Press.

Moser, C. and Kalton, G. (1977) *Survey Methods in Social Investigation*. London: Heineman.

Munday, J. (2006) 'Identity in focus: the use of focus groups to study the construction of collective identity', *Sociology*, 40 (1): 89–105. DOI: 10.1177/0038038506058436.

Murgado-Armenteros, E-M., Torres-Ruiz, F.J. and Vega-Zamora, M. (2012) 'Differences between online and face-to-face focus groups, viewed through two approaches', *Journal of Theoretical and Applied Electronic Commerce Research*, 7 (2): 73–86. DOI: 10.4067/S0718-1876201 2000200008.

Myers, D.G. and Lamm, H. (1976) 'The group polarization phenomenon', *Psychological Bulletin*, 83 (4): 602–27. DOI: 10.1037/0033-2909.83.4.602.

Myers, G. (2004) *Matters of Opinion: Talking about Public Issues*. Cambridge: Cambridge University Press.

Nemeth, C.J. and Wachtler, J. (1983) 'Creative problem solving as a result of majority versus minority influence', *European Journal of Social Psychology*, 13 (1): 45–55. DOI: 10.1002/ejsp.2420130103.

Nosek, B., Baaji, M. and Greenwald, A. (2002) 'E-research: ethics, security, design and control in psychological research on the Internet', *Journal of Social Issues*, 58 (81): 161–76.

Onwuegbuzie, A.J., Dickinson, W.B. and Leech, N.L. (2009) 'A qualitative framework for collecting and analysing data in focus group research', *International Journal of Qualitative Methods*, 8 (3): 1–21. DOI: 10.1177/160940690900800301.

Orentlicher, D. (2005) 'Making research a requirement of treatment: why we should sometimes let doctors pressure patients to participate in research', *Hastings Center Report*, 35 (5): 20–8. DOI: 10.1353/hcr.2005.0083.

Palmer, M., Larkin, M., de Visser, R. and Fadden, G. (2010) 'Developing an interpretative phenomenological approach to focus group data', *Qualitative Research in Psychology*, 7 (2): 99–121. DOI: 10.1080/147 80880802513194.

Palumbo, M. (2001) *Il processo della valutazione. Decidere, programmare, valutare*. Milan: FrancoAngeli.

Park, R.E. (1950) 'An autobiographical note', in R. Park (ed.), *Race and Culture*. New York: Free Press. pp. v–ix.

Parker, A. and Tritter, J. (2006) 'Focus group method and methodology: current practice and recent debate', *International Journal of Research & Method in Education*, 29 (1): 23–37. DOI: 10.1080/01406720500537304.

Parks, K.A., Miller, B.A., Collins, L. and Zetes-Zanatta, L. (1998) 'Women's descriptions of drinking in bars: reasons and risks', *Sex Roles*, 38 (9/10): 701–17.

Patton, M.Q. (2002) *Qualitative Research & Evaluation Methods*. Thousand Oaks, CA: Sage.

Pavsic, R. and Pitrone, M.C. (2003) *Come conoscere opinioni e atteggiamenti*. Bonanno: Acireale.

Pearson, J. (1999) '*Lurking anonymity and participation in computer conferencing: data from a case study on an initial teacher education course*'. Paper presented in CommNEd99, Hameelina, Finland.

Porcellato, L., Dughill, L. and Springett, J. (2002) 'Using focus groups to explore children's perceptions of smoking: reflections on practice', *Health Education*, 102 (6): 310–20. DOI: 10.1108/09654280210446856.

Pruitt, D.G. (1971) 'Choice shifts in group discussion: an introductory review', *Journal of Personality and Social Psychology*, 20 (3): 339–60.

Puchta, C. and Potter, J. (2004) *Focus Group Practice*. London: Sage.

Ragin, C.C. and Becker, H.S. (eds) (1992) *What is a Case? Exploring the Foundation of Social Inquiry*. Cambridge: Cambridge University Press.

Rapari, S. (2005) 'L'uso del focus group nella ricerca sociologica con i bambini: considerazioni sulla composizione dei gruppi e la preparazione della traccia per la discussione', *Sociologia e Ricerca Sociale*, 26 (76–7): 193–205.

Reid, D.J. and Reid, F.J.M. (2005) 'Online focus groups: an in-depth comparison of computer-mediated and conventional focus group discussions', *International Journal of Market Research*, 47 (2): 131–62.

Remenyi, D. (2017) *Field Methods for Academic Research: Interviews, Focus Groups and Questionnaires* (3rd edn). Reading: ACPI.

Riessman, C.K. (2008) *Narrative Methods for the Human Sciences*. Thousand Oaks, CA: Sage.

Ritchie, D.A. (2003) *Doing Oral History: A Practical Guide*. Oxford: Oxford University Press.

Robinson, W.S. (1951) 'The logical structure of analytic induction', *American Sociological Review*, 16: 812–18.

Robson, K. (1999) 'Perceptions of oral health care services in Bro Taf'. Unpublished report for Bro Taf Health Authority, Wales.

Robson, S. and Foster, A. (1989) *Qualitative Research in Action*. London: Hodder and Stoughton.

Rogers, W.A., Meyer, B., Walker, N. and Fisk, A.D. (1998) 'Functional limitations to daily living tasks in the aged: a focus group analysis', *Human Factors and Ergonomics Society*, 40 (1): 111–25.

Salvadori, C. (2006) 'Progetto Dama: Giovani, territorio e partecipazione'. Research report, Osservatorio Provinciale di Pistoia, Italy.

Sanjari, M., Bahramnezhad, F., Fomani, F.K., Shoghi, M. and Cheraghi, M.A. (2014) 'Ethical challenges of researchers in qualitative studies: the necessity to develop a specific guideline', *Journal of Medical Ethics and History of Medicine*, 4: 7–14.

Santoso, B. (1996) 'Small group intervention vs formal seminar for improving approving appropriate drugs use', *Social Science and Medicine*, 42 (8): 1163–8. DOI: 10.1016/0277-9536(95)00390-8.

Sargent, S., Samanta, J. and Yelden, K. (2016) 'A grounded theory analysis of a focus group study', *SAGE Research Methods Cases*. London: Sage. pp. 1–14. DOI: 10.4135/9781473997233.

Schatzman, L. and Strauss, A.L. (1973) *Field Research: Strategies for a Natural Sociology*. Englewood Cliffs, NJ: Prentice Hall.

Schneider, D. (2004) *The Psychology of Stereotyping*. New York: Guilford Press.

Schütz, A. (1962) *Collected Papers: I. The Problem of Social Reality* (edited by M. Natanson). The Hague: Martinus Nijhoff.

Schütz, A. (1975) *Collected Papers: III. Studies in Phenomenological Philosophy* (edited by I. Schütz). The Hague: Martinus Nijhoff.

Scraton, P. (2004) 'Speaking truth to power: experiencing critical research', in M. Smyth and E. Williamson (eds), *Researchers and their 'Subjects': Ethics, Power, Knowledge and Consent.* Bristol: Policy Press. pp. 177–96.

Seawright, J. (2016) *Multi-Method Social Science: Combining Qualitative and Quantitative Tools.* Cambridge: Cambridge University Press.

Shariff, N.J. (2015) 'Utilizing the Delphi survey approach: a review', *Nursing and Care,* 4 (3): 246–52. DOI:10.4172/2167-1168.1000246.

Shaw, M.E. (1981) *Group Dynamics: The Psychology of Small Group Behavior.* New York: McGraw Hill.

Shrank, W.H., Kutner, J.S., Richardson, T., Mularski, R.A., Fischer, S. and Kagawa-Singer, M. (2005) 'Focus group findings about the influence of culture on communication preferences in end-of-life care', *Journal of General Internal Medicine,* 20 (8): 703–09. DOI: 10.1111/j.1525-1497.2005.0151.x.

Silverman, D. (2000) *Doing Qualitative Research: A Practical Handbook.* London: Sage.

Silvia, P.J. (2007) *How to Write a Lot: A Practical Guide to Productive Academic Writing.* Washington, DC: American Psychological Association.

Sintjago, A. and Link, A. (2012) 'From synchronous to asynchronous: researching online focus groups platforms', *Cultivating Change in the Academy.* Available at https://cultivatingchangeseries.com/from-synchronous-to-asynchronous/ (accessed 30 March 2020).

Skinner, B.F. (1957) *Verbal Behavior.* Englewood Cliffs, NJ: Prentice Hall.

Smith, H.W. (1975) *Strategies of Social Research: The Methodological Imagination.* Englewood Cliffs, NJ: Prentice Hall.

Smith, M.W. (1995) 'Ethics in focus groups: a few concerns', *Qualitative Health Research,* 5 (4): 478–86. DOI: 10.1177/104973239500500408.

Smithson, J. (2000) 'Using and analysing focus groups: limitations and possibilities', *International Journal of Social Research Methodology,* 3 (2): 103–19. DOI: 10.1080/136455700405172.

Stewart, D.M., Makwarimba, E., Barnfather, A., Letourneau, N. and Neufeld, A. (2008) 'Researching reducing health disparities: mixed methods approaches', *Social Science & Medicine,* 66 (6): 1406–17. DOI: 10.1016/j.socscimed.2007.11.021.

Stewart, D.W. and Shamdasani, P.N. (1990) *Focus Group: Theory and Practice.* London: Sage.

Stewart, D.W. and Shamdasani, P.N. (2017) 'Online focus groups', *Journal of Advertising,* 46 (1): 48–60. DOI: 10.1080/00913367.2016.1252288.

Stewart, K. and Williams, M. (2005) 'Researching online populations: the use of online focus groups for social research', *Qualitative Research,* 5 (4): 395–416. DOI: 10.1177/1468794105056916.

Stokes, D. and Bergin, R. (2006) 'Methodology or "methodolatry"? An evaluation of focus groups and depth interviews', *Qualitative Market Research: An International Journal*, 9 (1): 26–37. DOI: 10.1108/13522750610640530.

Sullivan, L.E. (ed.) (2009) *The SAGE Glossary of the Social and Behavioral Sciences*. Thousand Oaks, CA: Sage.

Tajfel, H. (1974) 'Social identity and intergroup behaviour', *Social Sciences Information*, 13: 65–93.

Tajfel, H. (ed.) (1982) *Social Identity and Intergroup Relations*. Cambridge: Cambridge University Press.

Tajfel, H. and Turner, J.C. (1986) 'The social identity theory of intergroup behaviour', in S. Worchel and W.G. Austin (eds), *Psychology of Intergroup Relations*. Chicago, IL: Nelson-Hall. pp. 7–24.

Tedlock, D. (1979) 'The analogical tradition and the emergence of a dialogical anthropology', *Journal of Anthropological Research*, 35: 387–400.

Templeton, J.F. (1994) *The Focus Group: A Strategic Guide to Organizing, Conducting and Analyzing the Focus Group Interview*. Chicago, IL: Probus.

Terry, D.J. and Hogg, M.A. (1996) 'Group norms and the attitude-behavior relationship: a role for ingroup norms', *Personality and Social Psychology Bulletin*, 22: 776–93. DOI: 10.1177/0146167296228002.

Tolman, E.C. (1932) *Purposive Behavior in Animals and Men*. Berkeley, CA: University of California Press.

Torres, V. (2006) 'A mixed method study testing data-model fit of a retention model for Latino/a students at urban universities', *Journal of College Student Development*, 47 (3): 299–318. DOI: 10.1353/csd.2006.0037.

Trobia, A. (2005) 'Il focus group e l'analisi di rete: un fertile connubio', *Sociologia e Ricerca Sociale*, 26: 76–7, 54–71.

Truman, C. (2003 'Ethics and the ruling relations of research production', *Sociological Research Online*, 8 (1): 1–11. DOI: 10.5153/sro.773.

Turkle, S. (2011) *Alone Together: Why We Expect More from Technology and Less from Each Other*. New York: Basic Books.

Turner, J.C. (1982) 'Towards a cognitive redefinition of the social group', in H. Tajfel (ed.), *Social Identity and Intergroup Relations*. Cambridge: Cambridge University Press. pp. 15–40.

Turner, M.E. and Pratkanis, A.R. (1997) 'Mitigating groupthink by stimulating constructive conflict', in C.K.W. De Dreu and E. Van de Vliert (eds), *Using Conflict in Organizations*. Thousand Oaks, CA: Sage. pp. 153–7. DOI: https://psycnet.apa.org/doi/10.4135/9781446217016.n5.

Vaughn, S., Schumm, J.S. and Sinagub, J. (1996) *Focus Group Interviews in Education and Psychology*. London: Sage.

Venturini, G.L. (2002) 'Nvivo e la ricerca qualitativa computer-assistita', in M. Cardano (ed.), *Tecniche di ricerca qualitativa*. Torino: Libreria Stampatori. pp. 219–42.

Vicsek, L. (2005) 'Combining focus groups and surveys. A case example', *Sociologia e Ricerca Sociale*, 76/77 (XXIII): 105–19.

Vicsek, L. (2010) 'Issues in the analysis of focus groups: generalisability, quantifiability, treatment of context and quotations', *The Qualitative Report*, 15 (1): 122–41.

Vidich, A.J. and Lyman, S.M. (2000) 'Qualitative methods: their history in sociology and anthropology', in N.K. Denzin, and Y.S. Lincoln (eds), *Handbook of Qualitative Research*. Thousand Oaks, CA: Sage. pp. 37–84.

Vogt, D.S. and Colvin, C.R. (2003) 'Interpersonal orientation and the accuracy of personality judgments', *Personality*, 71 (2): 267–95. DOI: 10.1111/1467-6494.7102005.

Vygotsky, L.S. (1979) 'Consciousness as a problem in the psychology of behaviour', *Soviet Psychology*, 17 (4): 3–35. DOI: 10.2753/RPO1061-040517043.

Wagner, W. (2001) 'Nature in disorder: the troubled public of biotechnology', in G. Gaskell and M.W. Bauer (eds), *Biotechnology 1996–2000: The Year of Controversy*. London: NMSI. pp. 80–95.

Wagner, W., Kronberger, N. and Seifert, F. (2002) 'Collective symbolic coping with new technology: knowledge, images, and public discourse', *British Journal of Social Psychology*, 41 (3): 323–43. DOI: 10.1348/0144 66602760344241.

Walton, J. (1992) 'Making the theoretical case', in C.C. Ragin and H.S. Becker (eds), *What is a Case? Exploring the Foundation of Social Inquiry*. Cambridge: Cambridge University Press. pp. 121–37.

Warner, J., Weber, T.R. and Albanes, R. (1999) 'Girls are retarded when they're stoned: marijuana and the construction of gender roles among adolescent females', *Sex Roles*, 40 (1/2): 25–43.

Wasserman, S. and Faust, K. (1994) *Social Network Analysis: Methods and Applications*, Vol. 8. Cambridge: Cambridge University Press.

Watson, J.B. (1914) *Behavior: An Introduction to Comparative Psychology*. New York: Holt.

Webb, E.J., Campbell, D.T., Schwartz, R.D., Sechrest, L. and Grove, J.B. (1981) *Nonreactive Measures in the Social Sciences*. Dallas, TX: Houghton Mifflin.

Weber, M. (1904) 'Die Objektivität Sozialwissenschaftlicher und Sozialpolitischer Erkenntnis', *Archiv für Sozialwissenschaft und Sozialpolitik*, XIX: 22–87.

Weitzman, E.A. and Miles, M.B. (1995) 'Choosing software for qualitative data analysis: an overview', *CAM – Cultural Anthropology Methods*, 7 (2): 1–5. DOI: 10.1177/1525822X950070020101.

Wight, D. (1994) 'Boys' thoughts and talk about sex in a working-class locality of Glasgow', *Sociological Review*, 42 (4): 703–37.

Wiles, R., Heath, S., Crow, G. and Charles, V. (2005) 'Informed consent in social research: a literature review', ESRC National Centre for Research Methods, NCRM Methods Review Papers, NCRM/001. Available at http://eprints.ncrm.ac.uk/85/1/MethodsReviewPaperNCRM-001.pdf (accessed 30 March 2020).

Williams, K.D., Harkins, S. and Latané, B. (1981) 'Identifiability as a deterrent to social loafing: two cheering experiments', *Journal of Personality and Social Psychology*, 40 (2): 303–11. DOI: 10.1037/0022-3514.40.2.303.

Winters, K. (2019) 'Using narrative analysis on qualitative data to identify types of voters', *SAGE Research Methods Case*. London: Sage. DOI: 10.4135/9781526476821.

Wodak, R. (2004) 'Critical discourse analysis', in C. Seale, G. Gobo, J.F. Gubrium and D. Silverman (eds), *Qualitative Research Practice*. London: Sage. pp. 185–208.

Wodak, R., De Cillia, R. and Reisigl, M. (2009) *The Discursive Construction of National Identity* (2nd edn). Edinburgh: Edinburgh University Press.

Wooten, J. (2017) 'Performance-based focus groups', in R.S. Barbour and D.L. Morgan (eds), *A New Era in Focus Group Research*. London: Palgrave Macmillan. pp. 251–76.

Zammuner, V.L. (2003) *I focus group*. Bologna: Il Mulino.

Zelditch, M. (1962) 'Some methodological problems of field studies', *American Journal of Sociology*, 67 (5): 566–76.

Zuber, J.A., Crott, H.W. and Werner, J. (1992) 'Choice shift and group polarization: an analysis of the status of arguments and social decision schemes', *Journal of Personality and Social Psychology*, 62 (1): 50–61. DOI: 10.1037/0022-3514.62.1.50.

Index

Page numbers in *italics* refer to figures; page numbers in **bold** refer to tables.